ACU Series: 1

D1824740

Faith and Reason
Friends or Foes in the New Millennium?

Edited by Anthony Fisher OP and Hayden Ramsay

The ACU Series is a publication venture of Australian Catholic University working in collaboration with the Australian Theological Forum. Each volume presents a theological or philosophical engagement from a Catholic perspective with issues of the day. The Series aims to promote forms of cultural dialogue in which different voices of faith, spirituality, philosophy, science and art may be heard.

Series Editor: Anthony J Kelly CSsR

ATF Press
Adelaide

ACU Series: 1

Faith and Reason

Friends or Foes in the New Millennium?

Edited by

Anthony Fisher OP

and

Hayden Ramsay

ATF Press
Adelaide

First published 2004

National Library of Australia
Cataloguing-in-Publication data

Ramsay, Hayden, 1964-
Faith and Reason : friend or foe in the new millennium
Includes index
ISBN 1 920691 18 9

1. Faith and reason – Christianity. I. Fisher, Anthony, 1960-. II. Title. (Series : ACU series ; 1).

200.1

Published by
ATF Press
An imprint of the Australian Theological Forum
PO Box 504
Hindmarsh
SA 5007
ABN 68 314 074 034
www.atfpress.com

Printed by Openbook Print, Adelaide, Australia

Foreword

Anthony KellyCSsR

This book of conference proceedings is the first of what is hoped to be a continuing series. Australian Catholic University, with its various Schools of Theology and Philosophy, is especially grateful to the ATF Press for the efficient and encouraging manner by which an inevitably disordered sheaf of learned papers has now appeared in this accessible form.

Pope John Paul II's *Fides et Ratio* in 1998 occasioned the conference from which these proceedings have emerged. The encyclical is best read as an encouragement to genuine intellectuality and philosophical reflection. Why the Pope judged that this word of encouragement was opportune at this particular time is the long story to be told in many ways in the pages that follow. The Pope, though a philosopher of considerable status, is the voice of Catholic tradition insisting that in the universe of faith, genuine intelligence can and must breath deeply, and grow to its own proportions and promise.

'Faith' and 'reason' are heavily weighted words. They point to elemental aspects of human existence. The papers and discussions presented here draw not a little of their liveliness from attempts to clarify and correlate these basic activities or dimensions of human being. In all the complexities of the possible relationships and inter-weavings of faith and reason, two types of questions keep recurring. On the one hand, What is the value of human intelligence, and how is it endorsed and supported by faith? On the other, What is the distinctive intelligence or rationality of faith, and how does it relate to the perennial search for wisdom represented in its various philo-sophical forms?

The resources of the past and insights from the present combine here to make for a richly textured discussion of these fundamental issues. The publishing of this book suggests that faith and reason have been found agreeable and challenging conversation partners.

It is an act of hope, too. In this third millennium, the Catholic tradition of 'faith seeking understanding/rationality' will inevitably be confronted rationalities of science, economics and philosophical analysis, to name just three. There will be moments of stoney silence on both sides. Still, a larger conversation has begun; and here, in this book, is one aspect of its beginning.

Anthony J Kelly CSsR,
Professor of Theology,
Australian Catholic University
Series Editor
February 2004

Contents

Acknowledgments

The publishers wish to acknowledge the following publishers and individuals for their kind permission to use their papers in this volume of essays:

A version of John Haldane's article, 'The Diversity of Philosophy and the Unity of its Vocation', has already been published in *Faith and Reason*, edited by TL Smith (Southbend, IN: St Augustine's Press 2001). chapter 11.

Kevin Hart's article 'Fides et Ratio et . . .' appeared in the *American Catholic Philosophical Quarterly* 76:2, 2002: 199–220.

A different form of Michael Levine's article, 'Contemporary Christian Analytic Philosophy of Religion', appeared in the *International Journal for Philosophy of Religion*, 48, 2000: 89–119.

John M McDermott's article, 'Faith, Reason and Freedom', appeared in the *Irish Theological Quarterly*, 67, 2002: 307–332.

A version of Tracey Rowland's article, 'Alasdair MacIntyre's Tradition-Dependent Rationality and *Fides et Ratio*', is published in her *Culture and the Thomist Tradition: After Vatican II* (London: Routledge, 2003), chapter 6.

Preface

Hayden Ramsay

In 2000 the Australian Catholic University hosted a conference on *Faith and Reason: Friends or Foes in the New Millennium?* It was generously sponsored by the then Archbishop of Melbourne, Dr George Pell, and funds from the University's Professor of Philosophy, Raimond Gaita and its Vice-Chancellor Peter Sheehan. The conference was occasioned by *Fides et Ratio,* the 1998 Encyclical Letter of Pope John Paul II on faith and reason. The conference brought together the richest crop of local and international speakers to address such a topic ever in Australia and generated enthusiastic discussion with several hundred participants. It also helped to show-case the just opened St Patrick's Campus of the University in Melbourne and the new-born School of Philosophy across that University's several campuses.

Thanks are due to the conference committee, which included Professors Rai Gaita and Tony Kelly CSsR, Mrs Kath Allison, Mr Peter Coghlan, Rev Dr Anthony Fisher OP, Mrs Joan Manshon, Dr John Ozolins, Dr Hayden Ramsay, Rev Dr Denis Rochford MSC and Dr Mark Wynn. Anthony Fisher, who by the time of the conference had taken up the rôle of Director of the new John Paul II Institute for Marriage and the Family, and his assistants Kath Allison and Neville Condron, did the bulk of the organisation. Seminarians of Corpus Christi College were present in large numbers and acted as drivers and minders, (furniture) movers and shakers.

Finally, thanks are due to all the speakers and participants in the conference, especially to Professor John Haldane of St Andrews University who so generously persevered with his (several) conference presentations, despite hearing of the death of his mother only hours after arrival in Australia.

After the conference the participants revised their contributions for the present publication. This seeks, some time after the dust stirred up by the encyclical has settled, to reflect on the wisdom and challenges of *Fides et Ratio* itself and on the debates it has aroused in philosophical and theological circles. We are grateful to Melinda Grant and Jolanta

Nowak for their assistance in formatting, proofreading and indexing these papers.

Hayden Ramsay
February 2004

Introduction

Anthony Fisher OP and Hayden Ramsay

When US philosopher Jean Hampton died at a tragically early age she left behind an incomplete manuscript, published as *The Authority of Reason*.[1] Hampton's book is a major contribution to the theory of rationality. In it she argues that instrumental reason cannot be understood purely instrumentally (chapter 5). Most philosophers today reject a rational account of the human good, arguing reason is simply the intellectual activity of endorsing and choosing effective means to ends. These ends are established on some extra-rational basis: preference, desire, custom, impulse, external proddin . . . Hampton believed that even instrumental rationality points to *some* non-instrumental human good—the good that is an instrumentally rational agent—and that this is an intrinsic good it is rational to seek.

Had she lived, Jean Hampton might have enjoyed an interesting conversation on rationality with Pope John Paul II. The year Hampton's book was posthumously published, the Pope, happily still reigning, celebrated the twentieth anniversary of his Pontificate with an Encyclical Letter *Fides et Ratio*.[2] This letter is the first sustained papal document on philosophy for over a century and a major contribution to Catholic—and wider than Catholic—debate on reason and faith, philosophy and theology. The Pope's letter celebrates the breadth and authority of an objectivist account of reason and clarifies (at a time when it was sorely needed) that, for Catholics at least, a mature faith is always one that is rationally held, philosophically well-informed.

---

1.   Cambridge University Press, 1998.
2.   John Paul II, *Fides et Ratio:* Encyclical on the Relationship between Faith and Reason (Sydney: St Paul's, 1998). Unless otherwise indicated, numbers in round brackets refer to paragraph numbers of that letter.

1. Faith and reason

'Faith and reason are like two wings on which the human spirit rises to the contemplation of truth' (1). So John Paul opens his encyclical, proposing the attainment of truth as the goal of *Fides et Ratio*. But faith and reason clearly carry people to the truth in different ways. Reason, at least according to one prominent intellectual tradition, is our nature, and so our natural response to the world around us and to ourselves. Faith, on the other hand, is a divine gift, not always recognised or appreciated when received, often puzzling even to those who believe they are endowed with it, let alone to others. Just how do these two very different 'wings' function together to raise the spirit to contemplation?

The idea of faith independent of reason is ambiguous. If it refers to faith *with no in-put from rationality whatsoever*, then it is logically impossible: no one can have beliefs of any sort without formulating propositions, understanding and criticising propositions, endorsing reasons etc. If it refers to faith *whose content is not generated by means of natural reasoning at all but only by supernatural processes* ('revelation'), then it is hard to grasp how it can mean much to us: how can we accept (or reject), integrate (or fail to integrate), and follow (or not) beliefs from an alien source that are not expressed and justified in our own language and thought systems? If it refers to faith *which stands and falls not by reason but on some extra-rational authority*, then it may be coherent but must nonetheless be troubling: why should rational beings accept and follow beliefs that are counter-rational, not open to canons of rational criticism, rationally incommunicable to others?

The idea of reason without faith is also perplexing. If it refers to reasoning *without any unargued premises*, then it is, again, logically impossible. If it refers to reasoning *without beliefs received on authority from others*, then it may be possible but seems highly unlikely. If it refers to the pursuit of truth *systematically excluding from consideration certain sorts of enduring questions or all data that are unobservable, unmeasurable, uncontrollable or unusable*, it is certainly possible but many would wonder: why bother?

Fides et Ratio argues that faith and reason *are* compatible and, in a sense, inseparable. The encyclical claims that it is natural to human beings to want to understand things, and possible for them to do so because of the gifts of freedom and rationality they have received (16, 28–31). We naturally seek truth, at all times and in all things; just as we naturally seek health, companionship, activity, peace, God and other conditions—both principles and ends—of a good human life. The church, John Paul claims, is 'a partner in humanity's shared struggle to arrive at truth' (2). Her mandate in this is from Christ, whose mission it was to reveal the truth to all people. The truth he reveals is, of course, ultimately the truth about himself, a truth that transcends any human individual's or community's capacity fully to know, yet it is nonetheless somewhat available to anyone who submits their mind to God—a choice made possible by the activity in us of the Holy Spirit.

This submission, and the beliefs that constitute it and follow from it, are 'faith'. It is not 'another way' to the truth but 'the other way' to truth—and on this Catholic account, the only way to the whole truth, at least as much of the whole as we can know in this life. As such, it is clearly and inevitably a challenge to ordinary reasoning (23), but it is not an *alternative* to reason or *in conflict* with reason. If there are not two, potentially rival, truths ('truths of reason' and 'truths of faith') but instead truth is a unity (34), then faith and reason are neither alternatives nor contradictories. They may have, to some extent, different starting-points, different methodologies, different authorities, different standards of competence: but they do not ultimately have different goals, and even in these other respects they have much in common.

It follows from this that *everyone*, believer or not, is actually engaged in an intellectual pilgrimage towards what is, ultimately, knowledge of God; and *every believer* is like every non-believer, engaged in the daily struggle to develop and maintain a well-functioning mind that can serve such a pursuit. Some people reject the relevance of God to their daily lives—hence the permanent need for considering whether there are reasons for believing in God and what they might look like (in this book: Coghlan, Oppy, Lamb). Some Christians will reject the Pope's optimism about human reason (Adams), while others support it (Fisher, Martin), or suggest aspects of the reason-faith relation that require further analysis (Hart, Ozolins, Quilter). Ultimately, the issue goes back to the synthesis of reason and faith arguably achieved in the high Middle Ages[3] and what John Paul calls the subsequent 'drama of the separation of faith and reason' in the ages which followed (45–8). Is the medieval account of the human

---

3.　See, for example, Edward Grant, *God and Reason in the Middle Ages* (Cambridge University Press, 2001).

mind and its encounter with religion of enduring value? Has the receding of that medieval vision been loss or gain (or both)? Where to from here?

2. Philosophy and theology

The greatest achievement of the synthesis of reason and faith is the relationship between philosophy and theology that it suggests. The meta-philosophy that explains the places of wisdom-love and God-thought in our lives is restated in *Fides et Ratio* and is perhaps its most compelling contribution. In the Pope's vision, philosophy and theology are not rivals or irreconcilables, they are complementaries. Theology requires philosophy because we need to think rigorously in the search for truth. For theology this requirement is one of *resources* (for the terms, concepts, arguments, canons of criticism, and global theories for theologising are all philosophy-rich: 65), of *understanding* (for appreciation of much of Scripture, Tradition, doctrine and practice requires comprehension of the underpinning philosophical narratives and traditions: 65–68), of *content* (for theology without philosophy tends towards mere feeling, fad, even fanaticism: 77) and of *communication* (for non-believers will attend to and comprehend little theology initially, but can become intellectually attuned to theological discourse by philosophical discussion: 5, 92, 99).

Although it is less obvious, philosophy also needs theology. Excluding rational thought about God and religion smugly entrenches particular philosophical positions such as materialism and utilitarianism, and the particular forms of argument these require or support. Philosophy, in turn, is impoverished, by being itself instrumentalised, assigned only utility value. The resources of theology mean 'reason is stirred to explore paths which of itself it would not even have suspected it could take' (73). Theology's in-put opens up to philosophy topics in philosophy of religion and issues of transcendence and the place of spiritual experience and the spiritual endeavour in human life. It enlarges the horizons, scope, goals and language of the discipline. The theological notion of a free and personal God, for instance, opens up new philosophical issues of being; the notion of sin offers a new angle to the philosophy of evil; Christian anthropology and sociology has profoundly influenced our conceptions of dignity, rights and freedom; dogmas such as supernatural happiness and original sin challenge and enhance philosophical theory of human nature (76).

For all this, philosophy enjoys a proper autonomy from theology (77). A one-winged bird may not fly so well, but it is still a bird. More, the philosophical dimension might be said to be more primitive in man, deeper within human nature. Philosophy springs up with the natural urge to ask questions about things and to be satisfied only with answers we can believe true (3). But philosophy is not only the questions we ask and the answers we give from childhood to the grave, it is also that sense of wonder, that contemplative spirit that motors such question-asking and answer-giving. And such questioning and answering and wondering and contemplating is *not* merely utilitarian: we are seeking some truth and when we get it or part of it we are captivated by the getting of it, we feel drawn by reverence for what we have discovered, for truth itself, and for the capacity of the human mind to seek and recognise it.

This almost-mystical experience is at the heart of the pre-Christian legacy of Greek philosophy which made it such a natural ally for much Christian thought in the succeeding centuries. It is also an experience that carries our philosophising into the territory of theology. When we are shaken by transcendence and contemplation of truth, we are poised to recognise the sort of truths about God that no human reasoning alone but only God's self-revelation can disclose. This is a deeply *real* form of philosophy, and it is philosophising the Pope insists is practised by everyone. We do not all take part in the study of philosophical systems or follow the debates of professional philosophers, but we all engage in philosophical enquiry (27)—we are all stirred sometimes by desire for or awareness of profound truths—and this spirit of philosophical enquiry is also ripe with queries that are actually theological.

The philosophy-theology relation is nonetheless controversial. In the reformed tradition there is scepticism about philosophy's usefulness (Adams). This invites a Catholic response that celebrates the rôle of philosophy but is humble also about its limits (McDermott, McInerney, Moses). But it also invites a rejoinder that all theologians, Catholics included, must be wary of a philosophy-shaped theology: philosophy works with a more limited view of reality than theology and cannot be the principal determinant of a genuine theology (Gleeson, Kelly).

But even if philosophy is of very great importance to theology, has recent philosophising about religion been of much use? The analytic philosophy of religion characteristic of the Anglo-American academy has been criticised for its irrelevance to the actual concerns of religious believers and its lack of imagination (Levine). Others think it has more potential but suggest it should aim to do something quite different to its current self-appointed task: it ought to provide people with a way of living and acting in the world—the 'practice of wisdom' or of 'philosophical spirituality'—that is both autonomous of and yet complementary to theology's contribution (Haldane).

3. Realist-objectivist philosophy

John Paul's encyclical occasioned much more debate in the academy than is usual for papal documents. Some were delighted to see their discipline so warmly appreciated by an institution they associated with benighted dogmatism or anti-intellectual ritualism. Others were not so surprised by this Catholic enthusiasm for philosophy—especially coming from one of those rare popes who has been an academic philosopher—but were suspicious of his apparent support for a particular style(s) or school(s) of philosophy. The Pope writes that the church has no 'official philosophy' (51, 76): reason, like all human capacities is fallible, weakened by structures of sin, so no purely human system has the sort of definitive certainty of a revealed and defined matter of faith. Nevertheless, *Fides et Ratio* is fairly specific on the sort of philosophy it recommends, and it is explicit in its support for certain philosophical authors, theses and works over others.

For instance, the Pope specifies a realist-objectivist philosophy over the more sceptical accounts characteristic of modernity and post-modernity: for only realism can supply the necessary 'services' to theology and, he argues, to truth more generally. The encyclical often talks of contemporary distrust of reason and the collapse of confidence in the possibility of balancing rational thought with the claims of faith (55, 61). The Pope specifically mentions several currents of thought that he believes endanger philosophy itself and certainly limit its relationship to theology (85–91). These include eclecticism, historicism, scientism, pragmatism, nihilism, rationalism, fideism and relativism (55, 66, 71, 85–91). Many of these have infected popular culture not so much as full-blown philosophies but more as fragments of passing fashions or longer-standing ideologies, often only half understood and incoherently jumbled together.[4] These critical remarks, backed up by his enormous corpus to date treating some of these isms more fully, and taken together with his brief survey of the history of thought, make it clear the Pope is recommending not just the doing of philosophy, but doing it in particular ways. Only a philosophy that acknowledges the existence of a real world and of free and rational persons, that has the metaphysical space for exploring questions about God and the supernatural, and that acknowledges the possibility of attaining truth—including moral truths—will satisfy. And there, for many, is the rub . . .

But the Pope does far more than give ticks and crosses to various currents of historical and contemporary thought. He elaborates, for instance, an *implicit* 'philosophy of humanity', an unchanging core of philosophical principles such as those of non-contradiction, finality and causality, those concerning persons, truth, and goodness, which are not 'a philosophy' but are at the core of all philosophising (4). He explores the contribution of the history of philosophy and its various developed departments (eg ch 4). He makes a case for a philosophy that gives meaning to the lives of ordinary people and gives them a wisdom to live by (the 'sapiential dimension' and 'philosophy of life': 81–3). Such a philosophy should also explain and vindicate our capacity to know truth, goodness, beauty; it should establish the possibility of metaphysical claims that transcend empirical experience; and it should give some account of the relationship between strictly philosophical and more broadly theological engagements. In several places Thomas Aquinas is offered as an example of such an achievement (43, 44, 78); and more contemporary efforts praised when (only when?) they build on 'the best' from the past as John Paul sees it (59 etc).

Given all this, there has been criticism that the Pope is disingenuous in claiming the church has no official philosophy while endorsing one very specific philosophy. The issue, however, is perhaps more subtle, particularly with reference to 'implicit philosophy' and the citation of Aquinas (Ramsay, McInerny, Fisher). John Paul is not writing here as a professional philosopher, an academic offering original philosophy—something he has done as Korol Wojtyla; if he

---

4.   A situation famously described in Alasdair MacIntyre, *After Virtue: A Study in Moral Theory* (2nd ed, London: Duckworth, 1984).

were, he would no doubt have anticipated and taken up obvious criticisms as to precisely what he means by, for example, 'metaphysics', 'realism', pragmatism', 'rationalism', 'nihilism' etc (Hart, Haldane, Gaita, Ramsay).

For all this, the encyclical's highly complimentary view of philosophy and the work of philosophers may come as some surprise to those who presume and even dogmatically assert a dualism between religion and reason or the church and the academy—a surprise, indeed, to those on both sides of the divide, whether inclined to fideism or rationalism. The Pope's belief in philosophy's special place in the life of the mind generally and in relation to theology in particular has been and should be greatly welcomed. In particular, his call to 'philosophical spirituality' that explores 'the sapiential dimension' of human life, and his interest in a 'philosophy of life' are major contributions to debate and suggest fruitful new directions (Haldane, Heft). The encyclical should goad both anti-philosophical theologians and anti-theological philosophers to look again at what the other discipline might have to offer them. And it presents a real challenge to both religious and secularist 'fundamentalists' who all too often neglect the rôle of either philosophy or theology.

4. Magisterium and philosophy

If the Catholic Church—not alone amongst other religious traditions, though pre-eminent amongst them in this respect—has an enormous interest in philosophy, it will obviously be deeply unsettled when philosophy seems to contradict divine revelation. Yet rather than insisting that at that point philosophy kowtow to theology, the church continues to insist that philosophy is an autonomous discipline. It is so because reason, even unassisted by faith, is directed of itself to truth and has in itself the means of reaching truths. The Pope confesses that, whatever some churchmen might have said or done in the past, the church has neither right nor competence to interfere with professional philosophy. But when philosophies that seem to contradict revealed truths become widespread, the church naturally highlights the contradictions to philosophers, theologians and the faithful (ch 5).

The Pope is anxious that this continue and that it should not be greeted defensively. Such critique is a service; it is meant to offer a wider and different perspective to philosophers so that they have before them the full range of facts and principles before articulating their views (51). It may well invite a nuancing of the philosophical or theological claims made to date. Moreover, John Paul argues, since philosophers are those *professionally* open to and anxious for criticism and self-criticism, the Magisterium's voice will be as welcome as any other critical comments offered with argument, in charity and out of a shared concern for the truth.

But philosophers are as jealous of their territory and nervous of interference as any other academics. Even if the church's interventions in philosophy are generally more rational and benign than the interventions of some others—politicians, media, medical researchers, bureaucrats—they may still seem authoritarian or anti-intellectual to some. The Pope seems to be proposing not only a different way for philosophers to view those 'interventions' but also a different way for church officials to intervene. Supporting and encouraging good thinking must be the ecclesial institution's goal, not forcing conformity or uniformity. Since much Western philosophising has been undertaken by Catholics, often within Catholic institutions, often using and advancing ideas that are part of the Catholic inheritance, the church has a great interest in philosophical renewal and has often supported such renewal (58–60)—most recently in the teaching of the Second Vatican Council and in the writings of the philosopher-pope, John Paul II. That should continue and flourish. The church has also long insisted on the centrality of a philosophical education for its priests and in theological studies, and has supported numerous institutions, teachers and projects devoted to philosophy (including the proceedings published in this book)—projects and teachers that may not be automatically supportive of the church's own teaching. That too should continue.

For all that, not all philosophers will be convinced by the church's view of the rôle of philosophy and philosophical faculty (Adams) or at least of some parts of that view (Gaita). Catholic philosophers may accept the church's guidance (Haldane, Ramsay), but will still take great care to protect the integrity of their discipline and to avoid the creation of a 'Catholic philosophy' or philosophical ghetto, answerable to ecclesial hierarchs and not genuinely engaged in the academic discipline of philosophy. Theologians naturally enjoy a different relationship with the Magisterium (McDermott). Their task is the understanding of revelation, which means that their primary engagement is with the content of the sacred texts, traditions and teachings of their church. They have very specific duties to their ecclesial community. Yet the interrelationship of philosophy and theology means philosophy too is answerable to the church *as servant of truth*—as philosophy is answerable to all servants of truth. Philosophy's duty to heed here is intellectual, whereas theology's is also filial.

5. Reconciling 'foes' and confirming 'friends' for the future

Fides et Ratio concludes with various challenges to all those involved in the search for truth. John Paul has words for theologians, teachers, priests, philosophers, seminarians, scientists, indeed for all people since all are in some sense 'philosophers'. For professional philosophers and theologians, one imperative is to establish the common ground. The most obvious is the shared concern for truth—though that very notion is of course much contested today. There is a need therefore for philosophers and theologians to begin almost from scratch, explaining and articulating what and why they think and believe what they do. And they will help each other enormously if they do that. But who will listen to arguments for particular truths if truth itself is ridiculed or treated with indifference, even by high profile academics or university administrators, and when argument is scorned or avoided? (Gaita)

In many ways, philosophy's task is the harder of the two; but at least it is already begun. Philosophical theology, medieval studies, analytical Thomism, new anthropologies, renewed interest in metaphysical essentialism and moral realism, the revivals of *eudaemonism* and virtue ethics—these have all been well under way for over twenty years now, and already feature in the frontline of the programs and publications of mainstream academies.

Unlike in the Middle Ages when theology led the way, theology has in more recent times been slower to catch on to such new developments. Strangely this reluctance is evident even when the new philosophy's success is demonstrable. All too few systematic theologians yet engage with and learn from the rebirth of ideas about soul, life, death, immortality, atonement, eternity, prayer or god in philosophical theology; few moral theologians have realised that it is Aristotle and Aquinas, not Mill and Sartre, who are at the cutting edge of today's ethics; few pastoral theologians understand that the richness of Christian tradition on the body, person, freedom, sexuality, relationships and commitments is now well appreciated even in many secular philosophical quarters, and is always accorded at least a serious intellectual response.

Fides et Ratio will give significant encouragement to academics for decades to come, even if it fails to redirect the academy as radically as its author might pray for. Already big-name philosophers and theologians, including some represented in this book, are responding to its concerns. And there are many others, Alasdair MacIntyre, John Finnis and Aidan Nichols to name just a few, who are leaders in their fields. It will take time for others to internalise and respond to the challenges of the encyclical, challenges which go beyond technical questions within particular schools of philosophy or theology, to the very basis of academic life and the life of the mind.

For some decades past some of these academic debates have been more or less impossible: discussion of anything seen as dependent on 'Christian values' (let alone 'Catholic') has, at least until recently, been marginalised in self-consciously secular 'liberal' academies. But debate on faith matters, on religious topics, and topics of interest to religious believers can now take place in most universities. Thus concern over the nature and functions of the university in general, and of a Catholic (or other church-sponsored) university or academy in particular, and the implications of the university's public consecration to truth can now feature in debates between philosophers, theologians and others, and unite them in contending with pressures from educational administrators, political masters or the culture (Gaita, Ramsay). Engagement between Western, Judeo-Christian culture and other cultures and thought systems, such as that dialogue with Eastern thought invited by the Pope (72), is now a topic for thinkers other than church diplomats and empirical anthropologists. The specifically Christian notion of a historical approach to culture that does not dissolve into relativism can at last be debated, and the contributions of some out-of-the-closet Christians, such as Alasdair MacIntyre, taken seriously in the secular academy (Rowland).

Perhaps more than any of these, the old idea of a wisdom for loving and living by should be explained and made accessible to ordinary folk (Haldane). Socrates, Buddha and Jesus all offered a philosophy for living by, but the average issue of a philosophical periodical offers little—even indirectly—to help people lead a more fulfilling life. Moral, metaphysical and existential propositions are deeply needed by ordinary people, and philosophers can and should provide these in accessible ways, and not just refine them for their peers' benefit or for points for the annual research report. In due course, people's minds may well be opened up to specifically theological concerns and truths; but for those not yet interested in Scripture or ecclesial Tradition, there will at least be some wisdom and some deeper yearning to be found through philosophy. When we take part in this sort of conversation, our thoughts and choices have more than utility value. We are already choosing to *live* in a certain way.

The contributors to this volume adopt various stances towards *Fides et Ratio*, but each treats some question(s) it occasions conscious of the challenges of both faith *and* reason. In itself this may be one of the enduring fruits of the encyclical: the respectful and fruitful conversation it invites. Where debate about philosophy and theology will go next is uncertain, but the Pope has done academics, and thinkers generally, a great service by raising the questions and making the points he has, at the beginning of a new century of human civilisation and a new millennium of grace. By giving us something seriously to think about, including some 'hard sayings' and some real light for the future, John Paul II has offered thinkers a tribute much more satisfying than pats on the back or kicks elsewhere. And by indicating their great respect for the life of the mind, both the Pope and the writers of this volume have demonstrated in practice the friendship that is possible for faith and reason in the millennium ahead.

Sceptical Realism: Faith and Reason in Collaboration

Marilyn McCord Adams

1. *Fides et Ratio*: Friendly, familiar, but somehow flawed!

For an Anglican eavesdropper, *Fides et Ratio* is a mild-mannered document, decidedly more congenial than Cardinal Ratzinger's commentary on *Ad Tuendam Fidem* (1998) which reasserted the invalidity of our orders and banned discussion of women in office; certainly less provocative than ARCIC's *The Gift of Authority* which renewed the offer of papal services to decide crucial controversies on behalf of the whole church with *no less authority than that of the ecumenical councils!* For an Anglican *philosophical* theologian—and, no, that's not, it only seems to be, an oxymoron—John Paul II's call for a revival of philosophical theology, for a renewed recognition that philosophy is the backbone of theology, for a return to 'the good old days' when four years of philosophy prepared the way for theological training, is surely music to my ears (3–4, 60, 62, 77)! How welcome to a medievalist in these days of waning neo-scholasticism, that he should commend medieval models of integration between faith and reason, between philosophy and theology (43–44, 58, 78)! *Fides et Ratio*'s mentions of the Magisterium (50, 78–79) are not heavy-handed, but merely express the obvious point: that if dogma underdetermines philosophy, not every philosophical position is compatible with Christian doctrine. The encyclical comes peaceably, not to condemn philosophy nor even primarily to discipline it, but as a suitor hoping to re-enlist its help (5).

Likewise attractive to a middle-aging 'sixties' existentialist is John Paul II's further step of imbedding familiar epistemological ideas within a 'personalist' framework, which—like Anselm's Christian Platonism—treats intellectual inquiry as but one dimension of our quest for the meaning of life (1, 26)! We humans have a natural tendency to seek the Truth, to ask ultimate questions, and in so doing to over-reach ourselves, to stretch for an answer that can be found only in a transcendent source (1, 5, 25, 30). In this context, submission to authority sheds connotations of intellectual repression, to find its home in the process of human persons entrusting themselves to one another and to a personal God (31–33). Likewise, the problem of evil is exposed as one that arises *for* persons and demands *a person(s)-to-person(s)* solution (76).

Nevertheless, for converging Anglican and philosophical reasons, I find myself opposed to what may be *the* (is at least *a*) central argument of the piece. Surveying the malaise and misery, the shallowness and confusion of our human condition, John Paul II represents confidence about human competence generally, and the prospect of certainty in particular, as a condition of the possibility of a successful search for positive meaning in life (4–6; cf 67–68). We settle for less, because we don't think we can do it (55–56, 61). No point trying, when we can't succeed! *Fides et Ratio* counters, 'Buck up! Think of yourself as "the Little Engine that could"!'

My title is a pun. Regarding the competence of human nature and the adequacy of its *ante-mortem* capacities, I am (in a colloquial sense) sceptical, if I may say so, grimly realistic. Only partly in consequence of this, I disagree with the Pope's epistemological claims, and so am (in a technical sense) a sceptical realist: someone who believes that there is a fact of the matter about metaphysical claims, but denies our *ante-mortem* capacity to know *with certainty* which (if any) are true. So, His Holiness might well regard me as part of the problem rather than the solution, and that in more ways than one! Happily, I can take heart because I find the Pope's pragmatic inference uncompelling. On the contrary, evident human incompetence can be a powerful motivator. Human need for God's practical help is dire as well as metaphysically grounded. At the intellectual level, need to know and the frustration of cognitive dissonance join natural curiosity and the intrinsic desirability of the object to sustain effort, despite the fact that our goal is incommensurate with our capacities.

2. The horror of human nature

In *Fides et Ratio*, John Paul II celebrates the notion that human persons are meaning-seekers by nature. He recognises, at least in passing, that evil is a problem because it jeopardises meaning-making. I, for my part, remain sceptical about the excellence or even adequacy of human capacities, because human life is infested with horrendous evils, ever pregnant with their possibility. And this condition seems to me not to be superficial or accidental but rather rooted in human nature and the environment of real and apparent scarcity in which we are placed.

2.1 In the grip of the horrendous

By *horrendous*,[1] I mean evils that reasonably seem to be life-ruining —more precisely, evils the participation in (the doing or suffering of) constitutes *prima facie* reason to doubt whether the participant's life could (given their inclusion in it) be a great good to him/her on the whole. Paradigm horrors include both individual and massive collective suffering, the rape of a woman and axing off of her arms, psycho-physical torture whose ultimate goal is the disintegration of personality, betrayal of one's deepest loyalties, participation in the destruction of those one loves best, child abuse of the sort described by Ivan Karamazov, child pornography, parental incest, slow death by starvation, the explosion of nuclear bombs over populated areas.

I believe most people would agree that such evils constitute reason to doubt whether the participants' life can be worth living, because it is so difficult humanly to conceive how such evils could be overcome. In terms of Roderick Chisholm's contrast between *balancing off* and *defeat*,[2] horrendous evils *seem prima face, not only to balance off but to engulf* any positive value in the participant's life with which they are not organically connected. In most (if not all) cases their destructive power reaches beyond their *concrete* disvalue (eg the pain and material deprivation they involve) into the deep-structure of the person's frameworks of meaning-making, seemingly to *defeat* the individual's value *as a person*, to *degrade* him/her to subhuman status. Thus, the Nazi death camps aimed, not merely to kill, but to dehumanise their victims, treating them worse than cattle to break down their person-alities and reduce their social instincts to raw animal aggression and self-preservation. Organising and running such institutions also degraded the Nazis, who caricatured human nature by using their

---

1. I defined the category first in my paper 'Theodicy and Blame', *Philosophical Topics* Volume 14 (1988): 215–45 and discussed it further in 'Horrendous Evils and the Goodness of God', *Proceedings of the Aristotelian Society* Supplementary Volume 63 (1989): 297–310. Reprinted in *The Problem of Evil*, edited by Marilyn McCord Adams and Robert Merrihew Adams (Oxford: University of Oxford Press, 1990), 209–21.

2. Roderick Chisholm 'The Defeat of Good and Evil' revised and reprinted in Adams and Adams *ibid*, 53–68.

finest powers the more imaginatively to transgress the bounds of human decency. Similarly, inasmuch as taboos constitute hedges erected to maintain minimum standards necessary for human community, taboo violations degrade their perpetrators, by exhibiting their unfitness for human society; they appear subjectively to degrade by socially disorienting their victims, exploding role-expectations at the most fundamental of levels.

I think it is obvious that *human beings are radically vulnerable to and frequent participants in horrors*, so defined. *Human history is riddled with horrendous evil*, as history books and newspapers, introspection and the Bible itself, all testify—so much so, that virtually every human being is complicit in actual horrors merely by living in his/her nation or society. Few individuals would deliberately starve a child into retardation, or force mothers to hard labour, sewing piecework all night for a few dollars, or withhold life-saving drugs from suffering people. But we participate, indeed reap large benefits from a social, political, and economic organisation that does and allows such things as a matter of course.

The sobering fact is that *it is comparatively easy for human beings to cause (be salient members in causal chains leading to) horrendous evils.* Indeed, *an individual's capacity to produce suffering (horrendous and otherwise) unavoidably exceeds his/her ability to experience it.* Qualitatively this is obvious: what could a nineteen-year-old male soldier experience that is like enough to the mother's anguish at seeing her child bounced to death on the points of bayonets? Quantitatively also, Hitler organised the degrading liquidation of millions but was himself only one person who could not possibly experience everything he caused. Yet, *where suffering is concerned, capacity to conceive follows capacity to experience; therefore our ability to cause horrors unavoidably exceeds our powers of conception.* Just as the totally blind are cognitively deficient about colour no matter how many colour facts they know, because of their inability imaginatively to represent colours to themselves; so also we cannot *fully* grasp how bad are the evils of which we have had no experience.

Morality is not the cure for horrors, because the horrendous is not fundamentally a moral category. Not all horrors involve moral wrongdoing (eg the father who unwittingly and non-negligently backs his truck over his toddler son; the torments of schizophrenia or Tay Sachs disease). Even where perpetrators are morally wrong, since 'incorrigible ignorance diminishes the voluntary', we cannot be *fully* morally responsible for the horrors we perpetrate. Certainly, white segregationists who 'sicked' German shepherd police dogs on blacks or fire-bombed churches or lynched and shot activists knew enough about what they were doing to qualify as morally wicked. My claim is that there was a vast surplus left over, that Martin Luther King was right to quote Luke-Acts (Luke 23:24; Acts 3:17) and contend that in a very important sense, horror-perpetrators 'know not what they do'. Nor can morality domesticate the horrendous with 'just deserts': to visit horrors upon horror-perpetrators does not stop but rather spreads the infection, does not reverse but only multiplies the ruin. Letting liberated concentration camp prisoners make Hitler shove former camp guards live into crematorial ovens might let some taste revenge. But it would further devastate their prospects for positive personal meaning.

Overall, there is an incommensuration between human agency and the horrendous. Their power seemingly to ruin can be quite disproportionate to the area they occupy on the space-time worm of our lives (eg Sophie's choice of which of her children shall live and which be liquidated by the Nazis, the momentary turn of the steering wheel that transforms someone into a forever-after paraplegic). We are vulnerable to them, without being reliably able to avoid, prevent, or be fully responsible for them. To affirm human competence for meaning-making in a world such as this would require confidence that human beings are able to do or be something that would overcome (balance off or defeat) horrors. But the epistemic measure of how bad horrors are is that we are stumped as to how to integrate them into a defeating good. The metaphysical measure is that no package of merely created goods—much less any within our power—would be sufficient to balance off or defeat them. Divine goodness and divine resourcefulness are needed to make positive sense of horrors; an Inner Teacher is necessary to teach us how to collaborate and appropriate the possible meanings that He makes.

2.2 Natural explanation
My own diagnosis is that this predicament arises from our being personal animals; that it is the result of tying personality to a developmental life-cycle and placing us in an environment of apparent scarcity. We not only use bodies as instruments, as a pilot does the ship; our psyche reflects our

biology, at both conscious and unconscious levels, in ways scientists now predict and in others that go unnoticed even by them. Of course, this fact can be interpreted metaphysically in many ways. But it led at least medieval Aristotelians to reject dualism, and to say instead that our soul is the form of an organic body. In this world, we humans go through an animal life-cycle: birth, growth, maturity, decline, death. Psycho-spiritually as well as biologically, we are developmental creatures: we human beings start life ignorant, weak, and helpless, psychologically so lacking in a self-concept as to be incapable of choice. We learn to 'construct' a picture of the world, ourselves, and other people only with difficulty over a long period of time and under the extensive influence of other non-ideal choosers. Human development is the interactive product of human nature and its environment, and from early on we humans are confronted with problems that we cannot adequately grasp or cope with, and in response to which we mount (without fully conscious calculation) inefficient adaptational strategies. Yet, the human psyche is habit-forming in such a way that these reactive patterns, based as they are on a child's inaccurate view of the world and its strategic options, become entrenched in the individual's personality. Typically, they are unconsciously 'acted out' for years, causing much suffering to self and others before (if ever) they are recognised and undone through a difficult and painful process of therapy and/or spiritual formation. Having thus begun *immature*, we arrive at adulthood in a state of *impaired freedom*, as our childhood adaptational strategies continue to distort our perceptions and behaviour. We adults with impaired freedom are *responsible* for our choices, actions, and even the character moulded by our unconscious adaptational strategies, in the sense that we are the *agent causes* of them. Our assessments of moral responsibility, praise and blame cannot afford to take this impairment into account, because we are not as humans capable of organising and regulating ourselves in that fine-tuned a way. And so, except for the most severe cases of impairment, we continue to hold ourselves *responsible to one another*.

Our animal life-cycle combines with our instinct towards self-preservation to produce an underlying anxiety about death, based on our 'knowledge' that we contain the seeds of our own demise. These psycho-biological factors make resources *seem* scarcer than they are. Nevertheless, there is the additional fact that we live in a physical environment that is prima facie inhospitable to human life. Nature is more powerful than we and hostile to our survival; collectively, human survival has been won through wit and technology. Nevertheless, the understanding of nature is sufficiently beyond us that we cannot anticipate the consequences of measures taken for present survival; and past apparent advances have had environmental consequences that threaten future disaster. Moreover, we are placed in an environment of scarcity, with apparently not enough to go around so that everyone can live comfortably. No wonder there is a Hobbesian war for the survival of the fittest, resulting in the stronger exploiting the weaker etc.

If human vulnerability to horrors is not superficial but rooted in our very nature, while actual participation in horrors is inevitable when we are set in a world such as this, human being in this world seems scarcely an excellence to be celebrated but rather a cursed kind of thing to be!

2.3 False optimism?

Traditional theology, with its free-will approach to the origin of evil, can in one sense agree. John Paul II simply follows suit, when he identifies our present condition, not as natural or original, but as that into which the human race fell as a natural and punitive consequence of sin. He appeals to sin to explain the fragmentation of philosophy and culture, as well as our confused ineffectiveness in seeking the meaning of life.

Elsewhere I have argued that classical free-will approaches are impotent, when it comes to pinning primary responsibility for horrors on free creatures. Even if Adam and Eve were created in an otherwise utopic environment with relevantly informed, mature and competent free agency, still their original condition was one in which false choices would trigger horrors beyond their power to imagine. Thus, according to the traditional scenario, this situation of radical human vulnerability to horrors was part of our original condition—one set up, not by our forbears' free choices, but by God!

Whether 'we did it to ourselves' or 'came by it naturally', *Fides et Ratio* and its author walk a rhetorical tight rope. Sin answers the question 'why, if we're so competent, we're individually and collectively so mixed up?' (19, 22, 28, 51–54). But if the natural and punitive consequences of sin landed us in our present circumstances, and if sin still besets us, why think we have it in us to make the kind of progress the Pope's agenda requires? My own view is that John Paul II can maintain his optimism about human thought and agency only by ignoring the implications of our radical vulnerability to horrendous evils. I submit that where positive meaning-making is our project, our predicament is much gloomier than he suggests.

Nor is my pessimistic picture that of a closet Calvinist. Actually, it is the Pope's argument that closely parallels Calvin's at the beginning of the *Institutes*. My low doctrine of human nature and its *ante-mortem* condition was wrung from reflection on *experience*—my own and that of my inner city congregations; from what I read in the newspapers about former Yugoslavia and Rwanda; not to mention the more insidious sides of university and ecclesiastical politics! If my estimate is controversial, I can only ask the reader to consider whether my description does not ring true.

3. Sceptical realism

In *Fides et Ratio*, the Pope goes beyond material assertions—eg that God exists as first cause and ultimate end of all else, that humans are free, capable of grasping relevant moral truths, and immortal (sec 4)—belief in which would be a condition of the possibility of our not getting demoralised, to make two further claims. To appreciate the difference between them, it will prove helpful to appropriate some distinctions from Rudolf Carnap's discussion in 'Empiricism, Semantics, and Ontology'. Carnap's focus is on the philosophy of mathematics, in particular on disagreements about what ontological commitments would be required to give an appropriate semantics for mathematical axioms, postulates, theorems, etc. He treats the competing philosophical theories as contrasting conceptual schemes, each of which aims at consistency, coherence, explanatory power, and fruitfulness. Carnap then distinguishes two ways of treating the question, 'Do numbers exist?': as an *internal* question, raised from the inside a given conceptual framework—in which case the answer is 'yes' when raised within Platonising and 'no' within formalist schemes; and as an *external* question about which of the competing conceptual schemes is the true one. Because Carnap regarded conceptual frameworks as conventional constructs, he advocated liberality in ontology: 'the more the merrier'; 'let many flowers bloom'. There is no need to shave Plato's beard. But there is no obligation to comb it either. For, empiricist that he was, Carnap denied that external questions had meaningful answers, insofar as there is no conceptual-framework-independent Reality with a capital R correspondence with which could measure their truth or falsity. Later, DZ Phillips transferred this point to Wittgensteinian language games or forms of life. Many language games are played, and there are criteria of reality internal to each. But there are no game-independent criteria of reality, no Reality with a capital R, against which language games could be measured and correspond or fail to correspond.

3.1 Metaphysical realism

In the encyclical, when the Pope takes his stand against 'relativisms' (5) and insists that there is such a thing as 'objective' (25, 56, 69, 82), 'universal and absolute' (27, 75, 95) Truth that transcends human conventions, he seems to be forwarding and commanding *a metaphysical realist* point of view. He wants to affirm, not just that it is true *within Thomist conceptual frameworks* that God exists as first cause and ultimate end, or that humans are free, possessed of a capacity to be cognizant of relevant moral truths, and immortal. Rather his position is that these are 'objective' truths in the sense that they correspond to a conceptual-framework-independent Reality with a capital R (cf 87).

Here, he follows the great medieval philosopher-theologians —Anselm, Aquinas, Bonaventure, Scotus, and Ockham—who took metaphysical realism for granted. Had it been proposed to them, they would have denied that reality is at bottom socially constructed by contingent conventions, whether human or divine. They would agree that the 'content' of the divine essence and created natures is not a function of anyone's volition. For Anselm and Aquinas, the divine essence is truth and goodness; no genuine power could make it otherwise. According to them, created natures are defined as different ways of imperfectly imitating the divine. Scotus and Ockham disagree, insisting that because relations are metaphysically posterior to their relata, the 'contents' of created natures pertained to them 'of themselves': if they could exist of themselves, they would be such of themselves. If they owe their being to God, nevertheless, omnipotence does not include power to make bovine or human nature to be differently constituted. Even Ockham (whose nominalism has been too often caricatured) is almost indignant at the suggestion that genera and species—created natural kinds—should be a function of human convention. Likewise taken for granted as a non-conventional fact of the matter are the claims that natures form an excellence hierarchy with the divine essence at the top, and that divine and created contrast as infinite to finite, so that there is a 'metaphysical gap' between them.

Anti-realism in philosophy is supposed to win the advantage of dismissing sceptical worries. If there aren't any facts of the matter beyond what relevant human communities could (in principle) agree upon, we need harbour no concern about how to gain cognitive access to 'things-in-themselves' or otherwise framework-independent realities. To those who press the queries—'are there minds other than our own?', 'is there an external world?', 'does God exist?'—the reply comes, 'the language games are played!', 'the internal criteria are regularly applied and yield affirmative answers'.

Anti-realism in theology isolates religious discourse, not only from ordinary language, but also from that of the 'broad-sense' sciences, the better to immunise religion against historical and philosophical challenges, thereby allowing people to practise a supernatural spirituality without the slightest infringement on their intellectual freedom. Put otherwise, if all of the criteria of reality are *internal* to language games, then religion and science (or history) deal with separate realities, which do not conflict because they do not meet. Some theologians (John Hick prominent among them) are attracted to a hybrid position, which recognises that God or Reality with a capital R is too big to be invented by human beings, but concludes that the 'size-gap' is so vast that God-talk in particular and religious language generally cannot be literally true by correspondence with Reality with a capital R but at most mythologically or metaphorically true insofar as it is part of a practice that promotes positive spiritual development. Both theological anti-realism and its hybrids claim for themselves the moral high ground of tolerance for the world's great religions and for the diversity of cultures generally, indeed promote themselves as an antidote to overweening Christian imperialism.

In philosophy, anti-realism strikes me as a bad bargain, more as a concession to than a refutation of sceptical worries. On the one hand, it is a cheap victory, because it buys the right to say that we know the truth with certainty, by redefining what 'truth' and 'certain knowledge' are. On the other, its pays the exorbitant price of admitting that the Truth we wanted to reach is not even there. Of course, many philosophical anti-realists adjust so well as to claim that it was a confusion to think we ever really wanted Truth with a capital T in the first place!

Both philosophical and theological anti-realism lead—as John Paul II implies—to intellectual and personal fragmentation (81, 88). Religion gets turned into mythology, or worse yet, consciously manipulable ideology, while broad- or narrow-sense science is forwarded as the paradigm of intellectual respectability. The notion of God as the conceptual-framework-independent *ens realissimum*, the one Truth around which all others are integrated, the Eternal Logos, the One Whom we would greet person-to-person, the One about Whom human reason is above all created to speak as much truth as it can . . . the idea that some of our religious discourse has cognitive content . . . the medieval recognition that intellectual inquiry *is* a dimension of spirituality . . . all of these get deliberately 'washed out'. Certainly, the last fifty years show how difficult it has been for analytic philosophers to keep from consigning ethics to the same non-cognitivist fate! So, like my medieval mentors, like John Paul II, I cannot accept these costs. Like them, I count myself metaphysical realist to the core!

3.2 Scepticism or certainty?

In his *Critique of Practical Reason*, Kant argues that *belief* in God, freedom, and immortality is a condition of the possibility of perse-verance in moral living. In *Fides et Ratio*, John Paul II seems to be advancing the stronger claim: that *certainty* about answers to *external* questions about God, freedom, immortality, etc are conditions of the possibility of a successful search for the meaning of life (2, 27, 92). Professor McInerny has already pointed out (in his reaction-paper 'Implicit Philosophy' at his own conference on the encyclical) the oddity of the list of alleged certainties—including as it does some self-evident propositions (such as the law of non-contradiction) and some wildly controversial and very much contemporary minority report claims (such as that things here below have God as their first cause and ultimate end), theses that whole systems of famous philosophers have been explicitly bent on rejecting. Such metaphysical ground is shared at most in the domain of unconscious and highly obstructable ten-dencies to accept the philosophical theses in question! And the vast array of philosophical disagreements to which the encyclical itself points robs one of any conceptual-framework-independent reason for believing that we have any such tendencies.

When it comes to external questions and their answers, I count myself a *sceptical* realist. *Pace* Carnap, I hold with the Pope that such questions and their answers are meaningful, because there is a Reality with a capital R to which conceptual frameworks do or do not correspond. *Pace il Papa*, however, I agree with Carnap that neither reason nor experience can bring all rational persons to agree. I came to this conclusion while writing my book on *William Ockham*; but it could just as well have been a book on Aquinas or Scotus, because it was the scholastic method that triggered the apparent insight. Bouncing back and forth between arguments *pro* and *contra*, weighing and envisioning objections and replies, attempting to referee late thirteenth and early fourteenth century debates, I came to a conclusion that Ockham, his contemporaries and distinguished predecessors never drew: that well-formulated philosophical/theological positions of any interest are inherently controversial, because defences of them will eventually involve premises over which parties to the dispute are fundamentally at odds.

What holds for philosophical/theological theories also applies to forms of life or world-views broadly speaking. What reason does not settle for theory, experience does not establish where the world's great religions are concerned. When the Pope declares that only Christ crucified can finally make sense of life, that Christ crucified breaks free of all cultural limitations (12, 23), we have to be medieval enough to distinguish. Does he mean to deny that the spiritual fruits of holiness are to be found in roughly the same proportions in Hinduism and Buddhism? As Hick is fond of pointing out, this would constitute a flat contradiction of our *ante-mortem* experience. Such a denial would also undermine the encyclical's attempt to be appreciative of non-European (or at least, non-Mediterranean) cultures (cf 70–72). If he means merely that in the world to come, everyone will agree that God was in Christ reconciling the world to himself, then *ante-mortem* certainty about the answers to external questions is not required.

Nor do I understand these fundamental 'undecidabilities' to be due to damage to our faculties produced by any *actual*—individual and/or collective—participation in horrors. In a way, our inability to demonstrate answers to Carnapian external questions—about which philosophical system corresponds to Reality with a capital R— shows not that we are incapacitated for doing philosophy, but rather that we are very good at philosophy—skilled enough to develop a plurality of equally defensible conceptual schemes. Likewise, the range of pragmatically fruitful religions testifies not to human incompetence but rather to human resourcefulness in generating a rich variety of forms of life.

3.3 The pragmatics of scepticism

In *Fides et Ratio*, John Paul II numbers scepticism among the demons that account for our current malaise and confusion (5, 81). But the history of Western philosophy shows how the practical consequences of scepticism have been charted in at least three different ways. Some (the Pyrrho of legend) held that assent should be withheld from what is uncertain, and so concluded that sceptics should not hold any beliefs at all. Others allowed that belief was humanly inevitable but all the same irrational. Still others (including David Hume) granted that belief could be reasonable even where certainty is impossible. It is easy to see how scepticism of the first two types could be pragmatically disastrous or at least demoralising. Remember how, according to the story, Pyrrho starved! In counting myself a sceptical realist, however, I identify myself with approaches of the third type, and so hold not only that it is legitimate to hold beliefs, but that there is rhyme and reason to preferring some sorts of beliefs to others. Even if external-question certainty isn't within our grasp, there is a criterion to guide our aim, where Truth with a capital T is our goal.

Specifically, I embrace *coherence*, not as a theory of *what truth consists in* (as a metaphysical realist, I insist, truth is *constituted* by correspondence, once again, with Reality with a capital R), but a *method of pursuing truth*. My assumption is that human reason's best chance at truth is won through the effort of integrating our data with our many and diverse intuitions into a coherent picture with the theoretical virtues of clarity, consistency, explanatory power, and fruitfulness. The process is difficult because our materials are so complex and pull in many different directions. It is dynamic because the twin desiderata of consistency and richness force many trial adjustments and alterations, before a satisfactory organisation, mastering complexity with simplicity, is achieved. The assignment is also fluid, because data and intuitions that strike us as bedrock at one time may become less entrenched later, and vice versa, forcing 'Copernican revolutions' in our outlook.

Where philosophical theology is concerned, faith and reason will surely be in collaboration. To begin with, theory-making, coherent world-view construction is a rational enterprise that puts both analytical and synthetic philosophical skills to work. But the entrenched data will come from many quarters: in philosophical theology, from reason, experience, and authority, and so will include both philosophical intuitions (eg that human souls cannot be reduced to atoms and the void, that what is received is received after the manner of the receiver, that an infinite regress in essentially ordered causes is impossible) and dogmatic claims (eg God was in Christ reconciling the world to himself, the body and blood of Christ are really present under forms of bread and wine). Moreover, while sceptical realism does not assign reason the role of proving philosophical claims to all rational persons, it can still allot faith and reason a certain autonomy. For philosophical claims will have to secure their market share in competition with alternative advantageous philosophical ways of understanding things; while the assertions of faith will be laid down by primary authorities and / or tested in conversation with theological and spiritual traditions and current religious experience. Of course, demand for consistency brings faith and reason into conversation with each other (that's what makes it philosophical theology). But this does not eliminate independent conversations or rule out a variety of philosophical explanations of faith—as medieval school theology clearly shows.

Having abandoned the possibility of universal *sola ratione* convincement, the sceptical realist expects a plurality of positions to take the field and to commend themselves on the basis of their internal clarity, consistency, and coherence; on the basis of their explanatory power and fruitfulness. Most theories will exhibit costs and benefits, handle some problems and issues better than others: eg obviously and crudely, idealism does better with mind than with body; materialism the reverse; supralapsarian double predestination is strong on divine sovereignty but weak on human freedom and responsibility in relation to God; Eastern trinitarian theology is firm on 'three' but scrambles for 'one', while Augustinian approaches easily accommodate 'one' while somersaulting for 'three'. The goal of philosophising and theologising becomes so to develop one's own outlook as to be a credible competitor, overall getting roughly as good a rating for explaining, handling problems and difficulties as the others. Importantly, dispatch of this task is incompatible with arrogance toward and/or cultivated ignorance of alternative positions. On the contrary, it requires the intellectual flexibility to enter into the other theories, to appreciate their benefits as well as to assess their costs, to learn what, why, and how they handle issues well or badly. This exercise sparks ingenuity and inventiveness, which sees how to refine one's own approach to strengthen its vulnerable points, and win new advantages for itself.

Thus, sceptical realism can count it rational—or at least, not irrational—to endorse one of the plurality of well-developed positions. It follows further that no position can be discredited by the mere observation that there is some theoretical or practical alternative. One would have to establish it to be decidedly inferior to its competitors in ways that cannot be repaired. The obvious consequence is that there will be a variety of positions, each of which it could be rational to hold. Once again, what goes for conceptual frameworks applies also to forms of life or world-views conceived more broadly. Belief systems and value hierarchies, life-styles and practices that pull life into fruitful focus would rate high. So far as our *ante-mortem* observations take us, the world's great religions, with their varying patterns of strengths and weakness, might seem to be on a par with each other.

Sceptical realism is thus committed to pluralism where the *reasonableness* of conceptual frameworks and the viability of life-styles is concerned. Insofar as it operates with Carnap's distinction between internal and external questions, it also concedes that answers to the former are relative to the conceptual framework or form of life. Once again, what keeps sceptical realism from endorsing pluralism or relativism *simpliciter* is (unsurprisingly) its *realism*, the fact that it posits a Reality with a capital R over and against which the conceptual frameworks and forms of life are measured.

What the Pope laments as false modesty, sceptical realism applauds as epistemic humility, which thereby gains a practical advantage over the Pope's *Fides-et-Ratio* position, where cross-cultural appreciation is concerned. If we have the capacity for certainty that ultimate meaning is found in Christ crucified, and sin is the explanation of error, then the door is opened for blaming the non-Christian for not agreeing with us. By contrast, sceptical realism furnishes Christians with every motive to learn from non-Christians, the better to enrich their own philosophical theologies and life-styles with dimensions they might have missed.

3.4 Missing motivation?

Still, the pursuit of Truth is arduous; our radical vulnerability to horrors makes the search for positive meaning tortured. Augustine's question in *De beata vita* presses: how can we be motivated to accept the rigors of seeking the Truth, when certainty is sure to lie beyond our grasp? Camus's anxiety threatens: how can we persevere in our existential struggle to respect and affirm the sacred quality of human life, when we are all complicit in destroying it? This is the thrust of John Paul II's argument: we need to be *certain* about God, immortality, and our functional capacities, if we are to persevere to the end. Looking first to the theoretical level, I want to emphasise that while scepticism—about our ability to prove the Truth with a capital T of philosophical theses or systems to all rational persons—does foster intellectual flexibility and tolerance, it does not by itself breed philosophical insecurity or doubts. So far from reducing us to intellectual impotence, it challenges us to roll up our sleeves for the philosophical effort of developing our position up to a level of theoretical competitiveness. To the degree that we succeed, it licenses confidence in the existence of God as first cause and ultimate end, even—as John Locke and John Paul II both hoped—in the reasonableness of Christianity.

Returning to the broader context of personal meaning-making, my answer both overlaps and takes issue with the Pope's anthropology. Experience gives evidence of a life instinct, in human persons of a strong tendency to pull our subjective picture of the world together, to achieve and maintain sanity, to organise our desires and projects in such a way as to lead a happy life. The life instinct goes with being animals; our drive to find positive meaning lies at the core of what it is to be persons. Framework-internally, I am happy to join the Pope in speaking of a *natural* desire, in the sense of one built-in to what it is to be a human being. These keep us poised in the face of the challenge, seeking to do or be something of positive significance against amazing obstacles.

Nevertheless, a vivid appreciation of the horrendous—of our radical vulnerability to it and our frequent participation in it, of the fact that we are personal *animals*, containing within ourselves the seeds of our own demise, and the fact that our personality is tied to a developmental life-cycle—ought to convince us that these powers can be stumped, so stunned that we spin our wheels while fruitful progress comes to an end. And so I hold against 'Aristotelian optimism': given our radical vulnerability to horrors, there is no guarantee that our natural desire for *ante-mortem* flourishing will not be defeated. Try as we may, in this world we may fail, if not always, then for the most part.

My own anthropology is situated in the now disfavoured neighbourhood of Augustine and Anselm rather than that of my medieval Aristotelian friends. Experience supports my notion that, left to itself, personal animality—its merely created components of mind and body, spirit and matter—are a dysfunctional combination. Framework-internally, I conclude that these dualities were not even designed to function on their own, without the omnipresent and continual, at first unnoticed but eventually and more effectively witting, collaboration with the divine inner teacher, whose involvement with us is so profound and pervasive as to be an operative part of who we are. In my judgment, the radical heart of the matter is not the need for collaboration between faith and reason, but a naturally necessary and inevitable working relationship between the creature and God himself!

The Spirit surrounds, enfolds, nudges, tries to pull us into focus, as St Paul says, 'with sighs too deep for words'. The Spirit coaches us through those developmental transitions—terrible twos, adolescence, mid-life crisis, the letting-go of ageing—when—despite continuities —we remodel ourselves so drastically as almost to become somebody else. Recognised or not, the Spirit spark-plugs all our creativity, whenever we problem-solve our way out of a shoe-box; make a better mousetrap; invent cubist painting, atonal music; take our stand for life and love in the midst of hatred, betrayal, disability or terminal illness; or just plain put two and two together to get fifteen!

Back in the eleventh century, Anselm explained how awakened desire combines with acknowledged incompetence to move us into deeper relationship with the God who satisfies. Anselm realised that given the *ante-mortem* (what he took to be *post-lapsum*) condition of our human nature, we get bogged down in our search for Truth, fall asleep to our possibilities, numb our desires to get the most out of life. His works are meant to function as 'outer' teachers, to dangle before us the desirability of our object, to remind us of our fundamental orientation towards the Good Itself, to coach us towards a more rational approach which seeks the source and does not mistake the means for the end.

Anselm's spiritual maps chart how no sooner is our passion stoked than we are brought face-to-face with our incompetence, with our ignorance of how to seek, with the disproportion between our powers and our ultimate end. Panic lands us where Augustine, Anselm, and evangelists in every age are convinced we ought to be: implicitly or explicitly, crying for help. But, all the while, the Spirit of God surrounds us, unnoticed like the air we breathe. And this helps explain why—to the extent that we do, to the extent that horror-participation does not stop us in our tracks—we keep trying. Like infants groping for focus in an environment of loving persons, unless horror participation mixes or screens out the messages, we subliminally sense that—despite our frustration—our plight cannot be wholly desperate, because the one whom we seek is the one in whom we live and move and have our being!

Comments on 'Sceptical Realism: Faith and Reason in Collaboration'

John Hilary Martin OP

Dr Adams begins with an acute observation on the propensity for doing evil inherent in the human animal. She gives some praise to the Pope for defending realism, but at the end accuses (perhaps that is too value-laden a word, better to say she *finds*) the Pope a bit of a Pelagian who relies too much on classical philosophy for solving problems which are really religious. As we might expect from Anglican intellectualism and from one of our foremost scholars on Ockham, her differences with the Pope's document, *Fides et Ratio*, while significant, have much to offer.

For many years I have lived in California at Berkeley. It is a town named quite deliberately after Bishop George Berkeley (1685–1753), the famous philosopher of empirical idealism. He actually did spend five years in America, although not at Berkeley. He tried to overcome scepticism by relying not on reason as much as on idealism. The town was named after him because it saw itself as the *Athens of the West*. The teaching of philosophy has always been a great specialism of Berkeley and a great deal of it is done on a street called Telegraph Ave, a street that leads directly into the main gate of the University of California. Something called the *free speech movement* was born there, which was sceptical about much of American life, especially the purported benefits of a war then going on in Vietnam.

Telegraph Ave is lined with stalls and tables where students, and would-be students, sell souvenirs, tie-dyed shirts, crystals, home-made jewellery and much else (strictly nothing costing over $19.95). But much wisdom is exchanged between the people of the street and the vendors. One bit I overheard was an exchange between a vendor who was trying to flog some earings, said to be gold and studded with stones said to be emeralds. The street-wise local dismissed the vendor's spiel with the withering comment, 'You can call it what you like, but it ain't what it is'. The bottom line of the exchange: *Language doesn't construct reality; reality constructs reality*. Naming is pointless without some basis for it; reality isn't socially or intellectually constructed, at least not entirely. Even if you happen to convince yourself, and succeed in convincing everyone on the block, that the earings *are* gold and *do* have emeralds (for under $19.95)—the earings really *aren't* and *don't*. The implicit presupposition of the street-wise individual on the Avenue was that reality precedes what we say about it. He recognised no emeralds but rather a bit of flashy trash and he was not about to buy it. Sceptical, and with every reason, he was unwilling to buy and smilingly passed on his way.

If I understand Professor Adams's paper this is something of what she means by saying she is a *realist* and it is in this sense that she agrees with the Pope in *Fides et Ratio*. Reality comes first and is the basis of all reasonable thought. Having agreed to that, she finds there is still much to be sceptical about. Do we know reality well enough to make definitive judgments about it, about what we do with it? Can we trust our judgments about reality to make definitive judgments, especially in the moral order? Can we ever trust our judgments since we have mindlessly thrust the most horrendous evils on each other over the centuries—some of them flowing from communities quite conscious of what they were doing. These evils include items like aerial bombing during the war, the stolen generation, the holocaust, but perhaps more horrendous than all of those, the use of torture where persons set out to use pain to destroy the very personality of another. All this suggests we can put no trust in each other's knowledge of reality, maybe even of God.

Granted there is a reality independent of our thinking, what about our understanding of it? If reality is the basis of our thought, why do people disagree so much in their understanding of it? At the opening of the modern age, John Locke suggested a new strategy. It was high time, he thought, not to make reality the object of our thought as past philosophers had always done, but rather to look at knowledge from the other end, from the workings of the human mind. Locke's thought, of course, was well timed. After Descartes it was time to step back and concentrate on the organisation of human knowing. Whatever might be said about human minds (and much has been said since the 1700s) all agreed that human beings do not have *angelic minds*—do not have an intuitive grasp of reality, have to work things out step by step. We follow a rational process.

Rational processes leave room for error and misapprehension, even with the best thinkers. Only some aspects of reality ever filter through the knowing process. Now, as Locke suggested, examination of our mental filters is an extremely important thing to do. If done well, we learn what we will have (and not have) at the end of the filtering process. But Locke misguided us too. He diverted philosophical attention away from the object, away from reality, and spent the bulk of his time with the filter. It might be time again, as Adams suggests we do, to return again to the discussion of total reality, both the part we have filtered in and the part filtered out. Here, as the Pope has suggested in *Fides et Ratio*, the classical tradition of philosophy may be of help.

The stance of classical philosophers, like Anselm and Aquinas, is that reality is intelligible, but it's not entirely intelligible. In the last analysis we understand reality rather weakly and in a diluted manner. There still is lots of room for scepticism. Not only philosophers but ordinary people keep raising questions to which they know reason can give no definitive answers—questions about the character of life after death, or whether there is any life after death at all, whether the destiny of the human race falls within some overall divine plan or are human affairs are merely happenstantial, why we practice evil, why the holocausts, and why torture? Philosophy does not understand reality well enough to do more than give tentative answers to questions such as these.

But again, if knowledge is based on reality, why do we often do so poorly with questions such as these? While Adams is a realist about reality, she is not a realist about human knowledge of that reality. Human understanding of reality is not something which we can take blithely in stride and then act upon it as if that were a final truth.

This is a strong position and one I find attractive. Our noetic is constructive, it is the creation of custom, something we agree to—and so like all things human it can be defective. The reasoning which allows the taking of life in war, the taking of human life in the laboratory, reasoning that seems so right at the time decisions are made, can always benefit from a bit of scepticism. Adams's main difference with the Pope in these matters, as far as I can see, is with the quality of human knowledge. Reality does inform our minds, but not all that well. I also share Adams's hesitations about the range of reason, but from another stance. I agree that a great deal of what goes on in human experience is not reasonable, or directly intelligent at all. Our intellect, our mind, may hover over all our experience, but it never understands the object of experience very well. There is a mystery, an unintelligibility about much of the reality we brush up against. Its particularity escapes us. And so human judgments are necessarily provisional. They need to be assisted. Fortunately they are assisted in a variety of ways. First they are corrected by the collective wisdom of the human community. Ralph McInerny notes that answers to these issues can be found not only in the Thomistic tradition (the classical tradition to which the Pope may have been alluding), but we can also expect to find them echoed in many traditions. Reasonable understandings appear in many philosophic systems because there is a kind of commonsense in us that is always being informed by reality. But a partial understanding of reality from time to time will cause even this common understanding to go astray.

Are not the best aids to human judgment myth, religion and the judgments given in faith? I am not thinking so much at the moment of the judgments found in the Bible, but the faith given by God in every time and place. In this context I like the compact phrase of an Aboriginal elder—*Before Abraham, God was with the Aboriginal people.* The classical tradition of the *Dreaming* had much to tell that was beyond reasoning and even beyond collective custom. We are safe to say that God always is with all peoples—and is with them to this day. God can and will find ways to guide our reasoning.

This seems to be in line with one of the last points which Adams makes. There is a need for an inner teacher to improve and guide the judgments which we, or our community, want to make. It is that faith which will voice forceful criticisms of the reasonings which we construct. For the Christian that voice can be a public voice as well as inner. In the form of revelation, as the Pope might argue, it is the strongest and the final voice. But in the academy at least it will do its work off stage, so to speak, since faith is not assigned to do philosophy's work for it.

The Scandal of Philosophy: Reconciling Different Philosophical Systems According to *Fides et Ratio*

Ralph McInerny

When Pope Leo XIII called for the restoration of Christian philosophy according to the mind of Thomas Aquinas in 1879, the only question of pluralism was, so to speak, intramural. Leo's primary motive in turning Catholics to the thought of Thomas Aquinas was what he took to be the pass to which modern philosophy had brought the intellectual and social culture of the times. This left little motivation to seek allies among the designated foes. But it was quite another matter with those thinkers who had been positively influenced by revealed truth. The kind of thinking that Leo had in mind was not of recent origin, nor had it begun in the thirteenth century. That is why we should not be surprised to find that Thomas Aquinas—despite his prominence in the title of the encyclical—is not mentioned until paragraph 22 of the 37-paragraph letter.

1. Standing in a tradition

What the reader of *Aeterni Patris* notices is a kind of tension between naming Thomas Aquinas as *the* Christian philosopher and theologian, on the one hand, and merely citing him as the paladin of a vast number of thinkers of similar stripe, on the other. Indeed, when Thomas is first mentioned, Cardinal Cajetan's description of Aquinas is immediately quoted:

> Iamvero inter Scholasticos Doctores, omniuum princeps et magister, longe eminet Thomas Aquinas qui, uti Caietanus animadvertit, veteres *doctores sacros quia summae veneratus est, ideo intellectum omnium quodammodo sortitus est.* [n 22]

Thomas is seen as a compendium or summa of everything that has gone before him, such that what was scattered in different Fathers and doctors, is unified in him.

Anyone will recognise in this description what is essential to Thomas, namely to stand in a tradition, to see himself as working from a fund of knowledge handed on from before. Absent from Thomas is any compulsion to be original, a compulsion which could be said to characterise the great thinkers from Descartes onward: a palpable passion to stand out from one's fellows, above all from one's predecessors. The past is swept away as useless for the philosopher. Descartes of course insists that he is beginning *ab ovo*, and ever since philosophers have been divided into those who thought he made an omelette and those who thought he merely scrambled eggs. The one thing the great figures after Descartes agree with him on is that the past is positively useless to the philosopher. And of course Descartes himself is swiftly included in that past. Modern philosophy is not a tradition, but a series of starting points, or turns. We have had one turn after another, each of which promises that, the proper turn having been taken at last, philosophy can now begin.

I speak of course of the major figures. There have been Cartesians and Leibnitzians and Baconians, and Lockeans and Humeans and Kantians and Hegelians. But these mini-traditions are at war with one another and number among them those less ambitious and daring than the man whose name is given to the school. For the major figures, philosophy veers toward autobiography, in the sense that the intellectual odyssey of the thinker is one with what is thought. The Cartesian drama of methodic doubt obeys all the canons of Aristotle's *Poetics*. An attractive young man finds himself idle in winter quarters and, when he asks himself what he really knows—thinking back on his days at La Fleche—he is gripped by the panicky thought that there may be nothing of which he is so certain that he would die for it—not an ideal condition for a solider to be in. And so the drama begins. Candidates for certain knowledge are brought forward, hope rises, but then all judgments based on sense perception are swept away because Descartes's senses sometimes deceive him. Mathematical truths? Once more hope rises, only to be dashed by the malevolent demon. We have reached the nadir of the effort, all seems lost, but then, by his own efforts, the antagonist finds a plausible solution to his dilemma and the curtain rings down. In the gloom that had descended on Descartes a small light began to glow. Even if whatever he thinks to be true is false it is nonetheless true that he is thinking! That belief at least escapes the worm of doubt. Descartes emerges triumphant from the ordeal.

And, given the fact that Descartes is presenting himself as Thales *redivivus*, the first philosopher, it is only fitting that his story should include a divine sanction. And so it does. Parmendies, in the proemium of his poem, tells us that he has been swept up to heaven by the goddess and confided with a truth that he will pass on to us. Somewhat similarly, there stands at the outset of the new turn Descartes gave philosophy, the mysterious three-part dream which he interpreted as warrant for the tack he took. And like Pascal, Descartes wrote out the dream and still had it with him when he died in Stockholm. In gratitude for this quasi-revelation, Descartes vowed to make a pilgrimage to the House of Loreto, a vow he eventually kept.

2. Pluralism and *Aeterni Patris*

What greater contrast could there be between the father of modern philosophy and the thinker Leo XIII advocated in *Aeterni Patris?* If the encyclical can be said to resolve the problem of the plurality of thinkers prior to Thomas by presenting him as the summa of them all, this inspired a Thomistic revival and a wave of scholarship. What precisely was Thomas's attitude toward his sources? Is it really possible to see all the Fathers and previous doctors as singing from a single score that achieved its ultimate harmony in Thomas's thought? Is what Thomas made of a previous thinker what that thinker made of himself? Furthermore, the encyclical's tendency to gather together all of Thomas's near predecessors and his contemporaries into an amalgam called Scholasticism would also be questioned in later stages of the Thomistic revival, when the differences and peculiarities of the medieval masters were stressed.

As for the pluralism after 1274, the encyclical is equally irenic. Franciscans and Jesuits would be able to follow Scotus and Suarez, respectively, but this too would be done *ad mentem divi Thomae.* Complying with this led to a good deal of submerged animosity. Suarezians were capable of interpreting the real distinction between essence and existence in such a way that it comported well with the denial of the distinction—at least as Dominicans understood it. Perhaps the most significant way in which Franciscans carried on without much outward fuss was the speed with which they produced critical editions of Bonaventure, Scotus and later Ockham. While the

Leonine Commission which had been charged with the production of a
reliable text of Thomas got off to a good start, it was soon to be slowed
and then rendered all but irrelevant by a mounting tide of pedantry.
Marietti of Torino produced the manual editions which inspired the
Thomism of the second wave and when eventually, at great intervals,
volumes of the critical Leonine edition appeared they were annoyingly
unrelatable to the Marietti texts used in the decades of scholarship that
had been based on them, as if the study of Thomas had been in
suspension until the Leonine was ready. It would be difficult to point
to a Leonine volume that had the impact of Father Wyster's edition of
questions 5 and 6 of the exposition on Boethius's *De trinitate* or the
Marietti edition of the commentary on the *Metaphysics*. Now, thanks to
Father Busa's *Index Thomisticus*, the Leonine texts have gained a usefulness they never knew in print form, where Thomas was all but eclipsed
by interminable introductions which created the impression that until
they were mastered the text was unintelligible. And sometimes, after a
great display of erudition verging on pedantry, the text itself would be
trashed by its editor, thus proving how different scholarship is from
understanding. One was reminded of Nietzsche's comparison of
Greeks and classicists.

With the rise of 'medieval studies', a historical approach to such
authors as Thomas and Bonaventure and Scotus flourished and a
generation of students grew up whose interest lay in truths *about* the
texts rather than the truth *of* the text. The latter interest had all but
fizzled in the wake of Vatican II—this fizzling perhaps the condition
for the rapid rise of medieval studies, creating the circumstances in
which John Paul II issued *Fides et Ratio* in 1998.

3. Pluralism and *Fides et Ratio*

If the pluralism of *Aeterni Patris* was intramural, the variety that might
be found within the guild of Christian Philosophers, *Fides et Ratio* casts
a wider if ambiguous net. On the one hand, there is an insistence on
the plurality of philosophical systems, by no means confined to those
who exhibit the maxim of John of St Thomas, *philosophandum in fide.*
John Paul II links the church's interest to philosophising East and
West, early and late. The thought of Thomas Aquinas seems never to
receive an unequivocal preferential option: rather, it is seen in the flow
of philosophy, a flow which itself receives an initially positive
description. There are numerous statements suggesting that
philosophy has been developing from the beginning, rising from

height to height. Thus, at the very outset of the encyclical, we are told: 'In both East and West, we may trace a journey which has led humanity down the centuries to meet and engage truth more and more deeply.'[1] This cheerful note is sounded again and again, and it contrasts sharply with the encyclical's eventual account of the pathology of modern philosophy that goes far beyond the summary judgment about rationalism that we find in *Aeterni Patris*.

But first the more positive emphasis. The reader notes a perhaps surprising claim that the ultimate objective of philosophising is to learn about ourselves. But this humanism is quickly modified. In the opening paragraph, we are told that God has placed in the human heart 'a desire to know the truth—in a word, to know himself'. But then we read that it is by knowing and loving God that such self-knowledge will come. And, in paragraph 1: 'the more human beings know reality and the world, the more they know themselves in their uniqueness . . .' Where exactly does the encyclical stand on the turn philosophy took with Descartes? 'Modern philosophy clearly has the great merit of focusing attention upon man.' [n. 5] But later in the same paragraph, a caveat is given. 'Yet the positive results achieved must not obscure the fact that reason, in its one-sided concern to investigate human subjectivity, seems to have forgotten that men are always called to direct their steps toward a truth which transcends them.'

For all that, the encyclical begins under the aegis of the motto at Delphi: Know thyself. It is this capacity for self-knowledge that sets man off from the rest of creation and which is tied up with what *Fides et Ratio* calls 'the fundamental questions which pervade human life'.

What are they?

Who am I?

Where have I come from and where am I going?

Why is there evil?

What is there after this life?

John Paul II finds these questions in the sacred writings of Israel, in the Veda and the Avesta, in Confucius and Lao-Tze, in the preaching of Tirthankara and Buddha; in Homer, Euripides and Sophocles, and of course in the writings of Plato and Aristotle. Having their source in man's quest for meaning, they pervade world literature and their answers provide the direction men take in their lives. Philosophy is one way of addressing these questions, which are pursued by men 'so that their lives may be ever more human'.[3] That the human

—ourselves—is not the exhaustive theme of philosophising has been clarified by an earlier aside that 'the object of our knowledge becomes part of our life'.[1]

Once the philosophical pursuit of the fundamental questions has been introduced, the Greek conception of this pursuit as a love of wisdom is stressed. 'It is an innate property of human reason to ask why things are as they are, even though the answers which gradually emerge are set within a horizon which reveals how the different human cultures are complementary.'[3] The common, fundamental questions receive a variety of answers, as in different human cultures, but there is 'a horizon' within which different cultures embodying different answers to the fundamental questions are complementary, not competing or conflicting.

There is nonetheless a danger of absolutising one's own system. 'In different cultural contexts and at different times, this process has yielded results which have produced genuine systems of thought. Yet often enough in history this has brought with it the temptation to identify one single stream with the whole of philosophy. In such cases, we are clearly dealing with a "philosophical pride" which seeks to present its own partial and imperfect view as the complete reading of all reality.'[4] If every philosophical system is partial and imperfect, then no one of them could be sufficient. For all that, 'every philosophical *system,* while it should always be respected in its wholeness, without any instrumentalisation, must still recognise the primacy of philosophical *enquiry*, from which it stems and which it ought loyally to serve'.[4] Enquiry is defined in terms of the pursuit of truth with respect to the fundamental questions, all systematic answers to which are partial and imperfect. Philosophical enquiry thus looks like an exercise in comparative philosophy, an overview which takes into account the plurality of systems. Pluralism is legitimate so long as it recognises the partial and imperfect nature of each of the systems with respect to the truth, and does not seek to make one system prevail over others. But there is also an illegitimate pluralism of systems. 'A legitimate plurality of positions has yielded to an undifferentiated pluralism, based upon the assumption that all positions are equally valid, which is one of today's most widespread symptoms of the lack of confidence in truth.'[5]

It is nonetheless noteworthy that *Fides et Ratio* says things about philosophy which presumably are not said from the point of view of any system. Contrasting it with the knowledge provided by divine faith, the encyclical goes on. 'Based upon God's testimony and enjoying the supernatural assistance of grace, faith is of an order other than philosophical knowledge which depends upon sense perception and experience and which advances by the light of intellect alone.' [9] This description of philosophy of course presents a fundamental difficulty for the irenic approach taken by the encyclical. Descartes, for one, does not accept the view that philosophy begins with sense perception and experience, at least in any positive sense. Similarly, the encyclical contains conflicting remarks about the definitive turn taken by modern philosophy. Indeed, the Cartesian priority seems embraced in the following astonishing remark: 'Moreover, the first absolutely certain truth of our life, beyond the fact that we exist(!!!!), is the inevitability of our death.'[26] Doubtless this later remark must be glossed by earlier ones where our self-knowledge was recognised as depending on knowing of the world. And there are explicit rejections of the epistemological turn. 'Abandoning the investigation of being, modern philosophical research has concentrated instead upon human knowing. Rather than make use of the human capacity to know the truth, modern philosophy has preferred to accentuate the ways in which this capacity is limited and conditioned. This has given rise to different forms of agnosticism and relativism which have led philosophical research to lose its way in the shifting sands of scepticism.'[5]

This critique of modern philosophy gets sharper as the encyclical continues. Having turned away from the illuminating aid of revelation, modern philosophy has moved off in a direction that leads to idealism, to atheistic humanism, to positivism, indeed to nihilism.[45] But early and late, *Fides et Ratio* speaks of a plurality of paths to the truth.

> Since access to the truth enables access to God, it must be denied to none. There are many paths which lead to truth, but since Christian truth has a salvific value, any one of these paths may be taken, as long as it leads to the final goal, that is to the Revelation of Jesus Christ.[38]

Before saying more about such pluralism, we must ask what *Fides et Ratio* has to say about what we have called intramural pluralism, the pluralism of Christian philosophies.

In a manner reminiscent of *Aeterni Patris*, *Fides et Ratio* postpones mention of Thomas Aquinas until the encyclical is well under way. Thomas appears first in paragraph 43 of the 108 which make up the encyclical. Scholastic theology is not mentioned until n. 42, and only after Anselm is discussed are we told that Thomas occupies 'a quite special place'. Thomas 'had the great merit of giving pride of place to the harmony which exists between faith and reason'.[43] The discussion of Thomas runs from 43 to 44. We are reminded that the church has consistently proposed 'Saint Thomas as a master of thought and a model of the right way to do theology'. Pope Paul VI is quoted to this effect. Paragraph 43 seems to echo Jacques Maritain's *The Degrees of Wisdom*. Thomas is praised for having given primacy to the wisdom that is a gift of the Holy Spirit. 'This wisdom comes to know by way of connaturality; it presupposes faith and eventually formulates its right judgment on the basis of the truth of faith itself.'[44] But besides the Gift of Wisdom, there is also philosophical wisdom and theological wisdom. Finally, it is the realism of Thomas that is praised. 'Looking unreservedly to truth, the realism of Thomas could recognise the objectivity of truth and produce not merely a philosophy of "what seems to be" but a philosophy of "what is".'[44] But, in what may seem a deliberate effort to downplay the primacy that Thomas has played in the church, we are told that 'The Church has no philosophy of her own nor does she canonize any one particular philosophy in preference to others'. [49] Nonetheless, the faith provides a negative criterion for appraising philosophies: 'opinions and philosophies which contradict Christian doctrine' [50] and so forth are false. But yet again the note struck is that of pluralism.

> Moreover, as philosophical learning has developed, different schools of thought have emerged. This pluralism also imposes upon the Magisterium the responsibility of expressing a judgment as to whether or not the basic tenets of these different schools are compatible with the demands of the word of God and theological enquiry.[50]

Presumably, not all will fail this test, and the result will be a legitimate plurality of philosophical systems.

4. Appraisal of extramural pluralism

There is a qualified but repeated claim in *Fides et Ratio* that there is a plurality of philosophical systems which have been developed over the course of the history of philosophy. From the point of view of Christian faith, if a philosophical opinion or system contradicts it, that opinion and system may be judged false. This is, so to say, the application of an external criterion and should not be confused with a *philosophical* refutation of the opinion or system. But the believer will continue his analysis of that system in the conviction that it has gone wrong. That modern philosophy has gone off on sidetracks is another repeated claim of the encyclical. By deliberately separating itself from the help that faith provides reason, philosophy has drifted into a number of false positions: idealism, atheistic humanism, positivism, relativism and ultimately nihilism. But the wrongness of these positions is not confined to noting that they conflict with truths we know by faith. The encyclical has proceeded slowly to arrive at a number of truths about the nature of the knowing subject. In paragraph 33, we are provided with a summary of them:

1. It is the nature of the human being to seek the truth.
2. This search does not look just to partial truths or to the truth of individual acts.
3. It looks for an ulterior truth which would explain the meaning of life.
4. It is therefore a search that can reach its end only in an absolute.
5. Thanks to his nature and capacity for thought, man can recognize a truth of this kind.
6. Such a truth is found in company with others.
7. The capacity to entrust oneself and one's life to another person is the most significant and expressive of human acts.

One can easily think of philosophical systems which would fall short of exhibiting all of these—or indeed any of them. After all, there are nihilist systems, if that is not a contradictory phrase. Short of that, there are philosophies which begin with doubt. 'Life in fact can never be grounded upon doubt, uncertainty or deceit; such an existence would be threatened constantly by fear and anxiety. One may define the human being, therefore, as *the one who seeks the truth*.'[28]

All humankind by nature desires to know.

> People cannot be genuinely indifferent to the question of whether what they know is true or not. If they discover that it is false, they reject it; but if they establish its truth, they feel themselves rewarded. It is this that Saint Augustine teaches when he writes: 'I have met many who wanted to deceive, but none who wanted to be deceived'. [25]

It is just these common truths that the encyclical mentions at the very outset as providing a key to the way in which philosophical pluralism is to be assessed. Immediately after the warning that a species of philosophical pride is involved in preferring one system to all others, since each system is only an imperfect and partial grasp of truth, *Fides et Ratio* adds something of the first importance.

> Although times change and knowledge increases, it is possible to discern a core of philosophical insight within the history of thought as a whole. Consider, for example, the principles of non-contradiction, finality and causality, as well as the concept of the person as a free and intelligent subject, with the capacity to know God, truth and goodness. Consider as well certain fundamental moral norms which are shared by all. These are among the indications that, beyond different schools of thought, there exists a body of knowledge which may be judged a kind of spiritual heritage of humanity. It is as if we had come upon an *implicit philosophy*, as a result of which all feel that they possess these principles, albeit in a general and unreflective way. [4]

The implicit philosophy here referred to amounts to the claim that there are certain truths which all human beings can be expected to know, 'albeit in a general and unreflective way'. These principles provide a point of reference for the assessing or comparison of philosophical systems. This is something to which the encyclical refers several times at later points.

No less important than research in the theoretical field
is research in the practical field—by which is meant the
search for truth which looks to the good which is to be
performed...Here too it is a question of truth . . . [there
is a reference to *Veritatis Splendor*] It is essential,
therefore, that the values chosen and pursued in one's
life be true, because only true values can lead people to
realize themselves fully, allowing them to be true to
their nature. [25]

Moreover, we are given a clarification as to what was meant by the
'horizon' within which the various philosophical systems can be seen
as complementary. 'The unity of truth is a fundamental premise of
human reasoning, as the principle of non-contradiction makes clear.'
[34]

5. The implicit philosophy

When we consider the notion of an implicit philosophy as the set of
common principles knowable by all that constitute the criteria for
appraising the plurality of philosophical systems, difficulties follow
both for what we have called extramural and for intramural pluralism.
In the first place, far from providing common ground for a plurality of
differing philosophical systems, implicit philosophy provides a means
of rejecting all non-realist philosophical systems. Second, it will occur
to anyone that the principles enumerated seem to be drawn directly
from the pages of Thomas Aquinas. Thus, despite the apparent
acceptance of philosophical pluralism and its favourable attitude
toward historical developments in philosophy—admittedly balanced
by severe criticisms—and despite the seeming soft-pedalling of the
primacy of Thomas Aquinas, the net effect of the invocation of an
implicit philosophy is to make the thought of Thomas regulative in a
fundamental way. But how can this implicit canonical role of Thomas
Aquinas in the expression of implicit philosophy avoid the charge of
philosophical pride when one philosophical system is preferred to all
others?

Several questions impose themselves:
- Are the principles of the implicit philosophy principles of
  Thomism? Is Thomism just one philosophical system among
  others?

- Reflection discloses that Thomism properly understood is the possibility of a legitimate pluralism in philosophy.

5.1 Implicit philosophy is not a part of Thomism

The introduction of an implicit philosophy presumed to be in the possession of all is a reminder of the greatest and most fundamental difference between philosophy as Thomas understands it and philosophy since Descartes. We observed earlier that Thomas, unlike Descartes, sees himself as working within a tradition. Descartes, by contrast, sets aside everything he had learnt or heard and endeavours to start from scratch. *Après moi, la philosophie.* To stand in a tradition does not mean that one accepts the deliverances of previous philosophical *systems* or of a single *system*. Rather it means to stand on the common ground of human beings; that is, to presuppose that, prior to the beginning of formal philosophising, human beings are so created that they know truths about the world and about themselves, both about what is and about what ought to be. Philosophy *presupposes* this knowledge, articulates and clarifies it, but does not confer it on anyone.

The appraisal of philosophical systems—that is of alternative philosophies—is either theological or philosophical. If theological, it is a matter of assessing whether or not a philosophical opinion or system contradicts the faith. If it does, it is known to be false, the faith being true. This is a simple application of the principle of contradiction. And the principle of contradiction, *Fides et Ratio* reminds us, is prior to all formal philosophising because it is regulative of thinking as such, and it is regulative of thinking as such because it is first a truth about the things that are. The theological appeal to the principle of contradiction draws attention to the fact that religious faith is reasonable. A philosophical appraisal of rival systems is not a matter of pitting the principles of one system against those of another, as if these were chosen arbitrarily, but of appraising rival opinions and systems by appeal to the same principles that bind one's own thinking, because they must bind anyone's.

Thus, although it is of course true that anyone reading the list of principles that belong to implicit philosophy will be reminded of Thomas Aquinas's discussion of the first principles of theoretical and practical reasoning—chiefly the principle of contradiction in the former and the principles of natural law in the latter—these principles are presupposed by Thomas—as they must be by anyone—and are merely articulated and analysed by him. They are not then in any narrow sense principles of Thomistic philosophy.

5.2 Thomism is not a kind of philosophy

The principles of implicit philosophy are presupposed by Thomas Aquinas as he begins formal philosophising; indeed the former is regulative of the latter. Since these starting points or principles of Thomism are in the common domain, Thomism is not a *system* of philosophy, if a system is defined in terms of peculiar and distinguishing principles. Historians have distinguished Platonism from Aristotelianism, but Plato is to Aristotle somewhat as Descartes is to Aquinas; historians have distinguished the various medieval thinkers from one another in terms of the distinctive and regulative intuitions of each. Some historians, like De Wulf, thought there was a Scholastic philosophy common to them all; Gilson, denying this, thought one of them right and the others wrong. In the modern era, there is an overt effort on the part of philosophers to be unlike the rest of men—and one another. To the degree that a philosophy is a distinct philosophical system—commencing with principles formulated without reference to what is commonly known—the notion of a philosophical system becomes an increasingly bogus or marginalised intellectual effort. [cf n. 47] Particularly when philosophers have lost their way in relativism and nihilism, there is little point in seeking in them acknowledged common starting points. The time has then come for ordinary folk to rescue philosophy from the philosophers. 'The truths of philosophy, it should be said, are not restricted only to the sometimes ephemeral teachings of professional philosophers. All men and women, as I have noted, are in some sense philosophers and have their own philosophical conceptions with which they direct their lives.' [30]

5.3 Thomism and pluralism

When *Fides et Ratio* remarks on the fruits of following the urging of Leo XIII in *Aeterni Patris,* referring to the 'powerful array of thinkers formed in the school of the Angelic Doctor' [n. 58], it quickly adds that there have been other signs of 'a resurgence of philosophical thought' of Christian inspiration. 'Earlier still, and parallel to Pope Leo's call, there had emerged a number of Catholic philosophers who, adopting more recent currents of thought and according to a specific method, produced philosophical works of great influence and lasting value.' [n. 59] There follows an astonishing list. [a] Some devised syntheses that stood comparison with 'the great systems of idealism'. [b] Others established the epistemological foundations for a 'new consideration of faith in the light of a renewed understanding of moral consciousness'. [c] Others started with an analysis of immanence and 'opened the way to the transcendent'. [d] Finally, some sought to combine the demands of faith 'with the perspective of phenomenological method'.

Such a list may seem to take back unequivocal criticisms made earlier in the encyclical. Rivalling the 'great systems of idealism' or beginning with the 'analysis of immanence' or epistemology seems to conflict with the principles of that implicit philosophy which are presupposed by any formal philosophising. But perhaps the mention of the use of the phenomenological method provides the clue to understanding this list, not as an exercise in eclecticism and what Pius XII would have called a false irenism, but as an indication of how philosophising that begins from implicit philosophy is capable of learning things from philosophical efforts which seemingly or even actually disdain implicit philosophy. One of the first things Edith Stein did after her conversion was write a comparison of Thomas Aquinas and phenomenology. Of course, she broke with Husserl after his turn toward idealism in *Ideen,* and in her posthumously published *Eternal and Finite Being* sought to give her version of Thomism. This suggests that, although the new and the old in philosophy are not compatible if one of them denies the principles of implicit philosophy, they are compatible, the one enlarging the other, if both respect the principles of implicit philosophy. Of course, as Aristotle pointed out, we can also learn from a philosophical opinion by determining its falsehood, since to know that it is false is a gain in knowledge of the truth.

It is because it exemplifies in a pre-eminent way the power of the truths that make up the implicit philosophy that Thomism is able to benefit from other philosophical efforts—positively, when they are in conformity with implicit philosophy, negatively, when they are not. To be a student of St Thomas is to be interested, in principle, in every philosophical system, not eclectically, but because of the principles from which he begins and which provide the only sure basis, as *Fides et Ratio* asserts, for dealing with the plurality of philosophical positions which would otherwise be nothing but an intellectual scandal.

Faith and Reason: Naturalised and Relativised[1]

Gregory Moses

> One Buddhist sutra tells us that when conditions are
> sufficient, we see forms, and when conditions are not
> sufficient, we don't. When all conditions are present,
> phenomena can be perceived by us, and so they are
> revealed to us as existing. But when one of these
> conditions is lacking, we cannot perceive the same
> phenomena, so they are not revealed to us and we say
> they do not exist.
>
> From Thich Nhat Hanh, 1995, 42.

1. Introduction

This paper, the first part of a two-part research project, is inspired by a
distinction made by Professor Jan Van der Veken and his colleague
Andre Cloots from the University of Leuven, Belgium, between what
can be said about God on the basis of generally available experience,
versus what can be said on the basis of particular experiences of
particular people. According to Van der Veken and Cloots, about all
that can be said on the basis of generally available experience is that
'the primordial qualification of Creativity' or something like that is
intelligent. Even the sceptic Hume can't quite resist this much. But that
this is a Lure to goodness, truth and beauty, or Gracious, or
Compassionate or Holy, that can only be said on the basis of particular
experiences of particular people.[2]

---

1. This is a November 2001 update of a paper prepared for the August 2000
    Melbourne Faith and Reason Conference. It represents research in progress going
    back as far as 1996.

2. Jan Van der Veken, 'Whitehead's God Is Not Whiteheadian Enough', *Whitehead
    and the Idea of Process*, edited by Harold Holz and Ernest Wolf-Gazo
    (Freiburg/Munchen: Verlag Karl Alber 1981), 300–11; 'Creativity as Universal

This is a distinction that Van der Veken himself puts forward under inspiration from the mathematician, scientist and philosopher Alfred North Whitehead, chapter on God in *Science and the Modern World*,[3] which rendition Jan prefers to the more well known rendition in the last part of *Process and Reality*. In Part V of *Process and Reality*, Whitehead is himself overtly dependent on the particular experiences of particular people, namely *the brief Galilean vision*. In *Process and Reality* Whitehead goes too far, much further than is legitimated by his own speculative cosmology.

As Van der Veken has it, this distinction may be intuitively compared to the distinction between the knowledge that a perfect stranger might have of my good friend and the knowledge available to me as his or her good friend. This is a fair comparison, in so far as, among other things, it brings out the fact that faith is much more than just knowledge. It is also trust and already a kind of love. In process theological terms indeed 'faith' can cash out as something like clueing into the lure of the Divine Mystery in our lives and having the courage to entrust oneself to it, as in 'Do not be afraid, only have faith'.

However, as is regularly the case with imperatives and performatives, such 'entrustment' will bring with it certain cognitively relevant commitments (as for example with something so banal as 'please open the door'). Such commitments are based on particular experiences of particular people, the person who comes to faith and those of others whom he or she has come to know or know about. Such experiences meanwhile help to form and indeed are formed by, interpreted with the help of and even *enabled by* religious traditions of one kind or another. This constitutes religious traditions for cognitive purposes as dynamic traditions of experience and interpretation.

This distinction, now embedded in a distinction between religious and scientific traditions of experience and interpretation, is affirmed, extended and deepened with the help of recent philosophy of religion and recent philosophy of science. The epistemic consequences are then elaborated with the help of some theses on 'the hermeneutics of

Activity', in *Whitehead's Metaphysics of Creativity*, edited by Frierich Rapp and Reiner Wiehl (Albany: SUNY, 1990), 178–88; and Jan Van der Vecken, and Andre Cloots, 'Creativity as General Activity', in *Metaphysics as Foundation: Essays in Honour of Ivor Leclerc*, edited by Paul Bogaard and Gordon Treash (Albany: State University of New York Press, 1992), 98–110.

3.   Alfred Whitehead, *Science and the Modern* World (Cambridge: Cambridge University Press, 1926), 213–4.

reasonable believing' with a connection to David Hume's section on miracles in the first *Enquiry*.

When we do all this, the distinction also ends up getting relativised, and in what I think is a rather harmless sense, 'naturalised'. *From the point of view of generalised* or more generalised *reason*, for a person taken up into particular traditions of experience and interpretation, it is only to be expected that they believe as they do. Indeed given the tradition-specific criteria it may even be reasonable for them to so believe, in a sense of particularised rationality.

So the first allegation of this paper (Part 1) is that the distinction between faith and reason is not that of subjective versus objective, or non-rational versus rational, or supernatural versus natural, but more like particular versus general, or even, as it will turn out, more particular versus less particular.

In the context of questions raised by the multitude of religious traditions, this notion of particularised rationality already pushes us in the direction of the thesis of a Rawls'-like pluralism of reasonable believing. The notion of a pluralism of reasonable believing is a thesis about tradition-specific *rational credibility*, and is put forward at this point as a modest alternative to the usual exclusivism, inclusivism and pluralism on the question of who has the truth. This side of the parousia, we cannot demand of people that what they believe be 'true', which usually means what we take as true. All that we can require of each other is that our believing be reasonable. This will always be contextualised, with a good deal of 'luck' one way or the other.

This is not to say we cannot learn from each other, or that we should avoid or eschew dialogue. On the contrary, the logic of maintaining our reasonable believing in the epistemic meta-world created by the thesis itself may push us into even stronger dialogue. The suggestion of a further paper (Part 2) will be that this happens from out of a fairly delicate species of *inclusivist attitude* in respect of our own tradition, versus exclusivist, pluralist or generalised religious sceptic. What we have seen with our eyes, what we have looked at and touched with our hands (1 John 1:1, NRSV translation), albeit had inside a mutually validating tradition of experience and interpretation, will continue to have a hold over us over against what other people share with us in the way of testimony from outside. This is only natural, to be expected, and indeed reasonable in a double sense. What we have experienced personally will, other things being equal, have an epistemic advantage for us over mere testimony from others, at least to the point of giving us, and anyone else similarly experientially situated, an *epistemic right* to stay with it for the time being. Furthermore, it is precisely the richness of our own particular experiences and the interpretative structures they motivate that we have to contribute to any cross-traditions discussion in the human pursuit of truth. There may thus be a species of pre-eschatological imperative at work, it can well be our best way of standing in the truth. This is a carry-over from our own reasonable believing. But at no point do we dispute the in-principle reasonably believed character of the beliefs of our dialogue partners, any more than they dispute ours. The inclusivism, such as it is, will continue to be framed inside a pluralism of reasonable believing.

However, this latter is for a further paper and at this point is for the sake of context.[4]

We begin our story (for Part 1), then, with some remarks on contemporary philosophy of religion and recent philosophy of science before moving on to the so-called hermeneutics of reasonable believing. We then draw some consequences and applications. In a further paper, Part 2, we will then look at suggestions for a way ahead on the question of judging or deciding which religious tradition to belong to, if any, and push the project towards the justification of what

---

4.   The position which will be taken in Part 2, while independently elaborated in my own terms, is rather similar in general form to that of Nicholas Rescher in *Pluralism: Against the Demand for Consensus*, edited by Nicholas Rescher (Oxford: Clarendon Press, 1993). Cf the following: 'There is no good reason why a recognition that others, circumstanced as they are, are rationally entitled *in their circumstances* to hold a position at variance with ours should be construed to mean that we, *circumstanced as we are*, need feel any rational obligation to abandon our position . . . from the angle of rationality, I will (if indeed rational) have to take the line that in so far as a choice resolution is adequate for me it is also adequate for anyone in my experiential situation.' (119–120). And 'Nothing in perspectival pluralism as such compels us to see our cognitive commitments as *mere opinions*. There are indeed opinions of sorts, but there is nothing 'mere' about them. They are *judgements*—matters of reasoned conviction for whose acceptance we (warrantedly) take ourselves to have good reasons . . . An experiential pluralism of cognitive orientations is thus no impediment to doctrinal commitment.' (121). And finally, 'We not only have an *epistemic* justification to stick by our own opinions, we have in various circumstances a *moral duty* to do so.' (122).

we hope will be a non-melioristic[5] dialogal inclusivist attitude nesting within the continuing acknowledgment of a pluralism of reasonable believing.

2. Towards a pluralism of reasonable believing

2.1 Post-Katzian philosophy of religion
In the late 1970s and early 1980s the philosopher Steven Katz edited two books which between them have changed the shape of the philosophy of religious experience and the notion of a religious tradition,[6] almost as much as the work of Karl Popper changed the shape of philosophy of science. Since then, the question has been, not whether religious experience for the most part is constructed most of the time, but 1) the extent and manner by which it is constructed, within the religious tradition in which it occurs, and 2) the significance of this, if any, for the question of the cognitive value of religious experience.

In respect of the first issue, the extent and manner of construction, we may make a broad distinction between various *partial constructivists* (eg Katz himself, Peter Moore, John Hick, Dupre, Schillebeeckx) and the occasional *total constructivist* (eg probably Gimello, in Katz; also the linguistic constructivism of some deconstructionists). Partial constructivists acknowledge in theory at least that the externality also plays a part in the formation of experience, and in principle at least allow experiences to affect traditional interpretative structures, as well

---

5. I take it that the problem with what has recently come to be called 'meliorism' is that when it is made explicit and up-front, when voice is given to one's 'inclusivism' in the tone, for example, of the recent Vatican document *Dominus Jesus*, as frequently understood, one's behaviour is reasonably interpretable as arrogant and more importantly blatantly insulting to one's dialogue partners and therefore unethical and even anti-Christian (if one happens to be a Christian). (Cf John D'Arcy May, 24 October 2001). One is therefore involved in a species of religious contradiction in actu, where the very act of making the claim puts oneself in contradiction with the actional requirements of the tradition on whose behalf one is making the claim. Such an infelicitous state of affairs is obviously to be avoided if we can at all manage to do so.

6. Steven Katz, editor, *Mysticism and Philosophical Analysis* (London: Sheldon, 1978) and *Mysticism and Religious Traditions* (Oxford: Oxford University Press, 1983).

as the other way around. For the total constructivist, the movement is all one way. Traditional meditative practices and such-like are for the sake of enabling or constructing certain experiences, to enable us, for example, to experience the world the way the Buddha says it is (Gimello).

According to the broad run of partial constructivist post-Katzian philosophy of religion, for epistemological purposes a religion may be understood as a developing tradition of experience and interpretation. Interpretative structures prepare the way for and indeed enable and *get incorporated into* certain types of experience; experience evokes and sometimes brings about changes in interpretative structures. One may make a relative distinction between *originating experiences*, eg the experiences of the Buddha or of Jesus and the early Jesus community, and *founded experiences*, which happen and are to a large extent made possible by the existence of the tradition to which the originating experiences eventually gave rise. But even this is only a relative distinction, with the experiences of Jesus and the early Jesus community presuming the context in first century Judaism and the experiences of the Buddha presuming a context within the religious traditions of his time in India.[7]

'Interpretation' here, of course, is more than just world-views or theories. It includes attitudes, emotional stances, value judgments, meditation and other practices, various disciplines etc. Indeed, it consists in the whole gambit of what shapes the way deeply religious people in one of the religious traditions experience each other, the events of daily life, the world and the mysteries or what John Hick calls *the Real.*[8]

The debate is far from over, even in favour of partial constructivism. However, even if, contra Katz and his constructivist colleagues, there turns out to be some such phenomenon as pure empty consciousness unaffected by its context,[9] its significance and indeed its very point would seem to be still tradition-dependent.[10] Similarly with regard to neo cross-cultural classifiers (eg Wainwright,

---

7.   For this version see Louis Dupre, *Religious Mystery and Rational Reflection* (Grand Rapids: Eerdmans, 1998), 116–117.

8.   John Hick, *An Interpretation of Religion* (London: Macmillan, 1989).

9.   See especially Robert Forman, editor, *The Problem of Pure Consciousness: Mysticism and Philosophy* (Oxford: Oxford University Press, 1990).

10. Cf even Smart in Katz, 1983, *op cit*, as well as Pike Nelson, *Mystic Union* (Ithaca and London: Cornell University Press, 1992) regarding union without distinction.

Stoeber).[11] Cross-cultural classifications, if any, need to be made more circumspectly and acknowledging tradition incorporation in their detail and the significance of the various stages as relative to the tradition. For epistemological purposes then we would still be into traditions of experience and interpretation, whatever happened to the debate on both of these points.

Whatever, religious traditions are always particular, relating to the particular experiences of particular people taken up into various particular historically determined communal traditions of experience and interpretation. Religious experiences typically happen within or in contact with such particular traditions, and are formed by, interpreted with the help of, and help to, form such traditions.

2.2 Post-Popperian philosophy of science

Popper already had science 'built on a swamp', with so-called 'basic statements' only relatively basic.[12] Post-Popperian philosophers of science, such as Lakatos, Kuhn, Feyerabend, Toulmin, and a host of others have taken things even further. It seems that science or the sciences happen inside and between paradigms, research programs, traditions of enquiry etc, that all facts are theory laden and all experience and all experiments are also theory laden. Of course, this need not be the theory under test; it may be various background theories. But the point is still made. All enquiry is tradition-constituted, not only eg ethical enquiry (MacIntyre). The only difference is in the mode by which traditions constitute the enquiry.

Once again, paradigms, research programs, traditions constituting enquiries, are not just theories. They are also attitudes, disciplines, practices, ways of operating with each other including certain implicit criteria for what is allowable. Indeed, they are the whole gambit of what a scientist in a particular discipline puts on when she or he goes to work of a morning, much of it all but incapable of being brought to consciousness.

---

11. William Wainwright, *Mysticism: A Study of Its Nature, Cognitive Value and Moral Implications* (Madison, WI: University of Wisconsin Press, 1981) and Michael Stoeber, 'Introvertive Mystical Experiences: Monistic, Theistic and the Theo-Monistic', *Religious Studies*, Volume 29 No 2, (1993): 169–84.

12. Popper, *The Logic of Scientific Discovery* London: Hutchinson, 1972), 111.

Other work in the history and social situatedness of sciences might be slotted in at this point, including work by feminist philosophers and historians of science such as Carolyn Merchant and Nancy Howell.

Over against religious traditions: entrance into such traditions is typically more easily available than entrance into an entirely different religious tradition to that of one's birth. Such scientific traditions, particularly the mathematical and natural scientific ones, indeed tend to move fairly readily across cultural and religious boundaries. After all, the whole of one's life is not typically involved in such an entrance. The experiences on which they are based are more generally available, typically rather less tightly restricted in its criteria for availability than typically fully-fledged religious experience. However, it is only *relatively* more generally available, relative to the paradigm, research program, tradition of enquiry in which the particular scientist is implicated. Indeed, the scientific enterprise itself is in a certain way only relatively generally available to us human beings. Its coming about as a human practice was the product of certain historical contingencies, datable by some to the high Middle Ages. But once it has come about, it becomes available to others outside the particular cultural and historical context which first gave rise to it.

2.3 Moral, scientific and religious 'luck'

One quick if rather intuitive way to bring out the similarity, the only relatively distinct character of such human practices as science, ethics and religions is in terms of the apparent ubiquity of the notion of 'luck'.

The term, 'moral luck', has been brought into common discourse particularly by the philosopher Thomas Nagel. The notion is already in Hume in his refusal of a fast distinction between natural abilities and virtues (Hume is just following the ancients, including Aristotle, in this respect). However, religious people have probably known about it for ages, via such phrases as 'there but for the grace of God go I'.

There appears to be a class of phenomena which we might by analogy call 'scientific luck', roughly, being in the right place at the right time. This could be applied to science itself. It certainly would seem to apply to paradigm change in science, eg whether one happens to be old and embedded or young and enthusiastic at the time (Kuhn). It probably applies pretty well to a lot of particular scientific discoveries.

We could also talk of such a thing as 'religious luck', whereby when and where one is born and various contingencies along the way after that will often have a lot to do with one's religious convictions and commitments.

2.4 *Some differences making for a relative distinction*

In spite of such similarities as brought out by this analogy, however, the different spheres are still relatively *distinct*. The distinctiveness has probably two main sources.

As Van der Veken has pointed out, in religions we do have to do with particular experiences of particular people, taken up into rather particular and not all that easily available particular traditions of experience and interpretation. In the sciences, especially the natural sciences, we have to do with more generally and more easily and widely available experiences, albeit taken up once again into traditions of enquiry, paradigms, research programs etc.

This criterion of degree of availability, meanwhile, itself bears a rough relationship to another criterion, *the criterion of degree of abstractness*. Religious traditions have to do with the whole of *life in its concreteness,* in Whiteheadian Process terms, to guide concrescence in the midst of concrete life. Mathematics and the sciences, even when they deal with the whole of the created universe, do so only very abstractly. It seems, then, that the religious person sacrifices generality (though not always certainty) in favour of concreteness.

Further than this difference in respect of the criteria for availability of the relevant experiences, as well as similarities there are probably significant differences in *the manner in which the different species of tradition constitute the enquiries and experiences* specific to the tradition in question. However, what these differences are cannot be said *a priori*. If we want to know how a tradition constitutes its enquiries and affects its typical experiences, we have to go and see. Whether such differences are at all important has to be addressed after such a close look, not before. There is also the question as to whose or which criteria to use, or whether there are any neutral criteria at all. See below, for more (but again, mostly postponed to Part 2 of the project).

There may be one significant feature that distinguishes religious traditions from traditions of enquiry, eg in science, very interesting because not so usually noted. Religious traditions are, in a certain respect, *more empirical than science*, typically staying closer to their empirical base. As noted briefly already, religious traditions tend to have a special relationship with certain 'originating' experiences, which constitutes that tradition as the tradition that it is, eg Christian, rather than Buddhist or Moslem. To quote Louis Dupre, 'The process would constantly pass through new experiences and interpretations, all of which, however, remain both subjectively and objectively dependent upon the original, interpreted experience.'[13] A religious tradition, to this extent, is more analogous to a 'research program' in science (Lakatos) than to science itself, though only analogous, not the same. At the core of the tradition stands, not a set of fundamental formulae, but *a set of originating revelatory experiences*, including perhaps a primary interpretative structure indistinguishable from the experience (Dupre again). We do our best to be faithful to this, whatever else.

This is probably a bit too strong in respect of our distinction. Research programs or paradigms in science consist in more than formulae. Also included are ways of doing science and implicit conceptions of what science is, which can change from one research program to another. There is also the example, the 'scientific experience' of certain key people early on in the tradition, which becomes a paradigm (in one of the many senses of that word) for future science in that tradition. On the other side, revelatory experiences in religion are very soon turned into various core 'dogmas', which typically go beyond the primary interpretation in the originating experiences. This tends to once again *relativise* our distinction a little bit, but let us not throw it away altogether.

Another problem, just to complicate matters, is that certain religious traditions, eg Hinduism, may not have originating experiences in quite the same sense as the so-called 'historical' religions, such as Judaism, Islam and Christianity, and also Buddhism. Though certain sub-traditions such as Sankara Vedanta may be more in this line.

The bottom line on this point, then, seems to be that, in dealing with a specifically religious tradition, we should expect a closer relationship with immediate experience than is typical for a mature tradition in science. We should expect a religious tradition to be rather closer to its experiential base, whether guided by a definitive originating experience or not. However, to know what goes on really

---

13.   Dupre, *op cit*, 117.

in a particular tradition, once again we have to look and see. Also, the epistemological point of this has yet to be determined.[14]

2.5 Sharpening the distinction and relationship: Eberhard Herrmann
Since I wrote this paper, I have come to realise that there is a need for some more precise distinctions here. This is mostly as a result of reading an essay by Eberhard Herrmann.[15] Herrmann makes a clear distinction between scientific theory and what he calls 'views of life'. Scientific theory is focused on our knowledge of reality, views of life on our engagement with it. Views of life may be inspired by scientific theory, but are value-added, deal with the contingencies of life such as happiness and misery, suffering and death, give some idea of what human life might be like at its best and so serve to ground distinctions between good and evil, right and wrong. Herrmann argues for a non-representational realism in regard to both, though it is a different species of non-representational realism, not exactly the same.

In respect of science, he distinguishes three levels, namely supposedly real systems, models and scientific theory. Scientific theories are abstract structures or patterns, whether mathematised /axiomatised or not, which, under suitable interpretation, may give rise to models capable of generating testable hypotheses in respect of particular phenomena or supposed real systems 'out there'. The theories themselves are patterns or abstract structures rather than statements, and so are neither true nor false, and they become representational in any sense only when they are used to produce

---

14.   It may be interesting to note at this point that the Whiteheadian Process tradition to which Van der Veken and Cloots belong gives us the wherewithal to make sense of the inevitably particular character of religious traditions. The particularity is an inevitable consequence of concreteness, both in origin and in purpose. In process terms, a good and holy person is at minimum a person whose subjective aims are consistently in line with the initial aims or lure of the divine mystery. For Whitehead, such initial aims are always particularised to the situation in question. Beyond this, concrete life is always environmentally dependent, always particular, with this peculiar past to take account of and no other. Life, being concrete, is particular, while science and philosophy aim for generality. Theology, meanwhile, does its best to bridge the gap, frequently using the resources of philosophy for this purpose.

15.   Eberhard Herrmann, *Scientific Theory and Religious Belief* (Kampen, Netherlands: Kok Pharos, 1995).

models of particular segments of reality. However, they are crucially involved in our discussions of reality and so a 'non-representational realist' attitude is appropriate in their regard. This, Herrmann contends, rather than an instrumentalist attitude.

For Herrmann, views of life are also best understood in a non-statement perspective, and unlike theories cannot in general be used to generate testable hypotheses. However, the adequacy of the expressions in our views of life can still be tested. According to Herrmann, such testing can be made on grounds of 1) internal consistency, 2) coherence with what we otherwise have reason to believe, and 3) whether we can live it, whether one can recognise oneself in it, in other language (not Herrmann's), whether it can be integrated into one's personal and communal narrative identity. In so far as it is susceptible of such testing in respect of adequacy, and in so far as views of life function crucially in our more or less felicitous engagement with reality, a 'non-representational realist' attitude is appropriate here as well.

Right towards the end of his essay, Herrmann incorporates views of life into traditions:

> . . . our reflections on the contingencies of life always take place within the framework of a certain view of life functioning as a tradition within which we are able to give expression to our reflections. Traditions can be changed. They function both as the background against which we develop ways of communicating, thinking, reflecting and criticizing, and as the means by which these ways receive their specific feature. Thus, a tradition can give rise to criticism of itself and contribute to its own alteration.[16]

In the light of such comments, I take it that explorations of this paper are complementary rather than in competition with Herrmann's, whose positions seem to me quite moderate and whose arguments I find mostly convincing, except on one point, namely that the summation on views of life probably exaggerates the difference. Unless one is a total constructivist, there is still an element of experience-mediated reality constraint, and not only extra-religious experiences

---

16.   Herrmann, 122.

count in this. This is in spite of some incorporation of interpretation in experience, which with the possible exception of 'pure empty consciousness' is a general feature of experience as such anyway. This is to say that empirical criteria still do some useful work, also with views of life.

However, there is also one very interesting corrective point that Herrmann makes for us. Precisely speaking, competition is not directly between science and religion as such. It takes place between views of life, some of them more inspired by sciences than others. Some of these views of life are religious, some of them philosophical. Then there is the particular case of philosophical theology, which is according to Herrmann 'the intellectual manifestation of a religious view of life by means of philosophical tools'.[17] Philosophical views of life, including those of philosophical theology, sacrifice concreteness, immediacy of relation to particular experiences and vividness of expression in favour of (greater) generality of appeal. My original distinction between more particular and more general now functions as a relativised distinction also between religious and philosophical views of life.

2.6 A third ingredient: the hermeneutics of reasonable belief

This is rather earlier than the advances in philosophy of religion and philosophy of science. It can be dated at least as far back as Hume, the essay on miracles in the first enquiry. The locus classicus is the example Hume gives of the Indian prince, who quite reasonably refused to believe travellers' tales about water freezing, this being against all his own experience and the ideas about the nature of water which he had based on these experiences.[18]

For Hume, this is not sufficient to save miracles. Given that a miracle is an event against the laws of nature, no amount of evidence based on testimony will be enough to overcome the scepticism against it having occurred. What we could call the hermeneutics of belief will always, he thinks, be against belief in miracles. I have argued

---

17.   Herrmann, 14.

18.   See David Hume, *Enquiries Concerning Human Understanding and Concerning the Principles of Morals*, LA Selby-Bigge, PH Nidditch, 3ʳᵈ edition (Oxford: Clarendon Press, 1975), 113–114, and footnote on page 114. For more details see Greg Moses, 'On the Hermeneutical Implications of Hume's Essay *Of Miracles*', *Prudentia*, Supplmentary No 1994: 112–26.

elsewhere that Hume is mistaken.[19] But the point for us is that reasonableness in belief is not universalisable. It is partly a contingent matter, a function of one's place and time and one's history. Reasonable does not in fact mean valid for all minds. What is reasonable for one person may well be unreasonable for someone else.

This, in principle, is no big deal. The boy who cried wolf is another classic example. Indeed, something like the principle is illustrated everyday in courtrooms throughout the world. The person with the uncorroborated alibi knows exactly where they were at the time of the crime. It is quite reasonable for them to firmly believe in their innocence. Yet the more generally available evidence may be such that a judge and jury would convict beyond reasonable doubt. In such cases we have diametrically opposed reasonable beliefs.

Such examples may be good enough to get the notion of a 'hermeneutics' and consequent pluralism of reasonable believing into play. A better analogy for our cause might be found in the later work of John Rawls, Rawls himself depending on Joshua Cohen.[20] In his later work, Rawls seeks to ground his theory of justice in the prospect of an 'overlapping consensus' between diverse reasonable comprehensive doctrines in a democratic society marked by the fact of reasonable pluralism. According to Rawls:

> free institutions tend to generate not simply . . . a variety of doctrines and views, as one might expect from peoples' various interests and their tendency to focus on narrow points of view. Rather, it is a fact that among the views that develop are a diversity of reasonable comprehensive doctrines. These are the doctrines that reasonable citizens affirm . . . [21]

Such a diversity of 'reasonable comprehensive religious, philosophical and moral doctrines' is, he thinks, a permanent and inevitable feature of the public culture of modern democracy. 'Under the political and social conditions secured by the basic rights and

---

19.   Moses, *ibid.*
20.   See John Rawls, *Political Pluralism* (New York: Columbia University Press, 1993), 35–41, reference to Cohen footnote 37, 36, plus Lecture IV 'The Idea of an Overlapping Consensus', 133–172.
21.   Rawls *op cit*, 36.

liberties of free institutions, a diversity of conflicting and irrecon-cilable—*and what's more, reasonable*—comprehensive doctrines will come about and persist if such diversity does not already obtain.' The hope is that in a situation of reasonable pluralism, each of the reasonable comprehensive doctrines will be able to endorse the idea of a political conception of justice as fairness, each from it own point of view.[22] Given this, political liberalism does not require a transcen-dental standpoint for its support.

Of course, not all comprehensive doctrines and views count as reasonable.[23] In particular, 'When there is a plurality of reasonable doctrines, it is unreasonable or worse to want to use the sanctions of state power to correct, or to punish, those who disagree with us'. In fact, it sometimes seems that there is an element of circularity in Rawls's argument: a comprehensive view which, in a situation of reasonable pluralism did not endorse Rawls's political conception of justice would count as unreasonable. We will look, eventually, for another way of making the distinction. But the point, for us, is that what we have termed differing views of life would presumably count as candidates for Rawls's diverse and conflicting, but, what is more reasonable, comprehensive doctrines.

This excursus into political theory gives us at least the beginnings of a case for extending the notion of a hermeneutics of reasonable belief to such broad historical determinants of belief as religious and other traditions of experience and interpretation. What is reasonable for a person with one conceptual apparatus itself determined by a certain flow of particularised experience need not be reasonable for a person who lacks this conceptual requirement. In application to our problem: what is reasonable for a person taken up into one tradition of experience and interpretation may or may not be reasonable for a person taken up in another, and vice versa. Even where 'reasonable' is taken univocally, what turns out in practice to be reasonable can still be tradition-dependent.

Note, however, that this is just an in-principle claim at this point. The contention is that traditions of experience and interpretation are doxastic practices capable in principle of yielding reasonable belief. This is not to say that they all do so. Nor is it to say that all beliefs had

---

22.   Rawls *op cit*, 134.
23.   Cf Rawls *op cit* 39.

by people inside a particular tradition are reasonable. Particular traditions of experience and interpretation will have their internal rationality criteria, which will distinguish between belief and belief. Even more than that, there may well be broad relatively neutral criteria sufficient to eliminate at least some whole traditions.

3. Some consequences and applications

3.1 Consequences
This has a double effect.

On the one hand, for people who are willing to accept the story, 'science', and the broad realm of 'reason' and 'rationality' get to be somewhat demystified. Even sciences are human endeavours, the work of embodied human beings in the natural world with others taken up into particular histories and communal traditions. In spite of its glory, science is not the work of disembodied spirits or angel-like beings. The same goes for philosophies.

On the other hand, from the point of view of reason, it tends also to *naturalise* religions and the realm of religion and faith, while still managing to preserve their specificity. 'Faith' in its cognitive aspect comes out almost as a species of 'particularised reason'. Religious belief comes to seem only *natural, in the* specific neo-Humean but rather harmless *sense of, only to be expected in the circumstances*. The phenomena are such as to lead people aware of them to have certain kinds of expectation, without going into the question of the 'secret springs and principles'. There is a sufficient conjunction between the right interpretative structures and the having of certain experiences and belief consequent of such experiences, for the mind of a third party to be determined, in Humean fashion, to expect one when given the other.

At the same time, given the thesis of the hermeneutics of reasonable belief, this does nothing in principle to show the beliefs as unreasonable. People who have the concepts of 'table' and 'watch', in certain circumstances will experience tables and watches, and third parties will expect them to. Religious belief also might well be reasonable for the people who have it, in spite of its particularity, while not reasonable for the people outside, and vice versa for other beliefs. Indeed, religious people can still speak of grace, as a particular interpretation of religious luck, which interpretation of the 'secret springs and principles' actually at work is motivated by particular experiences of particular people.

Indeed, that a belief in either sphere is natural does not preclude it being reasonable. On the contrary, while not everything recognised as natural will be thought reasonable, recognising a belief as only natural is frequently a step along the way to recognising it as reasonable. The travellers with the Indian prince if they are really honest might well recognise that the prince was within his rights to disbelieve them. So also the prisoner with the jury if he or she was cool enough. So even more so third parties. Consider the steady progression: It is only natural that she/he/they should go that way. In the circumstances I would go that way also. One would indeed be a fool not to. In the circumstances it is a perfectly reasonable way for this person or group of people to so proceed. There seems to be possible, then, a subjective universalisability of belief within a specific situation criterion at work, with, presumably, a tradition-specific subjective universalisability criterion as a subset of this.

Such considerations I suspect are much to the betterment of religion. Religion is not an entirely other world, in spite of its distinctness. Epistemologically both it and what is typically called reason and science and rationality are involved in a complicated experience-interpretation dynamic. In both cases, what is meant by 'interpretation' is rather more than just bits of theory. In spite of their mostly relative differences, they would indeed appear to constitute a constellation of equally valid 'doxastic practices',[24] at least in principle, capable of realising reasonable belief in the people inside them.

3.1 Applications

The application to belief in God has already been well made by Jan Van der Veken and his colleague Andre Cloots. Whitehead's God is not Whiteheadian enough. The God of the Christians, or the Jews or the Moslems, is not available to people on philosophical grounds alone, but requires to be grounded in particular experiences of particular people. The God of the philosophers may well be the same as the God who properly deserves the name, the God of the Religions,

---

24.   William Alston, 'The Autonomy of Religious Experience', *International Journal for the Philosophy of Religion*, Volume 31, Nos 2–3 (1992): 67–99.

but only abstractly considered, the same reference but a long way from the same sense, as with your good friend to you and to a perfect stranger.

The process philosopher-theologian David Griffin already does a reasonable job, on similar lines, in respect of the after-life. Philosophy, in particular Whiteheadian process philosophy, leaves the question open, and can at best show it to be possible. The rest depends on particular experiences, albeit always received in a certain interpretative context. What one might add to this is a rather stronger emphasis on the idea that *the experiences themselves might be shaped by the interpretative structures that people take to them* but that, on the other hand, *this is not epistemologically crucial.* Further than this, the structures explained above might go a long way to explicate the reception of Griffin's work on the after-life and indeed the reception of his more recent work on parapsychology.[25]

On the basis of particular experiences of his own, had obviously within a particular context, the present author might like to affirm and strengthen Griffin's widening of the field of available experiences in this latter regard. It is not just near-death experiences and telepathy and such that count. Even more important are experiences of other people around death, typically the death of people close to them, fathers or mothers or spouses or brothers or sisters or other close family and friends, as well as the death of Christ and other religious leaders. In the right interpretative context, these can give a person an inkling of what resurrection is, of what reconciliation as a consequence of a death might be, and such-like. The point here is that such interpretations are much more convincing to people who have had the experiences or to people who have had similar experiences, than to people who can hardly imagine what they are talking about, and rightly so.

A further application might be in respect of claims to authority. Such claims also need to be somewhat naturalised. In the process, much greater recognition might need to be given, by the claimants themselves as well as others, to the historical and human component of such claims. They are sometimes historically and contingently determined and 'theory-laden' to an extraordinary degree. While some kinds of claims might still be made, any facile authority positivism

---

25.   David Griffin, *Parapsychology, Philosophy and Spirituality: A Postmodern Exploration* (Albany: State University of New York Press, 1997).

would seem to be thoroughly misplaced. Besides, there isn't any magic, it's all 'natural', the mystery has gone, though hopefully not the Mystery. But this is a whole other issue.

4. A reply to some objections

We cannot quite go home yet. I need to make some attempt to reply to some objections which Dr Mark Wynn was kind enough to make to an earlier version of this paper, given at conference in August 2000).

First, there would seem to be a crucial difference between the examples I used to get up the notion of a hermeneutics of reasonable believing and the case of inter-religious dialogue. In all three examples, Hume's Indian Prince, the boy who cried wolf and the unsubstantiated alibi, it is the testimony we discount, not the validity of their experience. We do not distrust their experience or the way they interpret it, we distrust their testimony to have had such experience. However, in the case of inter-religious dialogue, we take the testimony at face value. So they both have experience and the experience they say they have had. What legitimates us in giving preferential treatment to the perspective of our own tradition?

But in the case of views of life or traditions of experience and interpretation, both the experience in respect of its formation and how it is afterwards interpreted, including the fact that it is taken as evidence and what it is taken as evidence for, implicates the tradition in which the experience stands. Belief is contextually determined in a fashion which does not call into question the sincerity or honesty of the other party: precisely. What is needed, then, and the only way forward, is a way of evaluating the interpretative and formative tradition, together with its confirming instances. The experiences cannot be evaluated, for good or ill, in isolation.

This is where the fun starts. A non-chauvinistic application of agreed criteria to these complexes is likely, we hope, to eliminate the Jonestown extremes. But this may still leave plenty in the middle. The criteria will either be too abstract to eliminate anything other than the extremes or will be concretised in terms of the tradition itself and therefore circular or will be concretised in terms of another tradition and therefore chauvinistic. We are forced to acknowledge that not only are they, eg Buddhists, Moslems, Protestants, Catholics, Humanists, sincere and honest in their reporting but also reasonable in their believing, and that this is yet another instance to which the hermeneutics of reasonable believing may reasonably be applied.

So far so good: we are back to our pluralism of reasonable believing. But this in and of itself is not enough to put us above the fray. Indeed, so far as I can tell at this point, the project of constructing a genuinely useful meta-perspective which would treat the traditions even-handedly would seem to be doomed, as it seems to require something paradoxical. Namely, it would seem to require general, cross-cultural and cross-tradition criteria which are yet as concrete as the particular criteria deployed in the religions themselves.

As with the hermeneutics of meaning according to the followers of Gadamer, the best we can hope for, then, might be a broadening and probably a deepening of our own starting horizon, perhaps with a dash of a 'hermeneutics of suspicion' in respect of my own tradition as well as the others. But I don't jump so to speak into a kind of absolute horizon of being as such.

Of course, nothing said here prohibits development and growth over time through contact between religious and other traditions. On the contrary. But this will happen in an organic, communal, long-term fashion. We will be mutually respectful but also respectful of our own tradition. At no stage will it require one to leap into an impossible meta-perspective.

5. Conclusion

So where does this leave us? From the viewpoint of relatively more general reason, faith in its cognitive aspect seems to be a version of more particularised reason. But less particularised reason finds itself incompetent to decide in any final fashion in the realms of more particularised reason. Philosophy, which lives in less particularised reason territory, can bring greater clarity, and it may be, greater charity, but it can't make religious choices for us. We are still in the position of the person building the tower or the ruler going to war in the Christian gospels, weighing up alternatives in a manner which is reasonable but not generalisable except in a context-dependent sense. Mind-sets and interpretative structures determine experiences, and vice versa. Constraints on theory making and theory choice which determine such mind-sets can be very complicated and ill understood. Even when better understood, we are still not home and hosed. And, either there is no way of getting out of such mind-sets or else, just in case there is 'pure experience', the good interpretation of such phenomena depends crucially on the mind-sets into which it is taken. Very general criteria may perhaps be specified for helping us make our religious decisions, but their meaning, bias and exact application will itself be tradition-dependent.

So there is an element of 'luck', we are back with Thich Nhat Hanh's Buddhist sutra. And yet, for all that, decisions once made can be recognised as reasonable, by ourselves after the event and even it may be by third parties who cannot go our way.

Let us end, then, with a very similar quotation from a contemporary feminist philosopher Anne Seller (Seller, 1988, 183), herself quoting Kristin Luker:

> Reasonable people who are located in different parts of the social world find themselves differentially exposed to diverse realities, and this differential exposure leads each of them to come up with different but often equally reasonable constructions of the world.[26]

As Anne Seller goes on to say in her context, we also say, *quite so,* also for people caught up in different religious and also non-religious comprehensive traditions.

---

26. Anne Seller, 'Realism versus Relativism: Towards a Politically Adequate Epistemology', in *Feminist Perspectives in Philosophy,* edited by Morwenna Griffith and Margaret Whitford (Bloomington IN: Indiana University Press, 1988), 169–86.

Intimation, Argument and Faith

Peter Coghlan

At one crucial point in their famous debate on the existence of God, Frederick Copleston asks Bertrand Russell if he would 'agree with Sartre that the universe is what he [Sartre] calls "gratuitous"'. Russell replies: 'I should say that the universe is just there, that's all.'[1] The striking thing to me about this reply is not so much Russell's rejection of the idea, an idea which Copleston insists on, that the existence of the universe needs to be explained; rather, it is the blunt matter-of-factness of Russell's language—his failure to register even the slightest hint that the existence of the universe might provoke our deepest wonder and even awe. It is 'just there, that's all'.

I do not mean that Russell never *wondered about* the origins of the universe in the ordinary sense of asking whether the universe had a beginning in time or whether it has always existed. He surely did that; just as he surely wondered about the question of whether asking for a causal explanation of the whole universe was a legitimate one or not —a question he answered in the negative. No, what I miss from Russell's response to Copleston is any sense of his ever having *wondered at* the existence of the universe—any sense of his ever having been deeply moved by the fact that anything exists at all. Russell's failure here does not seem to me to be primarily one of argumentative acumen or rigor (he may or may not fail in purely intellectual terms) but a failure of imagination and feeling. He is simply blank to that movement of spirit that has led virtually all the cultures of the world, certainly all the world's tribal cultures, to celebrate in one way or another the wonder of the universe and to give thanks for it as in some sense a sacred gift. In the broadest sense of the term, Russell lacks a religious sensibility.

But why call this a *lack* in Russell, a *failure* of imagination and feeling? The fact that I can even propose an adverse judgment of Russell in these terms depends on a more or less widely shared

---

1.   B Russell & FC Copleston, 'A Debate on the Existence of God', in *The Existence of God*, edited by J Hick (New York: Macmillan, 1964), 175.

understanding of what constitutes depth and shallowness in human life. Someone who spoke of any of the other central experiences of human life—like birth, suffering and death, friendship, love, the experience of beauty and ugliness and of moral good and evil—in Russell's matter-of-fact way as being 'just there' would invite the same accusation that he was lacking in imagination and feeling—that he was being immature, flippant, shallow. We expect people to treat such experiences with at least some awareness of their seriousness and gravity; and we usually go further: we are moved by those who speak of such experiences with wonder. Their response confirms our own feeling that there are some dimensions of experience which touch us so deeply, which are so compelling, mysterious and unfathomable, that they demand to be spoken of in religious terms like the sacred.

We can be moved in the same way by profound works of art which explore these sacred aspects of experience and, at the same time, become experiences of the sacred in their own right. Some of these works suggest the sacred simply by deepening our awareness and appreciation of some aspect of human life or some aspect of the natural world. Rembrandt's portrait known as *Woman with a Pink* (1665–1669), for example, shows only a seated woman holding a carnation and looking pensively beyond it. But the depth of feeling conveyed in her quiet tender expression seems to capture the essence of the inward reflective life of human beings so that the painting, for me at least, becomes a moving and sacred emblem of what it means to be human. Like all of Rembrandt's greatest works, it is a painting of the most profound compassion. Or consider Van Gogh's *Peach Tree in Blossom* (1888). In an orchard of trees, one tree stands in the foreground, its spiky limbs and branches alive with bursts of white blossom and fresh pale green shoots. The whole tree seems charged with energy. It is a marvellous symbol of the living power of nature—a power that can only be spoken of, the painting seems to say, in terms of reverence and awe.

By contrast, some other works that touch on the sacred do so, not so much by deepening our sense of the world around us, but by seeming to take us out of that world. Take, for instance, the famous opening lines of TS Eliot's *Marina* with their poignant longing for a beauty that is half remembered and half glimpsed through the senses:

What seas what shores what grey rocks and what
islands
What water lapping the bow
And scent of pine and the woodthrush singing
through the fog
What images return
O my daughter

This is our world of pine scent and thrush song; and yet these simple and beautiful images evoke what seems to be the very taste of a mysterious—a sacred—world beyond.

Or take some of Mark Rothko's extraordinary explorations of colour. His 1953 painting entitled only, *White, Orange and Yellow*, for example, looks radiant even in a reproduction; and the more you look at the two bands of white and yellow, the more they seem to blaze with an unearthly serene brilliance. By contrast, a painting like *Black on Black* of 1964 draws you into its depth so that the black tones of the canvas become luminous and a new world begins to appear within the darkness—though it is impossible to say what that world is. These works consist of ordinary colours; yet Rothko's genius renders the ordinary transcendent, sacred.

Or consider the last movement, the great *Arietta*, of Beethoven's final piano sonata—number 32, Opus 111, in C minor. This starts quietly and slowly with a deeply pondered theme. Then the theme gradually begins to lilt as if gathering energy; and the lilt becomes a swing, and the swing a dance, until the whole movement breaks out into rhapsodic cascades of sound. From that point on, the music seems to press forward reaching ever higher into the upper registers of the piano as if striving for expression beyond the range of the instrument. It is music of the most wondrous and intense exploration, music that is ecstatically alive. Yet there is no resolution, and the Arietta ends softly with a single chord that, as Alfred Brendel says, ' . . .opens up the silence that follows, a silence we now perceive to be more important than the sound that preceded it'.[2]

Like Eliot's 'scent of pine and woodthrush singing through the fog', and like Rothko's luminous darkness, the transcendent silence that Beethoven leads us to is a profoundly elusive one—we think we can

2.   Quoted in W Kinderman, 'Brendel's Beethoven', cover notes to *Alfred Brendel II, Great Pianists of the Twentieth Century*, Phillips, cat 456 730–2, 1999.

hear it and yet it always escapes our conscious attempts to say what it means. In this sense, these works are *intimations* of the sacred rather than articulated revelations of it. They are, in the terms Eliot uses in *Four Quartets*, 'only hints and guesses'. This does not mean that there is no serious thought in these works; on the contrary, they are the product of profound reflection; but the kind of thought that is involved is imaginative rather than discursive, a matter, as William Blake puts it, of 'minutely organized particulars' rather than abstract argumentation.

And what is true of the works by Eliot, Rothko and Beethoven which touch in some way on the transcendent, is also finally true of Rembrandt's *Woman with a Pink* and Van Gogh's *Peach Tree in Blossom*—works in which the sacred seems rooted in this world. We may be able to point more precisely to what it is in these latter works—the inward life of the human spirit in the one, and the living energy of nature in the other—that makes us reach for a phrase like 'the sacred' to capture the full meaning of what we see; but why that inwardness and that energy should move us so deeply, why we feel that those who cannot see anything mysterious in these works are shallow, we are at a loss to say.

However, there are other works where our sense of the sacred seems to be more than an intimation, more than 'hints and guesses'. These are the kinds of works that spring immediately from a particular religious tradition and rely on the forms of that tradition—its beliefs, prayers and rituals—for their imaginative life. Such works may still, of course, be concerned with matters that remain unfathomable; but they approach those mysteries in the light of the articulated tradition of which they are part. I am thinking here of Fra Angelico's beautifully pure *Annunciation*, or the grandeur and glory of Bach's *Mass in B Minor*, or this, the opening stanza of John Donne's *A Hymn to Christ, at the Authors Last Going into Germany*, with its intense and hushed gravity—the gravity of a man coming to the full realisation of the meaning of separation, loss and mortality:

> In what torn ship soever I embark,
> That ship shall be my emblem of thy Ark;
> What sea soever swallow me, that flood
> Shall be to me an emblem of thy blood.
> Though thou with clouds of anger do disguise

> Thy face; yet through that mask I know those eyes,
> Which, though they turn away sometimes,
> They never will despise.

And what here is a quiet trust in God's continuing care, becomes at the conclusion of the same poet's *A Hymn to God My God, in My Sickness* a passionate faith which exalts even as it measures the full weight of suffering and death:

> So, in his purple wrapped receive me Lord,
> By these his thorns give me his other crown;
> And as to others souls I preached thy word,
> Be this my Text, my Sermon to mine own,
> Therefore that he may raise the Lord throws down.

I know of no finer expression of the human meaning of the Christian doctrine of the Resurrection than this great poem of Donne's.

One of the remarkable things about both of these stanzas is the way Donne creates a vivid sense of the presence of God as the 'thou', the 'Lord', to whom the poet is speaking. God becomes Donne's interlocutor. This is one key way in which a work like *A Hymn to God My God, in My Sickness* seems to be more than an intimation of the sacred—the sacred seems to be there, present in the dramatic body of the poem. Of course there can be critical argument about whether a particular work of art does realise the presence of the sacred or even an intimation of it. FR Leavis, for example, thinks that the famous opening of Eliot's *Little Gidding*—'Midwinter spring is its own season /Sepiternal though sodden towards sundown'—fails to achieve the 'metaphorical transference of the evoked this-worldly splendour to the postulated transcendental apprehension'. What we have in fact, Leavis says, is not an intimation of the sacred, let alone the presence of it, but 'mere assertion'.[3]

That is one level of argument. But if we assume that there can be genuine and truthful imaginative apprehensions of the sacred, whether intimated in some of the ways I have illustrated or realised in the more substantial way I have claimed for the two poems of Donne, then the further question arises as to the significance of those intimations or realisations. I have already suggested that our being moved or not by

---

3.   FR Leavis, *The Living Principle* (London: Chatto and Windus, 1975), 254.

the kind of works I have touched on here is one of the measures of depth and maturity in our responsiveness to human experience as opposed to shallowness and immaturity. But do such works have any other significance? Can they, for example, be taken in any sense as *evidence* or as *reasons* for religious belief? Do they lead to faith?

If we do think of them in that way, there are immediate problems. To begin with, intimations, no matter how moving, remain only that—elusive 'hints and guesses'; and even the more substantial presence of a personal God that is found in the two Donne poems can be seen as a dramatic fiction—a profoundly moving fiction, but still a fiction, like the presence of the Duke and his interlocutor that Browning so vividly creates in *My Last Duchess*.

Moreover, if we treat these works as evidence of some transcendent reality we must face squarely the fact that there are great works of art that offer us what might be called counter intimations. Lear's terrible cry of despair after the death of Cordelia—'Why should a dog, a horse, a rat have life/And thou no breath at all?' is one such intimation. Another, of a different kind, is the compelling sense of the utter blank finality of death that Wordsworth captures in one of his Lucy poems:

> No motion has she now, no force;
> She neither hears nor sees;
> Rolled round in earth's diurnal course,
> With rocks, and stones, and trees.

And, at the very end of his life, that great celebrant of the sacred dimension of human life, WB Yeats, wrote one poem—*The Man and the Echo*—whose ending, with its eerie, halting rhythm, challenges everything he ever wrote before:

> O Rocky Voice,
> Shall we in that great night rejoice? What do we know
> but that we face
> One another in this place?
> But hush, for I have lost my theme,
> Its joy or night seem but a dream;
> Up there some hawk or owl has struck,
> Dropping out of the sky or rock.
> A stricken rabbit is crying out,

And its cry distracts my thought.

There is no ultimate meaning or value either in this world or beyond it; there is only Lear's unanswerable question, or the rolling of the planet, or the profoundly disturbing cry of a stricken animal. (Could Russell's 'the universe is just there, that's all' be a counter-intimation of this kind? I think not: his language has none of the gravity of Wordsworth's 'With rocks, and stones, and trees.') If I continue to trust in some intimations of the sacred, it will not be because reason justifies that trust. It will be because I am 'intent', in Kierkegaard's marvellous image, 'upon holding fast the objective uncertainty, so as to remain out upon the deep, over seventy thousand fathoms of water, preserving my faith'.[4]

But perhaps it is a mistake to treat these intimations as evidence of anything other than our sense of the depth of our own human experience. Perhaps we should think of the intimations of the sacred to be found in Rembrandt's *Woman with a Pink* or Eliot's *Marina* or Beethoven's *Arietta* as continuous with the more substantial presence of the sacred in an openly religious work like Donne's *Hymn to God My God, in My Sickness* and therefore as part of an inherited language of religious faith. And perhaps we should think, as Rush Rhees does, of that inherited language and its many uses as *constituting* religious faith in the same way that the language of love and its many uses constitutes love.[5]

On Rhees's view, we go wrong if we think of religious faith as an attempt to answer metaphysical puzzles about the existence of the universe as a whole or the existence of certain phenomena, like natural order or moral good and evil, within it. The language we use when we speak of God as the 'Creator of Heaven and Earth' is not the language of causal explanation; rather, it is the language of wonder—not the *wondering about* that leads to the kind of philosophical argument that Russell and Copleston were engaged in, but the *wondering at* that Russell seems bereft of. The 'belief in a creator', says Rhees:

---

4.   S Kierkegaard, 'Concluding Unscientific Postscript', in *The Age of Ideology*, edited by HD Aiken (New York: Mentor, 1956), 240.

5.   DZ Phillips, editor, *Rush Rhees on Religion and Philosophy* (Cambridge: Cambridge University Press, 1997), 40.

is not the belief in a cause, even in the special sense
Aristotle has in mind. The belief in a creator might go
with the thought that . . . 'Isn't it extraordinary that
anything at all should exist.' If we call this an
expression of wonder, then it is the same wonder as is
expressed in 'This is all God's handiwork; this declares
the glory of God', or 'This—that there should be
anything at all—shows God's goodness.' And that
would not come into Aristotle's theology. A philosopher's contemplation of things may lead him,
perhaps, to infer the existence of a first mover. But if it
does . . . this is not what is being said in 'The Heavens
declare the glory of God.' And 'Isn't it extraordinary
that anything should exist' is not wondering what
could have caused it, or how it is possible. [6]

We do not teach children about God by talking of first movers or
necessary non-contingent beings or even grand designers. To do so
would be to trivialise our concept of God. God is not a metaphysical
entity but the 'Creator of Heaven and Earth'. No, we teach children
about God by using the religious language of our tradition—the
language of praise and worship, of thanksgiving and trust, of ritual
and prayer, which is constitutive of a certain way of life. 'What
religious people have in mind', says Rhees, 'is something like an
answer to questionings of the heart'.[7]

However, it does not follow from this that there cannot be any
argument within the religious way of life. There will always be
questions, and sometimes bitter disputes, amongst religious believers
about what can be properly said of God and what it means to worship
him. As Rhees quite rightly asks, 'Could you speak of worshipping
God—would it mean anything—without some sort of theology?'[8]

If this is so, then Rhees might allow that there is one kind of
wondering about that is appropriate here and that does not trivialise
our concept of God. And that is the kind of wondering about that
arises precisely when we ask, What is the proper focus of our

---

6.   *Ibid*, 4.

7.   *Ibid*, 31.

8.   *Ibid*, 45.

intimations of the sacred? What kind of object does answer to the deepest questionings of our hearts—to what Plato in the *Phaedrus* calls our 'flood of longing'?[9]

Plato found the appropriate focus of his intimations in the vision of absolute beauty and goodness 'whole and unspotted and changeless and serene'.[10] And Augustine, following him, asks in that beautiful passage in his *Confessions*, 'But what do I love when I love my God?', and answers:

> Not material beauty or beauty of a temporal order; not the brilliance of earthly light, so welcome to our eyes; not the sweet melody of harmony and song; not the fragrance of flowers, perfumes and spices; not manna or honey; not limbs such as the body delights to embrace. It is not these that I love when I love my God. And yet, when I love him, it is true that I love a light of a certain kind, a voice, a perfume, a food, an embrace; but they are of the kind I love in my inner self, when my soul is bathed in light that is not bound by space; when it listens to sound that never dies away; when it breathes a fragrance that is not borne away on the wind; when it clings to an embrace from which it is not severed by fulfilment of desire. That is what I love when I love my God.[11]

Plato's vision captures the kind of radiant serenity that we find in a painting like Rothko's *White, Orange and Yellow*; and Augustine's words capture the kind of mysterious sensual beauty that is intimated in the opening lines of Eliot's *Marina*.

Yet neither of these visions seems to be appropriate as a focus for the intense energy and power of Van Gogh's *Pear Tree in Blossom* or the ecstatic vitality of Beethoven's *Arietta*. To find a focus that will do justice to intimations like these, many turn to the figure of Yahweh in

9.   Plato, *Phaedrus & Letters VII &VIII*, translated by W Hamilton, (Harmondsworth: Penguin, 1973), 58.

10. *Ibid*, 57.

11. Saint Augustine, *Confessions*, translated by RS Pine-Coffin (Harmondsworth: Penguin, 1961), 61.

the Old Testament, especially as it is manifest, for example, in the voice that speaks to Job from the heart of the whirlwind:

> Have you ever visited the place where the snow is kept or seen where the hail is stored up, which I keep for times of stress for days of battle and war? From which direction does the lightning fork when it scatters sparks over the earth? Who carves a channel for the downpour, and hacks a way for the rolling thunder?
> Has the rain a father? Who begot the dewdrops? What womb brings forth the ice, and gives birth to the frost of heaven when the waters grow hard as stone and the surface of the deep congeals?[12]

The figure that speaks here is powerful, active, terrifying, holy. This is William Blake's God, the God who would dare create a Tyger that burns 'in the forests of the night'. It is the God of Abraham, Isaac and Jacob.

Yet could this figure also be the creator of that profound tenderness and compassion that we find in a work like Rembrandt's *Woman with a Pink*? To find an appropriate focus for that kind of intimation, others turn, again, to the mysterious and compelling personality of Jesus of Nazareth—to the figure which, on the one hand, manifests such extraordinary inner power and authority as he turns the Pharisees' attacks back against them and shames them into silence or as he stoops to write in the sand in the face of the mob intent on stoning the woman taken in adultery; and yet, on the other hand, to the figure that reveals such deeply human sympathy and vulnerability as he weeps at the tomb of Lazarus or cries out on the cross, 'My God, my God, why have you abandoned me?' It is, at least in part, this strange union of authority and vulnerability that leads many Christians to see in Jesus the fullest illumination of their sense of the sacred.

We may surely wonder in this way—wondering about the appropriate focus for our intimations of the sacred—without cheapening our concept of God. But now, how are we to understand the focus that we find does best answer the deepest questioning of our hearts? Is it simply a fiction created in language like the dramatic presence of

---

12. Job 38: 22–25 & 28–30, Jerusalem Bible.

God that Donne creates in his *Hymns*? Few religious believers would accept that God, whether the God of the Old Testament or the God that is manifest in the figure of Jesus, is merely a literary fiction—however profound that fiction might be. They would say that the language of the book of Job or of the gospels *reveals* the reality of God rather than creates it.

Nor, I suspect, would a Rush Rhees think of God as a literary fiction. For Rhees, God does not simply exist in the language of certain key texts. He exists in the common life—itself a kind of language—of worship and prayer that religious believers participate in—just as the reality of love is to be found, not only in key texts like *Troilus and Cressida* or *Romeo or Juliet*, but in our shared language of love which is part of our way of life.

However, many religious believers would also resist Rhees's way of putting things. For them, God exists independently of, and beyond, their shared life. The official Catholic tradition, for example, holds that God is a transcendent reality whose existence, in the famous words of the First Vatican Council, 'can be known with certainty from the created world by the natural light of reason';[13] and John Paul II is simply reflecting that tradition when he speaks in his encyclical, *Fides et Ratio*, of 'the need for a philosophy of genuinely metaphysical range capable . . . of transcending empirical data in order to attain something absolute, ultimate and foundational in its search for truth'.[14]

If the Catholic tradition is right in this, then we may not only wonder about the appropriate focus for our intimations of the sacred; we may also wonder, without impropriety, about whether there is some ultimate source of the sacred in our experience. In John Paul II's words, our 'speculative thinking must penetrate to the spiritual core and the ground from which it rises'.[15] Without that speculative thinking, we could never be sure that our belief in the reality of a transcendent God was anything more than wish fulfilment—a mere projection, as Feuerbach would have it, of our desires and longings.

Can the existence of a transcendent God be known through speculative argument with the kind of certainty that Vatican I speaks of? Given the notoriously contentious nature of such argument, and

---

13. Quoted in *The Catechism of the Catholic Church* (Strathfield NSW: St Paul, 1994), par. 36.

14. John Paul II, *Fides et Ratio* (Strathfield NSW: St Paul, 1998), par. 83.

15. *Ibid*, par. 83.

the difficulty of the abstract concepts involved, that claim seems a doubtful one. Moreover, as soon as we begin to use metaphysical notions such as 'first cause', 'uncaused cause', and 'necessary non-contingent being', we run the risk, as Rhees points out, of diminishing our concept of God—a necessary being is neither the terrifying and holy voice that speaks to Job from the whirlwind nor the authoritative yet compassionate figure revealed in Jesus.

A more modest view comes from Roger Trigg. Trigg agrees with the official Catholic tradition that 'the content of faith cannot exist securely apart from the conclusions of rationality'.[16] But he does not believe that the existence of a transcendental God who is the creator of the world can be proven by reason. The most that metaphysical argument can achieve, he thinks, is to establish the possibility, at most the probability, that such a being exists.

At the same time, Trigg is well aware that the being whose existence reason establishes is not the God of Abraham, Isaac and Jacob, nor the God made manifest in Jesus. That is why revelation is required. Revelation both confirms what reason makes possible and deepens our understanding of the nature of the creative cause of the universe so that we come to recognise that cause as personal, holy and good. It is only through revelation that we discover that the metaphysical being posited by rational argument is identical with the focus of our deepest intimations of the sacred—identical, that is, with the object of our longing and our faith, our worship and our prayer:

> A natural theology may create a space for the notion of a Creator, but it is still not much more than an empty space. We may conclude from the apparent unity of nature that it would have to be one reality rather than a series. It is still unclear, however, whether such a Being is personal. Is it indifferent to human beings? Is it even good? Questions are raised but not answered, unless we conclude that the nature of the physical world is such that it cannot allow any belief in a purpose within it. In other words, natural theology provides a case for thinking that, if there were a God, humans still need a

---

16. R Trigg, *Rationality and Religion: Does Faith Need Reason?* (Oxford: Blackwell, 1998), 184.

further source of knowledge about the character of
such a God. God has to be revealed in a more specific
and direct way. Revelation is thus not a substitute for
'natural' reason. It is an answer to the questions such
reason produces.[17]

We cannot know the God of faith without revelation; but it is
metaphysical argument, or 'natural theology' as Trigg calls it, which
has the logical priority. For it is that kind of argument which enables
us to recognise a revelation and to distinguish a genuine instance of it
from its false semblances. 'Without some conception of a Creator', says
Trigg, 'there must be considerable doubt about what, if anything, or
who, if anybody, is being revealed.'[18]

But now Trigg has a problem. For he also insists, as we have seen,
that metaphysical argument can do little more than 'create a space for
the notion of a Creator', a space which is more or less empty of content.
Yet if metaphysical argument cannot tell us whether the posited cause
of the universe is holy or good, or even whether that cause is personal,
it is difficult to see how that kind of argument can provide the criteria
necessary to recognise a revelation and to distinguish between true
and false instances of it. If reason has almost nothing to say about the
character of the being it makes space for, why should we expect a
revelation like that of Yahweh or Jesus? And if we cannot recognise the
supposed identity between our metaphysical concept of God and the
God of revelation, how can revelation confirm the existence of the
being that metaphysical reason says is possible or probable?

And there is a further problem here. The conceptual space Trigg
speaks of is not completely empty. It contains abstractions like the
notion of a first cause, or an uncaused cause, or a necessary non-
contingent being. But these are precisely the kinds of abstractions that
Rush Rhees thinks have really nothing to do with the life of faith—the
life of prayer and worship—which is centred on the God of Abraham,
Isaac and Jacob or on the figure of Jesus as the unique revelation of
God. The abstractions of metaphysics only trivialise the life of faith. As

---

17.   *Ibid*, 185.

18.   *Ibid*, 182. This view of Trigg's is broadly in line with the position John Paul II
      takes in *Fides et Ratio*—except that the Pope has much greater confidence in the
      power of metaphysical reason to establish the existence of God than Trigg does.
      See *Fides et Ratio* 8, 9 and 34.

Rhees pointedly asks: 'Suppose we prove that there is a necessary being and that in some sense everything depends on it—why call it 'God'?[19]

In the face of these difficulties, we might be tempted to reverse Trigg's logical order, which places metaphysical argument before revelation. Perhaps we should see revelation as logically prior to metaphysical argument. This would mean that the first step in establishing the existence of God is to have a concept of God that is serious and deep enough to function as the appropriate focus of our intimations of the sacred. Only then can we turn to argument to demonstrate that such a God may possibly exist, or even probably does exist.

But this move fails for the same reasons that Trigg's original argument fails. If the metaphysical argument which creates 'a space for the notion of a Creator' cannot be confirmed by revelation because we cannot recognise the identity between the abstractions that occupy that space and the God of Abraham or Jesus, then the reverse procedure will not work either: we cannot confirm the existence of the God of revelation by reference to the abstractions of metaphysical argument. Moreover, those abstractions, whether they come first or second in logical priority, will continue to diminish our understanding of the God of faith.

There are, of course, other moves and other arguments. We could, for example, attempt to show that the ideas of personhood and goodness follow from the notion of a necessary non-contingent being. I do not discount this possibility; but it would involve some highly abstract reasoning that would seem to lead away from the God revealed in Job or in Jesus rather than towards those revelations. Or we could follow Descartes in defining God from the outset as supremely perfect and so perfectly good, trustworthy and holy. This is still not the God of revelation; and Descartes's attempt to establish that the God defined in this way actually exists leads to all the well-known difficulties of the ontological argument. Or we could follow Richard Swinburne in arguing that because personal action is the simplest form of causation, reason requires that the cause of the universe be a personal being.[20] Again, this personal being is not the voice from the

---

19.   Rhees, *op cit*, 5.

20.   R Swinburne, *The Existence of God* (Oxford: Clarendon Press, 1979), 103–106.

whirlwind or the loving Father Jesus speaks of; and one billiard ball striking another seems to many people to be just as simple, perhaps a simpler, form of causation than the mysterious nature of personal action.

Perhaps the arguments that have the best chance of keeping faith with our intimations of the sacred, and with those 'revelations' that have provided the Western tradition with such profoundly satisfying focal points for those intimations, are those which spring directly from our experience of moral good and evil, from our experience of love, including the love of truth, and from our experience, not so much of the order in the world that the traditional design argument rests on, but of its beauty—a beauty which is celebrated, and sometimes deepened, by art. We wonder at such experiences; we may also wonder about them in the sense of seeking for an appropriate focus for them when they come to us in the form of intimations of the sacred; and we may wonder about them in the further sense of wondering where they come from and what, if anything, is their source.

This last kind of wondering about does not seem to me to diminish or cheapen the initial wondering at from which it springs; on the contrary, it takes that initial wonder with profound seriousness. It says, in effect: these experiences, whether in life or art, are so important to anyone who wonders at all, and occupy such a central place in the hearts and minds of those whose lives move us most deeply, that they cry out for explanation. Are they, as Rush Rhees suggests, essentially human achievements that have become part of the fabric of our common life? Or do they have a source, as some of our intimations imply, that transcends human life?

Of course those questions now invite metaphysical speculation and argument with all the attendant dangers that Rhees points out to us. Plato remains both an inspiration and a warning here. His vision of absolute beauty and goodness—'the end of all endeavour, the only object on which every heart is set' as he says in *The Republic*[21]—still stirs the imagination; but his attempt to argue that the Forms are the transcendent source of all beauty and goodness founders on the very metaphysical reefs that he himself saw—what is the nature of these transcendent abstract entities and how do they relate to actual instances of the beautiful and the good?

---

21.   Plato, *The Republic*, translated by Desmond Lee (Harmondsworth: Penguin, 1980), 304.

The challenge, then, is to find a mode of argument that does justice to our intimations and revelations of the sacred and yet maintains its intelligibility and coherence as it seeks to go beyond them to find their source. I have nothing new to add to answering that challenge here; and perhaps there is no answer.

If that is the case, then I think we have three options. We can say, with Rush Rhees, that the search for a transcendent source of our intimations is a misguided one because we cannot make sense of the metaphysical concepts we are forced to use in our argumentation, and, even more importantly, because those concepts trivialise our understanding of God. Or we can, with Kierkegaard, hold fast to a faith in a transcendent source of the sacred despite, or even because of, its rational uncertainty and simply accept our predicament—'out upon the deep, over seventy thousand fathoms of water'.

Or, finally, we can turn back to our intimations and what we judge to be their most appropriate focus, recognising their centrality in our lives, and acknowledging that we may never, at least in this life, have anything more than 'hints and guesses'. At one point in *Four Quartets*, this is TS Eliot's position. It is a more tentative position than the famous conclusion to the sequence with its ringing affirmation that:

> . . . all shall be well and
> All manner of things shall be well
> When the tongues of flame are in-folded
> Into the crowned knot of fire
> And the fire and the rose are one.

But I sometimes think that this earlier position is all the more moving for its very tentativeness and humility. And I end this paper with these lines of Eliot's from the third of the four Quartets, *The Dry Salvages*:

> For most of us, there is only the unattended
> Moment, the moment in and out of time,
> The distraction fit, lost in a shaft of sunlight,
> The wild thyme unseen, or the winter lightning
> Or the waterfall, or music heard so deeply
> That it is not heard at all, but you are the music

While the music lasts. These are only hints and
guesses,
Hints followed by guesses; and the rest
Is prayer, observance, discipline, thought and action.
The hint half guessed, the gift half understood, is
Incarnation.

'Truth in the Inward Part': Faith and the Scalpel of Suspicion

Winifred Wing Han Lamb

Introduction

Philosophers of religion like Merold Westphal[1] have noted with clarity that the 'masters of suspicion', Freud, Marx and Nietzsche, have presented a new kind of philosophical challenge to faith. While the dominant European philosophy of religion from Gaunilio through Hume and Kant and that continues to dominate philosophical discussion today takes Christian claims to task on the basis of lack of evidence and intelligibility, the masters of suspicion have attacked Christians themselves for their duplicity and for the way in which they use their faith as an instrument of self-interest. In this way, Westphal distinguishes *'evidential atheism'* from *'the atheism from suspicion'*. While the former practises a form of scepticism towards religious faith claims and addresses the propositions believed, asking whether there is sufficient evidence to make belief rational, suspicion addresses itself to the persons who make such claims and believe such things. As Westphal says, 'It (atheistic suspicion) seeks to discredit the believing soul by asking what motives lead people to believe and what functions their belief play, looking for precisely those motives and functions that love darkness rather than light and therefore hide themselves'.[2] The interest in finding the 'heart-springs of thought and action' beyond propositions and public truth claims is not prominent in Western philosophy, but it is there.

Francis Bacon, for example, in his critique of the Idols of the Tribe and the Cave warned that 'The human understanding is no dry light, but receives an infusion from the will and affections; whence proceed sciences which may be called "sciences as one would". For what a man

---

1. Merold Westphal, *Suspicion and Faith: The Religious Uses of Modern Atheism* (Grand Rapids: Eerdmans, 1993).
2. *Ibid*, 14.

75

had rather were true he more readily believes.'[3] Other philosophers make a similar point about the centrality of the will and consequently the need for suspicion towards knowledge claims of any kind. Schopenhauer, Ricoeur, even Hume and Kant acknowledge that inclinations represent a 'powerful counterweight' to duty and reason. For as Kant said, in all human endeavours 'everywhere we come upon the dear self, which is always turning up . . .'[4] If such insights into the depths of the human heart had been incorporated into philosophical critique we would have had a very different, and a wider debate within mainstream philosophy of religion.[5]

My concern in this paper is to construct a response from faith to atheistic suspicion (focusing on Nietzsche's critique of Christian piety), which of course challenges faith to respond in just those other directions. If, as Westphal says, the critique of faith from suspicion seeks to uncover the duplicity of believers by unmasking their motives for belief as well as the function that belief plays in the advancement of their interests, what form should the response from faith take?

The title of my paper contains a phrase from the well-known penitential psalm in which David faces up to his sin before God. The prophet Nathan had brought home to him the enormity of his sin(s) and in particular, the tyranny of his actions, viz the gross misuse of his kingly power to further his adulterous desires. In addition, it is brought home to him, in a self-authenticating moment of conviction, how as ruler, instead of caring for one of his subjects, he had treated him with violence, regarding him only as an obstacle in his way. In this psalm, David confesses his sin and puts himself under God's judgment

---

3.   Francis Bacon, *Novum Organum*, XLIX, LVIII, quoted in *ibid.*

4.   Kant, *Grounding for the Metaphysics of Morals*, translated by James W Ellington (Indianapolis: Hackett, 1981), 407, quoted in *ibid*, 22.

5.   See Stephen Williams's, *Reason and Revelation: A Window on Modernity.* (Cambridge: Cambridge University Press, 1995) which takes up this line of thinking. Williams argues that conventional accounts of modern atheism are too dominated by epistemology. He offers instead a different reading of intellectual history which locates Christianity's offence to modernity not only in epistemology and theodicy but also in Christianity's claim about God's historical act of reconciliation and forgiveness. Williams presents Western atheism as 'a spiritual movement of the soul as well as an intellectual movement of the mind'. (8) Williams's position is particularly pertinent to the atheism from suspicion and I will make reference to it at the end of the paper.

without for a moment shirking God's holy requirement—not only for an outward form of righteousness, but for 'truth in the inward part', ie truthfulness in parts of him that only God's holy gaze can reveal.

This psalm gives us a picture of faith's response to suspicion and it serves to show where faith concurs with Nietzsche and where it departs from him, how faith can, on the one hand can be grateful to Nietzsche for his insights about human nature while on the other hand refusing his logic. In this psalm, we find that God's holy gaze, while searing, offers a depth of insight that furthers both truthfulness and freedom. The psalm provides a phenomenology of Christian confession which while concurring with Nietzsche's insight into the tawdriness of the human heart, also serves to show that repentance does not have to be seen as the state of inverted revenge that Nietzsche diagnoses, but rather that it can be an act of freedom and dignity. God the judge is also the God the liberator.

Nietzschean suspicion is continued in postmodern forms in which truth claims are often interpreted as bids for power in one form or another. We find this in the philosophy of Michel Foucault. In his recent book on Foucault, Chris Falzon[6] recommends 'social dialogue' as the way forward, but such dialogue is based on the abandonment of any metaphysical and transcendent perspectives of the world because, as Falzon sees it, such meta-perspectives are responsible, not only for the self-deceptive closure that Nietzsche identifies, but also for forms of mastery and dominance.

It is undeniable, however, that David addresses the transcendent God, and it is before such a God that he feels judged and before whom he also submits and pleads. While this gives further fuel to Nietzschean and Foucauldian suspicion of self-deception and the instrumental use of religion for the purpose of self-interest, there is a point at which faith can do no other than invite examination into a believer's relationship to the transcendent God who sees, judges and liberates. There can be no knock-down arguments here—the sceptic will have to (in Wittgenstein's words) 'look and see', to observe how David puts himself under God's judgment in what to all intents and purposes is a position of non-manipulative vulnerability. David is a

---

6. Christopher Falzon, *Foucault and Social Dialogue: Beyond Fragmentation* (London: Routledge, 1998).

powerful man, but as a sinner, he eschews both mastery and self-justification.

The sceptic will also have to decide whether David's confession and his obvious guilt is 'sick' and inverted as Nietzsche claims. What a psychologically healthy person looks like involves a complex discussion about anthropology. In pleading for God's forgiveness David appeals to God's holiness and mercy but also asks to be put right, not only in outward forms of piety but also 'in the inward part'. Here spiralling duplicity ends—at the place of acknowledgment, confession and trust in God.

My intention is not to labour over an exegesis of this psalm, but I begin my paper with it because it shows, more clearly and appropriately than argument, the radical difference between the logic of faith and the logic of atheistic suspicion. The atheism from suspicion therefore introduces into philosophy of religion questions about philosophical anthropology and a needed discussion about what people are like and what difference faith makes to them. More will be said on this point. However, the rest of the paper will also advance a response containing arguments against Nietzsche's atheistic suspicion but it will also finish at the limits of argument.

In Part 1, 'They "already know what is good and just"—Nietzsche and the Pharisees', I will begin with Nietzsche's critique of Christian piety which is based on his notion of slave morality. His characterisation of 'pharasaism' is particularly insightful and, as a mirror to Christian piety, it bears out the recommendation from Westphal that Christians should read Nietzsche for Lent and for the purposes of self-examination.

Nietzsche said that both Zarathustra and Jesus were hated by the religious Pharisees because these prophets challenged the moral conservatism of the day and offered something new. This was abhorrent to the Pharisees because they were thoroughly invested in their view of the world in the manner of mastery and ownership. In a way, the Pharisees had a fundamentalist form of believing in which, as Nietzsche diagnoses, they 'already knew' everything that they wanted to know about God and about their fellow humans. In this the Pharisees exhibit, not only manipulative and instrumental religion, but also a totalising closure towards the religion of their day.

In Part 2, entitled 'Their hardness of heart—reading Nietzsche through Jesus', I will show how the significance of this state of epistemic closure is at the heart of spiritual closure, and it is described by the biblical notion of 'hardness of heart'. This condition comes with the warning that believers must attend not only to acts of piety and virtue but also to the state of their own heart, to inquire whether it is open to truth and to the address of the transcendent God. While, as mentioned above, postmodern critiques of transcendent views of the world are based on the assumption that such views encourage closure, pharisaic closure is addressed in Christian thought in such a way that transcendence is part of the solution rather than the problem.

In the remainder of the paper, in Part 3, entitled 'The limits of suspicion—"a base form of honesty"' and Part 4, '"Beyond suspicion" —where to from here?', I will more directly fault Nietzsche's critique of Christian piety on at least three grounds. My first criticism of Nietzsche is that while he shows insight into false forms of piety, his account is superficial because he does not look deeply enough. He is too prepared to accept what he catches with his passionate gaze as the final truth about believers. He does not look to see how believers themselves are concerned about their duplicity and how they themselves desire truthfulness and transparency. If Nietzsche had carefully considered Psalm 51, and indeed the wide literature of Christian devotion, he would see there the evidence of a longing within believers for grace to free them from the nexus of power relations that Nietzsche says is the total story of human relations and behaviour. In failing to look further, Nietzsche's critique of piety itself becomes totalising and transcendental, as if nothing of believers was left over after Nietzsche's critical summation. Having dismissed Christians as practising a full scale *'cunning of impotence'*, Nietzsche does not care to see how they deal with this fact about themselves in the life of faith and confession.

A second major problem with Nietzsche's critique is that beyond the critique there is something else going on, ie the critique is driven by his passionate hostility to Christianity because of what he saw as its corrupt anthropology. By the time he wrote *The Gay Science*, Nietzsche had moved to the stage in which his hostility towards Christianity was directed by private rather than publicly demonstrable reasons. About this he wrote, 'What is now decisive against Christianity is our taste, no longer our reasons' (GS III. 132). And if this is so, why should we take Nietzsche seriously beyond a certain point?

The third point of objection is related to the previous one. Nietzsche does not seem to recognise the limits of suspicion, although he did acknowledge that cynicism can be dangerous because it is 'the only form in which base souls approach honesty'.[7] As Westphal notes, there is something totalising and complacent about suspicion if it is carried to the limits. Even though we must watch the forms of closure and mastery that produces the worship of gods that are 'no gods',[8] we must also protest in the end against the relentless suspicion that itself becomes transcendental and idolatrous. This point will be discussed further in Part 3.

However, we now reach an impasse, because even if, in response to Nietzsche, Christians resolved to be truthful in their faith and profession, it will not do because, for Nietzsche, Christianity is finally irredeemable and totally diseased. In Part 4, '"Beyond suspicion" —where to from here?', I raise questions about how faith can engage with Nietzsche in the face of such opposition and against such deep hostility, and I offer some suggestions for the way ahead in philosophy of religion.

1. They 'already know what is good and just'—Nietzsche and the Pharisees[9]

Nietzsche's critique of Christianity and of Christian piety is based on his central themes of resentment and revenge and of the slave morality on which it is based. Even more basic is Nietzsche's assumption about human beings that they are driven by the will to power, indeed, 'the psychical extravagance of the lust for power!',[10] since 'the will to power . . . is after all the will of life'.[11] This is extended beyond human behaviour to include societies in which customs that arise out of the need to preserve themselves become the basis of morality. According to Nietzsche, the difference that is fundamental to morality is not

---

7.   Nietzsche, *Beyond Good and Evil: Prelude to a Philosophy of the Future*, translated by Walter Kaufmann (New York: Random House, 1967), 26.

8.   Karl Barth, *The Epistle to the Romans*, translated Edwyn C Hoskyns (New York: Oxford University Press, 1933), 37–52, discussed in Westphal, 3.

9.   I have drawn heavily on Westphal in this part and am much indebted to his insights.

10.   *Ibid*, 222.

11.   *Ibid*, 223.

between egoism and altruism as it is often posited, but between what is in accord with custom and that which defies it. In the case of religion and religious morality, Nietzsche's suspicion focuses on the discrepancy between the religious affirmation of altruism and the will to power that he detects at its origin. Altruism may look like self-denial on behalf of others but in reality, and at bottom, it is nothing but shrewd calculation.

While Nietzsche was a moral pluralist (in that he said that there are many different moralities,) he found two basic types which he calls master morality and slave morality. There is no need here to explain further the different structures of these two kinds of morality except to reiterate the known fact that Nietzsche admired master morality for its openness—its unashamed celebration of power, and most of all, its power of affirmative self-definition. In contrast, the weak are contemptible because they lack what makes life worth living for the strong, and being powerless, they use morality to wreak their impotent revenge. Slave morality is a reactive morality—hating the strong, it calls them evil and, as the injured party, it calls itself good. It uses a logic that is founded on victimhood and a 'stewing' resentment. Nietzsche despised it because it is self-deceptive and duplicitous and it thrives upon an imaginary revenge.

Nietzsche said that Christian piety exhibits this *'cunning of impotence'* because it makes a virtue out of weakness. Weakness and its impotent expressions are rationalised as a 'meritorious act'. Here, weakness 'is being lied into something meritorious . . . and impotence which does not requite into "goodness of heart"; anxious lowliness into "humility"; subjection to those one hates into "obedience" . . . [and] inability for revenge is called unwillingness to revenge, perhaps even forgiveness'. [12] This rationalisation of weakness, says Nietzsche, is a kind of 'prudence of the lowest order' because different modes of spiritual incapacity such as low self-esteem, cowardice, and laziness are turned into virtues following the inverted logic of slave morality. In other words, 'the goodness of the good stems from their lack of power to do what they (for that reason) designate as evil; it is their will to power that makes this lack of power into virtue and merit'. [13]

---

12.   Nietzsche, *On the Genealogy of Morals*, translated by Walter Kaufmann and RJ Hollingdale (New York: Random House, 1967), 13–14.

13.   Westphal, 247.

Similarly, and following the same inverted and slavish mentality, Nietzsche finds that it is low self-esteem that is at the bottom of many avowals of love and pity. Such inauthenticity works itself into an art form as it is generated by a restlessness that Nietzsche describes as 'roaming'. He says that the answer to such undignified 'thrashing about' is the cultivation of self-love. So he advises, 'One must learn to love oneself—thus I teach—with a wholesome and healthy love, so that one can bear to be with oneself and need not roam. Such roaming baptises itself "love of the neighbour": with this phrase the best lies and hypocrisies have been perpetrated so far'.[14]

Here Nietzsche comes close to sounding constructive and pastoral, and what he says resonates with what many people, Christian or non-Christian, believe to be the substance of psychological health. These insights are continued in Nietzsche's discussion on the nature and origin of pity. Again pity is a form of dissembling. While it parades as thoughtfulness in which 'we are thinking only of the other person', in actual fact, we are consciously thinking of ourself 'but are doing so very strongly unconsciously'. It too is a will to power and is generated by a flight from oneself because of low self-esteem. Pity is an act to give 'a taste of superiority' and for that reason, it hurts the pride of another. Nietzsche writes, 'Pity is obtrusive . . . pity offends the sense of shame. And to be unwilling to help can be nobler than the virtue which jumps in to help.'[15]

In Nietzsche's view, the desire for moral superiority also drives the other oft-admired virtues of humility and chastity. These are acts of hatred by which people monopolise virtue. It is a way of saying, 'we alone are the good and the just' and the very presence of such moral individuals exude a vengeful power dressed in legalistic moralism—'. . . they walk among us as embodied reproaches . . .'[16] The will to power through moral supremacy is exemplified in the Pharisees, whom Nietzsche describes as being 'all men of ressentiment . . . a whole tremulous realm of subterranean revenge'.[17] He sees the Pharisees as those who call themselves, and themselves alone, the good and the

---

14. Nietzsche, *Thus Spake Zarathustra*, translated by Walter Kaufmann (New York: Viking, 1966), III 11.2.

15. *Zarathustra*, IV, 7.

16. *Genealogy of Morals*, III 14.

17. *Ibid.*

just. The logic of slave morality and resentment is doubly powerful in the righteous religious because, as Westphal says, in the Pharisees is 'the confluence of moral and theological rectitude whose God is the validator of their virtues and the avenger of their enemies'.[18]

Not surprisingly, Zarathustra finds himself hated by the good and the just and he reminds us that he shares this distinction with Jesus. The reason for this is that both Jesus and Zarathustra hold transformative visions that signal something new and they ask awkward questions about the status quo and the moral life. Such questions are considered immoral by the Pharisees because, as quintessential moral conservatives, they 'already know what is good and just'.[19]

The Pharisees are thoroughly invested in the moral status quo not only because it is one that they know, and use their energies to shore up, but it is also one that affirms their virtue and their superiority. The Pharisees are moral constructivists 'imprisoned in their good conscience'.[20] Zarathustra tells us that the good and the right are the greatest danger to the future of mankind, and we can see why. They are so sure that they are on the side of right that, like fascists,[21] they will go to great lengths to preserve that 'right'. They will use all that it takes to keep out the new and the innovative as well as all moral challenge to their position and they will, in their fascist and fundamentalist certainty genuinely think that this is justified. A dangerous position indeed! It is one described as 'hardness of heart' in the Bible and it is also denounced time and time again by Christ as a serious condition of sin because it bars people from the kingdom.

Here faith concurs with Nietzsche. To 'already know what is good and just' is to be far from truth and truthfulness and far indeed from the kingdom of God. In addition, Nietzsche has drawn our attention beyond the epistemic state of the Pharisees to their bad faith and to their psychological disease. The Pharisees not only had closed minds but they also lived a big lie—the lie of resentment that lingers, festers

---

18. Westphal, 262.
19. *Zarathustra* Prologue 9.
20. *Beyond Good and Evil*, 135.
21. Westphal says that pharisaism, as Nietzsche characterises it, is a form of fascism. This point is insightful and it illuminates the dichotomous nature of inverted reasoning. As Westphal himself also points out, both Luther and Karl Barth shared this insight—viz that the dichotomous thinking of 'them' and 'us' in fascism is the essence of self-deceptive instrumentality and of idolatry.

and poisons. Even though one would not go the way of Nietzsche in then preferring open and immediate revenge to festering resentment, there is no doubt that the inauthenticity of the Pharisees is a far from attractive picture.

In what follows, I will take up these lines of concurrence, to discover what faith says about pharisaic closure and to discuss how it could respond to Nietzsche on the question of anthropology. When Nietzsche said that 'What is now decisive against Christianity is our taste, no longer our reasons', to what extent is his disgust founded on some-thing more substantial than mere taste in which we find common ground for dialogue with him?

2. Their hardness of heart—reading Nietzsche through Jesus

It is hard for Christians not to take Nietzsche seriously at certain levels. Westphal says that the strain of protest in Nietzsche's critique against Christian dishonesty is so strong that Christians should at least admire the extent to which he is committed to truthfulness. Indeed, says Westphal, Nietzsche takes truthfulness so seriously that it functions like a kind of Kantian categorical imperative so that his critique challenges Christians to consider whether they are as committed to honesty and openness.[22] In addition, there is no doubt that Nietzsche's critique stimulates in Christians a longing to be saved from the tawdriness that Nietzsche so graphically depicts and a longing for the freedom and dignity that comes from such transparency and openness.

In this section, I will explore a reading of Nietzsche through the teachings of Jesus, with a heuristic that is inspired by Nietzsche himself—viz his seriousness about truthfulness as noted above. However, such a heuristic entails a reflexivity by which the reader watches their own pharisaism so that suspicion is not only directed towards those designated as 'pharisees' but turned also upon themselves. To really take truthfulness seriously is for Christians to practice a demanding level of self-examination, recognising all the time the evasiveness of consciousness within themselves.[23] The Bible is

---

22.   See Westphal, 237, footnote 5.

23.   This is a reflexivity of an internal nature which involves self-examination, but truthfulness could also involve an external reflexivity in which one also tells the shortcomings of another. These forms of reflexivity are essential to dialogical

everywhere realistic about the machinations of the human heart, and no more so than in the gospel narratives.

Jesus' critique of the Pharisees we will find is remarkably consistent with Nietzsche's. He exposes the smugness and trium-phalism of pharisaic religion and the extent to which it is founded on the dichotomous morality of 'them' (the sinners) and 'us' (the righteous). However, we also find Jesus taking the disciples to task for similar tendencies—their spiritual complacency and the shameless instrumentality of their faith. Pharisaism, it seems, extends to all—'The heart is deceitful above all things and desperately corrupt,' wrote the prophet Jeremiah. No one is safe, it seems, and as the philosopher Michel Foucault also said, everything is dangerous.[24]

How far, then, could suspicion extend in the service of truthfulness? This question will be more directly pursued towards the end of the paper, but we will now turn to how Jesus responded to the Pharisees and to what he said about their form of piety.

In the previous section, I suggested that the mind-set of the Pharisees is a constructed moral prison which is not only distorting of the subjects but also provides a moral rationalisation (founded on a kind of fascist logic) which shores up all self-interested action in the name of righteousness. Westphal discusses with insight the danger of 'the morality of good and evil', showing how this thinking is based on the dichotomous categories of good and evil, of 'inside' and 'outside'. As we have seen, according to Nietzsche, pharisaic morality is a form of slave morality that is borne of a stewing resentment and that defines itself in relation to the object of resentment which it designates 'evil' from the entirely self-centred position of victimhood and aggrieve-ment. As Nietzsche has also shown, it is subterranean and seething and perpetuated by constant dissembling and manipulations. It is not an attractive picture. This self thrashes about, exhausted by restless efforts to maintain its constructed moral world. It is far from the quiet

---

truthfulness. I am grateful to Rev Andrew Murray for drawing my attention to the distinction between 'truth seeking' and 'truth telling'. For a discussion on this see his two 'Reflections' in *The Catholic Weekly*, 'The Life of Truthfulness', September 13, 1998 and 'Spare a Little Thought for Pilate', August 27, 2000.

24. Michel Foucault, 'On the Genealogy of Ethics: An Overview of Work in Progress', 1983, Afterword to Hubert L Dreyfus and Paul Rabinov, *Michel Foucault: Beyond Structuralism and Hermeneutics* (Chicago: University of Chicago Press, 1983), 231–32, fuller quote is found in Westphal, 287.

dignity that is borne of peace and trust.[25] Nietzsche is right to advise that we need a centring emotion like self-love to enable us to avoid such 'roaming' and such restless machinations.

Nietzsche was also right to point out that the Pharisees hated Jesus and were very much threatened by his view of the world. Westphal suggests that perhaps the most Nietzschean text in Christ's teachings is the parable of the two men in the temple,[26] which he told 'to some who trusted in themselves that they were righteous and despised others'—or in Nietzsche's words to an audience that 'already knew what is good and just'. The parable illustrates the inverted logic of a slave morality because the category of 'sinner' is used by the Pharisees to draw clear boundaries between themselves and those they categorised as morally inferior. This construction is based on a fictional dichotomy between self and other, corresponding to the clear categories of 'sinner' and 'saved', and this dichotomous way of seeing the world is used to shore up their self-esteem. So far so good.

However, as Westphal also points out, we also find Jesus going *beyond* the Nietzschean analysis in this parable. While Nietzsche sees no place for the sorrow of the tax collector, saying that the guilt that 'sinners' feel is merely the case of the weak turning their resentment inward, this surely cannot apply to the tax collector, who is not socially weak. His guilt, it seems, is genuine but it is not demeaning either because it is part and parcel of his insight into how he stands in relation to God and in relation to others. It is not a sick emotion, as Nietzsche diagnoses, but constitutive of his self-understanding and freedom. So when the tax collector called himself a sinner, he was giving the term a meaning that is beyond both pharisaic and Nietzschean vocabulary. Neither does the meaning of guilt in such cases bear out the inverted structure of slave morality. Rather it constitutes a powerful creative insight into oneself and into the human condition.

---

25. Stillness and quiet confidence are marks of spirituality. In Christian understanding, these qualities are a gift of grace, from being unconditionally loved by God. This state is described, for example, in Isaiah 32:4 which is contrasted with the state of the 'restless' and the 'rash' who do not understand the ways of God.

26. Luke 18: 9–14.

The meaning of 'sinner' in the tax collector's self-realisation thus challenges both pharisaic and Nietzschean understanding, and we find Christ doing this time and again. His invitation is always to those classed as 'sinners' and 'outcasts', including the tax collectors and the harlots. His teaching through various parables such as the parable of the father who asks his two sons to work in the vineyard reverses the dichotomous, inverted moralism of the religious people of his day. Another parable of the vineyard challenged, not only their epistemic closure but also their mastery and ownership of the kingdom, making its rules and reaping its benefits.[27] For such is 'hardness of heart' that besides being closed to the challenge of what is new and trans-formative, it also totalises by claiming full ownership of the truth.

Time and again, Jesus undermines the distinction between the righteous and the sinner which, while essential to the religious mind-set is inimical to the way of grace and forgiveness. As Westphal points out, he did this not only by what he said but also by whom he chose to associate with. For example, his affirmation of the woman who anointed him at Simon the Pharisee's house offended the strict rule of hospitality of the righteous. Herein lies the rub—pharisaism is hostile to grace and to forgiveness. The resistance lies within the very persons themselves who disallow salvation to others because their moral inferiority is the basis of their self-justification and esteem. Seeing things from the Pharisees' perspective, Westphal writes, 'How can I share salvation and thereby put myself on a par with those whose moral inferiority is the basis of the moral superiority that is my ticket, not just to the kingdom, but to a place of prominence and power within it?'[28]

If pharisaism opposes itself to grace and its generous spirit, what can we say about suspicion itself? How does it stand up to the heuristic of truthfulness that we have applied to Christians?

3. The limits of suspicion—'a base form of honesty'

The well-known parable of the prodigal son is a good place to start. This parable takes us further away from Nietzschean logic to an entirely different plane of thought. Here we find a notion of compassion that surpasses Nietzsche's categories. We all know the

---

27.   See Mark II:27–12:12 and Luke 20: 1–19.
28.   Westphal, 272.

story. The prodigal has returned and the father who had been expecting him greeted him half-way. The celebrations begin, but the focus then shifts to the righteous and pouting elder brother who is not celebrating. Rather he reminds his father of his exemplary behaviour 'all these years'. Pharisaically, he declares, 'I have never disobeyed your command'. In his response, the father neither questions nor dismisses his son's high standard of behaviour but simply says, 'It was fitting to make merry and be glad, for this your brother was dead, and is alive; he was lost, and is found' (Luke 15). This righteous behaviour is not dismissed for itself, it is simply surpassed by forgiveness and grace.

The mean-spirited nature of pharisaism that Nietzsche revealed is now found in the elder brother. The Pharisees do not only *'already know* what is good and just', they have also already assigned people to hopelessness and hell. Not so the father of the prodigal, who is open to change and to transformation in his prodigal.

In this story, compassion and mercy pose a challenge to suspicion. If suspicion is truly honest, it surely cannot continue relentlessly because to do so is to perpetuate the very dichotomies that Nietzsche identified in pharisaism. It then falls prey to the baseness that Nietzsche identified in cynicism. Relentless suspicion is also another form of self-righteousness which, like pharisaism, constructs a world of morality that is closed to possible contradiction. It too, 'already knows' that it is right to be suspicious of others and to be sure of its own judgment. It too stews in its own superiority, suggesting as much sickness as that which Nietzsche loathed in states of inferiority. Suspicion thereby becomes a totalising summation of the other that leads to circularity and closure, leaving no room for the new.

As noted earlier, the postmodern suspicion of meta-narratives and of references to a transcendent God is based partly on the fact that these are bound up with forms of mastery and with forms of self-deceptive closure. However, while the incredulity and suspicion of meta-narratives is seen as being quintessentially postmodern, there is something in it that is also deep within the roots of modern philosophical thought. Nietzsche himself was part of a trajectory of Western atheistic thought in which theism and humanism are seen as polarities. In some ways, Feuerbach anticipated Nietzsche in regarding the notion of God (a mere human construct) as hostile to human freedom and creativity.[29] Feuerbach thus equated Christianity with conventionality and self-deceptive servility.

The Christian response to this is rather more complex. While Christianity would not for a moment deny the totalising use of various meta-narratives within its own history, it continues to maintain that humanity is not diminished by a transcendent God, but rather found in him. In this context, Christian faith teaches that our knowledge of ourselves is bound up with our knowledge of God and dependent upon it. The idea, of course, is not that God is there to confirm our comfortable beliefs, but rather, that God addresses us from beyond, sometimes even 'as our adversary', to challenge and transform us beyond our inclinations and expectations.[30] Contrary to postmodern (and modern) assumptions, far from being the cause of human self-deception and closure, relationship to the transcendent God enables resistance to those tendencies.

The dangerous traps of self-deception, closure and 'hardness of heart' are well recognised within Christian faith and thought and the practices of devotion in which believers are warned to guard against them. We are reminded, for example, of Coleridge's famous aphorism on the danger of the kind of zeal that turns the love of truth into the love of the ego. In 1825 he wrote, 'He who begins by loving Christianity better than truth, will proceed by loving his own sect or church better than Christianity, and end in loving himself better than all'.[31]

Indeed, a major part of the Christian Scriptures and devotional literature is focused on resisting such tendencies towards instrumentality and egoism. Much of Christian devotional literature and practices reflect the yearning to pass beyond hardness of heart and forms of dissembling to the freedom of humility and worship.[32] As

---

29.   The phrase is John Calvin's and found in Anthony C Thiselton, *Interpreting God and the Postmodern Self: On Meaning, Manipulation and Promise* (Grand Rapids: Eerdmans, 1995), 123.

30 .   See *ibid*, 161.

31.   ST Coleridge, *Aids to Reflection in the Formation of a Manly Character* (London: Taylor & Hessey) 101.

32.   Westphal's 'Suspicion and Faith' is itself a good example, as are the writings of theologians that he cites, such as Luther and Karl Barth, as well as Stephen E Fowl and L Gregory Jones, *Reading in Communion: Scripture and Ethics in the Christian Life* (Grand Rapids: Eerdmans, 1991), also referenced in Westphal, 284;

Thiselton notes, Christians look to the love and grace of God which signals the end of manipulation because God loves unconditionally and does not 'compete'.[33] Yet Nietzsche has ignored this significant aspect of Christian faith and confession, choosing to stay at certain levels of inauthentic piety in order to dismiss the possibility of a healthy and genuine piety.

4. 'Beyond suspicion'—where to from here?

When St Paul wrote that '. . . knowledge puffs up but love builds up . . . ' he was expressing the truth that what we know carries a responsibility of care, and must only be used to advance the good of another. Accordingly, while suspicion serves a prophetic role, it must only be practiced in the service of truth and love. Perhaps Nietzsche recognised this when he said that cynicism is a base form of honesty. It is base because as a form of uncaring attack it victimises and disempowers. Ethically, there is something perverse in exposing fault and disease without giving hope because it could become the kind of totalising gaze that is rightly discredited in postmodern thought.

Nietzsche had great insight into human nature and, as we have noted, his passionate attack on Christianity, for all the caricature, was also driven by a ruthless honesty which Christians can admire. But why did he see nothing but sickness and nothing but bad faith? The answer lies, at least partly, in Nietzsche's ideal of anthropology which drove his hatred of Christianity for what he saw was its utterly perverse anthropology. As Karl Barth notes, Nietzsche became the most passionate champion of a humanity not only without God but 'without the fellow man' and Christian anthropology threatened his own ideal of the superman, the man of 'azure isolation', '6000 feet above time and man'.[34]

Reinhold Niebuhr is an obvious example of Christian insight into the capacity of the human self to deceive itself and to manipulate values and actions in the name of supposed 'morality' and 'truth'. See his *Moral Man and Immoral Society*, (London: SCM, 1963); for devotional literature, see eg Clifford Williams, *Singleness of Heart: Restoring the Divided Soul* (Grand Rapids: Eerdmans, 1994) and Andrew Murray's 'Reflections' above are good examples.

33.   Thiselton, 163.

34.   Karl Barth, *Church Dogmatics*, edited by GW Bromiley and TF Torrance, Volume III, Part Two, 240.

As stated above, Nietzsche's critique of Christianity which was driven by obvious personal hostility moved to a stage when he openly professed that by then what he had against it was no longer a matter of reason but of taste. In Nietzsche's eyes, it was patently obvious that Christianity constituted the greatest misfortune of the human race thus far. He despised it because, based on his understanding of power, Christianity was the religion 'of those who go under, of the colourless, the mistaken, the worthless, the under-world, the ghetto, the variegated mass of abjects and rejects, those who creep and crawl on the earth revolting against all that is lofty'.[35] By the time he wrote *The Antichrist*, his attack on Christianity had amounted to a crusade of Dionysius against the Crucified.

Stephen Williams points out that in this crusade, Nietzsche was all too conscious of his ancestry in which he saw his thought as marshalling and fulfilling historically deep and psychologically fundamental strains of resistance to the Christian tradition. In this vein, *The AntiChrist* defines Christianity as 'the will to vengeance, the will to hatred, the expression of decadence'.[36] As Williams says, it is clear that Nietzsche's powerful emotional resistance to Christianity derives, not from his rejection of a false theology, but of a scandalous anthropology (ie what Christianity says about the helplessness of human beings) and of a God that spoils life for Nietzsche. Williams writes, 'As creation and redemption define humanity in Christian perspective, so they define the new humanity in Nietzschean thought. The opposition to Christianity centres on its anthropology'.[37] Consequently, Nietzsche was preoccupied more with values more than concepts in his critique. He wrote, 'I call Christianity the one great curse, the one great intrinsic depravity, the one great instinct for revenge for which no expedient is sufficiently poisonous, secret, subterranean, petty . . .'[38]

Barth said that as the most consistent champion of 'prophet of humanity without the fellow-man' Nietzsche identified the fundamental difference between his ideal (which as we noted has a long ancestry) and the ideal of humanity that is found in Christianity.

---

35.   Nietzsche, *The Antichrist*, in *The Portable Nietzsche*, translated by Walter Kaufmann (New York: Viking, 1954), 124, 229 etc.

36.   Williams, 101.

37.   Williams, 89.

38.   *The Antichrist*, 62.

Barth then contends that it is the view that Nietzsche utterly despised—of 'the Crucified and His Host'—that Christian faith has to keep 'as unconditionally as he rejected it'.[39]

Are we now up against the limits of dialogue with Nietzsche and with his legacy in postmodern suspicion? To pursue this question properly would require another paper, so in conclusion, I will offer some brief suggestions for a way forward. These are based on my contention that while the atheism from suspicion, such as that offered by Nietzsche and the other 'masters of suspicion', Marx and Freud, is vociferous against faith, it also brings about some important shifts in philosophy of religion that could create new spaces for engagement. As I see it, there are at least three reasons for this.

Firstly, the atheism from suspicion broadens the discussion to include anthropology instead of remaining at the level of epistemological discussion alone. In response to Nietzsche's critique, the discussion will now need to address questions about human beings themselves, whether in fact theism diminishes them, whether atheism is necessary to freedom, etc. In addition, Nietzsche's critique has raised important questions about what constitutes psychological health and wholeness and the part that faith plays in these matters.

Secondly, such discussion could introduce a new 'rhetorical space'[40] in the engagement in which there is greater mutuality of engagement. As discussed earlier, the practise of suspicion is based on certain observations about human nature, motivation and behaviour. It proceeds on the conviction that the 'heart springs of thought and action' that represent a 'powerful counterweight' to duty and reason need to be brought to light. However, that ' . . . dear self which is always turning up . . . ' is present in all of us. Because philosophical suspicion is based on a fundamental mistrust about human nature and about how rationality itself is influenced and shaped by the will and the affections in subtle ways to advance our deep motives, *anyone* can invite suspicion. In other words, those who practice suspicion have opened up a point of commonality with those whom they fault. Accordingly, suspicion introduces a mutuality into the engagement between the interlocutors. A shared human nature implies some kind

---

39.   Barth, *Church Dogmatics*, 242.

40.   The phrase comes from Lorraine Code, *Rhetorical Spaces. Essays on Gendered Locations* (New York & London: Routledge, 1995).

of 'anthropological continuity'[41] between philosophers and believers which is generally unacknowledged in traditional philosophy of religion. In other words, while the sceptical philosopher may not share the beliefs of theists, and may even be hostile to these, authenticity and honesty requires him/her to own up to a certain degree of 'fellow feeling'. Wittgenstein, for example, recognised this important fact for philosophy of religion.[42]

Thirdly, the issue of the truth value of Christian claims shifts and broadens as a result of Nietzsche's critique to include the lives of those believers who profess them. The demonstration of that truth value is not provided by apologetics of an evidential nature because suspicion about the truthfulness of religious profession directs our attention elsewhere. The 'scalpel' of suspicion now requires Christian believers themselves to be truthful and plausible in that more demandingly incarnational way that St Paul meant when he challenged the church at Corinth with these words, 'You show that you are the letter of Christ . . . written not with ink but with the Spirit of the living God.'[43]

In short, the atheism from suspicion reminds Christian believers that the commendation of their faith must, in the end, resonate with the whole of the human self and not simply with rationality alone. So while evidential atheism concentrated attention on propositional truth, suspicion now directs Christian responses to viewing *persons* as bearers of the truth that is being claimed. It therefore elicits a more demandingly holistic response, presenting a new challenge to the relation between faith and reason in the new millennium.

Two contemporary Christian apologists who engage with contemporary suspicion in their writings and ministry remind us that apologetics cannot be purely academic, nor can it simply be a matter of arguments and words. Since Christianity is an incarnational faith, Middleton and Walsh conclude that in the end, the scalpel of suspicion and the charge that Christians practise an instrumental faith can only

---

41. The idea is found in Fergus Kerr, *Theology after Wittgenstein* (Oxford: Blackwell, 1989), 156–162.

42. On the implications of Wittgenstein's *Remarks on the Golden Bough* for how philosophy of religion should proceed, see Kerr above, 163; see also my '"Human Like Us": Some Philosophical Implications of "Naturalising" Fundamentalism', *Australian Religion Studies Review* 12 (1) (1999): 5–17.

43. 2 Corinthians 3:3.

be answered by the 'concrete, nontotalising life of actual Christians, the body of Christ who as living epistles take up and continue the ministry of Jesus to a broken world. That is the only . . . apologetic worth bothering about . . .' 154.

In the same vein and directing us again to the importance of truthfulness in the inward part, Cardinal Suhard has elegantly argued, 'To be a witness does not consist in engaging in propaganda, nor even in stirring people up, but in being a living mystery. It means to live in such a way that one's life would not make sense if God did not exist'.

Moral Inquiry in a Catholic University

Raimond Gaita

Is the idea of a Catholic university a contradiction in terms? The question might seem to betray an inclination to hyperbole. Nonetheless, I ask it seriously. Much of the Catholic intelligentsia would see its point. Much of it would not, I think, confidently answer that it is not.

The reasons for taking the question seriously are relatively easy to state. Take me as an example of a non-Catholic professor of philosophy in a newly established, state-funded Catholic university, appointed because his views were judged sympathetic to the 'Catholic ethos' of the university. In a number of publications I have argued that all human beings are inalienably precious. Although I acknowledge that this idea received its deepest expression in the religious traditions which spoke of the sacredness of every human being, I believe that it can stand independently of explicit religious commitment, independently of speculation about supernatural entities and independently of any metaphysical speculation that would attempt rationally to ground it. I have also been publicly and severely critical of Peter Singer or, more accurately, of what I have called 'the Singer phenomenon'. My enemy's enemy . . .

The 'Singer phenomenon' is the (to me astonishing) fact that Singer enjoys pretty much the untroubled esteem of most of the intelligentsia even though he believes that one could kill a perfectly healthy three-week-old baby for frivolous reasons, yet not wrong the baby. One might, for example, have been offered the job one had always desired. A newly born child would stand in the way of accepting it. Rather than pass up the opportunity, one could kill it—kill it, that is, *without wronging it*. In Singer's book, *Practical Ethics*, that belief is stated without embarrassment. He is right to believe that the extent to which people are now seriously prepared to consider his reasons for it marks a shift in the moral boundaries which define our culture.

.

Singer does not believe that because one would not wrong the baby it is morally permissible actually to kill it. Other reasons which do not focus on the baby would almost certainly sustain a prohibition against doing so. One could, perhaps should, give it up for adoption, thereby giving pleasure to a childless couple. Or one might set a bad precedent if one killed it just because it stood in the way of one's career prospects. Some people take comfort in those qualification. Others find they compound the horror.

Whichever way one goes on this, it would be hard to deny that it is startling to claim that one would not wrong the baby. It is therefore interesting that it appears not to have troubled an intelligentsia which, as I remarked earlier, generally accords Singer intellectually critical, but morally untroubled, esteem. Admittedly, Singer is not esteemed so generally because he professes that opinion. Many people believe that what he says about animals, about other forms of infanticide, about very sick or disabled children and about euthanasia more generally, should be taken morally seriously by any person who is both compassionate and reflective. The esteem Singer enjoys suggests that his admirers regard his belief that one would not wrong a perfectly healthy baby, under four weeks old, if one killed it for frivolous reasons, to be at worst an acceptable blemish on an otherwise fine and compassionate package of proposals. People who say that they find the morally repugnant character of that belief more troubling than any of the logical mistakes Singer makes on the way to it are treated with urbane condescension and sometimes even with intellectual contempt.

Until his departure to Princeton, Singer and I were neighbours. On one occasion after I had criticised 'the Singer phenomenon' severely in one of the quality newspapers, we went for a long walk along the beach, discussing our differences. Neither of us seriously hoped that we could overcome those differences, but we tried to state them clearly so that each could better understand the other. Suppose, however, that Singer had convinced me that he is right and that my hostility to his views is really based, as he believes but did not then say, on muddle and obscurantism. Suppose too, that because I had often criticised him publicly, not just for his logic but for the morally horrible nature of some of his views, I felt obliged to admit my conversion publicly when interviewed by journalists, as I sometimes am. Finally, suppose that I then began to profess Singer's views in my teaching.

Obvious though it is, I will state my point gently. Amongst the hierarchy of the Australian Catholic University and the associated religious hierarchies connected with it my conversion and its expression publicly and in my teaching would cause at least headache and heartburn. Would I therefore be conscience bound to resign? If I were, what would distinguish a Catholic university from those Catholic educational institutions whose specific purpose is to instruct their students in Catholic doctrine—a seminary, for example?

When Singer's appointment at Princeton was announced, some people protested against it in very strong language, partly because they knew that they would not have been born, or if they had been born, they would have been killed, if their parents practised what Singer preaches. Many of his supporters were outraged by the vehemence of their protests. It struck me then and still does, that those who were outraged often betrayed a failure of moral imagination and sympathy. Often they appeared unable to understand that morally serious and intelligent people could be morally repelled by the claim that one could kill a three-week-old baby for frivolous reasons and yet not wrong it. Finding that claim repugnant, they would seek words and deeds to express their repugnance.

The outrage also had its comical aspect. Singer relishes—indeed he glories in—the prospect of overturning 2000 years of belief in the sanctity of life, yet he (and his supporters even more) tut-tut most prissily when people blow raspberries, throw tomatoes or, God forbid, block the entrance to his lectures with their wheelchairs. We must have a revolution, Singer and his supporters appear to believe (a revolution that has *undoubtedly* already claimed many lives), but it must be conducted like an academic seminar. Such a mixture of incomprehension and foolishness inclines me to think that Singer and many of his supporters do not really understand what they are doing. Nonetheless, at the time when his appointment was announced I wrote, and I continue to believe, that it would be a dark day for universities everywhere if Princeton overturned its decision to employ Singer in response to such protests. What was then at stake, I believe, was not freedom of speech conceived as a political ideal—as a right of citizens —but academic freedom. To defend my claim that it would have been a dark day for universities, I would not have appealed to the rights of citizenship in a democratic nation, but to the concept of a university and the rights and obligations that go with it.

The concept of the *liberal* university, someone might say. Why identify that with the concept of the university? Should Catholic universities not be importantly different in what they count as academic freedom?

Perhaps they should, but not in ways that will ease the difficulty, I think. To explain why, I want first to distinguish between academic freedom as that might be expressed in the rights accorded to someone who speaks in a university at a lunch-time meeting, for example (academic freedom as it should be enjoyed most generally by the community of scholars that make up a university), and academic freedom more as expressed more specifically in an academic's right to profess certain opinions in his or her discipline. The longstanding traditions of Catholic moral philosophy, do not, in my judgment, constitute a discipline. They are traditions within the discipline as that is constituted by its historically distinguished figures and by those who are distinguished amongst its contemporary practitioners—those who enjoy the esteem of their peers, and who determine, to a considerable degree, the state of the play in the discipline. Singer now belongs to the latter group and there are many other distinguished philosophers who are sympathetic to his views. Indeed, it is now hard to study and work in moral philosophy without discussing Singer-type positions, and it is virtually impossible to teach it without doing so.

I take it for granted that it would be unthinkable, even in a Catholic university, to penalise students—whether they are first-year under-graduate or PhD students—for believing what Singer does and expressing their beliefs in an examination.

What should we say about their teachers? Again I would stress that I am not asking what academic freedom, conceived generally, could mean if a teacher in a Catholic university was not permitted to profess Singers views. I am asking: what does the autonomy of a discipline—autonomy applauded in *Ex Corde Ecclesiae* and In *Fides et Ratio* — come to if university teachers cannot actually profess, rather than merely present, Singer's ideas? What does respect for the autonomy of a discipline come to if those who have mastered it and teach it are not permitted to profess opinions which partly constitute the present state of their discipline?

Universities of all kinds must, if they are to deserve their name, protect the integrity of their disciplines. That entails that they must protect the right of those who teach them to profess views that are constitutive of those disciplines, or which are, in part, constitutive of **the** state of play in them at any particular time. They must tolerate Nietzschean criticism of Aquinas, for example, and Singerian criticism of the belief that every human life is sacred. That 'must' is conceptual. It is the same 'must' that someone appeals to when she says that an institution must encourage reflection and scholarship if it is rightly to be called a university. If I am right, then the differences between Catholic universities and liberal, secular ones will not ease the pressure to suspect that a Catholic university is a contradiction in terms.

Before I try to see if anything can ease that pressure, I want to distance my position from **some** others with which it might be confused. To do that, I want to reflect on the fact that it is sometimes right to believe that a discipline is in decline, even cultural disaster, and that its practice corrupts the youth. 'Does Oxford moral philosophy corrupt the youth?', asked Elizabeth Anscombe, a distinguished Catholic philosopher, in a paper whose title was formed by that question. Amongst the reasons why she thought the answer to be yes, is the fact that contemporary moral philosophy encourages students to take seriously the belief that one may do evil that good may come of it. In a later paper, 'Modern Moral Philosophy', she said, outraging I would guess ninety-nine per cent of philosophers, that anyone who thought, in advance, that it is permissible judicially to punish an innocent person for the sake of a greater good, shows a corrupt mind. By 'in advance' she meant in advance of actually being in such a situation. Actually in it, she said, one would be merely a 'normally tempted human being'. Seriously to propose the thought in philosophy classes is to show a corrupt mind. Anscombe's colleagues drew the obvious conclusion. She believed that most of them have corrupt minds.

Anscombe's position is not as illiberal as most of her critics have assumed it to be. I do not know if she thought so, but I believe it would have been consistent with her position for her to support someone's appointment to a distinguished chair in moral philosophy in one of the great universities of the world even though she believed that person had a corrupt mind. Strange though it might seem, there is no inconsistency in acknowledging that someone deserves a distinguished chair in moral philosophy and other philosophical honours (a knighthood perhaps) while thinking they are shallow and foolish and that they corrupt morally the students they teach.

Have I now betrayed that I do not understand how serious it is to corrupt young people? I believe that I do understand. As a university teacher, however, I have a responsibility to my students and to my discipline, to protect the ideals of university life as they shape and are shaped by a conception, like they one I have sketched, of the integrity of a discipline. That conception requires that someone who teaches a discipline in a university be permitted to profess ideas which are a central part of their discipline as that is determined by its distinguished practitioners.

The belief that it is outrageous to suggest that the honest practice of a discipline might corrupt the youth is connected with a myth —edifying and powerful—that supports it. It is the myth that a serious thinker—a *true* thinker—will fear to think nothing. She will follow reason wherever it takes her, no matter how frightened or morally disgusted she may be at the prospect of embracing the conclusions it delivers to her. If necessary—this myth insists—she will accept that the whole of morality is a sham. It is not hard to see how the myth functions in defence of Singer and against those who are morally appalled by some of his conclusions. It is often said that Singer and others who think like him about when we would wrong children if we killed them have followed their arguments with courage and integrity wherever those arguments took them.

Perhaps they did, but they did not reach their conclusions gritting their teeth as reason relentlessly compelled them to go somewhere they desperately did not want to go. Nobody is in that way compelled by arguments about anything remotely interesting in ethics. All the arguments in ethics have so many unclarities and depend on so many controversial premises, that only someone unusually lacking in imagination and intelligence could fail to find loopholes through which to escape with a perfectly clear intellectual conscience. More importantly, all arguments in ethics (and elsewhere) depend for their persuasiveness on the fact that their conclusions are not taken as reducing to absurdity the steps that led to them. An argument, for example, that led to the conclusion that it is permissible forcibly to take Aboriginal children from their parents with the intention that, together with other things, it should lead to the extinguishment of the Aboriginal peoples, would not now be considered seriously. If Singer's arguments for infanticide are now accepted as deserving of serious consideration, it is not just because of their logical force. It is because changes in the culture have disposed us to accept a conclusion that only thirty years ago discredited any arguments that led to it, no matter how logically powerful the arguments might have appeared.

That is one aspect of what I have called the edifying myth about the nature of reason. There is a second, more interesting, aspect of it that I will explore by commenting on the claim that a really serious thinker should be prepared to think herself into nihilism—into thinking that the whole of morality is a sham—if reason appears to compel her to do so.

Were my commitment to philosophy to temp me to such nihilism, I would give up philosophy, fearful of what I was becoming. Most —perhaps all—of my colleagues would do the same, I am quite confident. If they did not, I would seek better company. I have come across no one who is seriously prepared to profess such nihilistic scepticism in her own name. None of the great philosophers has done so. The myth survives because it is put impersonally or because is attributed to someone else—someone 'who is neither timid nor stupid', as one philosopher put it, or to the characters in Plato's dialogues. Given how pervasive the myth about reason is and for how long the prospect of nihilistic scepticism has haunted philosophy, the fact that I have never encountered or read a serous first-person profession of such scepticism is a fact that alternately astonishes and amuses me.

Socrates always asked his interlocutors to put aside for the duration of their discussion what they had heard, what *could* be said by someone or what could theoretically be argued for, and to answer, seriously, for themselves. When people are asked whether they believe that morality might be a sham, that our sense of the terrible wrongs people have suffered might answer to no genuine concept, then if they are also asked to answer seriously in the first person then invariably they say they do not and cannot believe it.

Only at such a point of seriousness, I think, can there be fruitful exploration of why one cannot, merely as the conclusion of an argument, seriously profess nihilistic scepticism. At that moment of sobriety, one discovers that one would fear to be a person who seriously professed such a conclusion, and that the fear of it is different in kind from the fear of thinking painful thoughts, for example. One also discovers that one's incapacity even to wish to be the kind of person who would follow reason to a nihilistic conclusion is different from an incapacity to question beliefs that are so deeply inculcated that one finds it psychologically impossible even to contemplate their sceptical examination. The latter are psychological obstacles, external to the content of the understanding they stand in the way of. But the fear of becoming the kind of person who no longer cares for morality, who thinks it all nonsense, is a fear internal to moral understanding itself. It is part of what constitutes our sense of the distinctive seriousness of morality, of the distinctive way it matters to us. That, I think, is what Kierkegaard had in mind when he said that just as the logician most fears a fallacy, so the ethical thinker most fears to fall away from the ethical.[1]

Because the fear to fall away from the ethical is internal to one's identity as an ethical thinker—to an understanding of the ethical and the kind of seriousness it has—it is not a psychological fear. It is, to be sure, a form of shutting one's mind, but it is not closed-mindedness of the kind that everyone agrees is intellectually culpable. For that reason, it is a misunderstanding of the nature of critical thinking to believe that a true, radical thinker, a true philosopher, will be faithful to the claims of reason even when she believes that it is taking her to nihilism.

Thinking oneself into nihilism is one kind of case. Thinking oneself into the belief that the Jews are vermin who pollute the earth and should therefore be exterminated is another. The former is constantly represented as a possibility that should haunt the philosophical conscience and inform our conception of radical thinking. The latter was professed by German theologians and philosophers and acted upon during the time of the Third Reich—a fact whose full signif-icance the church has yet properly to understand. Would anyone deny that those theologians and philosophers had corrupt minds? Is it plausible that the fact that they had corrupt minds is irrelevant to the *philosophical* assessment of their positions? Should a young German philosopher who shut his mind to the idea that Jews are vermin who deserve extermination have feared that he was forsaking his philo-sophical vocation for the sake of morality? Should he have thought

---

1.   This will scandalise some philosophers, I know. I have discussed the matter in some detail in *Good and Evil: An Absolute Conception* (London: Macmillan; New York: St Martin's Press, 1991) and more recently in *A Common Humanity: Thinking about Love and Truth and Justice* (Melbourne: Text Publishing, 1999; London and New York: Routledge, 2000).

that his identity as a philosopher and his identity as a human being are separable?

In a natural use of the expression, it is *unthinkable* to an ethical thinker that she should fall away from the ethical, unthinkable that she should think her way into the belief that the Jews or anyone else should be exterminated. Less extremely, the fact that only thirty years ago, the conclusion that one could commit infanticide was a *reductio* of any argument that led to it, shows that thirty years ago that conclusion was unthinkable. Ironically, philosophers who profess to think about everything have not thought much about the forms of the unthinkable. In part this is because they assume that appeal to them is either dogma or merely an extravagant way of saying that something is obvious or so well established that to question it is to question what has become common knowledge. Natural though that assumption is, I believe it is mistaken. Certainly it needs more examination that it has received. Questioning *that* assumption should be part of philosophy's critical self-examination. Understanding the ways we rule things out of consideration matters to an understanding of what it is to think well and badly. It therefore matters to an understanding of the difference between genuinely radical critique and the ersatz radicalism, the superficial enchantment with transgression, that is exposed the moment one calls upon its advocates seriously to profess their scepticism in the first person.

It is evident, I hope, how often defences of the liberal university draw on the unexamined rhetoric about the nature of critical inquiry that I have been trying to expose. Partly because I do not wish what I am saying to be identified with it, I have tried to show that it is both superficial and a kind of pretence. That done, I will return to my examination of whether there is a case for saying that the notion of a Catholic university is a contradiction in terms.

In the mid 1970s, the philosophy department in the University of Leeds was dominated by a group of Catholic philosophers. A student come out of a lecture on Thomas Aquinas complaining that it was impossible to escape the Catholics in the department. Martin Milligan, the translator into English of Karl Marx's 1844 manuscripts and then still a member of the British communist Party, gave the lecture. He shared, with no significant reservations, Marx's belief that religion is the opium of the masses. When I lecture on Peter Singer, I remember

Martin Milligan and hope that I might deserve a similar compliment to the one that disgruntled student unintentionally paid him.

When I try to characterise Singer's beliefs justly, when I develop arguments in his defence which I think are sometimes better than his, when I refuse to allow students to think they have the better of him when they have not, I do not do it only to knock him down later. Nor do I do it because I think that my students will not be adequately prepared to resist him if they underestimate the simple power and attraction of his arguments. I do it because I owe it to him as a colleague and because I will fail my discipline, dishonour my vocation as an academic and betray my students if I do not.

If I have students who do not see (perhaps because they are resistant to seeing) the strength of Singer's argument, I press the argument as forcefully as I can. I do not do so because I believe they must be open to its conclusion. That would be to require something of them that I do not require of myself. If a student says that she is afraid to believe that one wouldn't wrong a three-week-old baby if one killed it just because one didn't want it, I would explain to her that she should not feel that she has to chose between philosophy and morality. I would explain to her that she should not think that her fear of becoming persuaded by what she is convinced are morally horrible beliefs shows that she cares more for morality than she does for truth. And I would, of course, present the arguments against Singer. But if his arguments and those against him are presented justly, there is no guarantee that the arguments against him will be found intellectually or even morally convincing. In this domain there are no knock-down arguments. If it is one's obligation to teach moral philosophy of a kind that one fears may corrupt one's students, then one has no alternative but to risk corrupting them. Or, more precisely, one has no alternative in a university. In other institutions of higher education—a seminary, for example—it may be different.

The difficulties do not end there, however. We must now attend to the critical concepts that are appropriately brought to bear in university teaching and examining. The distinction between wisdom and cleverness, or between wisdom and expertise, for example, often depends on the application of a range of concepts which are hardly ever discussed in the main stream of analytical philosophy. Sentimentality, a disposition to pathos or to banality, are examples. Again, given the pride philosophy takes in thinking about thinking, this is as surprising as it is regrettable. But the fact that the (cognitive) failings that are marked by those concepts are ignored (for the most part) in the assessment of essays and examinations and in making appointments, is not a matter for regret, paradoxical though it may seem. The following example might show why.

I once had to mark a PhD whose title suggested it was a thesis in moral philosophy. It turned out to be on 'the problem of evil'. Because I am not a philosopher of religion, I looked over it in order to assess whether I was competent to examine it. The candidate argued, basically, that what one loses on the swings one gains on the round-abouts. Pain, he said, is an evil, but it often alerts us to illness. As I read the thesis I began to think its main arguments so banal that it must fail. Then the candidate started quoting eminent professors in the field, many of whom argued as he did, with only a little more sophis-tication. That did not incline me to review my judgment that the points that were argued to be morally significant were in fact banal, but it taught me that banality is no obstacle to achieving deserved distinction in the discipline. That being so, how could I fail, or in any other way penalise, that student for his banality? Yet the concepts I refused to use in the assessment of his thesis are, as I said earlier, critical to a distinc-tion between wisdom and cleverness, between wisdom and expertise and between what is shallow and what goes deep. Towards the end of this essay I will return to this point and attempt to reveal its importance.

Where are we then in our examination of whether the idea of a Catholic university is a contradiction in terms? Clearly there are fine Catholic academics in fine Catholic universities (and in secular universities as well, of course). I find no difficulty in accepting the requirement that academics employed in a Catholic university should have views at least consistent with, if not actually in sympathy with, its Catholic ethos at the time when they are employed. Considerable intellectual advantages accrue to a community of relatively like-minded thinkers, able creatively to explore possibilities in ways difficult to do when one is constantly looking over one's shoulder, meeting objections which often come from traditions alien to one's way of thinking. Members of a Catholic University must, of course, engage vigorously (mostly at times of their own choosing) with other traditions in other universities. Engagements of that kind are fund-amental to the idea of a university. For reasons of that kind one can say that a Catholic university is one kind of university while the secular liberal university, glorying in the plurality of opinions within it, is another.

Difficulties arise, however, when academics who had views sympathetic to the Catholic ethos when they were appointed change those views to ones which, though they are widely held in the discipline, are not sympathetic to the Catholic ethos and may even be hostile to it. Had they professed such views when they were interviewed when the applied for their post, they would not have been appointed to it. Should they be asked to resign? If they do not, should they be sacked? Both would, I believe, be inconsistent with the nature of a university of any kind, and with the requirement that one be just to the (professional) opinions of one's colleagues and to the unpredictable consequences of rising to that requirement. Tolerance of those who think themselves into positions which would have prevented their employment will reduce the likelihood that they will censor their own thoughts, fearful of the consequences of not doing so. Academics are no braver than most members of the community. The inglorious history of the universities suggests that they may be less so. If one makes them too fearful, one will corrupt them.

In our times it is not just the concept of a Catholic university that is problematical. The concept of a university itself has become so. Few people nowadays distinguish between a university and an intellectually high-flying institution of higher education, and of course, in Australia, as in the UK, institutions which are not at all intellectual high-flyers have been granted the title university. To develop my argument I must state dogmatically and briefly what I believe are two essential features of a university. First a university must celebrate the intrinsic value of the life of the mind. Secondly—and this distinguishes it from, say, a high-flying research institute even if the research institute teaches students—a university obliges its members to reflect on the importance of the life of the mind, hopefully to reveal that it is worthy of a lifetime's devotion by people who have more than mediocre aspirations. To answer Callicles' challenge to Socrates is one of the distinctive obligations of a university. Callicles said the study of philosophy encourages in young people a liberality of mind without which they could do nothing fine and noble. But if an older person continues with it, he went on to say, that person 'needs a whipping', for he is doomed to deserved obscurity, rather than flourishing in the public realm or in the market place where 'men win renown'. Students and their teachers often laugh at Callicles, but I think that in their hearts most of them believe that he is right. His point can be generalised to many of the disciplines of the humanities.

When I said a moment ago that a university is distinguished from some other intellectually high-flying institutions by the fact that it imposes on most of its members an obligation to reflect on the importance of the life of the mind in a human life, I meant that reflection on what it means to be a university teacher will reveal that obligation to be internal to a university teacher's vocation. Lucid enactment of that obligation constitutes the kind of communality that is invoked when one says that a university is a community of scholars.

Thinking about the nature and importance of the life of the mind is, in the broad sense of the term, an *ethical* concern. If it is done passionately, in response to a sense that it is an obligation intrinsic to an academic vocation, it will be an example of the Socratic claim that to inquire about how to live is amongst the most important things a human being can do. Not to do it, he said at his famous trial, is to live a life unworthy of a human being. The fact that such an ethical requirement is intrinsic to the nature of a university, but not necessarily to the nature of a research institute, even when it takes students, explains why universities may sometimes place greater restrictions on opinion than exist even in the political realm. Sometimes, of course, ethically motivated restriction on the expression of opinion are merely the sign of what has come to be called 'political correctness'. As it affects universities, the interesting thing about 'political correctness' is that even when it is illegitimately censorious, it is sometimes a corrupted acknowledgement of a connection between the life of learning and the moral life, a connection which is at the heart of the university.

The claim that in a university freedom of opinion should suffer less restrictions than it justifiably does in the political realm is at odds with practices endorsed by almost all academics. Who would agree to the appointment to a chair of medicine someone whose ground-breaking discoveries were made when he experimented on prisoners in the Nazi death camps? Would anyone now agree to the appointment to a chair of anthropology someone who argued that Aborigines are savages from whom children of mixed blood should be rescued for their own good? And would anyone agree to the appointment to a chair of moral philosophy someone who said that homosexuals are disgusting, that their behavior should be a criminal offence and that those who offended repeatedly should be castrated? I could give many more examples. In many cases, however, the person who is rightly denied an academic post on account of the opinions he or she professed should be allowed to profess those same opinions in the political realm. The denial of an academic post would not be an offence against academic freedom, but denial of their right to express their opinions in the political realm would seriously infringe their rights as citizens to free speech.

The examples I have given of when a person would justifiably be denied an academic appointment, not on moral or political grounds *external* to a conception of the nature of the university, but as an expression of that nature, would, I am sure, meet with broad agreement. Yet it is interesting that in response to the suggestion that Singer should not be appointed to a post at Princeton because of the moral character of his view, many academics—indeed all the ones I heard and read—argued quite generally that moral considerations should be irrelevant to academic appointments. There is therefore some tension between the rhetoric that is now second nature to many academics and the positions which, after only a little reflection, most of them will acknowledge they hold.

A number of things feed that tension. One is the conception of reason that I criticised earlier, the conception according to which there is nothing that a true thinker will fear to think. Another is the fact that we are increasingly bereft of a language which has the power to reveal the intrinsic good of academic life as something deeper than a higher pleasure, or even a higher passion. The language in which one could reveal what could seriously be meant by speaking of a love of truth threatens to die on us, and is increasingly an embarrassment to those who wish to articulate the ideals of a secular liberal university. That is partly because they think it is edifying rhetoric of no cognitive substance or premised on a conception of spirituality that requires metaphysical underpinning and which can therefore no longer have a serious role in the formulation of secular ideals. That, I suspect, is why, when people acknowledge that moral considerations sometimes quite properly play a part in the assessment of the beliefs of applicants for academic posts, they tend to see those considerations as external to the nature of the life of the mind properly conceived. But if one tries to elaborate a serious conception of the love of truth, one might find oneself, with Plato as a companion, at a point where one can see an intimate connection between goodness and truth.

Is it just rhetoric to speak of the love of truth, meaning a love of it rather than, for example, passionate intellectual curiosity. Evidently, I don't think it is. Nor, however, do I believe that we can answer that question unless we reflect on examples that can show why one might want to speak that way and what speaking that way can mean. I doubt that abstract investigations of the concepts of love and truth and others closely related to them could show why someone would speak seriously of the love of truth, rather than of a passion or enthusiasm for certain studies or inquiries. The inclination to speak that way must be awakened in us by something quite different. Often it will have been a fine teacher whose example revealed to us what a love of truth may be and what it may be to live a life in fidelity to it. This will be personal to each of us. But in our intellectual and spiritual tradition there are examples which are common to us. I shall give two. The first is Saint Augustine and the passage I shall quote is from his *Confessions*. It is from the section where he is thinking about time and has fallen into terrible metaphysical confusions:

> And I confess to Thee, O Lord, that I yet know not what time is, and again I confess unto Thee, O Lord, that I know that I speak this in time, and that having long spoken of time, that very 'long' is not long, but by the pause of time. How then know I this, seeing I know not what time is? or is it, perchance, that I know not how to express what I know? Woe is me, that I do not even know what I know not. Behold, O my God, before Thee I lie not; but as I speak, so is my heart. Thou shalt light my candle; Thou, O Lord my God, wilt enlighten my darkness.[2]

The passage and all that led up to it expresses a mind labouring in obedience to the claims of reason and of truth upon it. One could quote it with edifying effect against certain forms of irrationalism and against

---

2. St Augustine, *Confessions* translated by EB Pusey (London: Dent, 1962), 11. 25. 32.

anyone who has forgotten the role of character in the development of the intellectual virtues. But one could not reveal the power and the beauty of the passage without referring to the love that is manifest so purely in it. One might, therefore, say that the passage is a fine expression of the discursive capacities of mind in service to a love of truth. That would not be wrong, but it could be misleading. Simone Weil indicated why when she said that it is misleading to speak of a love of truth. One should speak instead, she suggested, of the spirit of truth in love. The passage I have quoted from Augustine's *Confessions* is an excellent one to quote in her support, for the spirit of truth in love is exactly what is expressed in it. That's what makes it so wonderful.

A Catholic university should be not be embarrassed to speak of a love of truth, of a vocation as something deeper than a profession, and of the virtues necessary to understanding both. Such unembarrassed speech is sorely needed, not only in Catholic universities, but also in liberal secular ones, if students are to hear the words with which to name and to appropriate the deepest treasures that universities can offer. But if that language is to live for us, it must be nourished by examples. In closing I want to say something about what I believe is involved in learning from example.

Earlier, I said that we fully appreciate the kind of value we ascribe to the pursuit of truth for its own sake, only when we see it in lives deepened by it. It is an important fact that we often learn most deeply when we are moved by what people say or do, in life and in art. Often, though, we are moved when we should not be, or in ways that we should not be, or more than we should be. Sometimes we are moved because we are sentimental, or liable to pathos, or in other ways vulnerable to the 'winged words' of rhetoric, as Adolf Eichmann called them. There are, I think, no standards that reason could firmly establish, even in principle, that could be sufficient to assure that we have been rightly or wrongly moved. There is no proof waiting to be discovered and written into text books, encyclopedias or private notebooks, that will tell us which things are really valuable and that we can consult whenever we are in doubt. There is nothing that will assure us, once and for all, 'what a man should be and what he should practice and to what extent, both when old and when young' (as Socrates put it to Callicles). Inescapably, we learn by being moved, and that would be so even in heaven. When we are moved we trust what moves us and trust that we are rightly moved. We trust wisely, however, only when trust is disciplined.

A considerable portion of my philosophical work has been devoted to exploring what disciplining trust comes to and to elaborating its implications for the distinction between legitimate and illegitimate persuasion. I have tried not so much to argue for a shift in the balance between head and heart in favour of the heart, as to make clear what we mean when we speak of an *understanding* of the heart, when, for example, we say that we have understood something in our head but not in our heart.

What marks the difference between blind and lucid trust in the examples that move us? Again, the answer is that we must turn to the critical vocabulary that tells us what it is to think well or badly: it will tell us what it is to be rightly moved and what are its many false semblances. Now, however, I must acknowledge a tension in what I have been arguing. The critical concepts whose grammar one must master in order to assess whether one is rightly or wrongly moved when, for example, one responds to what one takes to be an authoritative example of an academic vocation lived with great integrity, are the critical concepts that I said earlier should play little or no role in the assessment of a student's work or a candidates suitability for academic appointments, promotion or honours. They are the concepts that one must use when one assesses whether one is wrongly moved because one is prone to sentimentality, to pathos, to banality and so on. They are, as I suggested earlier, fundamental to the distinction between wisdom and expertise or mere cleverness and between depth and shallowness of understanding

Problematic though this may be in its implications, there is something that is, I believe, quite plain. If it is true that the language which will enable us to speak lucidly and with authenticity of a love of truth must be nourished by examples, and if it is true that we learn from examples only if we trust, critically and lucidly, what moves us, then any university that wants to be taken seriously when it talks of a love of truth must strive to ensure that trust is not undermined by a corrosive cynicism.

For many contemporary universities that will not be easy. In common with other institutions which succumbed to great external pressures, universities have been tempted to describe their submission to those pressures as relatively costless to their integrity. However, the universities are now marked by a pervasive mendacity in their descriptions of what they have done to save subjects and jobs and sometimes to protect their very existence. We academics tend to deny the extent of the untruthfulness, but everybody knows that it is now widespread in university life and that knowledge generates a debilitating cynicism about the higher ideals of the university. Cynicism erodes the trust necessary to learn from example. Mendacity corrupts the conceptual space in which examples may speak to us, and show us value where we had not seen it before and values we had not before understood, or even dreamed of. It is a far greater threat to serious notions of truth and truthfulness and so to a serious conception of the love of truth, than philosophical scepticism about truth of a kind often associated with postmodernism. When truthfulness seems to have little value, it is not surprising that philosophies should flourish which debunk even the desire for truth and objectivity, declaring the celebration of both to be attempts to disguise the exercise of power.

The Diversity of Philosophy and the Unity of Its Vocation

John Haldane

I

In the ordinary run of things Roman documents offer little in the way of philosophical interest. The present pontificate, by contrast, has been distinguished by the number of occasions on which John Paul II has invoked philosophical considerations in the course of addressing the church. Three encyclicals spring to mind: *Veritatis Splendor, Evangelium Vitae* and *Fides et Ratio.*

In the first two, moral philosophy is in view and certain contemporary normative theories are criticised.[1] Although the Pope makes efforts to limit himself to general considerations and to avoid affirming any specific philosophical position, it is unsurprising to find his own colours showing, and thus the potential for controversy is not altogether avoided. Consider, for example, the following passage from *Veritatis Splendor:*

> one has to consider carefully the correct relationship between freedom and human nature, and in particular *the place of the human body in questions of natural law.* A freedom which claims to be absolute ends up treating the human body as a raw datum, devoid of any meaning and moral values until freedom has shaped it in accordance with its design. Consequently, human nature and the body appear as presuppositions or preambles, materially necessary for freedom to make

---

1. For contrasting philosophical commentaries see A MacIntyre, 'How Can We Learn What *Veritatis Splendor* Has to Teach?', *The Thomist,* Volume 58, No 2, 1994; and J Haldane, 'From Law to Virtue and Back Again: On *Veritatis Splendor*' in *The Bible in Ethics,* edited by JW Rogerson *et al* (Sheffield: Sheffield University Press, 1995).

> its choice, yet extrinsic to the person, the subject and
> the human act . . . *A doctrine which dissociates the moral
> act from the bodily dimensions of its exercise is contrary to
> the teaching of Scripture and Tradition.*[2]

The concluding reference to the teaching of Scripture might suggest that the requirement to consider the body is a religious or theological one, and in that sense something extra-philosophical. Mention of the 'tradition' is more ambiguous: on the one hand it might be taken to mean the church's moral teaching as that derives from Catholic moral theology; or it may be interpreted as referring to the philosophical tradition of natural law ethics. But this disambiguation involves a contentious if not false disjunction. For until quite recently Catholic moral theology (understood as theory and not as casuistry) has largely consisted in a synthesis of natural law and scriptural interpretation.

Quite apart from the attitude of dissenters opposed to particular first order claims such as those concerning sexuality, the avowal of a particular form of rational justification of morality is somewhat controversial. It will not be enough, so far as *Veritatis Splendor* is concerned, to affirm some or other form of moral objectivism; one is expected (or is it required?) to subscribe to natural law. Moreover, while the insistence upon the relationship between right action and 'human nature' may seem a formal point satisfiable in indefinitely many ways, what is said *about the human body* suggests that some styles of reasoning that describe themselves as 'natural law ethics' will not do. Consider, for example, someone who argues that certain types of action are prohibited because they violate norms concerning the attainment of goods whose value is determinable by the practical rationality that we possess in virtue of our rational nature. Such a person will not yet have met the requirement set out in the quoted passage. For the 'natural' in natural law refers not only to the *source* of practical rationality but also to its subject matter. In the Pope's account of things ethics is essentially *about* the lives of rational animals, and our embodiment is not a further feature to which pure practical reason might then attend. If I have him aright, for John Paul philosophical anthropology is not something to which moral rationality might turn for empirical premises; rather, it is the source and precondition of morality.

---

2.   *Veritatis Splendor* (London: Catholic Truth Society, 1997), 75–77.

Indeed, the quoted passage expresses a yet more determinate philosophical conception: that of Thomistic anti-Cartesian personalism; Christian-Aristotelianism filtered through Husserl. For my own part, I find this *committed-voice* rather more congenial than the *committee-speak* of other church documents. Even so, I suggest that a question arises as to the appropriateness of such a level of philosophical specificity in a document addressed to the universal church, given that Catholic moral philosophers and moral theologians who are evidently cognitivists or objectivists nevertheless differ quite widely on the nature of moral reasoning and thus on the grounding of moral prescriptions and requirements.

I raise this matter at the outset because the third of the encyclicals, *viz Fides et Ratio,* is largely and not incidentally concerned with the nature and role of philosophy, and while the Pope repeatedly assures readers that he is not seeking to accord priority to any single philosophical system, writing that 'The Church has no philosophy of her own nor does she canonise any one particular philosophy in preference to others' (49), the suspicion arises that in truth he believes that only one approach (or family of approaches) will do.[3]

Since the text is directed to a range of constituencies beyond the formal addressees (the bishops), it is difficult to be altogether sure about this, however; and in face of that uncertainty one might not think it profitable or respectful to pursue the issue. Yet for those committed to the philosophical tradition which has the best claim to be *the* philosophy of Catholicism, *viz* Thomistic Aristotelianism, and for those interested in the development of Catholic philosophy and in the potential for engagement with philosophers outside the church, these matters are critical. They concern nothing less than the limits of acceptable philosophical pluralism and thus bear heavily upon the prospects for such enterprises as *ARCIC (Analytical Roman Catholic Inter-Philosophical Conversation).*[4] For it could be that like the other

---

3. Given *that* it treats of philosophy in general while *Veritatis Splendor* treats of moral philosophy (and theology) in particular, one might have expected that *Fides et Ratio* would have appeared first. It is of interest, therefore, that according to one source the latter was embarked upon first in the mid-1980s.

4. See J Haldane, 'Theism' in JJC Smart and JJ Haldane, *Atheism and Theism* (Oxford: Blackwell, 1996/7); 'Analytical Thomism', *The Monist* Volume 80, 1997; and 'Thomism and the Future of Catholic Philosophy', *New Blackfriars,* Volume 80, 1999.

ARCIC (Anglican Roman Catholic International Commission) this exchange may run into difficulty over the authority of the 'Bishop of Rome', that description now being used *de re,* and in connection with John Paul's metaphilosophical doctrine about the nature of true philosophy, or his theology of speculative and practical reason.[5]

II

The focus of my discussion is on issues raised in paragraphs 80 to 91 of ch VII 'Current Requirements and Tasks'. In the course of this—the penultimate chapter of *Fides et Ratio*—the Pope identifies three obligations for contemporary philosophy:

(i) to recover the sapiential dimension of the discipline (81);

(ii) to establish and maintain epistemological realism (2); and

(iii) to achieve genuinely metaphysical range (83).

It is tempting to partition these tasks into two; grouping the second and third as aspects of a single speculative enterprise, *the establishment of realism,* and taking up the first as an exercise for practical philosophy. But that would run counter to the view of their relationship expressed in the text, and I believe counter to the proper need for an integrated conception of philosophy as dialectic and the practice of the love of wisdom.

So far as the wider philosophical world is concerned, my own feeling is that the recovery of the sapiential dimension is the place to concentrate one's efforts and I shall make a first attempt on this task later. However, it is also necessary to say something about ii) and iii), since as the Pope observes:

> this sapiential function could not be performed by a philosophy which was not itself a true and authentic knowledge, addressed to [reality's] total and definitive truth, to the very being of the object which is known (82).

---

5.   For reservations about whether the Pope's conception of the autonomy of philosophy fully recognises its self-governance, as operating by reason according to its own methods and principles, see Anthony Kenny, 'The Pope as Philosopher', *The Tablet,* 26 June 1999 and Jean Porter, 'Letting Down the Drawbridge', *The Tablet,* 3 July1999.

So as to provide the required context for this discussion, let me give a brief overview of the chapter. Earlier in the encyclical we are introduced to the universality of the philosophical impulse, and to the power of its influence in shaping culture. This establishes one point of interest for the church, but a second lies in the ancient role of philosophy as handmaiden and messenger on behalf of faith. Precisely because he values the several traditional functions of philosophy, John Paul goes on to express concern at tendencies among philosophers and theologians to limit severely the function of philosophy as discerner of objective truth. These 'false trends', as one might term them (echoing the phraseology of Pius XII in *Human Generis)*, are discussed in chs IV, V and VI. This then sets the scene for the identification of current requirements and tasks listed above.

Thus philosophy is to establish our capacity to *know the truth (adequatio rei et intellectus)* and to achieve 'genuine metaphysical range capable of transcending empirical data in order to attain something absolute, ultimate and foundational in its search for truth' (82). These requirements exclude certain philosophical options: (i) *radical phenomenalism;* (ii) *relativism;* (iii) *eclecticism;* (iv) *historicism;* (v) *scientism;* (vi) *pragmatism;* and the more general vice to which he thinks these bad practices lead, *viz nihilism.*

No doubt it would not have been appropriate for the Pope to give detailed descriptions of these erroneous perspectives, in part for reasons of space, but also so as to avoid needless controversy in what is a work of doctrinal instruction and not a philosophical monograph. Nevertheless, this list of errors deserves much more discussion than it receives. Both clarification and more precise characterisation are needed. For one thing, the syllabus includes stances that seem to be of logically different kinds, some epistemological (eg phenomenalism), some metaphysical (eg scientism) and others perhaps stylistic (such as eclecticism). More to the point, however, if Catholic philosophers are to engage with the wider world they will need to start making distinctions within these categories and that I think will quickly return us to the issue of tolerable pluralism.

III

Certainly not every way of going on is as good as any other, but there are differences within the broad range of those who would agree with the necessity of the second and third tasks. Let me illustrate by observing one way in which philosophers with motives akin to the Pope's own have shied away from one kind of metaphysical realism precisely because it seems to lead to *scientism*.

Before doing that, however, I think it is appropriate to offer a couple of remarks about the 'syllabus of errors' cited above. The first on the list is 'eclecticism':

> By which is meant the approach of those who, in research, teaching and argumentation, even in theology, tend to use individual ideas drawn from different philosophies without concern for their internal coherence, their place within a system, or their historical context (86).

So described this hardly qualifies as 'a current of thought' (86 and 91) or as 'a position' (para 90), at least as those expressions are generally used and understood. Rather it represents a form of intellectual incompetence or irresponsibility and certainly not something that one could imagine anyone seriously proposing as an alternative philosophical approach. No doubt such intellectual vice should be warned against, but it seems out of place in a catalogue of contrasting philosophical approaches. There is, however, a different notion of 'eclecticism' appropriately applied to certain 'currents' or 'positions'. This connotes syntheses or blends of ideas or methods drawn from different historical approaches. Whether particular cases of this are reasonable is dependent upon actual specifics, but it would ill behove a Thomist to issue a blanket condemnation since Thomism itself and Karol Wojtyla's Lublin variant is highly so.

A second example of the need for 'fine-tuning' is provided by the inclusion of 'pragmatism' in the list of currents of thought. This might be apt were it not for the peculiar definition given of it:

> An attitude of mind which in making choices, precludes theoretical considerations or judgements based on ethical principles (89).

Certainly there is a use of the term 'pragmatist' (lower case 'p') in which it contrasts with action based on principle; but once again this does not represent a philosophical position so much as the avoidance of one. On the other hand, the current of thought known to philosophers by the title 'Pragmatism' (upper case P), and which is the subject of an entry in every philosophical dictionary or encyclopedia, is far from precluding theoretical considerations or ethical judgments. Whatever one's view of the thought of Pierce, James and Dewey, it is undoubtedly philosophical and one of its distinctive features is the philosophical emphasis given to values and norms.

What these examples suggest is that those who wish to commend *Fides et Ratio* to a philosophically educated readership will need to provide clarifying, qualifying terminological glosses. More substantial, however, is the task of determining the range of philosophical positions compatible with the encyclicals committed to epistemological and metaphysical realism. I cannot attempt this here but I would like to touch on the issue of philosophical realism since this is an unquestionable commitment of John Paul II and one of the main issues in contemporary secular philosophy.

First, then, realism is not an 'all or nothing' position. For example, one and the same philosopher might favour a realist position on causality but not on mathematics. That is to say, he or she might hold, in opposition to Hume, that causal relations obtain in nature prior to and independently of human thought, but also maintain that truth in mathematics is not a matter of correspondence with some mind-independent reality, but rather of provability in a constructive system, which is to say that mathematical facts are not discovered but created by thought. This raises the question of how realism either total or partial should be understood. A very common answer equates realism with facticity or truth, but a more metaphysical account would be in terms of mind-independent existence.

This is not the occasion to explore the details and difficulties of these options, but it needs to be pointed out that an exclusive and strict mind-independence criterion is liable to result in a position uncongenial to the orientation of the encyclical. The reason is that much of what we ordinarily take to be objective is not wholly mind-independent. Colours, tastes and other secondary qualities are partly constituted by subjective sensibility and many common descriptions of the 'world' express schemes of classification that reflect our interests rather than mind-independent natures. The Vatican is extensively and exquisitely decorated in marbles of various types, but marble is not itself a natural kind. Much but not all that is classified as 'marble' is limestone in a crystalline or granular state; and limestone is an aggregate of calcium carbonate and other chemical compounds. Thus, what, *from the point of nature,* are importantly different substances are grouped together by us because of their appearances as ones which themselves depend upon the form of our sensibility. Some metaphysical realists take this to be reason to say that 'marble' does not really exist. Pressed repeatedly this natural substance metaphysics becomes reductive scientific realism, which is only one step away from scientism. The Pope is right to reject the latter, but doing so coherently is liable to require relaxing the requirement on realism, or at least allowing that not everything that is objective is real (in the metaphysician's strict sense).

To repeat, my point is not to argue to a particular realist doctrine but only to suggest that when relaying the message of *Fides et Ratio* greater understanding must to be shown in identifying philosophical positions for praise or criticism. Quite generally, much more work needs to be done on the issue of the range of tolerable 'realisms' and none of us can afford to be triumphant about the 'tradition' or dismissive of other's ways of going on. Indeed, the common necessity of philosophy to make progress on these issues provides an opportunity for dialogue between Catholic philosophers and others.[6]

IV

Let me turn now to task (I) and to John Paul's call to academic philosophy to return to the ancient concern with the pursuit of wisdom. He writes:

> To be consonant with the word of God, philosophy needs first of all to recover its sapiential dimension as a search for the ultimate and overarching meaning of life (81).

I think this is perhaps the most valuable positive contribution of the encyclical and one that can and should be carried beyond the world of Catholic thought. With this in mind I would like to explore the relationship between philosophy conceived of as the practice of wisdom and the idea of philosophical spirituality as a demeanour

---

6.   In this connection see H Putnam, 'Aristotle after Wittgenstein' in *Words and Life* (Cambridge, MA: Harvard University Press, 1994) and J Haldane 'On Coming Home to (Metaphysical) Realism' *Philosophy*, Volume 71, 1996.

adopted in the face of reality as one's speculative metaphysics takes it to be.

There seems little difficulty in understanding the idea of spirituality and of the spiritual life within the context of religious thought. In Christianity especially these are given definite content by reference to the indwelling of the Holy Spirit and to practices of prayer, meditation and devotion by which the soul progressively partakes in the life of God not substantially but relationally as an adopted child might increasingly partake in the life of a family.[7]

When we turn to (non-religious) philosophy, however, a question arises whether any form of spirituality can find a home there. Yet even the most cursory reflection upon human experience and on the efforts of great writers and others to give expression to it, suggests that there is a domain of thought, feeling and action that is concerned with discerning the ultimate truth about the human condition and with cultivating an appropriate mode of being or demeanour in response to that truth. The phenomenology is compelling, the concerns are intelligible, and for some reason intelligent people persist in supposing that it must be a central part of philosophy to deal with these matters and therefore look to it to do so.

Philosophers themselves, at least academics in the dominant Anglo-American tradition, either ignore such appeals as one might the entreaties of a door-to-door evangelist; suggest they are confused in ways similar to those in which some metaphysicians suggest that people are mixed up when they ask about first or ultimate causes; or else, if they are inclined to grant something to the claim that questions of non-religious meaning and spirit do arise and call for attention, they point to moral theory or possibly to aesthetics as being the relevant departments to visit.

While this last option has the merit of recognising that there is something to be catered for, it makes a mistake in consigning it to moral philosophy as this is now understood, for that is concerned essentially with rightness of conduct, and first and foremost with conduct bearing upon other moral subjects. Notwithstanding its welcome breadth, contemporary virtue ethics remains a version of

---

7. I use the analogy of participation in the life of a family rather than that of a parent given that in Christian mystical theology partaking in the life of God involves entering into the mutual divine life of three persons.

moral theory and as such is concerned principally with action. Likewise, aesthetics is concerned principally with disinterested contemplation of objects of experience. Spirituality involves intellect, will and emotion and is essentially contemplative, but the process of discovering the nature of reality, evaluating its implications for the human condition and cultivating an appropriate demeanour in the face of these is not reducible to ethics, nor to aesthetics. Yet unless philosophers can show this enterprise to be confused or exclusively religious they are open to the charge of neglecting something of fundamental, indeed perhaps of ultimate, human importance.

V

The French classical scholar and historian of philosophy Pierre Hadot has made a series of very interesting studies of the aims and methods of the six ancient schools of philosophy, *viz Stoicism, Epicureanism, Platonism, Aristotelianism, Cynicism* and *Pyrrhorism,* arguing that each reflects and in turn seeks to develop a permanent possibility of the human spirit. These studies have been collected and translated into English under the title *Philosophy as a Way of Life* and I strongly recommend them.[8] I shall not even attempt to summarise his many conclusions but I do want to extract one or two points so as to advance my own discussion.

First, then, Hadot discerns in the various ancient traditions, but especially in the Stoics, a distinction between '*philosophy*' *(philo-sophia* conceived of as the formation of the soul, or the deep structure of character, with the addition of an orientation towards the good), and *discourse about philosophy* (understood as the investigation of the nature of things, and to a lesser extent our knowledge of them). This, of course, is related to the more familiar distinction between practical and speculative philosophy. But whereas modern, recent and contemporary thought has invested greatest effort and talent in the pursuit of speculation in the form of epistemology and metaphysics, the ancients, and again I am focusing on the Stoics, give priority to thinking about practice, and within that to the cultivation of wisdom and the development of the spiritual life. Epictetus observes that 'the lecture

---

8.   See P Hadot, *Philosophy as a Way of Life: Spiritual Exercises from Socrates to Foucault,* edited by AI Davidson (Oxford: Blackwell, 1995).

room of the philosopher is a hospital'[9] which is to say that his work is the cure of souls. Later he writes:

> How shall I free myself? have you not heard it taught that you ought to eliminate desire entirely? . . . give up everything . . . for if you once deviate from your course, you are a slave, you are a subject.[10]

Hadot's reading of such texts is both informed and imaginative. It also encourages him to make three claims of great interest. First, he construes much more of the writing of antiquity as belonging to philosophy in the sense of the practice of wisdom than has been common among historians of ancient philosophy. More precisely and more strikingly, he argues that these texts concern and in some cases *are* spiritual exercises. Second, and in direct opposition to the assumption which I mentioned that the notion of spirituality is in origin a religious one, he claims that in fact Christianity appropriated this area of reflective practice from pre-existing philosophical traditions and even that it took over 'as its own certain techniques of spiritual exercises as they had already been practised in antiquity'.[11] Third, he implies that the historical interest of all of this is perhaps its least significant aspect. In an essay responding to Foucault's use of his earlier work, Hadot writes:

> I think modern man can practice the spiritual exercises of antiquity, at the same time separating them from the philosophical [metaphysical] or mythic discourse which came along with them. The same spiritual exercises can, in fact, be justified by extremely diverse philosophical discourses. These latter are nothing but clumsy attempts, coming after the fact, to describe and justify inner experiences whose existential security is not, in the last analysis, susceptible of any attempts at theorization or systematisation . . . It is therefore not

---

9.   *The Discourses of Epictetus*, edited by C Gill (London: Everyman, 1995), 3, 23, 30.

10.   *Epictetus, op cit*, 4, 4, 33.

11.   Hadot, *op cit*, 206.

necessary to believe in the Stoic's nature or universal
reason. Rather as one lives concretely according to
reason. In the words of Marcus Aurelius, 'Although
everything happens at random, don't you, too, act at
random?' In this way, we can accede concretely to the
universality of the cosmic perspective, and the
wonderful mystery of the presence of the universe.[12]

This passage is full of promise, but a few comments are called for.
First, the exercises he refers to, what Foucault called *'pratiques de soi'*
(practices of the self)[13] are designed to liberate one from
(inappropriate) attachment to exterior objects and the pleasures
deriving from them. By regular self-examination one keeps a check on
the tendency to exteriority, and by contemplating the impermanence of
things one seeks to master or to possess oneself, attaining happiness in
interior formation. Writing up this examination, or better, perhaps,
examining through writing, is one form of spiritual exercise.

Where Hadot takes issue with Foucault is in claiming with the
ancient authors (including Plotinus) that the movement toward
interiorisation is inseparably linked to another movement, whereby
one rises to a higher psychic level, at which one encounters another
kind of exteriorisation, 'another relationship with the "exterior" or
what one might term the "real"'.[14] Without necessarily wishing to
reject it, one may reasonably call for further specification of this
transcendent movement. A major direction of development is likely to
lead to the inexpressibility of the mystical encounter with the 'One',
but other possibilities suggest themselves including moderate versions
of Platonist ontology and even naturalistic Aristotelianism.[15] Rather
than pursue this, however, let me voice a reservation about the claim
that spiritual formation may proceed independently of the truth of the
accompanying philosophical discourse (metaphysics).

---

12.   'Reflections on the Idea of the "Cultivation of the Self"', in Hadot *op cit*, 212.

13.   See M Foucault, *History of Sexuality,* translated by R Hurley (New York, 1984)
      Volume 3.

14.   Hadot, *op cit*, 211.

15.   In this connection, see John Haldane, 'De Consolatione Philosophiae', in
      Philosophy, Religion and the Spiritual Life, edited by M McGhee (Cambridge:
      Cambridge University Press. 1992) for discussion of Boethius and of the idea of a
      'contemplative gaze'.

Presumably even Hadot thinks there are some limits to just how wrong one can be at the speculative level while keeping on track in the practice of wisdom. Also there is reason to tie the two together as constituent components of a single enterprise, such that the content of spiritual formation is dependent upon its metaphysical compliment. The argument for this is quite straightforward. One reason for believing that the issue of spirituality arises within philosophy is reflection on a parallel relationship between religious belief and practice. Suppose someone was persuaded by philosophical or historical arguments that the God of Christian theism exists, but that he or she then seemed wholly unmoved by this acceptance. One would be inclined to say, I think, that religiously speaking the thing (conversion) has not yet begun. For *that* belief requires the formation of a demeanour appropriate to its content. Likewise I wish to say that a reductive materialist who really believes that his philosophy gives the ultimate truth about reality should be moved (by reason) to ask how in the face of this immensely significant belief he or she should compose themselves. It seems unintelligible to suppose that *nothing* follows for the enquirer from arriving at a fundamental view of reality, be it physicalist or theist. Not only does the question arise of how to compose one's spirit in the face of this, but the content of the metaphysical belief must condition the character of the resulting demeanour.

VI

The believer in Christian theism will be moved towards familiar Christian religious practices, and the reductive physicalist whose metaphysics is after all not so very different from that of the Old Stoics may wish to explore their spirituality. I think, therefore, that Hadot is wrong to try to loosen the link between philosophy and philosophical discourse; spirituality and metaphysics go together, as I believe the writers of antiquity would agree.

The example of the Stoics and of other figures in antiquity gives some reason for thinking that a kind of philosophical spirituality can be fashioned on a non-theological world view. Suppose, however, that this is an illusion. That raises the following question. If it should seem after all that the necessary condition for the possibility of spirituality is some religious truth, and if the need and possibility of spirituality should seem compelling, then might we have the beginnings of (a new version of) an (old) argument for religion?

Academic philosophy has travelled far from the concern of its founding fathers to provide a guide to life. Along the way it has lost sight of the very idea of spiritual values, and in its current phase it may have difficulty recovering or refashioning this idea. This very fact deserves to be examined and that examination might itself mark the beginning of a form of philosophical-cum-spiritual exercise: nothing less than an assessment of the value of what most academic philosophers currently practise in the name of their discipline.

Put another way and in the prophetic voice of John Paul II:

> philosophy needs first of all to recover its sapiential dimension as a search for the ultimate and overarching meaning of life. This first requirement is in fact most helpful in stimulating philosophy to conform to its proper nature. In doing so it will be not only the decisive and critical factor which determines the foundations and limits of the different fields of scientific learning, but will also take its place as the ultimate framework of the unity of human knowledge and action, leading them to converge towards a final goal and meaning (*F&R*, para 81).

Response to Haldane and Gaita

Hayden Ramsay

When *Fides et Ratio* appeared some philosophers and theologians rushed into print and comment in a matter of days, many in order to criticise it. Similarly, when John Paul's other two philosophical encyclicals—*Veritatis Splendor* and *Evangelium Vitae*—appeared, leading moral philosophers and bioethicists combed through them at lightning speed in search of errors. One principle we need to recall in reading this and other magisterial texts is stated by the Pope himself at *Fides et Ratio* 33: 'it must not be forgotten that reason needs to be sustained in all its searching by trusting dialogue and sincere friendships.' I reread chunks of *Fides et Ratio* early this morning before sharing my porridge with John Haldane, Professor of Moral Philosophy, in my home town of St Andrews. The encyclical clearly demands many and careful readings. A piece about philosophy or a piece of philosophy? Whichever, it is masterly, timely, something to celebrate together as well as to discuss critically.

Haldane notes the necessary connection between realist-objectivist philosophy and real human wisdom in the Pope's vision. If this is right, then one answer to Haldane's question 'why propose one particular philosophical theory in an encyclical which claims the church *has* no official philosophy' might be this: the 'sapiential dimension' itself places certain requirements on the philosophy we should construct and follow and it is in these that 'implicit philosophy' consists. Sapiential philosophy must produce systems which speak to people, and if a philosophical system is to say anything to people at all, there are certain principles it must acknowledge. For example, if your philosophy does not accept the *principle of non-contradiction*, you cannot state or accept propositions, therefore you cannot satisfy enquirers and answer their yearning to grasp life's meaning. If you do not accept that persons are *free and intelligent*, you have no reason to debate with them or to try to inform them, and you cannot understand anything they say or do as significant. If you do not accept principles of *teleology and causality*, your philosophical system cannot assume regularity in the world or in human affairs and so cannot offer analysis or give counsel.

If you do not accept some *fundamental moral norms*, you have little, if any, requirement to take others' enquiries and fates seriously, engage respectfully with them or pursue answers to their questions with diligent regard for the truth. The Pope clearly favours a fairly specific Thomist-personalist presentation of these truths. Whet-her he is right or wrong on that, the case for any good philosophy endorsing these realist-objectivist truths is strong.

Perhaps this is to say no more than Alasdair MacIntyre and many others do: that engagement between Thomists and philosophers outside the church is, so far, best accounted for and facilitated by the principles and dynamism of the Thomistic system itself. Just as St Thomas is the best model for the integration of philosophy and theology, St Thomas is the best model for the integration of philo-sophies. And indeed who would deny St Thomas is the best model of the sort of integration of philosophy and theology that is the encyclical's overall theme? If our concern is to put philosophy at the service of the faith while maintaining its own autonomy, what better model? If our aim is the realist-objectivist philosophy that is most useful for theology, what better model? If our aim is to affirm the natural order and yet give priority to the demands of the supernatural, again, what better model? Thus there is more to the Pope's endorsement of Thomism than the endorsement of some formal principles which are common to humanity (compare with McInerny) ——there is too a vision of the relation of philosophy to theology, of faith to reason, nature to grace.

I certainly agree that the Pope should not have offered in *Fides et Ratio* the major critique of the 'isms' he is well positioned to do and has often offered elsewhere. The Pope's point here is simply to expose the weak and/or naïve versions of these philosophies found in many theologians and other religious thinkers. Thus he has his sights not on the philosophically sophisticated views of contemporary philosophers, but on the thin and fairly incoherent collection of ideas increasingly passed off as 'philosophy' in religious thinking. And, speaking more generally, in the Pope's understanding of 'philosophy' as not a mere theory but the whole basis on which we approach our lives and form our choices, the philosophies of our age do not correspond to classic and well-argued philosophical positions. In both informal and formal thinking 'philosophy' today **is**, more often than not, simply (stylistic) eclecticism, (political) pragmatism, (spiritual) nihilism etc.

Again, I quite agree that since the whole philosophical community is involved in serious and highly technical debates over realism it would be a serious error for Catholic thinkers merely to repeat the word mantra-like, as if when Catholic tradition proclaims 'realism' it has a privileged answer to or exception from these debates. The bottom line of the Pope's commitment to realism seems to be philosophical-theological, with more of an emphasis on the divine than most modern philosophers are used to. He describes a realist philosophy as capable 'of transcending empirical data in order to attain something absolute, ultimate and foundational . . . in particular it is a requirement for knowing the moral good, which has its ultimate foundation in the Supreme Good, God himself'. (83) We need to recall, I think, that the point of the three guiding principles of philosophy in chapter 7 of the encyclical is to produce a philosophy consonant with the word of God and addressed to the needs of theology and contemporary theologians.

Here, what makes a philosophy realist seems to be its justification of our capacity to grasp first principles or foundations, as well as abstract concepts such as beauty, truth, values and God. Philosophers might indeed have been more comfortable had this approach been labelled 'foundationalism' and perhaps treated under the heading of epistemology (the Pope's second principle), with some suggestions about the sort of realist debates of modern philosophy offered elsewhere. Certainly, as all would agree, the philosophical biblio-graphies of Roman documents and their engagement with professional and international philosophical debates is often sadly limited—though in fairness, this is the first professional philosopher-Pope and things may yet change for the better.

To the by-now famous par. 81 on the sapiential dimension, I think Haldane's discussion of philosophical spirituality has made a major contribution. It is not simply that if we reach a certain philosophical conclusion ('democracy is untenable', 'IVF is wrong' . . .), integrity requires changes in our lives and conduct; it is rather that the very activity of practising philosophy—the adoption of a stance towards and within the intellectual life—involves making certain sort of choices about who we are and how we are to go on, including how we are to teach.[1] In any case, this point about philosophical spirituality means

---

1. This is clearer to grasp with some philosophies than others—to proclaim oneself a
    Thomist is to claim a place in an intellectual tradition and a commitment to a

that the ideal of impartial enquiry which some romantics about universities have—that lecturers are meant to list and critique all options, leaving the student with at most a brief biographical statement of where the professor happens to stand—is under serious threat. If philosophical spirituality is part of the philosophical life, that life surely demands commitment to and so passionate defence of some philosophy, and not just general explication of philosophical arguments. Here, perhaps, I am more with Haldane than Gaita.

I have a particular interest in the relation of philosophy to spirituality since I teach many seminarians and religious. As many will know, a disease of seminaries is the tendency to invoke separate categories of bite-sized morsels to help the students through: 'Did we do grace in philosophy or theology? Or was it in spirituality, or pastoral practice, or prayer in chapel?' An alternative view would be that philosophy, spirituality, prayer, pastoral care are all practised or invoked whenever one of them is practised adequately. Whatever are the reasons for an inappropriate segregation of activities which actually require each other, we are well settled into it. Is there any hope now of making philosophy spiritual or spirit-rich once again—yet alone of making theology philosophical, or pastoral practice theological?

The answer Pope John Paul would presumably give lies in his distinction between the philosophical debates of all folks and the philosophical systems of the professional philosophers. Where the latter abandon the sapiential dimension, we can be sure the former do not. The natural inclination to ponder and to wonder, especially in times of stress and distress, is never an exercise in jargon or sterility for ordinary folk. Here, at least, we encounter philosophy as attempting intelligently to change oneself; and perhaps it is by better attending to the philosophical debates of local and global communities, as James Heft recommends, that philosophical systems can recover something of the sapiential dimension. Which is really just to repeat the Pope's point: professional philosophical systems should serve and learn from humanly meaningful philosophical enquiries.

On Raimond Gaita's paper, I do think academic freedom means that universities must sometimes allow teachers converted to nauseating views to continue to teach these views—though pres-

certain sort of argument; to proclaim oneself a Stoic is to describe one's daily life. Why is that?

umably a Catholic faculty is entitled always to contain a core of those interested in contributing to Catholic-style philosophy. The university, however, has some other responsibilities here than protecting academic freedom. Gaita agrees. He believes that intrinsic to universities and academic life are ethical requirements which mean there are certain opinions which may not be professed—for example, anti-Jew, anti-Aborigine, anti-homosexual views. Thus these days we can put a homicidist but not a racist or a sexist in the chair of philosophy. This distinction between moral considerations intrinsic and extrinsic to academic life needs to be spelt out.

One way of doing so from Gaita's paper is this: (1) the professor of philosophy at a Catholic university should make the strongest philosophical defence he can of Peter Singer's homicidal views, but may not make philosophical defence of certain other (alleged) injustices; (2) this is so because the principles Singer appeals to are views which 'partly constitute the present state of the discipline' whereas, for example, anti-gay views do not.

My difficulty here is that Singer's sort of preference-utilitarianism / personism surely does not, even partly, constitute the discipline of philosophy, at least as it is recognised and practised by the vast majority of distinguished philosophers throughout the world. Who in the discipline, apart from Singer and some other bioethicists, are the distinguished philosophers who accept a form of preference-utilitarianism that claims, among other controversial claims, that infanticide of healthy babies does the baby no wrong? It is only outside philosophy (in politics, bioethics, public policy, moral theology . . .) that significant numbers tend in this direction. Thus why show Singer's view special favour? Why not rather class him with the other elitists who are now part of the generally discredited history of philosophy and teach him in that regard? Or perhaps address his views in healthcare studies, bioethics and politics, in all of which he is a major player? Why not characterise Singer's views of infants in terms of discrimination and rejection, as Gaita rightly describes anti-Aborigine and other such views? Or has Singer's response to major criticisms from natural law, virtue ethics, Kantian revivalists, Western and other deontologists really been sufficient to establish his place at the heart of philosophy?

My own dilemma as a teacher in offering Singer is that I might, unwittingly, help to keep alive a theory most philosophers of the first rank now reject. I choose to teach and do full justice to David Hume because of the brilliance of his arguments, though I dislike some of his own conclusions and the uses to which his modern sympathisers have put his texts. But I would not teach a view simply because it is popular, and certainly would not equate popularity with academic respectability.

Gaita's reason for believing we might give a great chair to a corrupt mind is this: 'I have a responsibility to my students and to those who came before and will come after them, to protect the ideals of university life as they shape and are shaped by a conception . . . of the integrity of a discipline'. I agree with this, but the ideal of university life may not be the only ideal to which academics—including Catholic academics—owe service; also, there are other parts of the academic ideal than protecting the rights of colleagues to hold and have disseminated appalling but popular views. For example, what of a colleague whose views are directed against the ideals of intellectual life and university, as Gaita has set them up, altogether? Or an academic at a Catholic university teaching, writing and speaking against the Catholic Church or its philosophy—*not* as a Camus might (see Heft), but as some of today's liberal-minded philosophers do?

And what of the (not unimaginable) case in which the whole discipline of philosophy becomes or is becoming corrupt? Do we continue—as philosophers—to promote and cooperate in the presentation of views those outside the (alleged) corruption would judge untrue to philosophy? Already these days we can find philosophy departments not with one liberal, one radical, one Christian natural lawyer, one Buddhist specialist, one feminist, but whole departments of contemporary liberals, or of postmoderns. If all moral philosophers were converted to contemporary liberalism, with my own view becoming an outpost mocked by all other leading practitioners, would I then teach only liberal moral philosophy, the only kind recognised by my peers, and sacrifice my deep philosophical convictions? Would this be the best way to live out my responsibility to my students? I think not.

Perhaps the difference between us rests upon Gaita's very high ideal of 'the university'. I would certainly be interested to hear more about this, and the relation of this view to such other views of universities as the mediæval universities, universities of the Scottish and other enlightenments, those Australian universities prohibited from teaching theology, late twenteith century, bureaucratised universities etc. Was even the classical academy an institution with an identity so strong it allowed teachers to do their very best (even better perhaps than these views' original defenders) to teach views they feared would corrupt the young?

I do agree entirely that universities should at least for a time get their minds off talk about 'professionalism' and 'professional ethical standards'. Indeed, for a Catholic university to throw in its hand with this and other manager-speak, as happens in most other universities, would be a double disaster. As Onora O'Neill's recent BBC Reith Lectures well demonstrated, this sort of 'standards' talk ('accountability', 'transparency', 'professionalism' . . .) only appears when trust has already broken down and an institution's ethos contaminated. And this sort of talk is quite ineffective in repairing the damage.[2]

Fides et Ratio has a highly quotable opening: 'faith and reason are like two wings on which the human spirit rises to the contemplation of truth'. They are *like* two identical wings; but they are not quite identical. For one thing, reason, unlike faith, is our nature, and reason, unlike faith, is corrupted and never completely succeeds in its endeavours. Belief that our nature is corrupted but can be, at least to an extent, healed by our philosophical endeavours makes Haldane's thoughts on philosophical spirituality and Gaita's thoughts on teaching philosophy quite urgent. In particular, how do Christians reconcile choice of a purely philosophical stance for living and for teaching (a 'philosophical spirituality') with our most profound belief that there is a higher spirituality that comes from recognising our dependence and so coming to live out, humbly, a religious faith?

One response was sketched, tentatively, by Haldane. If there is a compelling need for spirituality and this requires religion, there is a new case for religion. Thus religious spirituality trumps philosophical spirituality. I am not so sure. One might argue by analogy that there is a compelling need for art and this requires beauty, therefore there is a new case for beauty. But we can have art—however imperfect —without beauty, or with little beauty; and we can have spirituality —however imperfect—without religion, or with little religion. If that is so, then what is the case for a specifically religious spirituality—for perfection through religion—and what is its true relation to the philosophical spiritualities Haldane has so wonderfully described?

---

2. Onora O'Neill, *A Question of Trust* (Cambridge: Cambridge University Press, 2002).

Contemporary Christian Analytic Philosophy of Religion[1]

Michael Levine

1. Introduction

This paper examines three issues (biblical interpretation; evil; and religious experience) in contemporary Christian analytic philosophy of religion that are indicative of its lack of vitality, relevance and 'seriousness'—in a sense I shall explain. Contemporary philosophy of religion now is, and for the past thirty years has been, dominated by the religious agendas of Christian conservatives. Far from 'now becoming recognised once again as a mainstream philosophical discipline'—as a catalogue blurb (Philosophy 2000) announcing a new Ashgate Series in the philosophy of religion falsely proclaims—not only has mainstream philosophy long ignored such philosophy of religion, but so has the study of religion generally (for example biblical scholarship, theology and religious studies). That the religious find it largely irrelevant goes without saying—though there are various reasons for this. Instead of 'faith seeking understanding', one is reminded of W Somerset Maugham, whose characterisation of philosophy pertains to most types, but particularly to the apologetics of contemporary Christian analytic philosophy of religion—including theodicy. 'Philosophy is an affair of character rather than of logic: the philosopher believes not according to evidence, but according to his own temperament; and his thinking merely serves to make reasonable what his instinct regards as true.'[2]

---

1. This article was published as 'Contemporary Christian Analytic Philosophy of Religion: Biblical Fundamentalism; Terrible Solutions to a Horrible Problem; and Hearing God', *International Journal for the Philosophy of Religion* 48 (2000): 1–31. It is reprinted here with permission of the editors.

2. W Somerset Maugham, 'The Philosopher', in *On A Chinese Screen* (London: Jonathan Cape, 1922), 164.

2. Biblical interpretation, creationism and wax noses

John Haldane claims to accept the value of New Testament criticism and says he has no wish to insulate Scripture from it. I argue that he misrepresents such criticism and its findings in a way that moves towards religious fundamentalism.[3] On the one hand Haldane claims that in terms of a debate about atheism and theism what biblical scholarship shows about the evidential value of the New Testament is not a great deal. On the other hand he thinks such scholarship supports the evidential value of the New Testament and hence the claims of Christianity. There are very few critical historians who read any text, much less the gospels, at 'face-value' in Haldane's sense. Redaction criticism shows that the synoptic editors worked with a relatively clear set of traditional elements that they deploy in their own ways and for their own purposes.

Haldane's treatment of New Testament criticism, or what is now, after Robert Alter, sometimes termed 'excavative biblical scholarship'[4] clearly illustrates entrenched religious fundamentalism, and a lack of understanding of contemporary biblical scholarship. Although he claims to 'accept the value of New Testament criticism' and says he has 'no wish to insulate Scripture from it' (p 205), he misrepresents its findings. He construes 'the scholarly study of scripture' in such a way that 'it supports [rather than undermines] the claims of Christianity' (p 205). He supports his position partly by arguing against the view of SGF Brandon, referred to by Smart, that 'Jesus was a zealot put to death for threatening insurrection against the governing Roman authorities' (p 205). But his dispute with Brandon and others on this point is basically a historical dispute and not one about the findings or implications of excavative biblical scholarship. Even if Haldane is right about Brandon's account being less plausible than the (various) synoptic accounts, there are of course many other historical, sociological and psychological accounts and interpretations of the narrative(s) that explain things quite differently and perhaps more

---

3.   JJC Smart and JJ Haldane, *Atheism and Theism* (Oxford: Blackwell 1996). Although Haldane seeks to distance himself from fundamentalism I argue (below) that he is unsuccessful. That van Inwagen is a Christian fundamentalist, although he never explicitly acknowledges it, should be clear from the quotations and my discussion of his views below.

4.   Robert Alter, *The World of Biblical Literature* (New York: Basic Books, 1992).

plausibly than either Brandon's account or the gospel narrative. To claim, as Haldane does, that all such speculations, interpretations and historical accounts are less plausible than what he sees as the common core of the gospel narrative is question begging. There are various models of the actual social reality of Jesus and his movement, but little consensus.[5]

Excavative biblical scholarship involves, among other things, form, source and redaction criticism. It attempts to determine various things about the 'origin of the Bible: who composed these various books, when and where, for whom, with what pre-existing texts in hand, with what traditional genres as patterns, with what historical events in mind, to make which "ideological points", and so forth, on and on'.[6] On the one hand Haldane claims that in terms of 'a debate about atheism and theism' what biblical scholarship shows about the 'evidential value of the new Testament' is 'not a great deal' (p 207). On the other hand he obviously does think such scholarship, at least indirectly, supports the evidential value of the New Testament and hence the claims of Christianity—claims which *ipso facto* would support theism.

> [T]here is a theoretical question as to what to count as an early version of a Gospel . . . Nonetheless, there is a widespread consensus among theist, agnostic and atheist scholars that Paul's epistles were written in the 50s and 60s of the first century and that the gospels, in more or less the form in which we have them today, were composed between 70 (Mark) and 90 (John) AD . . . the thing to be struck by is how *close* these dates are to the life and death of Jesus . . . the authors of the gospels were not state propagandists or spokesmen for some powerful social group . . .

5. Cf John Gager, *Kingdom and Community* (New Jersey: Prentice Hall, 1975); Richard Horsely, *Bandits, Prophets, and Messiahs: Popular Movements at the Time of Jesus* (New York: Seabury Press, 1985); Burton Mack, *Who Wrote the New Testament?* (San Francisco: Harper, 1995); A Saldarini, *Matthew's Christian-Jewish Community* (Chicago: University of Chicago Press, 1994); and work by Burton Mack and John D Crossan.

6. Nicholas Wolterstorff, *Divine Discourse: Philosophical Reflections on the Claim That God Speaks* (Cambridge: Cambridge University Press, 1995), 16.

The trend of recent scholarship supports a more or less face-value reading of the gospels. What I mean by this is that there is evidently an ancient common narrative core, which reflects the beliefs of the contemporary followers of Jesus . . .

[T]here are no good scholarly reasons for doubting that this [common narrative core which reflects the beliefs of the contemporary followers of Jesus] is what was pieced together within the lifetime of people who could and may have known Jesus, and that this is why they sincerely believed. Whether one accepts it oneself is another matter, but if one does not that is no good basis on which to doubt that the gospel writers meant what they wrote. Arguments to the contrary tend to import historical speculations less plausible than the narrative, or to make philosophical assumptions about what could or could not happen and then reconstruct the text as deceitful or poetic [pp 206–208].

The dating Haldane cites is rather uncontroversial, though some would put Mark at 66 and John closer to 100. The New Testament books were in literary circulation by the mid-second century. Only Paul's letters and perhaps Mark were clearly written within forty years of Christ. But Haldane's conclusions are peculiar. There is a 40–60 year gap between Jesus' death and the formation of the extant gospels. Does this make them 'close' to the life and death of Jesus? (Paul never knew Jesus 'in the flesh' so he is not relevant in this regard.) Haldane claims that 'time and hindsight tend to improve the quality of historical writing and then as now there were plenty of people around to take issue with and correct the account of events' (p. 206). Even if Haldane is right in his overgeneralised view about the relation of time and hindsight to historical writing, the evidence from the gospels themselves hardly suggests that the time lapse helped those who wrote the gospels in their quest for historical accuracy—if indeed historical accuracy was a principal concern. Historians agree that for ancient historiography it was not.

Most New Testament scholarship agrees that there is a common set of 'sayings-sources' (Q) informing the synoptic gospels. This source contains certain sayings of Jesus, key narratives etc, and seems to stem from the oral tradition of a primitive Christian community. But the synoptics deploy these sources in different ways, cite the same sayings in different narrative contexts, and differ in all sorts of detail such that it is difficult to say that they—much less the very different gospel of John—stem from a 'common narrative core'.

Sophisticated students of oral and written tradition in antiquity know that tradition is not interested in reproducing events 'as they happened.' Rather, it is interested in transmitting events in such a way as to enable hearers to participate in their meaning in their own setting. This undermines Haldane's equation of the forms of Christian tradition found in the gospels with 'what the followers of Jesus saw and heard'. Ancient historians recognise that ancient historiography was thoroughly polemical. From a genre point of view, the gospels are not historiography—except perhaps for Luke-Acts.

The New Testament is evidence for beliefs of early Christian writers, though not in Haldane's literalist sense. The question is whether these beliefs should be authoritative for later readers. This is a theological or religious decision that is under-determined by one's views as to whether or not the gospel writers had their stories straight. Even if the common core did reflect the beliefs of the early Christians in the way claimed by Haldane, the question remains whether their interpretations of the events of Jesus's life advances or demonstrates the claim he was Messiah. This is a matter of one's religious convictions and not a historical question per se. Despite his disclaimer, Haldane conflates and confuses the question of religious conviction with the historical question. One can believe in the redemptive suffering of Jesus even if one believes that transmitters and editors mangled the literary traditions reporting it. The New Testament is a guide to framing the significance of Jesus's life and suffering for Christians, but its historical accuracy does not affect its religious authoritativeness in the way that Haldane (and fundamentalists) claim.

To make a long story short, it is controversial whether 'the trend of recent scholarship supports a more or less face-value reading of the Gospels' (p 207) in Haldane's sense that 'there is evidently an ancient common narrative core which reflects the beliefs of the contemporary followers of Jesus' (p 207). Redaction criticism claims that it is incorrect to suppose that the New Testament was more or less written down, with a few inconsequential embellishments, from oral reports of eyewitnesses, or those not far removed, telling it like they believed it happened. Redaction is itself composition. But Haldane appears to treat those who actually composed the synoptic gospels as mere scribes. He is either wrong, misleading, or far too vague in claiming that '*there are no good scholarly reasons* for doubting that this [common core] is what was pieced together within the lifetime of people who could and may have known Jesus, and that this is why they sincerely believed' (p 208). Consequently, where doubts are so based he is wrong in claiming that this is not a 'good basis on which to doubt that the gospel writers meant what they wrote.' Even if one leaves reports of miraculous occurrences to one side, excavative biblical scholarship (and literary theory) is overflowing with reasons why such a seemingly straightforward and for the most part literal interpretation of the gospels—the kind Haldane endorses—is incorrect. Part of the task of such scholarship is to determine just what it is that the various authors did mean. Haldane is not the only philosopher of religion to recently claim that their interpretations respect and take into account excavative biblical scholarship while actually ignoring or otherwise utterly misrepresenting it.[7]

Thus, Haldane is right in claiming that excavative biblical scholarship has implications for the evidential value of the New Testament, but wrong in his assessment of the evidence and so in what he takes that value to be. He is right of course in claiming that 'the suggestion that New Testament Scripture reports the Incarnation of the Son of God . . . is not something that can be ruled out on grounds of scriptural criticism' (p 209). But this does not mean that such criticism has no implications for the evidential value of such claims, including how they should be interpreted—their aim, purpose and the meaning of the texts themselves. Whether excavative biblical scholars are correct in eschewing the kinds of claims made by Wolterstorff and Haldane about the implications of their scholarship is debatable. But that such claims are eschewed is a fact they should acknowledge.

Creationism is usually linked with some kind of fundamentalist interpretation of the Bible. Although Haldane's views about creation appear not to be linked in any direct fashion, and although he explicitly distances himself from creationism, it is worth noting, in the

---

7.   Cf, Michael Levine, 'God Speak', *Religious Studies* 34 (1998): 1–16, in which I discuss Nicholas Wolterstorff's views on 'excavative biblical scholarship', in *Divine Discourse*.

context of this paper as a whole, that his views are creationist—or have much in common with types of creationism.

In *Theism and Atheism* Haldane claims that scientifically oriented atheists import extra-scientific assumptions in their arguments that evolutionary theory offers the best explanation, the one most likely to be correct, for the 'emergence of the reproductive from the non-reproductive' (p. 169); 'the step from non-living entities to living entities;' and for 'the transition from mindless to minded life' (p 99).

Despite his arguments that evolutionary theory fails to account for the transitions cited above, Haldane says he is not a creationist.

> I am not arguing the case for creationist science, the not impossible but foolish view that there is nothing to evolution; that God made the world as we find it today, a few thousand or a few hundred thousand years ago . . . I acknowledge that there is a history of evolutionary processes and that our evidence and inferential grounds for thinking this also provide reason for linking humankind with pre-human species . . . [but] biology, including its evolutionary dimension, cannot be understood or adequately accounted for in mechanical non-teleological terms. The emergence of life and the start of speciation call for explanations and what reductionism has to offer fails to provide these, giving at best a blank cheque to chance, which is to say offering no intelligible explanation at all [p 106].

Creationism is identified with the foolish view Haldane repudiates. But there are other forms of creationism, more plausible than the one Haldane rejects that Haldane agrees with on certain points. Thus, creationism typically and centrally involves the claim Haldane argues for—'that biology, including its evolutionary dimension, cannot be understood or adequately accounted for in mechanical non-teleological terms . . . [that] the emergence of life and the start of speciation call for explanations'. The explanations Haldane sees as called for are non-reductionistic—by which he means non-naturalistic, or in plain parlance—non-scientific. He does not mean, in this context, that the entire process of evolution, and what makes it possible, itself requires an explanation, a more basic explanation or a final cause—though he believes that too. He means that evolution cannot explain what evolutionary theory, bolstered by DNA research, maintains it does explain. Haldane's account of creationism is selective. And given what he says about the gaps in what evolutionary theory can account for he cannot distance himself from certain forms of creationism.[8]

Consider one further example in relation to interpreting the Bible. In *Divine Discourse* Nicholas Wolterstorff defends the acceptability of the belief that God speaks (ie God performs illocutionary acts). Against Ricoeur, Hans Frei, and Derrida, Wolterstorff argues that interpreting texts generally, but the Bible in particular, to find out 'what the author was saying' (ie authorial-discourse interpretation) is desirable.

Suppose one accepts authorial-discourse interpretation as the proper mode for interpreting texts generally and the Bible in particular. Can one know that one's interpretation is correct? '[A]s John Locke puts it, the outcome of biblical interpretation threatens to be `that the scripture serves but, like a nose of wax, to be turned and bent, just as may fit the contrary orthodoxies of different societies. For it is these several systems, that to each party are the just standards of truth' (p 226). Wolterstorff's treatment of the 'wax nose' problem is indicative of the admittedly deep theological presuppositions of authorial-discourse interpretation of the Bible, and also of how problematic such interpretation is. It is odd that he does not notice that the wax nose problem, or a version of it, is just as applicable to text sense and most other modes of interpretation. Nevertheless, his suggestions for overcoming the problem in connection with authorial-discourse interpretation are unacceptable.

Wolterstorff says that 'there is no way to avoid employing our conviction as to what is true and loving in the process of interpreting for divine discourse—no way to circumvent . . .the wax-nose anxiety . . . . [O]nly with awe and inspiration . . . only after prayer and fasting, is it appropriate to interpret a text so as to discern what God said . . . The risks cannot be evaded. But they can be diminished' given certain presumptions and tactics (p 236). What are these presumptions?

> [i] The presumption that the appropriator says what the person whose discourse is appropriated said . . .

---

8.   For further discussion of Haldane see Michael Levine, 'Critical Study of Atheism and Theism, JJC Smart and JJ Haldane', *Canadian Journal of Philosophy* 29: 157–170.

given our convictions as to what the appropriator
would have wanted and not wanted to say . . . [ii] A
presumption...that the speaker says what his sentence
means. There may be good reason . . . for departing
from . . . that presumption; but that then is what we are
attentive for . . . [iii] one minimizes the risk by doing
one's best to remain genuinely open to the possibility
that the beliefs with which one approached the
enterprise of interpreting for divine discourse are
mistaken . . . awareness of this diversity of interpretations remains relatively useless unless one also
struggles to become self-critical . . . so as to be able to
listen to those alternative interpretations, genuinely
listen. Parochialism, especially arrogant parochialism,
makes it inevitable that scripture becomes a wax nose
in our hands . . . [iv] one minimizes the risk of missing
or misinterpreting the divine discourse by cultivating
knowledge of ourselves and of the world . . . [and by]
coming to know God better [pp 237–239].

The ways in which he claims the risks can be diminished do not
diminish Locke's anxiety but attenuate it—and none more than the
admonition to avoid 'parochialism.'

The most arresting consideration is in point iii. Locke's point is
surely that parochialism, in one way or another, is the issue that
logically—not just psychologically—generates wax-nose anxiety. His
worry is *that all interpretation of Scripture is necessarily parochial.*
Wolterstorff, however, psychologises all of the above points and in so
doing he disregards the epistemological problem that Locke is
concerned with. Along with neglecting the genuine wax nose problem
(ie the epistemological problem), Wolterstorff posits ways of dealing
with parochialism that are as naive as they are themselves parochial.
He does not recognise that the parochial, especially the 'especially
arrogant' parochial (and what serious parochialism is not arrogant?)
never see themselves as such. Is there ever a question that as a result of
biblical authorial-discourse interpretation one will conclude something
one does not already believe—let alone something that conflicts with
what one already firmly believes?

Consider literalism and parochialism for a moment. This issue is
not going to turn out as Wolterstorff would like. Bertrand Russell's

authorial-discourse reading of Jesus's teachings on hell is vastly different and far more literal than that of Richard Swinburne's. Whose reading is more acceptable given the criteria Wolterstorff cites? 'The mind is its own place, and in it self Can make a Heav'n of Hell, a Hell of Heav'n' (Milton, *Paradise Lost* I, 254-5).[9] And reading van Inwagen or Plantinga on the problem of evil one could easily doubt that his extrapolation of the problem is anything like Job's understanding of the problem. Scripture *is* a wax-nose in the hands of contemporary Christian analytic philosophers of religion. Wolterstorff's treatment of Locke's wax nose problem does not in any way lessen the problem but exemplifies it.

The practice by some contemporary Christian analytic philosophers of religion of selectively and peculiarly interpreting the Bible to advance philosophical theses has its roots in Wolterstorff's and Plantinga's interpretation of Calvin and Luther on 'basic belief'.[10] This view has been enormously influential—exercising nearly a generation of philosophers of religion with a view that, whatever its merits, is falsely attributed to Calvin and Reformed theology. Plantinga and Wolterstorff claim that according to what they term 'Calvinistic or Reformed epistemology' (p 27) one is justified in believing in God apart from any of the other beliefs one has whatsoever (ie that belief in God can be properly basic for some people in some circumstances), that belief in God need not be based upon any of one's other beliefs in order to be justified. Plantinga claims not only that belief in God is properly basic according to the reformed view, but that ' the mature theist does not typically accept belief in God . . . as a conclusion from other things he believes; he accepts it as basic, as part of his noetic structure' (p 27). They explicitly base their claim on Luther's

---

9. See, Bertrand Russell, 'Why I Am Not a Christian', in *Why I Am Not a Christian and Other Essays* (London: George Allen & Unwin, 1975); Richard Swinburne, 'A Theodicy of Heaven and Hell', in Press, 1983), 37–54; and Michael Levine, 'Swinburne's Heaven: One Hell of a Place', *Religious Studies*, 29 (1993): 519–531.

10. Alvin Plantinga and Nicholas Wolterstorff, editors, *Faith and Rationality* (Notre Dame: University Notre Dame, 1983). For a critique of 'reformed epistemology' and the claim that reformed epistemology can be traced to Calvin or Luther—for example that they adhered to the Plantinga-Wolterstorff 'reformed epistemological' notion of 'basic belief' see my critical study of *Faith and Rationality* in *Philosophia* 16 (1986): 447–460.

Commentary on the Galatians in which he says 'kill reason and believe in Christ'. The wax-nose problem looms large if one effortlessly moves from that quotation of Luther either to Plantinga's interpretation of what Luther means, or (even more) to Plantinga's view about mature theists and basic belief. Luther does not mean that belief in Christ or God is not or need not be based upon reasons in the form of other beliefs one has. A belief can, in various ways, be 'contrary to reason' and yet one can still have reasons for believing it. What Luther does mean here has to be looked at in the broader context of how Luther understood the relationship between reason and faith.[11]

3. Terrible solutions to a horrible problem

The shift from the logical argument from evil against the existence of God to the empirical argument has been seen as a victory by those analytic philosophers of religion who now seek to establish that the existence of evil fails to make the existence of God improbable, or any less probable, than it might otherwise be. I examine several such arguments in an effort to establish the following: (i) Their victory is pyrrhic. They distort the historical, philosophical and religious nature of the challenge of the problem of evil; (ii) In attempting to meet the challenges of the empirical argument from evil against the existence of God they rely on disguised but well-worn strategies like the free will defence; (iii) A refusal to let any instances of evil count in any way, to any degree, against the probability of the existence of God, indicates that their rejection of the very basis of the empirical argument is ideological and contrary to traditional theism. Issues relating to falsifiability—and hence 'meaning'—are raised. (iv) Aspects of their arguments are morally repugnant; (v) The arguments are indicative of a lack of vitality, relevance and 'seriousness', in a sense I shall explain, of Christian analytic philosophy of religion.

Peter van Inwagen begins his discussion of the 'evidential problem from evil' with the following claim—a claim both false and vague. He says, 'It used to be widely held that evil—which for present purposes we may identify with undeserved pain and suffering—was incom-

---

11.   I am told that Plantinga has since abandoned the view that Luther or 'reformed theology' held the view he here attributes to them, but I have not been able to verify it.

patible with the existence of God'.[12] That is, he claims that although the logical argument from evil against the existence of a theistic God was once widely held 'it is no longer defended'. He says, however, that 'arguments for the following weaker thesis continue[s] to be very popular: Evil (or at least the evil of the amounts and kinds we actually observe) constitutes evidence against the existence of God, evidence that seems decisively to outweigh the totality of evidence *for* the existence of God'. William Rowe calls these arguments empirical arguments from evil against the existence of God and Van Inwagen calls them 'evidential' arguments.[13]

Van Inwagen does not say who those are who allegedly held that the existence of evil was incompatible with the existence of God. No doubt philosophers did hold this view, though it was never 'widely held' as van Inwagen claims, and it is of course unlikely that many in the wider community held it since logical compatibility /incompatibility about such matters is not something the wider community of believers/disbelievers would have views about. The serious problem of evil—the problem in Job and the one that Ivan faces in Dostoevski's *The Brothers Karamazov*—has always been concerned with some version of the empirical argument. After all, Job and Ivan are both believers. Job is talking to God and Ivan says, 'I am a believer. But there are the children, and what am I to do about them? That's a question I can't answer . . . Listen! If all must suffer to pay for the eternal harmony, what have children to do with it, tell me please? It's

---

12.   Van Inwagen, 'The Problem of Evil, the Problem of Air, and the Problem of Silence', *God, Knowledge and Mystery: Essays in Philosophical Theology* (Ithaca: Cornell University Press 1995), 66–95, 66.

13.   William Rowe says, 'It is one thing to argue that the existence of evil is logically incompatible with the existence of the theistic God and quite another thing to argue that the world contains evils that render the existence of the theistic God unlikely. The former is the logical argument from evil; the latter is the empirical argument from evil'. The empirical argument is also called the 'evidential', 'probabilistic', and 'inductive' argument. William L Rowe, 'The Empirical Argument from Evil.' In Robert Audi *Rationality, Religious Belief and Moral Commitment* (Ithaca: Cornell University Press 1986), 227–247, 227. Also see Rowe, 'Evil and Theodicy', *Philosophical Topics* 16 (1988): 119–132.

beyond all comprehension why they should suffer . . . It's not God that I don't accept . . . only I most respectfully return Him the ticket'.[14]

What Ivan is telling his brother Alyosha is that, as far as he can see, given God's existence there can be no intelligible reason for, or rational justification of, some of the evils that occur. Ivan is rejecting any humanly intelligible vindication of God's goodness in view of such evil. He is rejecting theodicy *per se*. At times Ivan appears to acknowledge the mere possibility that there may be an explanation for the evil, and so a vindication of divine goodness. But in the end he rejects this and the rejection is fundamentally morally based. Since he does not see any conceivable way, morally speaking, in which there could be a justification, he rejects the notion there is one, and defiantly rejects God as a result. Ivan does not want a merely logically possible explanation for evil but some plausible explanation for much of it. And he sees the lack of any morally plausible explanation—either real or imagined—as grounds for rejecting any meaningful possibility of there being one.

Ivan is making a point not unlike JS Mill's.[15] Mill claims that moral terms cannot apply to God wholly differently than they apply to people. To do so would be to equivocate absolutely on the meaning of the terms and so one might as well use completely different terms. Ivan is saying is that given the way we use moral terms—even extending their meanings somewhat—one cannot conceive of anything that would justify certain evils. At least where moral matters are concerned conceivability is a test of possibility since the meaning of moral is fixed by the ways in which we actually do *or conceivably could* use them. Furthermore, in the theology and falsification debate of the 1950s, when Flew talks about an assertion such as 'God loves us as a father loves his children' being so eroded by qualification that it was no longer an assertion at all' ('dying the death of a thousand qualifications') I see his point, or rather what is right about it, as in essence the same as Ivan's (Dostoevski's) and Mill's.[16]

---

14.   Feodor Dostoevski, 'Rebellion', from *The Brothers Karamazov*. In *God and Evil: Readings on the Theological Problem of Evil*, edited by Nelson Pike (New-Jersey: Prentice-Hall 1964), 6–16, 14–16.

15.   John Stuart Mill, 'Mr Mansel on the Limits of Religious Thought'. In *God and Evil: Readings on the Theological Problem of Evil*, edited by Nelson Pike (New-Jersey: Prentice-Hall 1964), 37–45.

16.   Anthony Flew, RM Hare, Basil Mitchell (1955). 'Theology and Falsification', in *New Essays in Philosophical Theology*, edited by Anthony Flew and Alasdair

Conceivability is by no means always a guide to possibility. But in moral matters, on my reconstruction of Ivan's view, it is a guide—and necessarily so—since moral concepts cannot transcend the human understanding and discourse constitutive of them.[17] Here is a clash of intuitions. Some think that given that God exists, it is inconceivable that the undeserving victims of the most horrible of evils will not somehow be recompensed for their suffering; while others claim that regardless of whether anything like a theistic God exists it is inconceivable that such victims be recompensed—and given this, it is inconceivable how such a God could exist. The nature of God is called into question.

If one takes the case of Job or Dostoevski's Ivan as paradigmatic of the problem of evil, then an effort to turn the problem into an issue of logical compatibility between the existence of God and evil rather than an existential problem integrally related to evidential concerns will result in a gross misrepresentation that misses the nature of the concerns of Job and Ivan altogether.[18] These are the existential

---

MacIntyre (London: SCM Press 1955), 96–105. Also see Kai Nielsen, *Ethics without God* (Buffalo: Prometheus Books 1973), chapter 1 'Morality and the Will of God,' for an argument that relates to Dostoevski's, Mill's and Flew's. See Feodor Dostoevski, 'Rebellion', from *The Brothers Karamazov,* in *God and Evil: Readings on the Theological Problem of Evil,* edited by Nelson Pike (New-Jersey: Prentice-Hall 1964), 6–16; Anthony Flew, RM Hare, Basil Mitchell, 'Theology and Falsification', in *New Essays in Philosophical Theology,* edited by Anthony Flew and Alasdair MacIntyre (London: SCM Press 1955), 96–105; Anthony Flew, 'Are Ninian Smart's Temptations Irresistible?' *Philosophy* 37, (1962): 57–60; Anthony Flew, 'Compatibilism, Freewill and God', Philosophy 48 (1973): 231–244; John Stuart Mill, 'Mr Mansel on the Limits of Religious Thought', in *God and Evil: Readings on the Theological Problem of Evil*. Edited by Nelson Pike (New-Jersey: Prentice-Hall 1964), 37–45.

17. It is clear on which side of the *Euthyphro* problem Ivan (in *The Brother's Karamazov)* and JS Mill stand. The gods command things because they are good. They are not, and cannot, be good merely because the gods command them.

18. For an account of various interpretations of God's answer to Job see Wesley Morriston, 'God's Answer to Job', *Religious Studies* 32 (1996): 339–356. Michael L Peterson, 'Evil and Inconsistency', *Sophia,* 18, (1979): 20-27, makes the point about the priority of the empirical over the logical argument from evil as follows. He says (27)

'The more interesting and important formulation of the problem of evil is not as an *a priori* problem of the internal consistency of theism. The problem is more

concerns that suffering raises. How can God be conceived of in the theistic manner—perfectly good, omnipotent and omniscient in the face of such evil? How is one to understand it? And how can one come to terms with such a god in the face of such evil? The problem of evil is first and foremost an existential problem and theodicies are meant to address these problems. In so far as the medium is (or partly contains) the message, in opting for an antiseptic approach to the problem of evil—one that does *not describe* the evils in question—van Inwagen and others (RM Adams, and Alvin Plantinga) distance themselves from the existential dimension of the problem. This in turn trivialises the problem of evil. This is not to deny that there has been some work on the existential/pastoral problem of evil. Here too the problem of evil is often distorted in more or less the same way and for more or less the same reasons (eg Marilyn McCord-Adams). Simplistic solutions are offered—such as the claim that God will make it up to people in heaven for the horrors unjustly suffered on earth—and animal suffering really doesn't matter.[19] These solutions again ignore Dostoevski and Job, and fly in the face of Mill's important admonition.

There is a corollary to the above. The distinction between so-called defence and theodicy is unfounded and irrelevant. If defences are simply meant to show that evil is compatible with the existence of God in a 'broadly logical sense'—the story they tell is possible in a broadly logical sense—then they are basically irrelevant to the problem of evil

---

powerfully formulated as an *a posteriori* matter regarding the acceptability or probability of theism in light of relevant external considerations. The problem must be moved from the sphere of purely formal logic into the arena of human thought and decision, into the realm where rational and moral persons assess theism in the light of their values, ontological commitments, and existential orientations. Indeed, this rendition of the problem of evil pervades the classical and contemporary literature . . . the atheologian . . . at best . . . can claim that theism is unacceptable or improbable according to the external considerations which are present and central to his evaluation, and not that it is essentially irrational. The theist, on the other hand, may claim that theism is reasonable because it makes quite good sense of experience, is morally acceptable, and so on.'
Also see Michael L Peterson, *The Problem of Evil: Selected Readings* (Notre Dame: University of Notre Dame Press, 1992).

19. See, Marilyn McCord Adams. *Horrendous Evils and the Goodness of God* (Ithaca, NY: Cornell University Press, 1999); Peter Forrest, *God without the Supernatural: A Defense of Scientific Theism* (Ithaca, NY: Cornell University Press, 1996).

and of minor interest.[20] In practice there is no genuine distinction between defence and theodicy. The free will defence is not a defence but a theodicy, or part of a theodicy, and no amount of calling it a defence will make it so. It seeks to justify God's goodness in the face of evil. While van Inwagen claims to recognise a distinction between defence and theodicy, he implicitly undermines it when he says that his own (partial) theodicy can also be read as a defence if one does not share his belief in its theological underpinning.[21] The interesting issues in defences will involve questions that do not directly concern the problem of evil at all—such as the plausibility of compatibilism or modal scepticism. The point is this: when you read a so-called defence there is nothing more in terms of argument or alleged fact that must be added to turn it into a theodicy. All that needs to be added is one's assent that it is, in view of one's other beliefs, a plausible (not merely logically possible) explanation of how evil could exist in the face of a perfectly good, gracious and all-powerful God.

I take it that both Job and Ivan reject free will as the cornerstone of an adequate theodicy. Even if, following Plantinga, the types of agents one takes to be responsible for freely choosing evil is broadened in an effort to account for natural evil as well as moral evil (ie natural evil is the devil's freely chosen work)—it is too facile to address Job's and Ian's existential concerns. Indeed, evil only becomes a problem at the point where despite free will, the issue (ie the project of reconciling the existence of God and evil together) becomes incomprehensible. Thus, in relation both to the defence/theodicy distinction as well as to the alleged abandonment of the logical version from evil against the existence of God, Plantinga and van Inwagen scratch mightily where only straw men are itching. The distinction and the abandonment are

---

20.   Cf van Inwagen, 'The Magnitude, Duration, and Distribution of Evil: A Theodicy', 96.

21.   Van Inwagen, 'The Magnitude, Duration, and Distribution of Evil: A Theodicy', in *God, Knowledge and Mystery: Essays in Philosophical Theology* (Ithaca: Cornell University Press, 1995), 96–122, says, 'Those who do not share my allegiance to these data [the data of Christian Revelation] may wish to regard this essay as providing one more defence, in Plantinga's sense' (97). In the same volume also see van Inwagen, 'The Problem of Evil, the Problem of Air, and the Problem of Silence, 66–95; 'The Place of Chance in a World Sustained by God,' 42–65; 'Ontological Arguments', 22–41.

both non-starters.[22] If they did not obfuscate the problem of evil they would be harmless. Traditionally, as in Job and Dostoevski (see Ivan in *The Brother's Karamazov*), moral evil is regarded every bit the problem, indeed it is the same problem, as natural evil—namely, 'Why does God allow it?' The alleged free-will defence is not seen an acceptable solution to the problem of moral evil as it is by contemporary Christian analytic philosophers of religion. Such philosophers thus misrepresent the traditional problem of evil in more ways than one.

The idea that in showing that the existence of evil (the amounts and kinds we observe) is logically compatible with the existence of a theistic God, or that they cannot be shown to be logically incompatible, is a point so trivial it is barely worth making. Even those like JL Mackie[23] who have sought to show that there is a logical incompatibility between the existence of God and evil are better interpreted as trying to show that certain standard theodicies that rely on free will do not work—and so Mackie argues that God could have created people so that they always freely chose to do the good. And in so far as Mackie's view rests on compatibilism—the position that free will is compatible with causal determinism—and compatibilism remains a viable option, there is no reason to suppose, as van Inwagen does, that nobody any longer defends Mackie's thesis. The reason it may *appear* that no one any longer defends it is simply because they have nothing more to say on it. The silence is not indicative of capitulation but of assumed victory. In any case, Mackie need not deny that *even if* God could have created human beings who always freely chose the good there might still be some over-riding morally relevant reason why God did not do so. And so the existence of God and evil may be a logical possibility. But who cares?

The premise that is at the core of the empirical argument is that there seems little reason to suppose that God could or would in fact have allowed the evil that does exist to exist given what we have reason to believe he could do. God, if God existed, would have done it differently. So Mackie's and others' so-called logical arguments are

---

22.   For further discussion of partial theodicies that I see as misleading as well as mistaken, see Michael Levine, 'Swinburne's Heaven: One Hell of a Place', *Religious Studies* 29 (1993), 519–531; 'Must God Create The Best?' *Sophia* 35 (1996): 28–34.

23.   JL Mackie, 'Theism and Utopia', *Philosophy* 37, (1962): 153–158; *The Miracle of Theism* (Oxford: Oxford University Press 1982).

perhaps more plausibly interpreted in context, without loss, as empirical or evidential arguments—or aspects of such arguments. The logical arguments of Mackie and others, given a little latitude, are not so much against the strict logical incompatibility of the existence of God and evil as they are against the plausibility of assuming the world would be as it is given the existence of a theistic God. They are arguments that are variations on or aspects of empirical arguments. Evil is evidence against the existence of God because there is no good reason to suppose, for example, that God would allow or needed to allow, for the amounts and types of evil that exist. Thus, the entire distinction between the empirical and logical arguments and the alleged retreat to empirical arguments after the alleged defeat of logical arguments is simply a kind of media beat-up by conservative Christian analytic philosophers of religion. More significant is the fact that van Inwagen and others misrepresent and avoid the traditional problem of evil.

Van Inwagen says 'if there is no least amount of evil that would serve whatever purposes an all-powerful and perfectly good being might have in allowing the existence of evil of the kinds and in *more or less* the amounts that actually exist, then such a being might very well allow particular evils that are individually pointless'.[24] There may be 'no least amount', but surely the significant objection is that qualitatively and/or quantitatively *less* would suffice for any imaginable purpose God may have. The fact that there is no clear cut-off point between too much and enough is beside the point. What drives the argument is that far too much evil—quantitatively and qualitatively speaking—appears to be otiose. Van Inwagen's claim that there may be (is) 'no least amount of evil that would serve' God's purposes is beside the point. It is inapplicable to the most significant versions of the empirical argument. Empirical arguments seek to show that given evil of the kinds and in *more or less* the amounts that actually do exist it, it is implausible to suppose that God exists since qualitatively and/or quantitatively so much of it seems pointless (ie there is no imaginable purpose of God's that it would serve). The heart of the empirical argument is that it appears utterly implausible (degrees of implausibility do matter)—and if Ivan is right maybe even impossible—to

24. Van Inwagen, *God, Knowledge and Mystery: Essays in Philosophical Theology*, 18.

suppose that the evil that exists could have a point in serving the purposes of an all-powerful and perfectly good being—for example, that such evil could lead to a greater good, or to any 'good,' at all.

Van Inwagen's arguments for modal scepticism, 'the thesis that we are largely ignorant of modal matters that are remote from the concerns of everyday life'[25]—are scattered throughout his essays. Like

---

25.   Van Inwagen, *God, Knowledge and Mystery: Essays in Philosophical Theology*, 11. See the other essays in this book as well. The contemporary locus *classicus* of the kind of scepticism concerning possibilities that van Inwagen takes up is, I think, to be found in Ninian Smart, 'Omnipotence, Evil and Supermen', *Philosophy* 36, (1961): 188–195. Also see Anthony Flew, 'Are Ninian Smart's Temptations Irresistible?', *Philosophy* 37 (1962): 57–60; and JL Mackie, 'Theism and Utopia,' *Philosophy* 37 (1962): 153–158.

Although van Inwagen ('The Magnitude, Duration, and Distribution of Evil: A Theodicy', 97) says, 'The theodicy I shall present is not in any large part my own invention' he does not say who his sources are. His disclaimer to novelty appears to conflict with his statement (*God, Knowledge and Mystery: Essays in Philosophical Theology*, 19) in his introduction that 'I have called to the reader's attention the themes in the essays that I believe to be different from anything that occurs in the works of other writers on the same topics'. In relation to two of his central themes—(i) 'Modal scepticism' and (ii) the view that some evils happen for no reason whatsoever—van Inwagen is mistaken if he sees them as novel. Smart discusses modal scepticism, though not by that name, but so does just about every other author who tackles evil and free will. As van Inwagen notes, Swinburne raises thought experiments that implicitly deny modal scepticism, and it is clear that most authors on evil line up on one or the other side of the thesis of modal scepticism. Mackie ('Theism and Utopia', *The Miracle of Theism* (Oxford: Oxford University Press, 1982)) for example, denies it, as does, on van Inwagen's own account, Swinburne and Plantinga.

As for his allegedly novel view that some evils happen for no reason whatsoever and serve no purpose: van Inwagen ('The Place of Chance in a World Sustained by God', 65) says '. . . a moral for students of the problem of evil: Do not attempt any solution to this problem that entails that every particular evil has a purpose, or that, with respect to every individual misfortune, or every devastating earthquake, or every disease, God has some special reason for allowing it. Concentrate rather on the problem of what sort of reasons a loving and providential God might have for allowing His creatures to live in a world in which many of the evils that happen to them happen to them for no reason at all'. This quotation could be taken as suggesting that a plausible rejection of the argument from evil against the existence of God must not rely on the kinds of claims that are often used against the logical version of the argument; for example, that it is *possible* that such and such an evil leads to a greater good so God must allow it. But, van Inwagen's

his attempted refutation of Swinburne on logical possibility most appeal to one's introspective capacity concerning what is and is not possible.[26] However, the appeal is not simply an appeal to intro- spection since van Inwagen is actually concerned in denying that our modal intuitions based on introspection are reliable. Modal scepticism plays a crucial role in van Inwagen's theodicy overall. This is because if we have good reason to believe that the laws of nature could be otherwise than they are—for example, could be such that there were never any killer viruses or tornadoes—then without causing massive irregularities in nature (ie without being in van Inwagen's loaded terms a 'deceiver'), it would appear that God could have and would have chosen those more congenial alternate laws.

Van Inwagen would agree that with few exceptions modal logicians and other philosophers (eg Plantinga and Swinburne) with views on logical possibility reject modal scepticism.[27] He says:

> I should say, we have some sort of capacity to know modal truths about familiar matters. I know that it is possible that—there is no intrinsic impossibility in its being the case that—the table that was in a certain

---

'moral for students of the problem if evil' is far more applicable to those who wish to refute the empirical argument. It is more applicable to those who claim that it is *plausible* to suppose that such and such an evil leads to a greater good so God must allow it. Still, one wonders why van Inwagen thinks he needs the 'moral' he issues. After all, the most common theodicies involve the Free Will Defence, and in that defence it is not assumed or argued but *denied* 'that every particular evil has a purpose, or that, with respect to every individual misfortune, or every devastating earthquake, or every disease, God has some special reason for allowing it'. The Free Will Defence maintains that there is an overall reason for God allowing such evils, but no special reason or purpose for any particular evil. Van Inwagen's 'moral for students of the problem of evil' is applicable only to the crudest of those who offer defences against the argument from evil. Who, after all, seriously maintains that every particular evil has a purpose?

26. Van Inwagen, *God, Knowledge and Mystery: Essays in Philosophical Theology,* 19–21. For a recent discussion of issues in modal epistemology that are relevant to van Inwagen's claims, see the essays in 'The Role of the Empirical (And of the A Priori) in Epistemology', *Southern Journal of Philosophy XXXVIII, Supplement* (2000).

27. George Seddon, 'Logical Possibility', *Mind* 81 (1972): 481–494.

position at noon have then been two feet to the left of
where it in fact was . . . But I should say that we have
no sort of capacity that would enable us to know
whether it is possible for there to be a being that is both
concrete and necessarily existent . . . or whether it is
necessary that the laws of physics have the same
structure as the actual laws. To my mind, philosophers
who think they can hold such concepts or states of
affairs as these before their minds and determine by
some sort of intellectual insight whether they are
possible are fooling themselves . . . The illusory
character of the conviction of some philosophers that
they have such a power is sometimes disguised by talk
of 'logical possibility,' for it is often supposed that
there is a species of possibility that goes by this name
and that one can determine a priori whether a concept
or state of affairs is logically possible. But there is no
such thing as logical possibility—not, at least, if it is
really supposed to be a species of possibility. I don't
deny that there is such a thing as logical *impossibility*.
This is an epistemological category: the logically
impossible is that which can be know to be impossible
on the basis of logical considerations alone—or, to be
liberal, logical and semantical considerations alone . . .
What I dispute is the contention that if a concept or
state of affairs is not logically impossible, then it is
'logically possible'. It hardly follows that, because a
certain thing cannot be proved to be impossible by a
certain method, it is therefore possible in any sense of
'possible' whatever.[28]

But few would claim that 'because a certain thing cannot be *proved*
[my emphasis] to be impossible by a certain method, it is therefore
possible'. What is generally assumed—that van Inwagen disputes—is
'that if a concept or state of affairs is not logically impossible, then it is
"logically possible"'. However, this is not an epistemological or a
mistaken epistemological thesis, as Van Inwagen would have it, but an

---

28.   Van Inwagen, *God, Knowledge and Mystery: Essays in Philosophical Theology*,
        12–13.

ontological one. Epistemologically what is generally claimed is that if something is not known to be impossible, and cannot currently be shown to be impossible, then it is prima facie possible. Things that we currently see no reason to suppose are impossible may well turn out to be impossible—just as, for example, we may hold logically incompatible beliefs—belief about states of affairs that could not possibly be instantiated. But why conclude, on the basis of these epistemological considerations, that there is no such thing as logical possibility—things or states of affairs that are logically possible? Supposing that epistemology (or epistemic justification) and ontology (or truth) may diverge on even the deepest levels, then even if something cannot be proved to be impossible by any method whatsoever (ie even if it is, for whatever reason, impossible to prove it impossible) that thing or state of affairs may, for all we know, be impossible.

Van Inwagen conveniently conflates epistemology with ontology—and he does so for a purpose in connection with his account of natural evil. He says 'if you think that it would be possible to design a planet, and a universe to contain it, that was both capable of supporting human life and contained no earthquakes or tornadoes, I can only point out that you have never tried'.[29] This theme is an elaboration on, or alternative version, of the one that for all we know 'it is necessary that the laws of physics have the same structure as the actual laws' and that natural evil would result from the operation of these necessary laws. Van Inwagen puts a twist on this with his 'just-so story'—a story integral to his theodicy that since their rebellion from God (ie after the fall) people can no longer protect themselves from things like tornadoes. Van Inwagen claims that 'it is probably not true that we should be better off for a complete elimination of natural evil . . . Our ancestral ruin is *primarily* a moral as opposed to a cognitive ruin'.[30] Even if he is right about the latter claim, what is one to say about the bizarre former claim? Try telling it to cancer, AIDS or earthquake victims.

---

29.   Van Inwagen, 'The Magnitude, Duration, and Distribution of Evil: A Theodicy', 106.
30.   Van Inwagen, 'The Magnitude, Duration, and Distribution of Evil: A Theodicy', 107.

But once the ontological issues are sorted out from the epistemological ones—once the question of 'possibility' is distinguished from knowing what is possible or impossible, or the possibility of knowing what is possible, then van Inwagen will have to come up with more than a simple reliance on his thesis of modal scepticism if he is to convince us that what we take to be prima facie possible is not, after all, really possible—let alone that 'there is no such thing as logical possibility'. He must give us positive reasons, and not allude to what some scientists may think, for supposing that the laws of physics could not be other than they are, or that given the laws of physics that do exist, earthquakes and deadly viruses must occur. Regardless of whether or not scientists would in fact side with van Inwagen on this issue, I am inclined to think what scientists think about these matters is not privileged—any more than medical doctors' ethical views are—-since it would have be shown that it was their scientific, rather philosophical views, that were intrinsically connected to their modal conclusions. Could the fundamental material constituents of the universe not behave differently from the way they do? Where is the contradiction in supposing such a thing or why suppose there is one?—which is not to deny that there may be one.

Similarly, he will have to give positive reasons why, contrary to Swinburne, he claims (1995: 20) he cannot imagine 'that it is coherent to suppose that the moon is made of green cheese'.[31] He says, 'I think that anyone who thinks he can imagine that the moon is made of green cheese has a very sluggish imagination: the active imagination demands a pasture for the antecedently necessary thousands of thousands of millions of cows, demands a way to preserve a piece of cheese in boiling heat, freezing cold . . . Only a philosopher of very little imagination would think he could imagine the moon being made of green cheese . . . [or] think he could imagine turning into an omnipresent spirit'.[32] I do not believe that imagining the moon to be made of green cheese requires imagining any of the things—like thousands of millions of cows— that van Inwagen claims are involved. He has given no argument in the present context why it should. In the absence of any specific reasons to suppose the idea incoherent, why suppose it

---

31.   Van Inwagen, *God, Knowledge and Mystery: Essays in Philosophical Theology*,
       20.
32.   Van Inwagen, *God, Knowledge and Mystery: Essays in Philosophical Theology*,
       20–21.

to be logical impossible? There is no logical impossibility in the supposition that the moon is made of cheese even given the laws of nature as they currently are—albeit the moon would probably be a very hard cheese indeed. At any rate, until one has substantial *arguments* rather than conjectures to offer on behalf of modal scepticism—arguments that would presumably break down the distinction between nomic and logical necessity; and the relation between logical impossibility and possibility as it is currently ordinarily understood—there is no ground for accepting the view that there cannot be a world much like ours, only without viruses and tornadoes.

Van Inwagen claims that 'the epistemology of modal statements is a subject about which little is known'. In particular, he claims that we do not know 'how we know' something is possible.[33] He says, 'I am convinced that, however it is that I know the modal status of certain statements about everyday matters, this method or mechanism or technique or device or system of intuitions . . . is of no value at all when it comes to judging the modal status of propositions remote from the concerns of everyday life'.[34] I think that we know a great deal more about the epistemology of modal statements than van Inwagen thinks we do, and that his scepticism in this regard has an ulterior motive. Van Inwagen simply assumes that we do not know 'how we know' something is possible even in everyday matters. But this seems false. We know that it is possible for the table to be two feet to the left of where it is because we can see that there is no contradiction in supposing it is possible for the table to be two feet to the left of where it is. At other times we 'compare' ideas or examine what certain beliefs we hold entail or imply to see if those beliefs are compatible with or entail something that could not possibly be the case. And van Inwagen has not shown that the mechanisms that we use to determine everyday modal matters is inoperable or in any way different in non-everyday matters. It may be more complicated in the latter case. This is to be expected. But why suppose it is different in kind? Even if it could be shown that we are frequently mistaken in the latter case but rarely in the former, it would not follow that 'how we know' would be different.

---

33. Van Inwagen, *God, Knowledge and Mystery: Essays in Philosophical Theology*, 13–14.
34. Van Inwagen, *God, Knowledge and Mystery: Essays in Philosophical Theology*, 14.

Ivan's moral scepticism is impervious to van Inwagen's modal scepticism. This is because even if, despite its implausibility, one grants modal scepticism which holds, for example, that for all we know natural laws are necessary; morally speaking, one would still not be able to regard certain state of affairs resulting in a world envisioned by modal scepticism as 'good'. Even if God's hands were bound, as it were, to create a world (if he was to create at all) in which laws of nature and human failing led to evils as described by Ivan, we would, according to Ivan, have to assert that such a state of affairs was evil—and that whatever else God may be, God could not be 'good'. To call such a God good would be to equivocate absolutely on the meaning of 'good'. *Even if* God's omnipotence does not extend to creating human beings that always freely chose the good, or were far better natured than they were, such a being could still not be called good. It is not just that, for example, the case of the child being tortured cannot be called good. Van Inwagen would agree with that. It is rather that on Ivan's or Mill's account, a Being who would allow for such a thing—even when modally constrained in certain ways—could not be called 'good' or 'God' in anything like its theistic meaning.

Many of the contemporary theodicies on offer, despite being slight and often insignificant variations on old themes, have not been sufficiently morally examined despite their being, to say the least, morally problematic. George Schlesinger says:

> It may be maintained that A is permitted to cause another person suffering, with the view of providing opportunities for others to respond in a noble way, only if A is absolutely certain that he is capable of compensating the victim fully for his suffering. By fully compensating I mean that the victim will eventually agree that the experience of having to undergo the suffering A subjected him to in the service of his stated goal, together with the subsequent experience of receiving compensation, are no less preferable to the experience of having neither. It is obvious that only God is in the position to guarantee this.[35]

---

35.   George Schlesinger, New *Perspectives on Old-Time Religion* (Oxford: Oxford University Press 1988), 51–52. Cf, Charles Taliaferro, *Contemporary Philosophy of Religion* (London: Blackwell 1988), 316–317.

Swinburne holds a somewhat similar position and van Inwagen holds an even stronger position. Swinburne says:

> It is because being of use is a good for him who is of use and increases his well-being, that when someone's suffering is the means by which they are of use that the net negative weight of their suffering-and-being-of-use is not nearly as great as it would otherwise be; and so our Creator, if he has given us many other good things has the right to use us to a limited extent for the sake of some good to others. Kant was surely correct to emphasise that one must treat individuals as moral ends in themselves and not use them for the good of others. But the latter phrase must be interrupted as 'on balance'. It is permissible to use someone for the good of others if on balance you are their benefactor, and if they were in no position to make the choice for themselves.[36]

Kant would disagree. But even if one does agree that it is not always wrong to use someone for the good of others one has to look at the situation in regard to the others Swinburne has in mind. What exactly does Swinburne mean by 'limited extent' in the above? The idea that it was not wrong to butcher the child in front of the mother because it will benefit the butcher is . . . well, what can one say? Ivan claims it a morally incomprehensible view. He may be mistaken and the view may simply be wrong. The idea that the view Swinburne presents is, or could be, part of any traditional Christian theodicy is dubious. Does Swinburne take his view as applicable to—and so as an apologetic for—the concentration camps? It reads that way. These views are philosophically and religiously reactionary, and unchristian to boot. The fact that such views have not drawn harsh criticism from contemporary Christian analytic philosophers of religion indicates both a lack

---

36.   Richard Swinburne, 'Theodicy, Our Well-being, and God's Right's', *International Journal for the Philosophy of Religion* 38 (1995): 75–91, 87. Cf, van Inwagen, 'The Magnitude, Duration, and Distribution of Evil: A Theodicy', 121–122.

of interest by the wider philosophical community and also how inbred contemporary Christian philosophy of religion, and much of the criticism directed at it, has become. If van Inwagen and Swinburne were political figures, there would be protesters on the street. I mean this literally and not polemically. After all, what they have done is to offer not just a prima facie, but an ultimate justification for the holocaust and other horrors. What should be explained is how this has gone virtually unnoticed in the literature.

Van Inwagen rejects the following principle both as a universal moral principle and as it applies to God—at least in certain circumstances. 'It is wrong to allow something bad to happen to X—without X's permission—in order to secure some benefit for others (and no benefit for X).' For example, he says:

> The circumstances in which it is most doubtful are these: The agent is in a position of lawful authority over both X and the 'others' and is responsible for their welfare . . . the good to be gained by the 'others' is considerably greater than the evil suffered by X; there is no way in which the good for the 'others' can be achieved . . . [for example] we might consider cases of quarantine or of the right of eminent domain . . . It is not to the point to protest that these cases are not much like cases involving an omnipotent God . . . They are counter-examples to the above moral principle, and therefore, that moral principle is false.[37]

But relevant moral differences between cases of quarantine and eminent domain on the one hand, and genocide and torture (for the benefit of the torturer?) are not hard to find—especially when the agent is God.

Let me sketch a response. Can it be plausibly argued that the victims of genocide and torture are treated as ends in themselves? Does van Inwagen reject the view that people are ends in themselves and must be treated as such? In the case of a quarantine or eminent domain it could be argued that the individuals involved are still

---

37.   Van Inwagen, 'The Magnitude, Duration, and Distribution of Evil: A Theodicy', 121–122.

treated as ends in themselves.[38] But can this be argued in the case of genocide? Is genocide, torture, and rape in any sense morally equivalent to quarantine or eminent domain as van Inwagen seems to imply? And for van Inwagen to satisfy his own conditions (above), doesn't a moderately plausible case have to be made that 'the good to be gained by the "others" is considerably greater than the evil suffered by X . . . [and that] there is no way in which the good for the "others" can be achieved?' Van Inwagen's consequentialist views rest on moral principles antithetical to sensible consequentialism—one that preserves certain duties towards individuals. Christian moral theory rejects such latitudinous consequentialism altogether. Schlesinger's, Swinburne's and van Inwagen's theodicies are seriously morally flawed and seriously anti-Christian. Van Inwagen's and Swinburne's suggestion that masses of people can be used in the way they suggest (ie for the benefit of others—for their torturers) is horrific and extraordinarily anachronistic.

Ivan (Dostoevski), and perhaps Job, reject such solutions as bogus and incomprehensible. Ivan says, 'And if the sufferings of children go to swell the sum of sufferings which was necessary to pay for truth, then I protest that the truth is not worth such a price. I don't want the mother to embrace the oppressor who threw her son to the dogs! She dare not forgive him! Let her forgive him for herself, if she will . . . but the sufferings of her tortured child she has no right to forgive; she dare not forgive the torturer, even if the child were to forgive him!'[39] Schlesinger, Swinburne and van Inwagen would all appear to acknowledge the force of Mill's view that moral terms cannot apply to

---

38.   Kai Nielsen, *Ethics without God* (Buffalo: Prometheus Books 1973), 38–41 has argued that the idea of God having created man for a purpose (eg fellowship with God) is 'offensive in that it involves treating man a kind of tool or artifact. It is degrading for a man to be regarded as merely serving a purpose'. Nielsen seems to me to be mistaken since the idea is that in creating humans with such a purpose and in fulfilling such a purpose humans would be fulfilling their own good ends as well. But van Inwagen's account is very different. In his theodicy people really are tools for another's purpose. There is no identification—except in a highly attenuated and abstract/definitional sense—between their own ends and the ends of others they unwittingly or unwillingly serve.

39.   Feodor Dostoevski, 'Rebellion', from *The Brothers Karamazov*, in *God and Evil: Readings on the Theological Problem of Evil*, edited by Nelson Pike (New-Jersey: Prentice-Hall 1964), 16.

God wholly differently than they apply to people.[40] To do so would be to equivocate absolutely on the meaning of the terms and so one might as well (should) use completely different terms. They think, however, that their theodicies do not equivocate on such moral terms. This is what Ivan is denying. Morally speaking their theodicies are incomprehensible. Nothing that one could legitimately recognise as 'good' could result from the evils in this world—nothing. There is evil that is genuinely gratuitous and cannot be seen as plausibly consistent with an omnibenevolent (etc) God.

Van Inwagen does not consider that he may be equivocating on the meaning of moral and related terms. In an exuberant footnote he says, 'when we no longer see through a glass darkly, when we know as we are known, when God's sorrows are made manifest to us, we shall see that *we* have never felt anything that we could, without shame, describe as sorrow'.[41] How could what we call 'sorrow' not really be 'sorrow'? Ivan would reject van Inwagen's view on the ground that it entails a peculiar kind of global moral scepticism (if *this* does not count as sorrow what does?) and denounce it as morally indefensible. It is morally indefensible for a variety of reasons that over-determine its moral indefensibility. At the heart of at least some such arguments would lie the fact that the very possibility of moral discourse requires that one not equivocate on the use of morally relevant terms. Some evil cannot be mitigated—cannot be squared with God's goodness, power and knowledge. And surely the fact that God may suffer far more than ordinary people in no way entails, as van Inwagen implies, that now that the mother no longer sees 'through a glass darkly' she will be *ashamed* at describing what she previously felt at seeing her child ripped to shreds by the landlord's dogs as sorrow. On van Inwagen's account, the victims of hideous evil did not feel anything that they could 'without shame' call sorrow—or so they may one day come to see. Does this extend to suffering and pain as compared with God's? What kind of comparison is this? Van Inwagen's interpretation of what occurs when we 'no longer see through a glass darkly' distorts its

---

40.   John Stuart Mill, 'Mr Mansel on the Limits of Religious Thought', in *God and Evil: Readings on the Theological Problem of Evil*, edited by Nelson Pike (New-Jersey: Prentice-Hall 1964), 37–45.

41.   Van Inwagen, 'The Magnitude, Duration, and Distribution of Evil: A Theodicy', 120n14.

meaning and standard interpretations beyond recognition. Here is another example of Locke's wax nose problem.

This view is a hideous distortion of a form of Christian theodicy—of any theodicy remotely plausible. It also affirms precisely what Ivan (Dostoevski) and JS Mill denies is possible; that once one no longer sees as through a glass darkly we will be able to see how and why God is just and things were in a sense good despite the evil in the world. According to Ivan, for this to be possible, we should be able to imagine a scenario in which the evil that occurs can somehow be take as good when seen perhaps *sub specie aeternitatis* or from a God's eye perspective. But this is what Ivan, contrary to Swinburne, van Inwagen and Schlesinger, claims is impossible. The claim is that no 'reward', no retribution, can make things right.

Van Inwagen claims that the point of his essay is 'that the patterns of suffering that exist in the actual world do not constitute even a prima facie case [ie "evidence"] against theism'.[42] Whatever the merits of such a position, it is a repudiation of the traditional theistic problem of evil since both the existential and logical dimensions of the problem are generated by the recognition that the patterns of suffering do constitute a serious prima facie case against theism; not necessarily against the very existence of God but against conceiving of God as traditional theism conceives of God. Whatever one wants to say about Job's consternation or Ivan's rebellion, they were not simply confused or unenlightened (at least not on a traditional theistic account) in thinking that the patterns of evil constituted a prima facie case against theism. Furthermore, there is no reason for van Inwagen to make such a claim, since he can acknowledge that evil does present a prima facie case against theism but that such a case can be defeated. His assertion is misleading since he does not deny (1995b: 92–95) that evil presents a prima facie 'difficulty' for theism—but rather denies that evil constitutes prima facie 'evidence' against theism.[43] Yet surely the prima facie 'difficulty' is generated by the prima facie evidence 'against'—whether or not that evidence proves to be anything more than prima facie forceful or even relevant?

---

42. Van Inwagen, 'The Problem of Evil, the Problem of Air, and the Problem of Silence', 70 n6.

43. Van Inwagen, 'The Problem of Evil, the Problem of Air, and the Problem of Silence', 92–95.

Van Inwagen takes on this objection. He asks rhetorically:

> But if a phenomenon is a 'difficulty' for a certain
> theory, does not that mean that it is evidence against
> that theory? Or if it is not evidence against that theory,
> in what sense can it raise a 'difficulty' for that theory?
> Are you not saying that it can be right to accept a
> theory to which there is counterevidence when there
> are competing theories to which there is no counter-
> evidence?[44]

That sounds good, but it is really a recipe for rejecting just about any
interesting theory. Just about any interesting theory is faced with
phenomena that make the advocates of the theory a bit uncomfortable.

Van Inwagen conflates the issue of 'evidence' against a theory with
the question of criteria for accepting or rejecting a theory. Who would
maintain that one should reject a theory merely because there is some
kind of evidence against it? Nothing in his account of why it is
important or practicable to accept some theories when 'faced with
phenomena that make the advocates of the theory a bit uncomfortable'
supports his distinction between 'difficulty' and 'evidence'. He seems
to be using 'evidence' (or rather 'evidence against') as synonymous
with 'evidence' that in fact renders a particular theory improbable
given what we know. But this is prescriptive and peculiar.[45] And what
van Inwagen means by 'difficulty' turns out to be nothing more than
evidence that proves to be merely prima facie evidence. Prima facie
evidence is, however, evidence nonetheless—and empirical arguments
seek to show that the evidence from evil is not just prima facie. Such
arguments seek to show that so-called defences, prima facie defences,
are not genuine defences because they are improbable given what we
know (eg Van Inwagen's account of natural evil is improbable given
what we know). And of course it is a gross distortion of the problem of
evil to suggest that theists are simply 'faced with phenomena [evil]
that make the advocates of the theory [theism] a bit uncomfortable'.

---

44. Van Inwagen, 'The Problem of Evil, the Problem of Air, and the Problem of
     Silence', 93.

45. The *American Heritage Dictionary* defines evidence as 'A thing or things helpful
     in forming a conclusion or judgment: *The broken window was evidence that a
     burglary had taken place. Scientists weigh the evidence for and against a
     hypothesis.*'

Van Inwagen misleadingly states another outrageous thesis that proves to be innocuous once he qualifies it. He says 'I argue that—from the point of view of traditional theism—among the states of affairs that have no explanation is the existence of evil: sin and death and disease . . . I argue also that many particular evils—the existence of the rabies virus . . . Have no explanation. (That is: the existence of these things is not a matter of metaphysical necessity; neither God nor any other rational being decreed or willed or brought about their existence . . .' But of course to say that 'the existence of these things is not a matter of metaphysical necessity' is a far cry from suggesting that from the point of view of traditional theism, evil, sin etc 'have no explanation'. The point of a theodicy is just to provide such justification *cum* explanation.[46]

Van Inwagen says:

> [T]hese difficulties do not render their beliefs irrational . . . they can acknowledge the difficulties . . . they might go on to offer some speculations about the causes of the phenomena that raise the difficulties . . . reasons God might have for allowing evil. Such speculations need not be (they almost certainly will not be) highly probably on the '-ism' in whose defence they are employed. And they need not be probable on anything that is known to be true, although they should not be improbable on anything that is known to be true. They are to be offered as explanations of the difficult phenomena that are, *for all anyone knows*, the correct ones. In sum, the way to deal with such difficulties is to construct defences . . . To show that an acknow-ledged difficulty with a theory is not evidence against it, it suffices to construct a defence that accounts for the facts that raise the difficulty . . . a defence [remember] may not be improbable, either on the theory in whose

46. Van Inwagen, *God, Knowledge and Mystery: Essays in Philosophical Theology*, 15.

cause it is employed or on anything we know to be
true.[47]

Constructing a defence that accounts for the facts that raise the
difficulty will only suffice to show that an acknowledged difficulty
with a theory is not evidence against it if the defence is genuine—that
is, if it is not improbable.[48] But of course what empirical arguments
seek to establish is the improbability, given what we know, of so-called
defences or theodicies. His own defence/theodicy concerning natural
evil is sheer fantasy against the background of science, history, and
geology.

Van Inwagen appears to be claiming that the theist is committed, a
priori, not to allow any evil or fact about evil or reflection on evil to
count as evidence against theism (ie how God is conceived). One can
always construct defences. His distinction between 'difficulty' and
'evidence' is Pickwickian. But Ivan's and Job's point—along with Mill
and Flew, is that the evil *must* count. When faced with the so-called
'difficulty' or evidence that evil presents for the theist, why should the
strategy of the theist be to construct defences? Neither Ivan nor Job
adopted such a strategy. Both deny that there can be a satisfactory
intellectually rational solution to the problem. Their strategy is to
existentially take the problem on board.

Van Inwagen's treatment of natural evil is even more difficult to
take seriously than Plantinga's. In attributing natural evil to the devil,
Plantinga reduces natural evil to a type of moral evil. Although the
notion of the devil as a force to be reckoned may have faded in more
'progressive' forms of Christianity, it is not difficult to see how such a

---

47.   Van Inwagen, 'The Problem of Evil, the Problem of Air, and the Problem of
       Silence', 93–94.
48.   The issue is more complex as van Inwagen ('The Problem of Evil, the Problem of
       Air, and the Problem of Silence', 94) points out. 'A defence may not be
       improbable, whether on the theory in whose cause it is employed or on anything
       we know to be true. In a particular case, it may be that no one can think of any
       hypothesis that satisfies these two conditions, and what was a mere difficulty for a
       theory will thereby attain to the status of evidence against the theory . . . two or
       more difficulties may jointly constitute evidence against a theory, even if none of
       them taken individually counts as evidence against it. This could be the case if the
       defences that individually 'handle' the difficulties are inconsistent, or if—despite
       the fact that none of the defences taken individually is improbable—their
       conjunction is improbable.'

notion might be regarded seriously in a context in which one believes in angels and other supernatural beings. Furthermore, as I see it there is no prima facie conflict between belief in angels and devils on the one hand and the story of the history of things that evolutionary biology, cosmology and other science presents us with on the other. But van Inwagen's story does conflict with science, cosmology and history. He claims that (i) natural events like tornadoes were present even before the fall and, (ii) for all we know, were and still are, necessarily present given what the laws of nature must be. This latter claim is a conjecture that he says has support from some scientists.[49] He couples the plausible assertion that tornadoes and certain viruses etc are not evil in themselves with the far-fetched claim that tornadoes etc resulted in evil only after the fall because—due to man's separation from God—human beings became cognitively impaired in such a way that they were no longer able to avoid natural occurrences like tornadoes and killer viruses.

Although he explicitly states that he regards the creation story (Adam and Eve) as a myth, it is hard to see how his view concerning natural evil can be consistent with what we know about the evolution of the species, the history of the earth etc.[50] Just what aspect of the

---

49. Van Inwagen, 'The Problem of Evil, the Problem of Air, and the Problem of Silence', 78–81.

50. 'To allay the possible curiosity of some readers, I will mention that I regard the story of Adam and Eve in Genesis as a myth, in the sense that, in my view, it is not a story that has come down to us via a long historical chain of tellings and retellings that originated with the testimony of participants in the events it describes. In my view, the rebellion of creatures against God happened far too long ago for any historical memory of it to have survived to the present day' (van Inwagen, 'The Magnitude, Duration, and Distribution of Evil: A Theodicy', 100 n4). But elsewhere (106) he claims that his account of natural evil being a result of the fall is a kind of 'just-so story'. Is it a just-so story or is it an actual historical event? Apparently, the two are not incompatible according to van Inwagen. 'Dennett's just-so stories are tales told to illustrate possibility, tales told against a background that may be described as the standard model of evolution. My just-so story is of a similar sort, but the "background" is provided by what I have described as "the data of Christian revelation"' (106 n7). Apparently van Inwagen is claiming that it is 'possible' that this is what actually historically happened and that this is consistent with Christian data. Is he serious? In which translation of the Bible is the idea that Adam and Eve or our historical ancestors, before rebelling against God, knew how to get away from earthquakes and avoid

creation story does van Inwagen regard as a myth if he claims that
there actually were people who, due to their living in harmony with
God, were able to avoid natural occurrences that would harm them?
Were there people on earth in some prehistoric and pre-fall time that
knew how to avoid killer viruses and how to avoid landslides and
earthquakes? Does the archaeological, geological and evolutionary
biological evidence support such claims? Van Inwagen has entered the
world of creation science.[51] It is a world and a treatment of evil that
relatively few believers would regard as a remotely plausible
constituent of a theodicy.

One of my particularly contentious theses is the claim that the
arguments about evil that I critique are indicative of the lack of vitality,
relevance and 'seriousness' of contemporary Christian analytic
philosophy of religion. I think I have illustrated why—at least so far as
the problem of evil goes—this is so. For one thing, the argument from
evil that they treat is, by and large, not the argument from evil that
concerns believers. For another thing, the fact that at least some of the
proposed solutions are, if I am correct, morally repugnant, means that
they will probably not be relevant to the concerns about evil that
ordinary believers have. (Go try to tell a concentration camp victim
that their suffering is not real in order to win them over.) In addition,
where their proposals are to the point (eg van Inwagen's modal

---

killer viruses? Van Inwagen's 'just-so story' really is on a par with how the tiger
got its stripes.

51.   Van Inwagen makes some surprising disclaimers that appear less remarkable and
perhaps even appropriate, after reading his account of natural evil. He says ('The
Magnitude, Duration, and Distribution of Evil: A Theodicy', 97), 'I do not claim
to be the first human being in history to have fathomed God's purposes. Nor do I
claim to be the recipient of a special revelation from God; I do not claim to be a
prophet whom God has charged with the task of disseminating an explanation of
His ways. The method of this essay is simply philosophical reflection on the data
of Christian revelation—or, more exactly, on what one tradition holds (in my
view, correctly) to be the data of Christian revelation.' Van Inwagen is not
specific about the 'data of Christian revelation' or tradition he is referring to
except to say it is 'Christian'. But Christian analytic philosophers of religion
frequently play fast and loose with terms like 'tradition' (ie what tradition? whose
tradition? 'data' according to whom? and they make historical claims that are
simply false. Take a notable example: To base 'Calvinistic or Reformed
epistemology'—specifically the idea that belief in God can be a 'properly basic
belief'—on anything that Calvin or Luther thought is false—as I have argued
above.

scepticism), they are elaborations or mutations on old themes.[52] But if they have mistaken the problem—discussing something largely irrelevant instead—and if their solutions involve proposals that must be rejected on moral grounds, how could their concerns possibly be vital or taken seriously?

4. Hearing God

In *Divine Discourse*[53] Wolterstorff addresses the epistemological question of how beliefs that God speaks 'are to be appraised' (p 261). He considers the case of a woman who believes that God spoke to her (pp 274–5) and he claims that she is 'entitled' to the belief—'entitled' partly on the basis of her other 'background beliefs' and because a psychologist told her that nothing was wrong with her. '[A] person is *entitled* to his belief that p just in case S believes p, and there's no doxastic practice D pertaining to p such that S ought to have implemented D better than S did . . .the obligations in question are *situated* obligations . . . a function of various aspects of the particular situation of the person in question' (p 272). On Wolterstorff's account anyone may be entitled to believe anything given a certain context, and a set of 'background beliefs'. Even if this is true, all it does is covertly obfuscate the real issue.

In the case of the woman who believes God is speaking to her, the relevant philosophical question has to do with objective justification and the notion of rationally acceptable evidence rather than entitlement. Consider William Alston's account of justified belief. '[B]eing justified in believing that p is for that belief to be based on an objectively adequate ground, one that is (fairly) strongly indicative of the truth of the belief' (p 267).[54] How one might distinguish a veridical experience of being spoken to by God, and be justified in believing the experience to be veridical, from cases of nonveridical experiences and unjustified belief? It *sounds* illuminating to say that she is entitled to believe God spoke to her, but once clear about the nature of 'entitlement' it is evident that it is not. For all that Wolterstorff has

---

52. Cf, HJ McCloskey, HJ 'God and Evil', *The Philosophical Quarterly* 10 (1960): 97–114; *God and Evil* (The Hague: Martinus Nijhoff 1974).

53. Nicholas Wolterstorff, *Divine Discourse: Reflections on the Claim That God Speaks*.

54. William Alston, *Perceiving God* (Ithaca: Cornell University Press, 1991), 99.

said, the 'Yorkshire Ripper' is also 'entitled' to believe that God spoke to him--and may be correct in his belief. So too may Margaret Thatcher if she believes, as some others undoubtedly believe and are 'entitled' to believe, that God speaks to her. They could have gone to the same Harvard Health Plan psychologist as the woman in Wolterstorff's example, believed they were being commanded by a loving God, and judged that 'accepting that the experiences are veridical, have the consequences that one would expect if the experiences were indeed of God speaking' (277).[55]

5. Conclusion

It is possible, of course, to treat the arguments discussed above as separate and discreet—and to examine them independently on their merits. Perhaps there is reason to do that—and indeed that is just what I have done above—though in my view some of them seem unworthy of serious consideration. Nevertheless, a critique of those arguments has not been my primary purpose. My purpose, instead, is to step back from these arguments in their particularity and to see what can be gleaned from such samples about the state of contemporary philosophy of religion generally.

There seems to be a view—a view if not prevalent or representative (though it probably is both prevalent and representative), that is at least widely held: that the advent of Christian analytic philosophy of religion with its sophisticated recourse to logic, epistemology, and metaphysics, has been good for philosophy of religion. Generalising from a biblical hermeneutics that essentially shuns over a hundred years of biblical scholarship, the treatment of the problem of evil and views on religious experience just discussed, it is clear why I do not think this is so. Like van Inwagen[56] I too have 'a moral for students of the problem of evil'. Look to the original (classic) statements of the problem in order to understand it. Do not be taken in by contemporary approaches that fundamentally alter or obfuscate the problem. Above all, ask yourselves whether alleged solutions are moral solutions—and get serious.

55.   Cf, Michael Levine, 'Can There Be Self-Authenticating Experiences of God?', *Religious Studies*, 19 (1983): 229–234.
56.   Peter van Inwagen, 'The Place of Chance in a World Sustained by God', 42–65, 65. See note 25 above.

God, God* and God'

Graham Oppy

One family of challenges to theistic belief derives from considerations concerning the claim that there is an omnipotent, omniscient, eternal, perfectly free, *perfectly evil* sole creator of the universe *ex nihilo*.[1] These challenges begin with the claim that a case can be made for the existence of this being—call it God*—which 'parallels' the case which can be made for the existence of God. (Perhaps one might think that it would be more accurate to say that the claim is that the case for God* is just as good or bad as the case for God, and that part of the case for God* is contrived simply by mimicking or parallelling the case for God. For, *prima facie* at least, it seems that there are extra wrinkles which are needed in the case of God* to construct arguments from Scripture, or revelation, or religious experience, or religious authority, etc. However, proponents of the challenges to theism which are under consideration ought to reply that the kinds of 'evidence' adverted to here are equally well explained on the hypothesis that God exists—where the explanation goes via God's good intentions to help us—and on the hypothesis that God* exists—where the explanation goes via God*'s evil intentions to harm us. I shall suppose that we should allow this generous construal of the notion of a 'parallel' case, and that no harm will follow from this concession.)

---

1.   See, for example E Madden and P Hare, *Evil and the Concept of God* (Springfield ILL: C Thomas, 1968), S Cahn, 'Cacodaemony', *Analysis*, Volume 37 (1976): 69–73, E Stein, 'God, the Demon and the Status of Theologies', *American Philosophical Quarterly* Volume 27 (1990): 163–7, C New, 'Antitheism', *Ratio* Volume 6 (1993): 36–43, C Daniels, 'God, Demon, Good, Evil', *Journal of Value Enquiry* (1997): 177–81. Also, compare discussions of 'the Perverse God', in the literature on Pascal's wager (for references, see J Jordan, *Gambling on God: Essays on Pascal's Wager* (Lanham: Rowman and Littlefield, 1994)), and discussions of a-being-than-which-none-worse-can-be-conceived in the literature on ontological arguments (for references, see G Oppy, *Ontological Arguments and Belief in God* (New York: Cambridge University Press, 1995)).

One kind of response to this family of challenges on behalf of theistic belief would be to deny that the mimicking *arguments* are genuinely parallel—eg to claim that the ontological or cosmological or teleological or . . . argument for God is stronger than the corresponding argument for God*, or that the problem of evil is a weaker argument against God than the problem of good is against God*. It seems to me that the kind of response looks *prima facie* rather unpromising; in any case, I propose to proceed under the *pro tem* assumption that this kind of response won't work. (Those who disagree with my judgment here should for now take me to conducting a 'conditional' investigation: what can be said in response to these kinds of challenges to theistic belief if one concedes that the mimicking arguments for God* do genuinely parallel the traditional arguments for God?) Instead, I shall focus attention on a line of response which aims to establish that there are reasons for thinking that the concept of God* is incoherent in a way in which the concept of God is not. In particular, I shall consider the suggestion that the notion of an omniscient and perfectly evil being can be shown to be incoherent in ways which tend not at all to establish that the notion of an omniscient and perfectly good being is incoherent. If this suggestion is correct, then—other things being equal (as the proponents of the objection hold that they are!)—it seems that the hypothesis that God exists is clearly to be preferred to the hypothesis that God* exists.

I propose to argue that, even if these counter-arguments do establish that the hypothesis that God exists is clearly to be preferred to the hypothesis that God* exists, this is not enough to show that theists are home free—for there are many other alternative Gods for whom 'parallel' cases could be constructed, and for which this particular counter-argument is ineffective. I shall then go on to consider the consequences of this claim for the status of the debate between theists and their opponents. (I shall also argue that there are serious questions to be raised about the counter-arguments against God*. However, I shall not place too much emphasis on these questions in this paper.) In order to get to these considerations, some preliminary scene-setting is required.

I

For the purposes of this paper, I shall suppose that *theists* are those who are committed to the claim that there is an omnipotent, omniscient, eternal, perfectly free, perfectly good, sole creator of the universe *ex nihilo*. Moreover, I shall suppose that an equivalent statement of this first supposition is that *theists* are those who are committed to the claim that God exists.[2] Some people who choose to call themselves 'theists' may wish to vary the defining description which I have used here; however, provided that we agree that God is at least omnipotent, omniscient and perfectly good—and that no other being has any of these properties—this disagreement will not affect any of the subsequent discussion.

At a first stab, we might suggest that to believe a proposition is to assign it a probability strictly greater than fifty per cent; that to disbelieve a proposition is to assign it a probability strictly less than fifty per cent; and that to suspend judgment on a proposition is to assign it a probability of exactly fifty per cent. However, it is unrealistic to suppose that we always assign perfectly precise numerical probabilities to propositions. Suppose instead that the probability that one assigns to a proposition is vague over an interval (p, q).[3] Then a second stab would be this: to believe a proposition is to take p strictly greater than fifty per cent, to disbelieve a proposition is to take q strictly less than fifty per cent and to suspend judgment on a proposition is to take p less than or equal to fifty per cent and q greater than or equal fifty per cent. No doubt there is room for further refinement.[4] However, supposing that this second stab will be

---

2. This assumption about 'equivalence' skates over a number of tricky issues: what sense of equivalence do I have in mind? what analysis of singular terms am I presupposing? am I assuming that there can be 'descriptive names'? and so on. For the purposes of this paper, I do not think that any harm will come if we suppose that 'God' is simply an abbreviation—hence substitutable in all non-quotational contexts—for the given description, even though in fact it seems pretty clear that this claim is false.

3. No doubt we do sometimes assign precise probabilities to propositions. We can represent these precise assignments by degenerate intervals (r, r).

4. For discussion of some of the issues involved, see A Hajek, 'Agnosticism Meets Bayesianism' (forthcoming). Note that the view outlined in the main text has the resources to accommodate intuitions about 'leanings'—eg the interval (10, 51)

adequate for our purposes, we shall have: a *theist* assigns a probability to the claim that God exists which is vague over an interval which is bounded below by fifty per cent; an *atheist* assigns a probability to the claim that God exists which is vague over an interval which is bounded above by fifty per cent; and an *agnostic* assigns a probability to the claim that God exists which is vague over an interval which includes fifty per cent. (Clearly, there is at least one other category —namely, those who assign no probability to the claim that God exists. For want of a better term, I shall call such persons *innocents*.)

I shall assume that the primary purpose of arguments is to change minds. That is, I shall suppose that the primary purpose of theistic arguments is to convert atheists, agnostics, and innocents to theism. (Likewise, the primary purpose of atheistic arguments is to convert theists, agnostics and innocents to atheism; and the primary purpose of agnostic arguments is to convert theists, atheists and innocents to agnosticism. I take it that there can be no innocent arguments. I shall henceforth concentrate on the theistic case—but the same consid-erations will apply, *mutatis mutandi*, to agnosticism and atheism.) A really successful theistic argument would be one which required anyone, on pain of irrationality, to become a theist. However, any argument which required some reasonable people to revise up the bounds of probability which they assign to the proposition that God exists would count as having some degree of success. (An argument which forces a revision up of the bounds of probability is one which forces a revision from vagueness over the interval (p, q) to vagueness over the interval (p', q'), where either p' is greater than p, or q' is greater than q, or both.)[5]

---

represents agnosticism leaning towards atheism. Note, too, that it isn't obvious why one should want to say that (47, 49) represents agnosticism—it seems at least equally plausible to claim that it represents tentative atheism. Finally, note that the fact that adoption of the view outlined in the main text entails that belief is not closed under conjunction, is arguably a welcome consequence (in view of problems like the lottery paradox and the paradox of the prefect). Despite all this, the view is still subject to difficulties—but not ones which will impact on the current discussion.

5.   Of course, there are further distinctions which could be drawn here. The strongest successful argument would require everyone to assign probability (1, 1) to the claim that God exists. (Some proponents of ontological arguments have thought that their arguments did this.) Perhaps the weakest successful argument would be one which required some reasonable persons to revise up ever so slightly one of

In our assessment of arguments, we suppose that the targets of the arguments are rational belief-revisers—ie we suppose that the targets of the arguments are disposed to revise or update their beliefs in accordance with the canons of rational belief revision. Of course, exactly what these canons are is a matter of considerable dispute. (For example, Bayesians hold that updating must proceed by way of conditionalisation.) And an even more controversial question is whether there are further constraints to be placed upon reasonable sets of belief. (For example, some Bayesians hold that reasonable sets of beliefs are regular—ie do not assign probabilities vague over the degenerate intervals (0, 0) and (1, 1) to anything other than *a priori*, necessary, analytic falsehoods and *a priori*, necessary, analytic truths respectively. However, Bayesians are characteristically loathe to add much in the way of constraints on prior probabilities.) For my purposes, I shall suppose that we do not need to worry about further constraints on sets of beliefs: if a person who is disposed to revise or update their beliefs in accordance with the canons of belief revision has an unreasonable set of beliefs, then there are considerations which can be presented to them which will force them to revise or update their beliefs (in ways which remove the unreasonableness). Of course, there is bound to be some idealisation here: actual people are reasonable to a greater or lesser extent at different times, and reasonableness is perhaps only one amongst several desiderata which actual belief sets aim to satisfy. So we idealise the targets of the arguments in some ways: we demand that they care about the reasonableness of their beliefs (at least with respect to the questions at issue), etc. However, we are also bound to use the actual judgments of what we take to be reasonable people—including, no doubt, ourselves—as a guide to the responses of our 'ideal' reasonable agents (for what else could we use?).

Various potential pitfalls loom. Sometimes when you disagree with me, I take this as evidence that you are subject to failings of rationality.

---

the bounds on the interval which represents their doxastic attitude towards the probability that God exists. (Of course, being a weakly successful argument in this sense might not be much of a recommendation of an argument—particularly if we don't insist on much in the way of constraints on reasonable prior probabilities.) And there is a wide range of possibilities in between. It is beyond our current concerns to pursue this kind of taxonomy here.

Other times, when you disagree with me, I just say that this is one of those things about which reasonable people can differ. It is hard to say how we draw the line between these kinds of cases. I am inclined to think that, at least *pro tem*, it should be conceded that there can be reasonable atheists, agnostics, theists and innocents (even under certain kinds of idealisations). Certainly, my own experience suggests to me that clever, thoughtful and insightful reasonable people can belong to any of these categories. At any rate, I shall begin by supposing that one should think that the dialectical situation is some- thing like this: reasonable theists present arguments for the existence of God to reasonable non-theists, who then offer the parallel arguments involving God* in reply. All parties to the debate are presumed to be dispositionally rational, ie disposed to revise their beliefs in accordance with the canons of belief revision. We shall perhaps need to rethink this conception of the dialectical situation later on. But, for now, we can turn our attention to the details of the arguments given by the participants in the debate.

II

Various recent authors have contended that there are difficulties for theism which arise from consideration of the claim that God*—an omnipotent, omniscient, eternal, perfectly free, *perfectly evil* sole creator of the universe *ex nihilo*—exists. These alleged difficulties are of at least two quite different kinds, which need to be carefully distinguished.

One suggestion is that there is an argument *against* belief in God—ie an argument against theism—which can be based upon consideration of God*. Roughly, this argument goes as follows: There is no more reason to believe in God than there is to believe in God*. (Every consideration which can be adduced in favour of God counts equally in favour of God*; and every consideration which can be adduced against God counts equally against God*). But, in circum- stances in which there is no more nor less reason to believe in God than there is to believe in God*, it would be positively irrational to believe in God. So it is wrong to believe in God—there ought to be no theists.

Another suggestion is that there is a *reply* to theistic arguments for belief in God which can be based upon consideration of God*. Roughly, this reply goes as follows: Every argument for God can be paralleled by an equally compelling argument for God*. So no one who is not already a theist has any more reason to believe in God then they do to believe in God*. But, in these circumstances, it would be irrational to come to believe in God on the basis of theistic arguments. So no non-theists should be persuaded by theistic arguments to change their minds and come to believe in God.

Since God* is typically invoked by non-theists in discussions in which they are replying to theistic arguments, there is often uncertainty about just what the arguments involving God* are intended to establish. After all, one very good way to reply to your argument for the conclusion that p is to provide a compelling argument that not p. So, even though it would suffice for the purposes of replying to theistic arguments to show that non-theists ought not to be persuaded by theistic arguments to change their minds and come to believe in God, it would also be (more than) enough for these purposes to show that there ought not to be any theists. In any case, even if actual debates sometimes involve confusion about these issues, the theoretical points are clear enough: there are two quite different contexts in which arguments involving God* appear—and different considerations must be appealed to in the assessment of these arguments in these different contexts.

Having noted these two different uses to which non-theists might put arguments involving God*, I shall now put this distinction aside. (It would only needlessly complicate the discussion to try to take it into account here.) However, we shall return to it later.

III

In the face of the challenges raised by God*, one might be tempted to argue in something like the following way: Suppose we grant that there is such a thing as moral knowledge (and hence that there is such a thing as moral belief, properly so-called). Suppose we grant further that there is a necessary connection between moral belief and motivation—moral beliefs are necessarily motivating in such a way that one can only believe that an action is good or right if one is inclined to do or to approve that action, other things being equal. Then it seems that we have the basis for an argument that there can be no such being as God*. On the one hand, God* is supposed to be omniscient. Hence, in particular, if there is moral knowledge, then God* knows—and hence believes—every moral truth. But then, if moral beliefs are necessarily connected to motivation, it follows that

God* is motivated to pursue the good and the right—and that is inconsistent with the claim that God* is perfectly evil.

An argument which bears some resemblance to the one just given is provided by Daniels.[6] Daniels argues in the following way: It is a conceptual truth that everyone most wants what is good—and hence it is also a conceptual truth that everyone most shuns what is bad. But it follows from this that no-one can knowingly do what is bad—and from this it follows that God* cannot exist.

Daniels' argument is subject to some immediate difficulties. In particular, it seems that there are many different ways of understanding the claim that everyone most wants what is good; but it is far from clear that there are ways of understanding this claim on which it is both true and yet also entails that God* cannot exist. First, there are questions about how to understand 'most wants'—does the claim concern the strength of first-order desires, or the content of all-things-considered desires, or the content of interests objectively conceived (so that one can be completely oblivious to what it is that one 'most wants')? Second, there are questions about how to understand 'good'—does the claim concern what is good by one's own lights ('what seems to one to be good', 'what seems to one to be good now'), or what is good by some more objective standard ('what is good from the standpoint of eternity')? Putting together these claims in different ways yields statements of quite different standing, ranging all the way from ostensible tautologies—'what one wants most now all things considered is what one wants most now all things considered'—to obvious falsehoods— 'what one most strongly desires is (and must always be) what is good from the standpoint of eternity'.

In order to get an objection to the existence of God*, it seems that what Daniels needs is the claim that 'what one desires, all things considered, is (and must always be) what is good from the standpoint of eternity'. After all, if the requirement of perfect goodness is to have any bite, it must require conformity to some kind of objective standard (I am not perfectly good just because I always do what is good by my lights!). But mundane considerations about weakness of will and our moral failings show immediately that it is not true that what we desire, all things considered, is (and must always be) what is good from the standpoint of eternity. Perhaps there is some further difficulty with the idea that there might be a being which always desired, all things

---

6.   See C Daniels, *op cit.*

considered, that which is worst from the standpoint of eternity—but it is not at all obvious what this difficulty is (and there seems to be no way of repairing Daniels' argument in order to demonstrate it). Henceforth, then, I shall concentrate on the argument from moral cognitivism which I outlined above.

IV

The argument against God* presented at the beginning of the previous section has some controversial premises. Not everyone agrees that there is moral knowledge, moral truth and moral belief. (Some philosophers have held that knowledge does not entail belief. Given this implausible claim, and the further implausible claim that it is only moral belief, and not moral knowledge, which is essentially motivating, one could claim that the argument is invalid—God* might be omniscient and yet have no moral beliefs! Other philosophers have held—on independent grounds whose nature need not concern us here—that God* has no beliefs at all. Again, one might try to use this view to undermine the argument against God* while not disputing the truth of the premises of the argument. However, it seems to me that, if one is disposed to think that moral beliefs are essentially motivating, then one ought also to think that moral knowledge is essentially motivating, even if one holds that knowledge does not entail belief. At any rate, it seems to me that the prospects for this kind of reply to the argument against God* are not very bright.)

Famously, Humeans deny that there can be essentially motivating beliefs—it is desires which are essentially motivating states, but beliefs and desires are distinct existences—and hence they either deny that moral beliefs are essentially motivating, or else they deny that there is any such thing as moral belief (properly so-called). If one accepts that moral beliefs are not essentially motivating, then the argument against God* collapses—why shouldn't God* prefer the destruction of the world to the scratching of his little finger, even though he knows perfectly well that this is wrong? And if one accepts that there is no such thing as moral belief (properly so-called), then of course there is no such thing as moral knowledge (properly so-called)—and hence there is no reason why there should not be an omniscient yet completely immoral being.

There are other routes to the claim that there is no (such thing as) moral knowledge. It is a commonplace that many philosophers have been error-theorists or non-cognitivists about moral discourse. If there are no moral propositions or properties—or if there are moral properties and propositions, but the properties are necessarily uninstantiated and the propositions are necessarily false—then there can be no question of moral knowledge. If what we take to be expression of moral knowledge is merely the expression or projection of our emotions or desires or preferences, then there is no truth-apt content to ground talk of moral truth and moral knowledge. From a number of currently occupied and often-defended standpoints in meta-ethics, the argument against God* is plainly mistaken.

Of course, these meta-ethical questions are enormously controversial. If the point of the arguments involving God* is to persuade theists to change their minds, then that argument can only be sustained if these controversial views can also be defended. (It seems plausible to me to think that theists are unlikely to be error-theorists or non-cognitivists about ethics. Perhaps, indeed, we have here an argument that they ought not to be error-theorists or non-cognitivists about ethics.) On the other hand, if the point of these arguments is simply to respond to theistic arguments for God, then the controversial status of these views is less pressing. (If one is firmly persuaded of the correctness of an error-theoretical or non-cognitivist treatment of ethics, why shouldn't one rely on this persuasion in replying to arguments for the existence of God?) Perhaps it would be nice to have a response which relied on less controversial assumptions, but it seems perfectly satisfactory nonetheless.

V

The argument involving God* is only one of a family of arguments (or challenges) which can be made to theism. Suppose we accept—on the basis of the argument given above, together with our allegiance to moral cognitivism—that there can be no such being as God*. There are still other beings which raise problems for theism. Consider, for example, God'. God' is a being who is as much like God as can be, except that God' is perfectly evil. Given the concessions just made, God' is neither omniscient nor omnipotent—there is moral knowledge which God' does not possess, and moral actions which God' is unable to perform. (Perhaps there are moral questions which God' is unable to answer. Whether or not this is so depends on tricky questions about the supervenience of the moral on the non-moral which I shall not consider here.) Nonetheless, God' is *very* powerful and *very* knowledgeable—and so the question arises whether there is a substantially stronger case to be made for the existence of God' than there is to be made for the existence of God.

It seems to me to be plausible to suggest that the case for God' which parallels the traditional case for God is about as good as the corresponding parallel case for God*. Given the concessions which we have made concerning moral cognitivism, it seems plausible to claim that God' is a perfectly evil being (a being than which none more evil can be consistently conceived). Consequently, it seems clear that we can develop parallels to familiar ontological, cosmological and teleological arguments for God. In the case of other familiar theistic arguments—moral arguments, arguments from religious experience, arguments from scripture, arguments from testimony to religious miracles, and so on—the arguments are not so much 'parallel' arguments as they are competing arguments of comparable cogency. (So, for example, if there really is religious experience as of a perfectly good God, this is just the kind of deception in which you would expect a perfectly evil being to engage.) There are many details to be argued over here—just as in the case of the arguments for God*—but I shall proceed under the assumption that the case for God' is pretty much as good as the case for God*.

Perhaps there is some 'flaw' in the case for God' which resembles the difficulty that moral cognitivism raises for God*. It seems doubtful that non-theists who wish to run the kind of line which is being pursued here ought to be very concerned about this possibility. After all—as Hume observed in his *Dialogues Concerning Natural Religion*—there are clearly many, many alternative hypotheses which one could formulate about the attributes of a sole creator of the universe (especially if we allow that a 'sole creator' can be a committee, or a body corporate, or the like). For many of these conceptions, one can construct a case which parallels—or at least robustly competes with—the traditional case for God. So, even if the case for God' fails, there are plenty of standbys waiting in the wings. (Perhaps you might think that it is obvious that the case for these standbys cannot be as strong as the case for God* or God'. However, we haven't yet seen what kind of objection might be made to the case for God'; as things stand—contrary to what one might have initially expected—the case for God' might be stronger than the case for God*. Perhaps there are other Gods out there for which the case is stronger still.) And, in any case, we have yet to see whether there is any comparable objection to the case for God'.

VI

Once God' and his ilk appear on the horizon, one might wonder whether it was such a good idea to pursue the moral cognitivism objection to God*. If there is to be a defence of God against the proliferating alternatives, it seems likely that it will not proceed piecemeal. (Of course, there might be a mixed strategy—knock out virtually all of the alternatives with a general argument, and then mop up the very small number of recalcitrant cases which remain. However, I shall start from the optimistic standpoint which supposes that there is a pure general strategy which can succeed.)

What kind of general defence might there be? I suspect that the best bet at this point is to invoke some kinds of considerations concerning simplicity, or opposition to scepticism, or insistence on believability, or the like. The hypothesis that God exists is simpler than the hypothesis that any of the alternative Gods exists, and this is a reason to prefer it to them, other things being equal (as they apparently are!). The hypothesis that one of the alternative Gods exists is a kind of sceptical hypothesis, which is doxastically parasitic on the hypothesis that God exists. (Whenever one has an explanation or theory, one can cook up alternative explanations or theories which 'work' equally well. Consequently, one can only avoid scepticism if one is prepared to accept that these cooked-up theories and explanations can be set aside.) The hypothesis that God exists is a live and believable hypothesis, unlike the hypotheses concerning the alternative Gods; since no-one could take these alternatives seriously, we are warranted in setting them aside. And so on.

Of course, the above list of considerations is rather heterogeneous: it may be that God* is not ruled out by the simplicity test even though it is ruled out by the others. Moreover, none of the considerations has been developed in any detail. (There are notoriously difficult questions about criteria for simplicity, criteria for determining when explanations and theories have been gerrymandered, reasons for thinking that unbelievability is a good ground for ruling out hypotheses, and so on.) However, I shall suppose that we have enough to be going on with.

VII

At this point, I think that we need to recall the two different uses to which non-theists might put arguments involving God*, God', and their ilk. Suppose, first, that non-theists are only interested in defending themselves against theistic arguments—ie they have no (immediate) interest in persuading theists to give up their belief in God. In this case, it seems to me, it is clear that the invocation of God*, God' etc does make prosecution of the theistic case much more difficult. On the one hand, a much more substantial burden is incurred if one undertakes to persuade non-theists to give up on ethical non-cognitivism (and other ostensibly acceptable philosophical views which must be advanced in order to construct arguments to defeat particular alternative Gods). And, on the other hand, the claims about simplicity, gerrymandering, etc seem unlikely to have much force since, in an important sense, simplicity and the appearance of gerrymandering are very much in the eye of the beholder. (More exactly, judgments about simplicity, gerrymandering, etc are sensitive to what else it is that one believes.) It seems to me, at any rate, that the claims about God, God*, God', and many other Gods besides, are pretty much on a par as far as simplicity, absence of gerrymander, and believability are concerned—and it also seems to me that most reasonable non-theists are likely to agree.

(Perhaps a useful point of comparison here is with what I shall call 'tools for prognostication'. It seems to me that hypotheses about the possibility of predicting the future using tea-leaves, crystal balls, sheep entrails, the constellations of the heavens, the writings of prophets, the utterances of trees, and so on are pretty much on a par as far as simplicity, absence of gerrymander, and believability are concerned. Adverting to these various different tools for prognostication is one good move to make in defending oneself against the arguments of someone who wishes to argue that one—but only one—of these tools yields reliable information about the future. Of course, one might well point out that this move is parasitic on the further assumption that there is no good evidence for—nor plausible mechanism which could be used to explain how one comes by—knowledge of the future (via the listed mechanisms). But exactly the same point can be made by non-theists against theists: by the lights of non-theists, there is no good evidence for—nor plausible mechanism which could be used to explain how one comes by—knowledge of God. It seems entirely natural to think that one who is disposed to claim that there is no good evidence for the existence of God will also be disposed to say that one might as well believe in God*, or God', or . . . given the available evidence. While these two claims are distinct, there is a clear sense in which they fit naturally together.)

Suppose, on the other hand, that proponents of the arguments involving God*, God' and their ilk are interested in attacking theists, ie in trying to persuade theists to give up their theism. Then it is much less clear that the invocation of God*, God' and their ilk adds substantially to the attack. After all, reasonable belief in God will fit into a network of beliefs which very likely conspire to produce the judgment that the hypothesis that God exists is simpler, less gerrymandered and more believable than the hypotheses about the existence of alternative Gods. At any rate, it seems to me that I have more reason to trust the verdicts of those theists whom I deem to be reasonable—ie more reason to suppose that the fact that these people make those judgments shows that those judgments can reasonably be made by reasonable people—than I have to insist that reasonable theists take on my judgments about the simplicity, etc of various hypotheses. (Moreover, I can note that those who are disposed to believe in God given the available evidence will naturally judge that it is much more plausible to suppose that God exists given the available evidence than it is to suppose that God*, or God', or . . . exists given the available evidence.)

By this point, readers are bound to have noticed that I have now committed myself to the claim that theists will not (and indeed ought not to) concede that the case for God can be paralleled by the case for God*, or God', or . . . , if what is meant by this is that they have no more reason to believe in God than there is reason to believe in alternative Gods given the available evidence. By the lights of theists, 'the case for God' must seem much superior to the case for alternative Gods—else, they would not be theists. So the *prima facie* appearances to which I alluded at the beginning of this paper are deceptive—there is a clear sense in which reasonable theists can and must deny that the case for God*, God', etc is as good as the case for God.

VIII

There are many problems here. The main one which we are now confronting is how to think about the epistemological and dialectical context in which the arguments under consideration are to be located. It is perhaps natural to think in the following way. A representative reasonable theist presents the case for believing in God to a representative reasonable non-theist. The non-theist responds by providing a parallel to the case just provided but which supports the existence of some alternative deity: God*, or God' or . . . The theist then is faced with the challenge of finding some difference between the case for God and the cases for the alternative Gods.

I suggest that one ought to be very suspicious about this talk of 'the case for God'. In the case of many things which we believe, the grounds which we have for those beliefs far outrun our abilities to articulate those grounds. (For example, it seems that it is no requirement of rationality that one ought to be able to recall the grounds for any belief which one has come to hold.[7]) Moreover, even in cases in which this is not so, it is often the case that the process of articulation could be extended indefinitely (there is always more which could be said). Consequently, talk about 'the case for God' too readily leads to confusion of epistemological and dialectical ('dialogical'?) questions which ought to be kept distinct.

I conclude—albeit tentatively (and without in any way supposing that the forgoing constitutes either an adequate discussion or defence)—that it may well be the case that theism and non-theism are both reasonable responses to the evidence which people have, and yet that any case which theists put forward for the existence of God can be 'paralleled' by cases for the existence of other Gods about which: (i) theists reasonably judge that the cases are not genuinely parallel (but often for reasons which they have not yet, and perhaps which they shall never have, successfully articulated); and (ii) non-theists reasonably judge that the cases are genuinely parallel (where this judgment is typically a natural expression of—or companion to—their

---

7.   See, eg, Harman (1986) for further discussion of this kind of consideration.

view that there is insufficient evidence for belief in the existence of God).[8]

---

8.   Two points in particular which need further work: (1) I do not think that my line of argument could be adapted to defend the reasonableness of belief in any hypothesis (eg I do not think that reasonable and suitably informed persons can believe in astrology). My judgment that there are reasonable theists whose belief in God is reasonable is crucial to my argument. (2) There is a distinction between descriptive and normative conceptions of 'reasonableness' which might have important consequences for my argument. (Why suppose that my intuitions about the reasonableness of my friends have any normative significance?) I hope to consider these issues elsewhere.

Whose Faith? Which Reason?

John Ozolins

Fides et Ratio explicitly claims that there is an objective truth and that revelation gives us certain knowledge about God and human salvation. Moreover, it argues that for an adequate theology a philosophical stance is needed which is not only sympathetic to its concerns but which also accepts the possibility of a rational explanation of the truth of the claims of faith. Thus, what is revealed by God can also be reached by a philosophical method which is prepared to admit that truth can be attained and is confident that there is an objective order in the world which can be discerned through the use of reason.

The following argument which arises on reflection on the claims of *Fides et Ratio* seems to lead to the elimination of reason in favour of faith alone. In outline, it may be put as follows: (1) The claim that there is one, true interpretation of revelation does not mean that at any particular historical moment we can be certain our understanding of revelation accords with the truth. (2) There is no privileged philosophical method which enables the truths of revelation to be confirmed through the use of reason. (3) Added to these, what might be meant by reasons in relation to the truths of revelation is not clear either and more generally, the notion of reason itself is far from unproblematic. The conclusion which can be drawn from these three premises is that it looks very much as if we are forced to rely very heavily on faith, rather than reason, in our understanding of what the truths of revelation claim. This does not force us back to fideism, however, if we take religious faith to have a similar structure to a scientific theory. By this we mean that religious beliefs have to be justified just as scientific beliefs have to be justified. Moreover, if we accept that knowledge forms a seamless web, then religious beliefs are as much a part of our overall theory of the world as scientific beliefs. In many respects religious beliefs are more fundamental than scientific beliefs because they address most immediately questions about our being in the world. As *Fides et Ratio* suggests, religious faith provides the impetus, as well as the ground, for the search for truth, but it is not divorced from the quest for knowledge and understanding of the natural and human world. This being so, religious propositions do not rest on a credulous acceptance of miracles and signs, but demand justification in the same way that we would demand it in the case of scientific propositions. It is this demand which allows us to escape fideism. What is offered here is a bare sketch of the issues which need to be addressed. An analysis of the connections between religious faith, scientific theory and an overall theory of the world is complex as what follows will show, but proposing that the structure of religious faith is similar to the structure of science provides us with a way of seeing the essential unity of knowledge and accounting for differences in religious beliefs. Moreover, it provides us with a way of systematically subjecting differing interpretations of faith claims within a faith tradition to objective scrutiny. It is also possible to see why different traditions are largely immune to change.

1. Whose faith: One true interpretation of revelation

The claim that there is one, true interpretation of revelation follows tautologously from the fact that it is given by God to the church, and so the truth is held within the faith community. Although revelation is complete it has not been made completely explicit and it remains for Christian faith to gradually grasp its full significance over the course of time.[1] Revelation itself is no body of doctrines or set of principles verbally communicated to us by God, but nevertheless language is central in proclaiming its significance for the people of God. *Dei Verbum* tells us that the 'plan of revelation is realized by deeds and words having an inner unity: the deeds wrought by God in the history of salvation manifest and confirm the teaching and realities signified by the words, while the words proclaim the deeds and clarify the mystery contained in them'.[2] Thus, although it is evident that revelation cannot be reduced to propositional statements, nevertheless it remains true that such statements provide a legitimate means of

---

1. 'Yet even if Revelation is already complete, it has not been made completely explicit; it remains for Christian Faith gradually to grasp its full significance over the course of centuries', and 'God has revealed Himself fully by sending His own Son, in whom he has established His covenant forever. The Son is His Father's definitive Word; so there will be no further Revelation after Him'. *Catechism of the Catholic Church* (Homebush: St Paul's, 1994), #66 and #73.

2. *Dei Verbum*, Dogmatic Constitution on Divine Revelation, 1965, #2.

giving it some conceptual form.[3] The difficulty, however, as *Fides et Ratio* acknowledges, is that it is in the interpretation of words and in discerning their meaning, not to mention their connection with the deeds of God in the history of salvation, that proves to be problematic. Thus, although the truth resides in the lived experience of the people of God, in the case of the truths of revelation as expressed by propositions in language, it is evident that more than one interpretation is possible and, since our assessment of them can only occur within a language, we cannot be sure that the interpretation we have of them is true. It is this difficulty and the demand, always, to give contemporary meaning to the word of God that has over the centuries prompted reflection, debate and the need for an authoritative assessment of competing interpretations.

The *Magisterium* of the church has the task of determining which interpretation ought to be accepted as authentic, but this is by no means a straightforward task and any pronouncement is always subject to revision or refinement. Over the course of 2000 years, the number of documents issued by bishops, councils and popes on doctrinal matters has been huge and it is no small undertaking to sort such documents into an order of importance. Some documents, pronouncements of ecumenical councils, for example, carry more weight than a letter from an individual bishop to his diocese. In determining what these documents mean, we not only have to understand them in their historical context, but also establish what they mean for us today. This hermeneutical work is far from easy.[4] Congar tells us that we need to recognise the historicity of every human conception and word. This applies even to the dogmas of councils and the very texts of the Scriptures. We approach truth, he says, we do not gain it in one go and we need the inputs of others.[5] Having the right philosophical tools for the task is crucial, but will not guarantee that we have reached a final truth.

---

3.   R Gaillardetz, *Teaching with Authority* (Collegville: The Liturgical Press, 1997), 74–75.

4.   FA Sullivan, *Creative Fidelity: Weighing and Interpreting Documents of the Magisterium* (Sydney: EJ Dwyer, 1996), 4–5.

5.   Y Congar, 'Towards a Catholic Synthesis', in *Who Has the Say in the Church?*, edited by J Moltmann, and H Küng (Edinburgh: T&T Clark, 1981), 70.

Fides et Ratio calls for a development of a metaphysics which is able to ground new developments in hermeneutics and the philosophy of language in order to create the opportunity for the truths of revelation to be expressed universally.[6] Although the church teaches that revelation is complete, nevertheless, all of what it means for us has not been given to us and, indeed, its fullness will not be revealed to us until Christ comes again. This is a faith claim in itself and furthermore, it is through faith that we are able to accept the presupposition that human language is capable of expressing divine and transcendent reality in a universal way. What this neatly reveals is the interdependence of faith and reason, since the philosophical tools that are to be adopted to express the truths of revelation themselves depend on faith.

Dei Filius asserts that there is a two-fold order of knowledge, we know one level by reason and the other by divine faith, but the divine mysteries can never be known fully by reason—*'we walk by faith and not by sight'*.[7] Faith takes priority over reason, even though there can be no real disagreement between faith and reason, since it is the same God who is the source of revelation as well as reason. Despite this, *Dei Filius* forbids the faithful from defending scientific conclusions which

---

6.   'The importance of metaphysics becomes still more evident if we consider current developments in hermeneutics and the analysis of language. The results of such studies can be very helpful for the understanding of faith, since they bring to light the structure of our thought and speech and the meaning which language bears. However, some scholars working in these fields tend to stop short at the question of how reality is understood and expressed, without going further to see whether reason can discover its essence. How can we fail to see in such a frame of mind the confirmation of our present crisis of confidence in the powers of reason? When, on the basis of preconceived assumptions, these positions tend to obscure the contents of faith or to deny their universal validity, then not only do they abase reason but in so doing they also disqualify themselves. Faith clearly presupposes that human language is capable of expressing divine and transcendent reality in a universal way canalogically, it is true, but no less meaningfully for that. (103) Were this not so, the word of God, which is always a divine word in human language, would not be capable of saying anything about God. The interpretation of this word cannot merely keep referring us to one interpretation after another, without ever leading us to a statement which is simply true; otherwise there would be no Revelation of God, but only the expression of human notions about God and about what God presumably thinks of us' (*Fides et Ratio*, 84).

7.   *Dei Filius*, chapter 4, #1–4.

are known to be contrary to the doctrine of faith. Faith claims are more fundamental ontological claims than empirically based scientific conclusions and, like any such claims, are less open to revision. If we want to maintain a strong unity of knowledge thesis then we give up scientific theories which contradict faith claims and so, if there are two levels of knowledge these are not equal, with what is known by faith taking precedence over what is known by reason. This does not mean that empirical scientific matters cannot change or deepen our understanding of faith claims. Since they reveal aspects of God's creation to us, they reveal the truth and so can help us understand faith claims—we have to be open to what science can reveal to us. The dangers of being too rigid about this are well known and do not need elaborating.[8]

The claims of the *Magisterium* to be able to definitively state what is within the tradition need to be examined since it may be the case that *even if we accept that it is able to do this*, this does not, in the end, prove to be sufficient to guarantee that we are able to understand what has been definitively promulgated. For example, neither the doctrine of transubstantiation nor the doctrine of infallibility, of particular interest in the discussion of how we can be guaranteed that what we understand by a particular faith claim is true, is able to be satisfactorily and without controversy clearly explained. More central mysteries such as the Incarnation can only ever be inadequately grasped and remain opaque to us.[9] Reason proves to be insufficient and the last yard has to be taken in faith. If this is so, then the possibility of reason providing us with a satisfactory explanation of the truth of the claims of faith is correspondingly weakened, since we cannot be sure that what we have provided a justification for is the true interpretation. There is no comfort to be taken here in the faith claim that the church is guaranteed by Jesus himself to possess the truth. Human beings are still left with the task of grappling with the mysteries of faith. The core of Christianity, 'the deposit of faith', is taken to be non-negotiable, but even this requires interpretation, since it is by no means easy to

---

8.   See, for example, the case of Galileo, as well as more modern cases such as theories of evolution. We need to be prepared to examine competing claims to see how they can be reconciled.

9.   St Paul tells us that now we see through a glass darkly. 1 Corinthians 13:12.

establish what is to be taken as central.[10] What is required is a faith assent. It is no wonder that the *Magisterium* talks of the need of the faithful to be meek of heart in accepting the church's teaching on various doctrinal and moral matters, rather than subjecting them to a hostile sceptical scrutiny.[11] The church has always taught that a conscience must be fully formed before a person should act, and this involves taking seriously the church's teaching on faith and morals as well as, it should be added, findings in other areas of knowledge. The church is aware of the possibility of different interpretations, but claims that its interpretation is authoritative—a claim rejected all too often, as various schisms and splits within the church have shown. A deeper problem which arises within a tradition are the different perspectives about important doctrinal matters which are possible and which are almost entirely dependent on the lived experience of a particular culture or time. For example, there is the contrast between understanding the Mass as a sacrifice and as a celebration[12], the sacrament of penance as confession and reconciliation.

The recourse to trust and faith in accepting a particular interpretation as authoritative is evident when the church makes a statement on doctrinal matters. *Lumen Gentium*, for example, says:

> Bishops who teach in communion with the Roman Pontiff are to be revered by all as witnesses of divine and Catholic truth; the faithful, for their part, are obliged to submit to their bishops' decision, made in the name of Christ, in matters of faith and morals, and to adhere to it with a ready and respectful allegiance of mind. This loyal submission of the will and intellect must be given, in a special way, to the authentic teaching authority of the Roman Pontiff, even when he does not speak ex cathedra in such

---

10.   See *Humani Generis*, #18 and #21.

11.   *Humani Generis* says: The truths that have to do with God and the relations between God and men, completely surpass the sensible order and demand self-surrender and self-abnegation in order to be put into practice and to influence practical life. Pius XII, *Humani Generis*, Encyclical Letter, Rome, 1950, #2.

12.   Understanding the church as a community—*koinonia*—is central to Vatican II and to the celebration of the unity of the faithful in Christ through the eucharist. See R Gaillardetz, *Teaching with Authority* (Collegville: The Liturgical Press, 1997), 8–14.

wise, indeed, that his supreme teaching authority be acknowledged with respect, and sincere assent be given to decisions made by him, conformably with his manifest mind and intention, which is made known principally either by the character of the documents in question, or by the frequency with which a certain doctrine is proposed, or by the manner in which the doctrine is formulated.[13]

In cases where there is limited ability to understand, the church urges us to loyally submit both our will and intellect, which is to say our reason, to authority.

Later in *Lumen Gentium*, the doctrine of infallibility which acts as a guarantee that that the church pronounces as being definitive is true, is expounded:

Although the bishops, taken individually, do not enjoy the privilege of infallibility, they do, however, proclaim infallibly the doctrine of Christ on the following conditions: namely, when, even though dispersed throughout the world but preserving for all that amongst themselves and with Peter's successor the bond of communion, in their authoritative teaching concerning matters of faith and morals, they are in agreement that a particular teaching is to be held definitively and absolutely.[40] This is still more clearly the case when, assembled in an ecumenical council, they are, for the universal Church, teachers of and judges in matters of faith and morals, whose decisions must be adhered to with the loyal and obedient assent of faith.[41][14]

Originally promulgated by Pius IX in 1870,[15] the doctrine has not been without considerable controversy and has itself been subject to

---

13.   *Lumen Gentium*, #25.
14.   *Ibid.*
15.   '. . . we teach and define as a divinely revealed dogma that when the Roman pontiff speaks EX CATHEDRA, that is, when, 1. in the exercise of his office as

interpretation. A broad interpretation can be made, as well as a narrow one.[16] For example, on a narrow view, the doctrine could be taken to mean that the pope does not need the agreement of the church on matters of faith and morals, either before or after any infallible pronouncement. That is, papal authority is emphasised to such an extent that infallibility is seen as a personal power of the pope to pronounce unerringly and arbitrarily on matters of faith and morals. The original definition of 1870 could be construed in this way. On the other hand, even though *Lumen Gentium* upholds the doctrine it is set in the context of the pope speaking, as head of the church, on behalf of the faithful. That is, he expresses a truth which is already within the communion of believers: 'This infallibility, however, with which the divine Redeemer wished to endow his church in defining doctrine pertaining to faith and morals, is co-extensive with the deposit of revelation, which must be religiously guarded and loyally and courageously expounded. The roman pontiff, head of the college of bishops, enjoys this infallibility in virtue of his office, when, as supreme pastor and teacher of all the faithful—who confirms his brethren in the faith (cf Lk 22:32)—he proclaims in an absolute decision a doctrine pertaining to faith or morals.[42] For that reason his definitions are rightly said to be irreformable by their very nature and not by reason of the assent of the church, in as much as they were made with the assistance of the Holy Spirit promised to him in the person of blessed Peter himself; and as a consequence they are in no way in need of the approval of others, and do not admit of appeal to any other tribunal. For in such a case the roman pontiff does not utter a pronouncement as a private person, but rather does he expound and defend the teaching of the Catholic faith as the supreme teacher of the universal church, in whom the church's charism of infallibility is

---

shepherd and teacher of all Christians, 2. in virtue of his supreme apostolic authority, 3. he defines a doctrine concerning faith or morals to be held by the whole church, he possesses, by the divine assistance promised to him in blessed Peter, that infallibility which the divine Redeemer willed his church to enjoy in defining doctrine concerning faith or morals. Therefore, such definitions of the Roman pontiff are of themselves, and not by the consent of the church, irreformable.' *Decrees of the First Vatican Council*, ch.4.

16.   G Denzler, 'Bulletin: The discussion about Bernhard Hasler's publications on the First Vatican Council', in *Who Has the Say in the Church?*, edited by J Moltmann and H Küng (Edinburgh: T&T Clark, 1981), 84.

present in a singular way.[43]'[17] Added to this is the recognition, firstly, of the role of the episcopate in the assent to what is proclaimed: 'The infallibility promised to the Church is also present in the body of bishops when, together with Peter's successor, they exercise the supreme teaching office. Now, the assent of the Church can never be lacking to such definitions on account of the same Holy Spirit's influence, through which Christ's whole flock is maintained in the unity of the faith and makes progress in it.[44]'[18] and secondly, though not subordinately, of the people of God: 'Furthermore, when the roman pontiff, or the body of bishops together with him, define a doctrine, they make the definition in conformity with revelation itself, to which all are bound to adhere and to which they are obliged to submit; and this revelation is transmitted integrally either in written form or in oral tradition through the legitimate succession of bishops and above all through the watchful concern of the roman pontiff himself—and through the light of the Spirit of truth it is scrupulously preserved in the church and unerringly explained.[45] The roman pontiff and the bishops, by reason of their office and the seriousness of the matter, apply themselves with zeal to the work of inquiring by every suitable means into this revelation and of giving apt expression to its contents;[46] they do not, however, admit any new public revelation as pertaining to the divine deposit of faith.[47]'[19] There is a much broader and richer understanding of the doctrine expressed here.

An obvious objection to the doctrine of infallibility is that it fails to lay to rest doubts and dissent about matters of faith and morals, for it cannot itself be thought to be infallible. That is, it cannot itself be held to be guaranteed to be free from error and so requiring the *fidei obsequio* to the truth by the faithful. Few papal pronouncements have been identified as expressing infallible dogmas, with only two, the dogma of the Immaculate Conception (1854) and the dogma of the Assumption of Mary (1950) being generally accepted as such.[20]

---

17.   *Lumen Gentium*, #25.

18.   *Ibid.*

19.   *Ibid.*

20.   FA Sullivan, *Creative Fidelity: Weighing and Interpreting Documents of the Magisterium* (Sydney NSW: EJ Dwyer, 1996), 83–88.

The church's history is full of controversies, errors and heretical views, with *Humanae Vitae* perhaps being the most famous recent example of controversy and one which continues to be in one way or another a source of conflict. Any comparative study of church teaching shows that there have been shifts and reinterpretations within doctrinal and moral matters also. Two examples are the church's teaching on capital punishment and the concept of a just war. This is as it should be, since we can expect our understanding of faith and morals to become deeper on reflection on accumulated human experience. Whatever way we think of the church, it is on a pilgrimage to the truth and the most we can say in answer to the question of whether we grasp the truth of revelation is 'not yet'.

This suggests that no present interpretation expresses the fullness of God's revelation and so we can conclude that the acceptance of the truth of any interpretation relies more heavily on faith than on reason. This is because in matters of interpretation we trust that the magisterium will be a sure guide and while there are good grounds for believing this, these do not provide us with the certainty which we crave. This could force us back to fideism, but as we shall see later does not.

2. Which reason I: No privileged philosophical method

Fides et Ratio stresses the importance of truth over and over again, since it is truth which plays a crucial role in how human beings negotiate the world and to establish what values are worth living their lives by.[21] This point is therefore crucial—knowing the truth enables us to be more fully human and so real fulfilment demands that we know what it is to be fully human. There are two difficulties here. Firstly, knowing

---

21. '"All human beings desire to know", (23) and truth is the proper object of this desire. Everyday life shows how concerned each of us is to discover for ourselves, beyond mere opinions, how things really are. Within visible creation, man is the only creature who not only is capable of knowing but who knows that he knows, and is therefore interested in the real truth of what he perceives. People cannot be genuinely indifferent to the question of whether what they know is true or not . . . It is essential, therefore, that the values chosen and pursued in one's life be true, because only true values can lead people to realize themselves fully, allowing them to be true to their nature. The truth of these values is to be found not by turning in on oneself but by opening oneself to apprehend that truth even at levels which transcend the person. This is an essential condition for us to become ourselves and to grow as mature, adult persons.' *Fides et Ratio*, 25.

what we mean by truth and secondly, how we can come to know the truth. These questions are not what I wish to tackle here, though what follows cannot be entirely understood without some assumptions about the nature of truth. According to *Fides et Ratio,* there is no privileged philosophical method which enables the truths of revelation to be confirmed through the use of reason.[22] This statement can be understood in two different ways, as suggesting that there are many different philosophical approaches which will enable truth to be attained or, pessimistically, as suggesting that there are no philosophical ways which will enable truth to be attained. The latter pessimistic view we can dismiss, for it would imply that reason can never enable the truths of revelation to be confirmed. We would be forced to rely on faith alone, contrary to what *Fides et Ratio* asserts. The former interpretation does not mean that all philosophical approaches enable the confirmation of the truths of revelation. Indeed, *Fides et Ratio* explicitly excludes certain philosophical viewpoints as being inimical to the task of explicating revelation because they have lost their concern for reflecting on the nature of being and instead have concentrated on epistemological questions shorn of their foundations in a belief in truth.[23] The conclusion we can draw is that there are only

---

22. In #49 *Fides et Ratio* explicitly states that the church has no philosophy of her own nor does she canonise any one particular philosophy in preference to others. This is at odds with *Humani Generis,* which explicitly mentions Thomism. See *Human Generis* #31.

23. '. . . Sundered from that truth, individuals are at the mercy of caprice, and their state as person ends up being judged by pragmatic criteria based essentially upon experimental data, in the mistaken belief that technology must dominate all. It has happened therefore that reason, rather than voicing the human orientation towards truth, has wilted under the weight of so much knowledge and little by little has lost the capacity to lift its gaze to the heights, not daring to rise to the truth of being. Abandoning the investigation of being, modern philosophical research has concentrated instead upon human knowing. Rather than make use of the human capacity to know the truth, modern philosophy has preferred to accentuate the ways in which this capacity is limited and conditioned.

'This has given rise to different forms of agnosticism and relativism which have led philosophical research to lose its way in the shifting sands of widespread scepticism. Recent times have seen the rise to prominence of various doctrines which tend to devalue even the truths which had been judged certain. A legitimate plurality of positions has yielded to an undifferentiated pluralism, based upon the

some philosophical methods which are candidates for the task of explicating revelation.

What would a metaphysics able to ground new developments in hermeneutics and philosophy of language which are capable of expressing the truths of revelation look like? Here the best guide, we are told, is St Thomas Aquinas.[24] This suggests that there is very little in modern philosophy which would serve as a basis for providing an alternate route to the truths of revelation. While it is plain that philosophy is not monolithic and that this is not the place for a thoroughgoing account of what philosophical candidates there are which are capable of providing a means of expressing revelation, there are different ways of doing philosophy which enable us to see different aspects of the problem of the human condition. This may be so even of a philosophical stance which assumes a defeasible account of truth, such as pragmatism. Of course the main point of the encyclical is that if a metaphysics does not allow for the possibility of truth, then it contradicts one of the first tenets of faith, namely that there is truth. As we have seen, revelation from God presupposes that God has revealed what is true to us—this follows necessarily from God's nature. A metaphysics which claims there is no truth must be ruled out.

Deflationary accounts of truth which do not dismiss truth but reduce it to warranted assertibility or rational acceptance can also be ruled out.[25] Given these different ways of understanding what truth is

---

assumption that all positions are equally valid, which is one of today's most widespread symptoms of the lack of confidence in truth.' *Fides et Ratio*, 5.

24. *Fides et Ratio* #43-#44. John Paul II reinforces the importance of Aquinas in his Apostolic Letter, *Inter Munera Academiarum*, 28 January 1999, saying, 'Merito quidem ille appellari potest "apostulus veritatis". Enimvero, Doctoris Angelici contuitus positus est in certitudine esse praecipuam concordiam inter fidem et rationem . . .' [Without doubt Aquinas deserves the title 'Apostle of Truth'. For certainly the thought of the Angelic Doctor consists in the conviction that there is a fundamental harmony between faith and reason.] And later, '. . . magistrum nostrae aetati efficiant Sanctum Thomam'. [St Thomas is a teacher for the present time.]

25. For some philosophers, warranted assertibility just is truth, since the purpose of belief is to be able to fulfil one's desires and so we are warranted in accepting those beliefs which are conducive to success. This is called *Zweckrationalität*— the sort of rationality displayed by the actions of someone who strives to attain his goals in a way calculated to achieve them. See A Plantinga, *Warrant: the Current Debate* (Oxford: Oxford University Press, 1993), 132–133. Warranted assertibility is parasitic on the concept of truth, since any explanation why we should

and that they are incompatible with a Thomistic account of truth, it is worth briefly examining whether they are incompatible with claims about the truth of what God has revealed to us. For example, consider the contrast between an assertion that there are certain truths, but we cannot know them fully because of our limited intellects, and an assertion that truth consists in what we know via our limited intellects, but because of this is always provisional. On the first account, there is truth, but it is unable to be known, on the second, there is only warranted assertibility. The first account has the advantage of being compatible with the faith claim that God would not deceive us, but in the examination of a particular proposition about what God has revealed has no advantages over warranted assertibility, since the same criteria are used for establishing whether the proposition is to be held to be true or whether it is accepted as warranted. Nevertheless, a deflationary account of truth such as warranted assertibility must be dismissed, for the notion of truth in *Fides et Ratio* is primarily concerned with truth as expressed by interpersonal relationships and in particular the truth that is found in the encounter with Jesus Christ.[26] That is, the claim that there is truth is embedded in a much wider and richer understanding of the world. This, however, takes us back to faith claims and a particular way of understanding the world which is not itself given to us by reason.

Aquinas himself holds that there is a twofold mode of truth, some truths that we can know by human reason and some truths about God that exceed the ability of human reason to know. He notes that even in the former case, the capacity of individual human beings varies and so there will be some individuals who will be unable to ever know the truth. Given that God is good, however, it is possible to know the truth about God through faith.[27] An obvious conclusion from this is that there can be no privileged philosophical method, since what truths there are will always exceed the capacity of reason to discover and hence whatever philosophical method of reasoning is employed it will never explain what is made known by faith without remainder.

---

accept warranted assertibility will need to assume the concept of truth in some form.

26. *Fides et Ratio*, #30–34.

27. Thomas Aquinas, *Summa Contra Gentiles*, translated by Anton C Pegis (New York: Doubleday and Co, 1955), Book I, chapters.3–5, 63–71.

The question, of course, is whether we have a problem if there is no central philosophical method which we can employ enabling the truths of revelation to be confirmed through the use of reason. It is evident from *Fides et Ratio* itself[28] and also *Aeterni Patris* that the church has not been backward in making use of a wide variety of philosophical methods in order to not only interpret revelation, but to also make it accessible to everyone. Thus, although Thomism may have some features which commend it as a model way of doing theology, it is not the only way of understanding revelation.[29] In recent times there has been much debate about the merits of Liberation Theology and whether Marxism is able to provide any insights into revelation, particularly in relation to the church's teaching on social justice. While there are a number of encyclicals which wholeheartedly condemn Marxism,[30] nevertheless, there are elements of Marxism which usefully provide a way of understanding the human condition and which resonate with the Christian concern for social justice. Leo XIII's great encyclical *Rerum Novarum*, for example, while condemning Marxism and Communism in the guise of Socialism, in its very strong call for justice for oppressed workers echoes the same concerns as the Marxists.[31] Existentialism in its original atheistic forms has also rightly been condemned, but this has not stopped Christian thinkers, such as Jacques Maritain, for example, from using existentialism to give an account of the human person and his or her relationship to God. All of these philosophical methods have provided insights and perspectives on the meaning of what God has revealed to us. There is no problem in using these different philosophical methods, provided that they assume that there is truth and that it can be accessed by human reason. Although these assumptions rest on faith, the choice of a philosophical method which takes seriously the pursuit of truth is not the result of a dogmatic credulousness, but a deep and considered reflection on the human condition.

---

28.   Explored in *Fides et Ratio* in chapter 4. Explicitly mentioned are the Greek philosophers, particularly Plato and Aristotle, #39–#42.

29.   *Fides et Ratio* says that Aquinas was able to effect a reconciliation between the secularity of the world and the radicality of the gospel. #43.

30.   For example, *Rerum Novarum, Laborem Excercens* and *Solltitudo Rei Socialis*.

31.   '. . . there is general agreement, that some opportune remedy must be found quickly for the misery and wretchedness pressing so unjustly on the majority of the working class . . .' Leo XIII, *Rerum Novarum*, 3.

3. Which reason II: The problematic nature of the concept of reason

Although we tend to assume that we know what we mean when we speak of human reason, it is not obvious what is meant and moreover, there is a distinction between the concept itself and the process of justifying or warranting our knowledge claims by the giving of reasons. There are, therefore, effectively two things to consider: what reason itself is and secondly, the question of what are suitable candidates as reasons for justifying a claim that revelation makes. These questions are not disconnected from one another, for at least one theory of knowledge, reliabilism, holds that a belief is justified if it is produced by a reliable cognitive process. That is, a process which more often that not produces a true statement about the world, where by this is meant a relation between a belief and the situation which makes it true. Deduction, for example, is a reliable cognitive process, whereas wishful thinking is not.[32] Perception is similarly a reliable cognitive process, since the beliefs which we hold to be true as a result of perception enable us to successfully negotiate the world. The justification of the claims of revelation on this account would be based on some reliable cognitive process or processes.

Human reason on this reading we take to be the cognitive capacity that human beings have to reliably make sense of the world, to draw inferences and make deductions, based on experiences that they have. This is one way of understanding what reason is. Another is suggested by Plato, for example, in the *Republic* and in *Meno* where he talks of reason as a species of remembering in his doctrine of *amnesis*. Reason exists in the immaterial realm, the realm of eternal forms where true knowledge lies. The soul, because it is immortal, already apprehends the forms, but, because it is imprisoned in the body, is distracted by the illusions of the material world. The struggle to overcome these distractions is a long and arduous journey, as the simile of the cave illustrates.[33]

Human reason is complex and is not just the capacity to use logic, it is the capacity to make connections between apparently unconnected

---

32. J Pollock, *Contemporary Theories of Knowledge* (London: Hutchinson, 1987), 114ff. See also D Armstrong, *A Materialist Theory of the Mind* (London: Routledge and Kegan Paul, 1968), chapter 9, 187–207; D Armstrong, *Belief, Truth and Knowledge* (Cambridge: Cambridge University Press, 1973), 159–161.

33. See Plato, *The Republic* and *Meno*.

experiences.[34] Unlike a computer, human reason is not linear, but involves a vast array of neuronal connections which are able to store memories and enable human beings to learn and reflect. Despite a popular view that the mind is like a computer, there is ample evidence that it is nothing like a computer. For example, while a computer can process vast calculations effortlessly, this is not so for the human brain, and yet human beings have little difficulty in recognising other human beings—a task which computers presently are unable to do easily. Once a computer develops a fault in its memory it stops working, whereas a human brain can lose, through stroke, much of its capacity, but still continue to function normally.[35] It can be plausibly argued that most human reasoning is anything but algorithmic and involves weighing up considerations which may in some respects be non-commensurable.[36] Unlike computers, human beings do not simply accurately and efficiently process information, proceeding in logical steps to a conclusion. In many cases, human reasoning proceeds by leaps of intuition, sometimes having little connection to the data that it has before it. The cognitive processes are often not clear, even to the individual using them, and there is a question mark about their reliability.[37] Data, information and knowledge are not synonymous, interchangeable terms, so it is not surprising that human cognitive processes should be so different from those of computers. Lyotard warns us about the increasing commodification of knowledge and its reduction to quantities of information. He also says that knowledge encompasses far more than just denotative statements, it includes such human things as *savoir-faire, savoir-vivre, savoir-écouter,* etc.[38]

---

34. Hume takes this tendency of human beings as expressing what cause is—constant conjunction and contiguity. See DA Hume, *Treatise on Human Nature* (Harmondsworth: Penguin), 19xx.

35. The computational view of the mind was first seriously advanced by Hilary Putnam, later repudiated by him. See H Putnam, *Representational and Reality* (Cambridge, Massachusetts: MIT Press, 1992).

36. There are difficult moral cases which are precisely of this kind.

37. For example, a famous example of serendipity is Kékulé's discovery of the structure of Benzene in a dream. Many highly original thinkers have little idea of the source of their ideas.

38. See Jean-François Lyotard, *The Postmodern Condition: A Report on Knowledge*, translated by Geoff Bennington and Brian Massumi, Forward by Frederic Jameson (Manchester: Manchester University Press, 1984), 4–18.

Human reason involves more than just a cognitive process for decision-making, though of course, practical reason is one of its hallmarks. It also consists in the capacity of human beings to be creative and imaginative, to express their innermost feelings through the writing and performing of music and drama, through dance, through painting, through prose and poetry and through other creative arts.[39] Through these activities human beings are able to reflect on the human condition and to find ways of communicating its meaning and significance to each other. Human reason is an integral part of all these processes, it is a part of how human beings are in the world.

That human reason should be seen as being similar to information processing is a relatively modern view of reason, drawing on recent research in artificial intelligence and the neurosciences which place the seat of reason in the brain. Dennett is probably the most well known exponent of a physicalist account of mental events such as beliefs and desires, arguing that every mental event is some functional, physical event or other.[40] For example, a chess-playing computer possesses certain information which is directed to certain goals by the software program that is being run on the computer. Dennett does not contend that the computer has mental states, rather that what is meant by mental states can be captured in terms of physical events. Such a thoroughgoing physicalist view of human reason, whilst not necessarily implying that human reason operates algorithmically according to some embedded computing program, does mean that reason can never be another path to the truths of revelation since revelation itself is forbidden in a closed physical world.[41]

Although the physicalist account of reason suggests a structuralism which is Kantian, it stops short of transcendental idealism, opting

---

39. The possession of rational powers, according to Aristotle, is peculiar to human beings. The capacities that human beings possess to be creative and imaginative are powers which are actualised when persons play music, paint, etc. See A Kenny, *The Metaphysics of Mind* (Oxford: Oxford University Press, 1992). See also Aristotle, *De Anima*, Book II, Chapter 3 and *Metaphysics*, Book IX, chapter 8.

40. D Dennett, *Brainstorms* (Brighton: Harvester Press, 1978).

41. See D Hodgson, *The Mind Matters* (Oxford: Oxford University Press, 1993), chapter 3, 63–96, for a discussion of what he terms consensus views of the mind.

instead for a transcendental realism rejected by Kant.[42] For Kant, reason is the structure which enables us to construct from the myriad of sense impressions (themselves extending only as far as our senses allow) a coherent world, but there is no guarantee that human cognitive capacity somehow gives any glimpse of the thing-in-itself. Kant says, ' It still remains a scandal to philosophy . . . that the existence of things outside of us . . . must be accepted merely on *faith*, and that, if anyone thinks good to doubt their existence, we are unable to counter his doubts by any satisfactory proof'.[43] What follows from this is that we need not suppose that there may not be other kinds of non-human cognitive capacity—we may never be able to communicate with Martians, for example, because their ways of cognising may be so different to ours that no communication is possible.[44] The physicalist, on the other hand, supposes that phenomenal experience somehow yields knowledge of the world as it actually is and so we could communicate with Martians, since whatever cognitive process they employed in representing the world, it would be the same world, but this is a leap of faith, as Kant says. That is, the world constructed from human phenomenal experiences will be the same as the world constructed by the Martians from their phenomenal experiences since it corresponds to how the world really is.

The physicalist conception of human reason is problematic because, as the foregoing discussion illustrates, it does not allow for the possibility of reason being used to lead us to an understanding of the claims of revelation. This is because the physicalist restricts the world to what can be known through phenomenal experience and human reason itself to no more than a physical process. Revelation, which points to mysteries beyond the reach of mundane experience, remains like Kant's noumena, forever inaccessible to reason. Not only is it forever inaccessible, there does not seem to be any reason to assume that revelation is about anything at all, as diehard positivists would

---

42.   The distinction is that the transcendental idealist says that whatever the world is like it is not necessarily like what our experience tells us it is like. The transcendental realist holds that by and large reality corresponds to our conception of it. See B Magee, *The Philosophy of Schopenhauer* (Oxford: Clarendon Press, 1987), 73–104.

43.   I Kant, *Critique of Pure Reason*, translated by Norman Kemp Smith (London: MacMillan, 1958), 34.

44.   A similar thought is expressed by Thomas Nagel in 'What's It Like to Be a Bat?', *Philosophical Review*, 83 (1974): 435–450.

want to assert. Fortunately, there is no need to restrict our understanding of human reason or human experience to a narrowly physicalist one. There are at hand other ways of expanding the scope of reason and the reach of human experience. What is a difficulty is in providing a rationale for choosing one conception of reason over another which does not rest in some way on faith. For example, choosing a Thomistic (or Aristotelian) account on the grounds that this would be the most congenial to an explanation of the claims of revelation would seem to be self-defeating. On the other hand, giving an account of human reason independently of any ontological and epistemic commitments is impossible.

Assuming that what we mean by human reason is settled to our satisfaction, we are faced with the related problem of providing an account of what warrants us in claiming that the reasons we have for believing in the truth of revelation justify our belief. The justification of the claims of revelation will not rest on empirical evidence of the kind that we would want to say warrants a claim that all crows are black, for example. It comes as no surprise that how we might go about justifying a propositional claim in physics is different from how we would justify a propositional claim in a religious context.[45] Hirst, for instance, identifies forms of knowledge as distinct ways in which our experience becomes structured round the use of accepted public symbols. Forms of knowledge involve: (1) certain central concepts—eg God, sin, etc; (2) a distinct, logical structure in which the concepts are related to one another; (3) expressions and statements which are testable against experience in some way; (4) distinct techniques and skills for exploring experience and testing knowledge claims within them.[46] Despite trenchant criticism of the view that knowledge can be compartmentalised in this way and the growing acceptance of an anti-reductionist holism paradoxically fuelled by the last great logical positivist Quine, it seems counter-intuitive to suppose that what serves as warrant for religious belief is no different from what serves as

---

45. John L Pollock, *Contemporary Theories of Knowledge* (London: Hutchinson, 1986), 10–13.
46. Paul Hirst in 'Liberal Education and the Nature of Knowledge', in RD Archambault, *Philosophical Analysis and Education* (London: RKP, 1972), 128–129.

warrant for scientific belief.[47] Fortunately, holism need not lead us to suppose this, but to place the spectrum of human knowledge in a broader social context so that each form of knowledge occupies a place within a greater whole.[48] MacIntyre, for example, places the practice of virtue within the context of a tradition, that is, within a community holding certain beliefs and practices in common.[49]

Applying the forms of knowledge analysis to religious claims tells us that what might be held to be a reason to believe in a religious context will be different to what might be a reason to believe in some other context. Hence, in the justification of religious propositions, we will appeal to something different to what we appeal to in another form of knowledge. On the other hand, a holistic position will mean that there are similarities between forms of knowledge, that is, the need to establish the truth of what is claimed is no less urgent for religion as it is for science. This allows the possibility that the structure of religion and the way in which we come to hold religious beliefs is essentially the same as the structure of science and the way in which we come to hold scientific beliefs. Moreover, this will be so in any other form of knowledge. Critics, such as postmodernists, have claimed that there are no clear boundaries between forms of knowledge and this may be so to the extent that developments in one form of knowledge may well inform developments in another form of knowledge. This latter view in fact supports the idea that it is possible to gain knowledge of religious truths through the use of reason—or more precisely, that it is possible to be convinced of the truth of religious propositions through the use of reason, just as it is possible to be convinced of their truth through revelation. For example, belief in God's existence would be supported by scientific evidence that creation could not have occurred *ex nihilo*. This would not lead to certainty, but might provide scientific support for a belief held on religious grounds that God exists. In general, reason in a religious context is taken to mean the process of thought by which the claims of

---

47.   For a discussion of holism, see J Fodor and E Lepore *Holism: A Shopper's Guide* (Oxford: Blackwell, 1992). The description of Quine as the last great logical positivist is Putnam's. See H Putnam, *Realism with a Human Face* (Cambridge, Mass: Harvard University Press, 1990), 269.

48.   See N Murphy, *Anglo-American Postmodernity* (Boulder, Colorado: Westview Press, 1997), chapter 1, 7–48, for a survey of anti-reductionist, holistic views.

49.   A MacIntyre, *After Virtue*, second edition (Notre Dame, Indiana: University of Notre Dame Press, 1984).

religion are tested, elucidated and explained. If we are only interested in reporting what X believes, for example, that X believes in the Incarnation, does not require X to give us any reasons, but if we want X to give us his justification in believing this then we ask for reasons. Scientific evidence, though not itself directly the reason for holding a belief can be a supporting condition for holding the belief in the Incarnation—that is, it makes sense to us to believe because of this condition.[50] Science and religion need not be hostile to each other.

In the continuing debate about what count as justificatory reasons for a belief it is not surprising to find a number of theoretical positions, some of which are well known in epistemology. For example, justification of belief can be divided into doxastic theories and non-doxastic theories, as well as internalist and externalist theories of knowledge. In the case of doxastic theories, the justifiability of a belief is a function exclusively of what beliefs one holds and one can include both foundationalist and coherence theories of knowledge under this heading. In the case of non-doxasitic theories, it is denied that the justifiability of a belief is a function exclusively of what beliefs one holds. In response to the question of what else the justification of a belief could be based on apart from one's other beliefs, non-doxastic theories provide two solutions: an internalist one, in which the belief is justified in terms of epistemic norms that tell us which cognitive processes are correct and which are incorrect, and an externalist one, which denies that the correctness of a cognitive process is an essential feature of justification.

The internalist/externalist distinction in relation to reason is important. On one understanding of the world, namely an internalist one, we take claims that X knows that p as dependent on either self-evident propositions or that this proposition coheres with other propositions. That is, we embrace foundationalism or coherentism —classic doxastic theories. On an internalist non-doxastic model, X knows that p depends either on reliabilism, that is, that we can reliably take it to be the case that p, where reliability depends on the structure of human beings being normally a certain way and as yielding conclusions of arguments which enable the world to be negotiated successfully. In an externalist model, the correctness of the cognitive

---

50. For example, a supporting condition for the Incarnation might be belief in God, but this does not itself justify belief in the Incarnation.

process by which we arrive at our conclusions need not be accessible to us. In this case, we would explain how it was that we were able to successfully negotiate the world by reference to some kind of evolutionary story. Another externalist model relies on Bayesian inference—we say we know that p because it is more probable than not-p.[51] In relation to faith, belief in the Incarnation is justified on the grounds that given other beliefs about God's redemptive action in the world it is more probable than not believing in the Incarnation. The giving of reasons—the justification of claiming to know that p—is itself justified in relation to one of these epistemological theories. Whichever model we decide upon depends on how convincing we find the arguments for these, but since we have to take a meta-theoretical stance to this argument itself, there needs to be some way of breaking through the regress—otherwise we depend on faith. Since there is no final arbiter, no Archimedean point, we need recourse to a tradition, a way of life, to justify the stance we take.

One result of assuming that structurally justification of religious belief will proceed in the same way as any other kind of belief is that one theory of knowledge justification will suffice for all forms of knowledge, even if the content of beliefs are different. This can be interpreted as meaning that the same standards of justification apply in religious contexts as apply in scientific contexts, even if, as is palpably obvious, the way in which we test for the truth of scientific belief is different to how we test for the truth of a religious belief. A scientific proposition, such as 'Water boils at 100 degrees Centigrade' will be confirmed by the observation that indeed water boils at 100 degrees

---

51.   The general form of Baye's Theorem says:

$$Pr(B_j | A) = \frac{Pr(B_j)Pr(A|B_j)}{\sum Pr(B_i)Pr(A|B_i)}$$

. The probability of event B_j given A will depend on the product of the initial probability of B_j and the probability of A given B_j over the sum of the products of the initial probabilities of events B_i and the probabilities of A given B_i. In a simplified version, assuming only two events, we have

$$P(B|A) = \frac{P(B)P(A|B)}{P(A)}$$

. Taking probability to refer to subjective degrees of belief, what the equation suggests is that our degree of belief in B increases in the face of increased information. For example, suppose we are asked to guess the suit of a card face down in front of us. Our chance of being correct will improve if we are told that it is a red card. Similarly, the degree of belief in a religious statement will increase if there are other beliefs which provide evidence for it.

Centigrade. On the other hand, a religious proposition, such as 'Christ rose from the dead', will be confirmed by some other means, such its consistency with other faith claims. Arguably, this suggests that the standards of justification need to be different because science and religion are incommensurable.[52] This is a simplification, however, for generally speaking, we do not test scientific propositions one by one, nor, if we are consistent, do we test religious propositions one by one.[53] Both scientific propositions and religious propositions have to be seen as being embedded within wider theories about the nature of the world, and although they may be seen as providing explanations of different aspects of the world, they are also seeking to explain the same world. That is, it is possible to do science without referring to religion, just as it is possible to do theology without referring to science. Nevertheless, both are poorer if their interdependence is not acknowledged. We shall return to this theme below.

If we see reason in a broader context, it is also clear that what we will offer as reasons for justifying particular knowledge claims will also have to be broader. Hence, in cases involving perception, for example, perceptual claims will be justified by the observations that have been made. In other cases, such as claims that something follows deductively from something else, justification is in terms of the accuracy of the logical proofs. In other cases, such as interpreting what an artist is trying to convey in a painting, there may be general agreement, but the possibility of interpretation enters in a way it does not in other cases. Here the possibility of differing points of view arises more readily. It is not what constitutes a reason which is difficult to establish, but whether or not it affords a justification which is not so easy to determine. The broader view of reason recognises that there are different ways in which we will arrive at a justification for our beliefs, and that limiting ourselves to one way or another, such as perception

---

52. See, for example, SJ Gould, 'Nonoverlapping Magisteria', *Natural History*, 1997: 18; L Gilkey, *Creationism on Trial* (San Francisco: Harper, 1985); N Murphy, *Beyond Liberalism and Fundamentalism: How Modern and Postmodern Philosophy Set the Agenda* (Valley Forge, PA: Trinity, 1996).

53. As Quine has argued persuasively. See, for example, WVO Quine, *Word and Object* (Cambridge, Mass.: Harvard University Press, 1960); WVO Quine, 'Two dogmas of Empiricism' in *From a Logical Point of View*, second edition (Cambridge, Mass.: Harvard University Press, 1980), 20–46.

or deductive logic, will limit what we can claim to know and close aspects of the world to us.

4. Escape from fideism: A scientific model for faith

Having explored the objections which the three premises we began with have raised for the prospects of complementary roles for faith and reason, it is clear that the assertion that we are forced to rely very heavily on faith, rather than reason, is much exaggerated. It is true that faith is the basis for the acceptance of the first half of (1) and the assertion that the church's teaching authority is backed by the Holy Spirit also relies on faith. Insofar as the church's teaching forms a consistent body of beliefs, one could argue that it displays internal coherence. Additional beliefs, to be accepted as true, need to fit with the other beliefs that are held to be true. One could say that the predominant theory of truth which seems to be exhibited is a coherence one, since additional new propositions have to be consistent with propositions already accepted as true. It is difficult to see how the hermeneutic circle can be escaped, though this is not a problem peculiar to religious faith. It is, however, far from any correspondence notion of an objective truth corresponding to how the world is.[54] What we have is an ontological theory about the world of which the *Magisterium* provides a particular interpretation. There is a reliance on the invariance of certain propositions—but even here, there may not be invariance over time. The faith is not monolithic and arguably to make it so requires constant attention from the *Magisterium*. Nevertheless, although the claim that the *Magisterium* provides us with the best interpretation of revelation we have itself requires a faith assent, it is not without justification and it is this which prevents us from sliding into fideism.

In relation to the second premise, although it is explicitly stated that there is no privileged philosophical method, there is a danger that in recommending a Thomistic approach to the nexus between theology and philosophy many fruitful insights into Christian beliefs and an understanding of the claims of Christianity may be lost. Theology needs to be open, therefore, to what different approaches to philo-

---

54.   It is probably problematic to speak of correspondence here, since religious assertions do not correspond with the physical world—at least as interpreted by someone like AJ Ayer, but this might simply be a difference between ontological ideas about the world.

sophy may reveal. This is nowhere more important than in giving an account of the nature of truth. Nevertheless, not all philosophical theories will be compatible with the claims of faith and will be excluded *a priori* from consideration as ways in which the truths of revelation can justified. It is difficult to avoid the conclusion in this case that argument is of less importance than what the faith calls us to believe. It is the challenge of this which has to be met.

In the third part of the argument we showed that there are different conceptions of reason and that what can be understood by justificatory reasons for believing in the propositions of faith have to be underpinned by an epistemology sufficiently robust to allow for such propositions to be included amongst those items which are claimed to be known. If the choice of such an epistemology was arbitrary, it would rest on faith, not necessarily on religious faith, but a belief that the world is of a particular kind without any further justification. Unless it can be justified on other than religious grounds, excluding a purely physicalist view of the world because it is incompatible with religious faith at first sight seems capricious. If so, then the argument that reason has been excluded in favour of faith alone is plausible. In what follows, we will sketch an argument which strengthens the view being put that there is no need to regard the theoretical elaborations of the concepts of truth and reason as being made arbitrarily.

Postmodernism, as has already been suggested, claims that there are no boundaries between disciplines and this can be understood to mean that all areas of knowledge are interrelated. If religious knowledge is accepted as a genuine area of knowledge,[55] then it will be coextensive with science. Putting aside the distinctions that can be drawn between theology and religion, this should not be taken to mean that religious knowledge should be approached in the same way as scientific knowledge, but rather that there will be common elements to all areas of knowledge. Torrance argues that there is a *scientia generalis*, common to all sciences, but that each special science has its own mode of rationality or objectivity, and its own aim and method as a *scientia specialis*.[56] Theology is a science because it begins not from religious faith, but what that religious faith is about, namely God and

---

55. There is not space to develop an argument for this here, though much of the foregoing discussion could be taken to support such a view.
56. TF Torrance, *Theological Science* (Edinburgh: T&T Clark, 1996), 113.

how God reveals God to us.[57] Pannenberg agrees, and thinks that the hypothesis of God can be evaluated positively if it increases the intelligibility of the natural world.[58] The strong unity of knowledge thesis can be maintained by the realisation that both theology and science seek to tell us about the world which human beings inhabit and so at one level cannot be separated from each other since each will inform the other about that world. Nevertheless, each will have its own methods, language and criteria for truth, as well theories and hypotheses and ways of testing these. The mistake the fideist makes is in supposing that there is a radical separation between science and religion.

We do not really need to model religion on science. What has to be recognised is that both are fundamentally alike in that both seek to understand and explain the world: in the case of science, we have an attempt to explain the natural world, in the case of religion, we have an attempt to explain more difficult questions about why the world is here at all. In this sense, it subsumes science within it. Thus, the scientific impulse to find the truth is explained not as an aberration, but as a result of human beings being in the world and seeking the source of that being. The search for truth is a search for God, the ground of all being. Obviously, not all scientists, let alone other individuals, will view the search for truth as a search for God, whatever they believe about truth. Nevertheless, the impulse to know and understand requires some explanation, if only in terms of an evolutionary account which dispenses with God altogether.

In giving an account of the relation between science and religion, the starting point is our experience of being in the world. From this experience we are forced to take a stance towards the world, to ask questions about its origin and what it is, to explore its furthermost depths and outermost limits, to categorise what is in it, to explain satisfactorily to ourselves the meaning and significance of our presence within it as well as our relationship to it and what it contains and, finally and most importantly, to acknowledge the mystery of the source of its being. These are all interconnected questions, and answers to one will affect answers to others. Thus, a belief that truth is

---

57.   TF Torrance, *op cit*, 29.
58.   W Pannenberg, *Theology and the Philosophy of Science* (Louisville: Westminster/John Knox, 1976); W Panneberg, *Systematic Theology*, volumes 1–3 (Grand Rapids: Eerdmans, 1991–1996).

unimportant affects what else is believed, a belief that there is only a physical world affects what we believe about its mysterious origin. This suggests that at the highest level of abstraction, we have to see science and religion as part of a seamless web.

At such a level of abstraction, assuming that we can satisfactorily show how science and religion are interrelated and together, along with other areas of knowledge, form a coherent all-encompassing theory of the world, it is apparent that falsification of the whole theory is most unlikely. There is the question of what would constitute falsification in any case. When Copernicus and later Galileo challenged the existing theory of the world, it was resisted, not because individual scientific views were being challenged, but because the whole world order was under challenge. There are similar challenges today sparked by scientific advances which call us to reflect on what it is to be a human being.[59] Differences of opinion, which indicate a difference in the overall theory of the world, lead to ideological clashes which are not easily resolvable, if they are resolvable at all. There is no easy way of deciding between rival traditions, as MacIntyre has shown. The solution he offers is to argue that one tradition can be shown to be superior to another if there are fewer inconsistencies and contradictions within it.[60] This, of course, may not be the case; both may be equally inconsistent and contain similar numbers of contradictions. Furthermore, the intention of entering into dialogue with another tradition may not be to overthrow it, but engage in a conversation with equals who have a valuable, if different perspective on the world.

Reason can support faith and by reason's reflection on revelation, human beings are brought closer to God. Since religion encompasses science, its methods of determining truth can be brought to bear on the

---

59.   For example, discoveries in genetics and the mapping of the human genome without doubt have had, and will have, profound impact on the way in which human beings see themselves. The ability to recognise defective genes within the foetus has been hailed as a considerable advance in the fight against genetic diseases; however, this is not because early detection will enable doctors to cure the disease, but because it will enable the foetus to be aborted in good time to prevent the birth of a defective, genetically diseased person.

60.   A MacIntyre, *Three Rival Versions of Moral Enquiry* (Notre Dame, Indiana: University of Notre Dame Press, 1990); A MacIntyre, *Whose Justice? Which Rationality?* (London: Duckworth, 1988).

propositions of religious belief. Science and religion inform each other, but religious principles, since they are more fundamental to our ways of being in the world, are the least changeable. Wittgenstein said that logic, the language game we are in and the background of our beliefs lay at the base of what we can come to know about the world and, moreover, our knowledge is provisional for knowledge is in a different category to certainty. More importantly, he says that the riverbed of our beliefs can also be shifted.[61] This would imply, however, a complete shift in our whole theory of the world, including our religious beliefs, but these lie at the deepest levels of our being and are least amenable to change because they are intimately linked with our conceptions of ourselves. Paraphrasing Wittgenstein, it is far less difficult to shift the continent on which the riverbed lies than change our deepest convictions. One very good reason for this is that a shift in some things, such as belief in the Trinity, involves a change in the allegiances which are a part of our self-identity. If we start out as Christians, we end up as non-Christians, for by denying the doctrine of the Trinity we deny the divinity of Christ.

It is clear that reason cannot be eliminated in favour of faith alone since faith claims have to be justified otherwise they are no more than credulous opinions, which cannot be taken seriously. Christian faith begins with revelation, but requires reason in order to interpret its meaning for us, and faith follows our acceptance of this meaning. This does not happen if there is no openness to the possibility that there is a God who reveals, who is truth and whom we can encounter in the person of Jesus. Faith and reason are inextricably linked, for an essential element in the examination of the claims of faith is the assumption that the truth can be known and that reason can be a route to establishing truth. This means that not all philosophical methods nor all theoretical constructs of the nature of the world can be assumed. This does not pose a real problem for us, since in order to develop any theory of the world we have to begin with some metaphysical and religious assumptions about the world, just as in science we begin with metaphysical assumptions about the world and the possibility of knowing about it. It is clear then that we are never forced back into fideism.

---

61.   L Wittgenstein, *On Certainty* (New York: HarperTorchbooks, 1972), #97.

Faith, Reason and Freedom

John McDermott

The Catholic religion spans the globe, and not just numerically, geographically, and spiritually in Christ, but also in joining various religious *Weltanschauungen*. With Judaism and Islam, Christ's church emphasises obedience in a community of believers but also insists on dogma, faith's positive intellectual content, and opens man to mystical union. With Hinduism and Buddhism, the church insists on under-standing and aims for union with God but also calls for the obedience of faith: man cannot save himself through private mysticism or asceticism but must respond in obedience to a gift mediated through a community.[1] Besides spanning East and West, speculation and obedience, Catholicism embraces the most primitive and the most intellectually sophisticated approaches to God: her theology creates the most refined thought and calls to mystical heights, yet her sacramental praxis lets God be encountered really in the bread and wine of sacrifice. God beyond all human perception becomes tangible. With natural religions the church affirms the fundamental goodness of

---

1. These characterisations of non-Christian religions are admittedly broad. R Zaehner, *Hinduism* (1966; rpt. London: Oxford University Press, 1962), makes very clear the speculative transformations of Hinduism in history: cf especially 38–41, 44–56. Though Theravada Buddhism refused to enter into various speculative questions deemed irrelevant to man's liberation, later variations of Mahayana Buddhism took them up: cf K Ch'en, *Buddhism*, (Woodbury: Barron, 1968), esp 30–85. Islam strongly emphasises obedience and law in fidelity to the Koran and tradition; beyond strict monotheism and Mohammed's apostleship various creeds are tolerated, though philosophy has in good part been rejected: cf. A. Guillaume, *Islam*, second edition (Harmondsworth: Penguin, 1956), 55–77, 88–142. Despite Guillaume, 147f, Sufi mysticism is still regarded with suspicion by 'orthodox' Moslems. Cf. J Marechal, SJ, *Studies in the Psychology of the Mystics*, tr. A. Thorold (1927; rpt. Albany: Magi, 1964), 271–279, on the mystic Hallaj and Islam's incapacity to unite obedience with mysticism due to the lack of a sacramental system. Cf. also H de Lubac, SJ, *Catholicism*, translated by L Sheppart (1947; rpt. New York: New American Library, 1964), 151–163, on Catholicism's ability to unify other religions.

creation, yet with religions of salvation she preaches the absolute need of conversion. With monotheists she preaches the possibility of a total response to God that unifies and liberates the whole person; but acknowledging the strengths of polytheism, she explains the interior divisions in man, which he does not control, in terms of original sin and concupiscence. She knows that the only possibility of synthesising the experienced unity and diversity of existence lies in the mystery of the tri-personal God intervening in the world.

The paradoxical tensions in Catholicism emerge clearly in the relation of faith and reason. Faith's truths transcend reason and cannot be deduced by it (DS 3004f, 3008, 3015-3017, 3035, 3041), but faith's assent cannot be blind (DS 3010). Not only can reason arrive by analogy at some understanding of divine mysteries but it also can discover the 'foundations of faith' and recognise 'the most certain signs of divine revelation' (DS 3009f, 3019, 3033f, 3036). The relation of reason and faith reflects the more fundamental relation of natural and supernatural orders. Since mind and reality correspond in truth, reason grasps truths of the natural order and faith affirms truths of the supernatural order, mysteries hidden in God and now revealed (DS 3015, 3027, 2029). The church insists on the mutual complementarity of the two orders despite their real diversity (DS 3019). For the revealing God endowed man with reason (DS 2017). Indeed, the incarnate Word in whom the church believes spoke to people in human words. He meant to be understood in ways accessible to human reason: through his words and actions people are led to believe in him. Moreover, only by insisting on the value of human reason can the church uphold the value of human freedom in the work of salvation. The importance of this connection has become clear in ecumenical discussions with Protestants.

The fundamental point at issue between the church and the reformers in the sixteenth century concerned the effects of original sin upon man's ability to cooperate with grace. Preaching man's total corruption, the reformers denied him any capacity to cooperate with grace. Justification is entirely God's work and no man can merit or glory in his sight. Luther emerged from the Augustinian tradition understanding human nature as a spiritual dynamism oriented to God or to the world; once original sin has skewered man's orientation, turning him from God to creatures, nothing in man can turn him back to God; his will is part of the natural dynamism and, as skewered, cannot straighten itself. As heir also to late medieval nominalism, Luther recognised that man's intellect cannot know God with certitude on its own, it has to be guided by God's grace and revelation.[2] Citing the late Augustine and sharing Luther's views on man's corruption, Calvin affirmed the will's incapacity to please God and perform good works unless moved by grace. But whereas Luther's theology was more existential, concerned with the anthropological conditions of grace's reception, Calvin started from God's omnipotence in his more abstract, systematic presentation. God accomplishes what he wills, making man do the good or actively condemning him to sin and damnation.[3] This stress on the objectivity of God's omnipotence

---

2. B Gerrish, *Grace and Reason* (1962; rpt. Chicago: University of Chicago, 1979), 10–56, 114–137, 168–171; A McGrath, *Luther's Theology of the Cross* (Oxford: Blackwell, 1985), 128–131, 148–175; A McGrath, The *Intellectual Origins of the European Reformation* (Oxford: Blackwell, 1987), 175–187; B Lohse, *Martin Luther's Theology*, translated by R Harrisville (Minneapolis: Fortress, 1999), 70–72, 106f, 163–168, 196–205, 244f, 250–257; *A Compend of Luther's Theology*, edited by H Kerr (1943; rpt. Philadelphia: Westminster, 1966), 88–91.

3. In *Institutes of the Christian Religion*, edited by J McNeill, translated by F Battles (Philadelphia: Westminister, 1960), J Calvin allows some tensions to emerge on the degree of man's corruption. On the one hand he affirms that the heavenly image is obliterated (II, 1, 5), nature is corrupted (II, i, 7–9.11; ii, 1.6–8.27), man is completely estranged from the end of his creation (II, i, 3). Yet the fall does not result in the destruction of man's whole nature insofar as God's mercy allows some traces of his image to remain (I, xv, 4.6; II, ii, 17); so reason is only partially weakened and corrupted (II, ii, 12). The oscillation on this position doubtless permits Calvin to explain God's loving redemption: He is hostile toward the corruption of his work, not the work itself (II, i, 11; xvi, 3f; xvii, 2). Early in the *Institutes* emerges Calvin's emphasis on God's infinity (I, xiii, 1–3.13.18.21) and omnipotence, which is divine providence (I, xvi, 3f, 6–9; xvii, 6f, 9.12f.; xviii, 1–4). Before the fall Adam enjoyed something like freedom of indifference, being capable of bending his will to one side or another (I, xv, 8). Such freedom does not hold for fallen man, who in no way controls free choice (II, 16, 6); in the same paragraph Calvin rejects the notion that God moves man by moving his nature while man turns the movement where he pleases. This apparently rejects the Augustinian notion of freedom, understood as the natural will's choosing of the good. Indeed Calvin's emphasis on God using bad men and their evil deeds as his instruments as well as the notion of double predestination would make it seem that Calvin favours for man a freedom of indifference, but this freedom is impotent in the face of divine omnipotence, imagined as an irresistible force from

allowed Calvin to affirm man's natural capacity to arrive at a knowledge of God as Creator, not as Redeemer, from the created things of the world (Rom 1:20).[4]

The philosophical turn to the subject initiated by Descartes and completed by Kant tremendously influenced modern Protestant thought. However much the Reformed theologian Karl Barth disagrees with the Lutheran Rudolf Bultmann for the anthropological starting point of his theology, he is of one mind with him on man's utter inability to know God apart from revelation. For him the Catholic *analogia entis* is the idolatrous invention of the devil and the chief reason for not becoming a Catholic. Calvinists and Lutherans now agree on this point because both wish to prevent man's freedom from cooperating in any way with grace. If man cannot know God apart from revelation, man has no reason outside of God for loving God and thereby attaining salvation. Faith and salvation are entirely God's work. Man is not free as long as he has no reason for his choice. He must be set free when God moves his will to believe, choosing what God wants. This rectification of the will is considered true freedom insofar as the will is itself only in choosing the good for which it has been intended.[5]

Against the Protestant negations Catholic theology has resolutely upheld man's ability to cooperate freely with grace and, consequently, his 'possibility of knowing God with certainty by the natural light of human reason from created realities' (DS 3004). Only if man can know God naturally can he understand what revelation proclaims about God—as a minimum 'God has spoken thus'—and so freely accept or

---

without.—Luther has some strong expression on God's omnipotence even with regard to prelapsarian man, but he refrains from attributing man's sin to God: cf Lohse, 166–168, 251–253, 256f.

4.   Calvin, I, ii, 1; iii, 1; iv, 4; v, 1.5.9.12.15. But he also plays down the certitude of that natural knowledge in I, v. 12.15. McGrath, *Luther's Theology*, 161–164, points out that Luther also allows a certain natural knowledge of God as a 'preconception' or 'point of contact' for revelation's appropriation; 'nevertheless, the effect of that revelation is to destroy such preconceptions, and replace them with the "crucified God"'.

5.   J McDermott, SJ, 'Jesus: Parable or Sacrament of God?', *Gregorianum* 79 (1998): 543–551, 556–560; K Barth, *Church Dogmatics*, edited by G Bromily and T Torrance, translated by G Bromily *et al* (Edinburgh: T&T Clark, 1956–1977), I/1, xiii, 40f, 168f, 243f; I/2, 43f.

reject the alleged revelation. In intellectual darkness freedom cannot operate. Mere arbitrariness enslaves man to his passions and reduces him to the level of the beasts.

Essential as are the faith-reason and natural-supernatural distinctions to Catholic theology, Catholic theologians do not agree on their meanings, and the post-Vatican II havoc is due in great part to that disagreement. Their disagreement reflects the underlying problem introduced by Kant into modern thought. Only by examining the inner-ecclesial debate within a wider context can we attempt a synthetic solution to the problems raised. But first it will be profitable to show why a faith beyond philosophy is needed by man to live life humanly.

1. The limits of reason

There are deep conundrums in life which the reason of natural philosophy can never solve: the reality of moral evil, the meaning of suffering, and the question of man's continued existence after death. Let us examine each in turn.

1. Understood as 'what should not be', moral evil resists all explanation. At least since the days of Aristotle 'explanation' involves the discovery of a cause, and a cause implies a necessity. Were the link between cause and effect not necessary, the alleged cause would be at most a *conditio sine qua non*. Since a real cause delivers necessity, any total explanation of evil would result in the absurdity that 'what should not be must be'. Admittedly dialectical systems, from Heraclitus on, seek to explain evil as the necessary correlate to good, but the distinction between both is ultimately relativised from a higher viewpoint and the meaning of words is lost. Thomists try to avoid the problem by considering evil first as physical or natural evil, defined as a *privatio boni debiti*, and then understanding moral evil as the choice of a lesser natural good contrary to reason or the divine law with a defective motive. But it is as impossible to choose a privation as it is to explain how one rationally chooses something that is less good. This explanation also fails to explain our experience of deliberately choosing what is wrong. Ultimately sin is irrational and cannot be explained.[6] That is why any attempt to defend God with reference to

---

6.   Cf, eg, Thomas Aquinas, *Summa Theologiae* 1, 14, 10; 48f; I–II, 75; C Journet, *The Meaning of Evil*, translated by M Barry (New York: Kenedy, 1962),

the 'commensurability' of evils and goods must always fail to satisfy fully. No more than a black hole, can evil be measured by man's mind.[7]

2. Suffering not only jars with the human desire for wellbeing but also resists rational explanation. In those philosophies seeing man as a basic unity of body and soul, pleasure results from the unimpeded operation of a natural faculty that knowingly possesses its connatural good (*ST* I–II, 31, lc.l; 32, 1). Pain, on the contrary, results when the faculty's natural operation is frustrated and fails to obtain its proper good (cf *ibid*, 35, lc.3). Pain's rationale cannot ultimately be discovered by such systems. For to mind corresponds some element of reality grasped by the mind. The mind grasps the natures of sensible realities, and natures are basic principles of motion which necessarily seek a goal in which to rest. Their final cause necessarily attracts them; otherwise there would be no understanding of the development inherent in natures. Insofar as pain frustrates a nature in its natural operation, the mind cannot grasp what is contrary to nature. If the mind were to find a cause, ie a necessity, for the pain, this necessity would be in contradiction to the necessity of the nature.[8]

Dualistic systems easily explain the pain which man suffers by making it necessary. Plato's soul is always striving to liberate itself from the body that restricts it and return to the world of the forms.[9] Kant's formal moral imperative is, as universal, necessarily in

---

especially 27–49 (the French title *Le Mal* is mistranslated since Journet holds that evil has no meaning in itself); Y Congar, OP, 'The Problem of Evil', in *God, Man and the Universe*, edited by J de Bivort de la Saudee (New York: Kenedy, 1953), 393–421, especially 397–400; J Maritain, *Existence and the Existent*, translated by L Galantiere and G Phelan (1948; rpt. Westport: Greenwood, 1975), 85–122; — —, *Dieu et la permission du mal* in *Oeuvres Complete* , XII, edited by J Allion et alii (Fribourg: Editions Universitaires, 1993), especially 43–73; J McDermott, SJ, 'Metaphysical Conundrums at the Root of Moral Disagreement', *Gregorianum* 71 (1990), especially 718–732.

7.   Cf, eg, H McCloskey, *God and Evil* (The Hague: Nijhoff, 1974), 83–128.

8.   St Thomas holds that (physical) evil, as corruption or privation of a good or its proper end (*ST* I, 48, 1, 2.4), has no form, no cause *per se*, neither formal, final, nor efficient (49, lc; 3c; 48, 1, 2), no existence, no intelligibility *per se* (48, 1c; 14, 10, 4); it is infinite (48, 1, 4), and even God knows it only indirectly *per bonum oppositum* (14, 10c.1).

9.   Plato, *Phaedo* 60–68, 80–84; *Symposium* 199–205, 210–212.

opposition to the individual desires of the subject, and the greater the struggle against one's desires, the more moral is the subject.[10] Alongside the form-matter dualism are dynamic dualisms, like Hegel's and Nietzsche's, orienting the finite subject to infinity. Not only does dynamic finitude necessarily involve collisions with opposed finite realities, but also the very desire for the infinite goal implies a felt lack, that is suffering. The postulation by Kant of an afterlife in which God recompenses the good for their sufferings runs into insurmountable difficulties: what sort of God must it be who inserted us into this world of necessary sufferings? If God can really reward the good in the afterlife, why does he not do it now?[11] In Hegel's system the conflict of

---

10. I Kant, *Kritik der praktischen Vernunft*, ninth edition, edited by K Vorlander (1929; rpt Hamburg: Meiner, 1963), 97–99, 178f: 'Here virtue is worth so much only because it costs so much'. Cf also his *Foundations of the Metaphysics of Morals*, translated by L White (Indianapolis: Bobbs-Merrill, 1959), 13–16, 29–31, where duty involves constraint and resistance to the natural desire for happiness. Though Kant's objective nature is mechanistic, he brings in the traditional notion of nature to ground desire, especially the desire for happiness that justifies subjectively his belief in God. Yet his opposition of morality (duty) to inclination (for happiness) is not consistent: he allows that securing one's own happiness 'is at least indirectly a duty, for discontent with one's condition under pressure from many cares and amid unsatisfied wants could easily become a great temptation to transgress duties'. (*Ibid*, 15) So he oscillates between subjective intention and objective obligation in his understanding of duty. That may be occasioned by his understanding of the subjectively given law as universal and a priori, which is almost equivalent to an objective duty. For more cf R Sullivan, *Immanuel Kant's Moral Theory* (New York: Cambridge, 1989), 118–122 — — Cf *Foundations*, 72–83, for Kant's awareness of the incomprehensible duality between the intelligible world of freedom and the world of the senses. — The strife between duty and pleasure is all the more dolorous in view of the 'radical, inborn evil' which Kant postulates in every human being, an evil whose origin none can understand, especially after Kant rejects the historical account of Genesis. Indeed, Kant contradicts himself in describing the evil as 'inborn' (*angebornes*), yet resulting from the free choice which a man makes when he comes as it were 'immediately out of the state of innocence' and makes himself good or evil: *Die Religion innerhalb der Grenzen der blossen Vernunft*, edited by R Malter (Stuttgart: Reclam, 1981), 33–66, especially 39, 50, 53–56.

11. This is the basis of Ivan Karamazov's complaint in F Dostovesky, *The Brothers Karamazov*, translated by A MacAndrew (1970; rpt New York: Bantam, 1981),

claims arises necessarily within the development of finite consciousness, and his God, who is also necessarily coming to himself in history, is submitted to the necessity of suffering.[12] Dualisms can never explain how the two parts of man ever came together. Dynamic dualisms, moreover, fail to show how the finite can ever attain its infinite goal; indeed, if the infinite God is infinitely far, he is also infinitely close and should not have to be sought. Atheistic or agnostic dualisms utterly fail to give reasons for suffering. Durkheim's postulation of collective thought to ground the morality demanding the sacrifice of the individual justifies the horrors of totalitarian national states.[13] Freud's formal distinction between the id and the moralising superego gives rise to an unrelenting struggle and results in the death wish.[14] The dynamic self-transcendence of Nietzsche's superman beyond good and evil leads only to willing one's own will and desiring forgetfulness before the mindless, endless repetition of the same.[15] So suffering has become life and life senseless.

Is man a duality of body and soul or a body-soul unity? In the former case it is easy to comprehend how the soul survives the body's destruction, but impossible to explain how the soul ever became enmeshed in the body in the first place. If the soul is the body's form, it is impossible to explain how it can survive the body's corruption. St Thomas attempts to finesse that problem by joining man's individual act of existence to the body over the soul; thus upon death the soul,

---

284–297. The view under attack is not Christianity, but reflective of German Idealism with many clearly Kantian presuppositions.

12. In G Hegel, *Phanomenologie des Geistes*, sixth edition, edited by J Hoffmeister (Hamburg: Meiner, 1952) conflict is build into the system throughout: cf especially 335–342 (the state's universal morality in conflict with familial duty) and 535–548 (God's suffering).

13. E Durkheim, *The Elementary Forms of Religious Life*, translated by J Swain (New York: Collier, 1961), 235–272.

14. Cf HU von Balthasar, *Theodramtik* I (Einsiedeln: Johannes, 1973), 475–482, for a good brief summary and critique of Freud's 'system'. Freud's superego is easily interpreted as Kant's moral consciousness prescribing the law to itself, the ego, in opposition to the individual's natural desires, the id. Cf Kant, *Foundations*, 68f, 72–74, for the basis of this opposition.

15. Cf, eg F Nietzsche, *Thus Spake Zarathustra*, translated by T Common, in *The Philosophy of Nietzsche* (New York: Random House, n.d.), 27–31, 37f, 43–45, 52f, 90f; — —, *Beyond Good and Evil*, translated by H Zimmern, *ibid*, 24–27, 62.

joined originally to existence, might survive (*ST* I, 75, 6c; 76, 2c.2; 4c; 6c.3; 7c). But that solution, however ingenious, encounters certain difficulties. First, man's soul in a separated state would be a pure form, hence a universal, unless it were individuated. Matter signed by quantity is the principle of individuation, but that individuation falls away with the body. Can one employ the act of existence to ground individuality? This solution unfortunately results in a double principle of individuation, and beings, especially mental beings, should not be multiplied without necessity. Second, the state of a bodiless soul could not be considered happy in every way since an essential element is lacking to its natural operation (cf *ibid* I–II, 4, 5, c.1.2.4–6).[16] Naturally any argument for the soul's incorruptibility is rendered more difficult by the experience of a sinful world and the intellectual confusion which sin introduces.

These three conundrums of evil, suffering, and personal immortality constitute the decisive questions of interest to most human beings because they pertain to their fate and provide the horizon of meaning within which their choices are made. They raise questions about a God who may or may not exist, who may or may not love us. Each conundrum touches the individual and his destiny, and natural philosophy is always brought up short before the mystery of individuality: *individuum est ineffabile*. Faith is needed, and its content must come from beyond man.

---

16. Cajetan repeatedly states that philosophical arguments for the soul's immortality are not of themselves persuasive; only faith can assure men of that truth. For the soul's operation is not entirely free of the body, but bound to the phantasm. Cf J Weisheipl, 'Cajetan', *New Catholic Encyclopedia*, edited by W McDonald, II (New York: Mc-Graw-Hill, 1967), 1054. And Cajetan was a conceptualist thinker, holding for a fundamental concept of being. Transcendental Thomists have a greater difficulty with immortality since, for them, being is known in a judgment, ie a *conversio ad phantasma*. On St Thomas's position cf J McDermott, SJ, 'The Analogy of Human Knowing in the *Prima Pars*', *Gregorianum* 77 (1996): especially 263–267, 270–276,502–507, 511–514. In no way do we deny personal immortality as a truth knowable to philosophy—cf later in this essay—we only indicate the inability of a philosophy based on natures to prove the soul's immortality.

2. The reason-faith relation

As is clear from the very terms used, 'supernatural' depends for meaning on 'natural' insofar as it surpasses the nature. Correspondingly faith is understood from reason. In good part the modem problematic has been defined by Immanuel Kant. To justify the success of Newton's physics in the face of Hume's empiricist critique, which results in nominalism, Kant transcendentally deduces the distinction between noumenon and phenomena. Whereas the noumenon, the unknowable source of sense impressions, represents Hume's empiricist world, the phenomena are ordered by the inherent categories of reason, that are a priori, ie universal and necessary. Scientific knowledge is explained as the subsumption of sense impressions, ordered by the a priori forms of sensibility (space and time), under the categories. Man necessarily gives the meaning to reality and all people think the same way. Phenomenal knowledge alone is objective. Hence where Newtonian physics succeeds, metaphysics fails, arriving at rational antinomies, since it seeks to employ the categories apart from sensible impressions. Nothing said about God, the soul, and freedom can be objective knowledge.

If the phenomenal world of space and time is ruled by exceptionless laws, Kant does not deny freedom, God, and personal immortality. On the contrary, he postulates their existence in the noumenon, that infinite reality corresponding initially to prime matter. As infinite, outside all finite knowledge, it cannot be distinguished from God and it offers a 'place' for freedom and the transcendental unity of apperception, ie the 'I' providing the unity of knowledge in the juncture of sense impressions, imagination, and categories. Kant holds that man is free to follow or not follow the a priori moral law that his practical reason dictates.[17] Because the universality of the law

---

17.   Kant's freedom is primarily freedom of indifference. Not only does every free act stand by itself but also freedom is fundamentally autonomy insofar as it gives the law to itself and is not dependent on instincts or inclinations; it is a type of efficient causality in the intelligible world enjoying a spontaneity of action before the formal laws offered by the practical intellect. As spontaneous arbitrariness, freedom is without an external cause and can always choose the opposite but is called to submit to the moral law. Cf Kant, *Kritik*, 57–59, 101, 115, 121f, 135–137, 151; — —, *Foundations*, 59–67, 71f; — —, *Religion*, 26–28, 43, 50f, 63f, 184.

contradicts the particularity of each one's desire for happiness and morality involves sacrifices, Kant considers it morally unacceptable that the just man go unrewarded. Hence he postulates a God capable of proportioning happiness to morality, a Creator (Urheber) of the natural world with its necessary laws, who also grounds the freedom of the moral law. Since God cannot be affirmed in objective knowledge, his existence has to be believed. This belief is not a moral duty but it fulfills a moral need.[18]

Kant's 'rational faith' is not Christian faith. It is accessible to everyone without Christ's historical mediation. 'Pure reason is the source out of which it springs.' Hence, while Kant allowed for a revealed, or scriptural, religion in view of the common people's reluctance to trust pure reason, reason serves as the interpreter of Scripture. Indeed supernatural faith, based on revelation, is in principle refused by Kant; it cannot legitimately be demanded of man. Man has no objective knowledge of God in himself; hence there is no theoretical doctrine of God that is inalterable, and historical knowledge is based upon contingencies and cannot be sure. Nor does man owe any duty to God, who has no needs and cannot be influenced by men. Religion consists only in recognising one's duties as divine commands; hence its content concerns only practical duties for man's moral betterment.[19] One can extend and summarise the argument against supernatural revelation thus:

What is revealed is either knowable or unknowable to human reason.[20]

If it is knowable, supernatural revelation is superfluous since man can know of himself what is allegedly revealed. At best a prophet or

---

18. Kant, *Kritik*, 142–157, 163–167; — —, *Religion*, 4–8, 190.

19. Kant, *Kritik*, 145, 148f.; — —, *Religion*, 113, 133f, 142f, 145f, 148–156, 201f, 225f, 248f, 255f.

20. Kant holds that God is speculatively or theoretically unknowable, and speculative analogy cannot be used to speak of him in comparison with sensible things; at most he can be considered the supreme moral lawgiver and described proportionately: cf *Kritik*, 154–162; *Religion*, 80–82, 126–128, 182–196, 222, 258f. In *Religion*, 215–217, 225–227, Kant indicates clearly that he understands Christian faith as directed to propositions, which he rejects insofar as they claim to say anything about God beyond what has to do with good conduct.

teacher sees more clearly than others and teaches them what they can in principle know from their own experience.[21]

If it is unknowable, it is immoral to affirm as true what cannot be known as true. God cannot demand from man an immoral act.[22]

Since the universality of phenomenal law prohibits all miracles, generations of German exegetes rewrite the gospels and project idealised images of themselves. Kant reduces Jesus to the realised ideal of humanity and a great moral teacher. He founded a church, but not a religion, since religion is one and is found in all human hearts. Jesus summarised all Kantian religion and duties in the command to love God (ie duty for duty's sake) and to love one's neighbour as oneself. In as many other ways as possible Kant assimilates Jesus' teachings to his own.[23] As a result, all faith, especially ecclesial, historical faith is relegated to private conviction and enjoys no objective standing in public debate.

Not everyone is satisfied with Kant's vision. Many see that the distinction between phenomenon and noumenon cannot be sustained. Jacobi astutely realises that to understand Kant's thought, one must understand the noumenon, but whoever understands the noumenon is already outside Kant's system.[24] How can the unknowable be affirmed

---

21.   Kant, *Religion*, 201–205, 209–214.

22.   Kant, *ibid*, 111f, 201f, 248f. Kant's argument is here extended to embrace truth telling about revealed dogmas; since Kant already excluded these from his rational religion, he just excluded immoral acts, like Abraham's sacrifice of Isaac, from the possibility of divine revelation.

23.   Rationalism's denial of miracles precedes Kant, but Paulus, the greatest rationalist exegete, was strongly influenced by Kant, as were others: cf A Schweitzer, *The Quest of the Historical Jesus*, translated by W Montgomery (1910; rpt. New York: Macmillan, 1961), 49, 103f, 324. Kantian influence can scarcely be overlooked in A Harnack, *The Essence of Christianity*, translated by T Saunders (1900; rpt New York: Harper and Row, 1957), 71–73, 76, 98–101, and makes itself felt even in F Prat, SJ, *Jesus Christ: His Life, His Teaching, and His Work*, translated by J Heenan (Milwaukee: Bruce, 1950), 276–278. Kant, *Religion*, 74–89, 105, 169–171, 208–214; he is aware, 143–145, 205f, 209–214, that his attempt to subsume Jesus' preaching under his own moral categories is not quite adequate, but he justifies the attempt by saying that everyone does it.

24.   S Atlas, 'Friedrich Heinrich Jacobi', in *The Encyclopedia of Philosophy*, edited by P Edwards, IV (New York: Macmillan, 1967), 236, cites Jacobi: 'Hence we cannot enter into the *Critique* [*of Pure Reason*] without assuming things-in-themselves, but we cannot retain that assumption upon leaving the *Critique*'.

to exist? Its very affirmation implies some awareness of its infinite reality. Hegel regards religion as the spirit's provisional perception of a reality greater than the articulation of a historical consciousness, a perception to be ultimately subsumed (*aufgehoben*) into the clarity of the concept (*Begriff*) that is absolute knowing, or Wissenschaft.[25] Schleiermacher explains religion as grounded in man's inborn feeling of absolute dependence, a feeling which Jesus' life and preaching awaken in individuals otherwise distracted by sin.[26] Kierkegaard, reacting against Hegel, sees man caught in the paradox of seeking always the infinite, the eternal, the universal, but being thrown back upon the finite, the temporal, and the particular. These paradoxical tensions keep man open for faith, but to make sense out of them man must sacrifice reason to accept in faith the realisation of those tensions in Christ, God and man.[27]

Catholic theology reacts in various ways to these intellectual currents. G Hermes develops Kant's practical reason to ground the need for revelation and the church; Gunther tries to employ Hegel to prove Catholic doctrine; Bonnetty and Bautin prefer fideism to enlightenment reason; Ghiberti and Rosmini rely upon an illuminism. All are rejected by the magisterium for excesses and errors. As the intellectual struggle develops, the magisterium increasingly uses a revived conceptualist Thomism as its principal instrument. Though early proponents incorporate many Suarezian elements into Thomism and many theologians remain eclectic, with time and precision the various currents of Baroque theology more clearly re-emerge. All concur in a basic epistemological realism and trust conceptual validity. Conceptual clarity drives the attack against Hegel and Romantic theories.[28] Moreover, as the political failure of 1848 takes the wind out of Romantic enthusiasms, baroque Thomism finds itself well adapted to the age. In the last half of the century European thought turns back to Kantian scientism. Cajetan, whose influence upon the revived

25. Hegel, 159–171, 348–350, 376–383, 400–413, 460–564, especially 553–564.
26. F Schleiermacher, *The Christian Faith*, edited by H Mackintosch and J Stewart (Edinburgh: T&T Clark, 1928), 5–18, 52–60, 123–141, etc.
27. S Kierkegaard, *Concluding Unscientific Postscript*, translated by D Swenson (1941; rpt. Princeton: Princeton U, 1968), 169–224.
28. Cf G McCool, SJ, *Catholic Theology in the Nineteenth Century* (New York: Seabury, 1977), for a very good overview.

Thomism was dominant from the sixteenth century on, had studied at Padua, a centre of the new science. His adaptation of Thomism to his age prepares it for the late nineteenth century. Cajetan, like Kant and nineteenth century scientism, trusts concepts and universally valid laws. Thomists also distinguish this. However valid the universal laws of nature, the contingency necessary for freedom is grounded in both matter and the existential order: though natures act necessarily in the essential order, they need not exist at all.[29] This same reference to contingency opens the way for supernatural revelation in history and faith. Before touching that issue some philosophical presuppositions of conceptualist Thomism should be reviewed.

For conceptualist Thomists being, ie all of reality, is grasped in an analogous concept that tends to be interpreted along the model of an abstract concept of an essence. Truth consists primarily in the

---

29. For Thomas's double attribution of contingency to matter and existence cf. J McDermott, SJ, 'Christ and Culture,' *Studia Missionalia* 44 (1995): 95f, nn. 7, 8; for existential contingency add also *ST* I–II, 109, 2, 2. J Maritain, *Sept Lecons sur l'Etre* (Paris: Tequi, 1934), 136f, 143f, 152–159, distinguishes contingent being from the chance rooted in the indeterminacy of the coincidence of diverse causal sequences, which result in the singularity of the fact (the equivalent of matter's here and now). Later in *Existence and the Existent*, translated by L Galantiere and G Phelan (1948; rpt Westport: Greenwood, 1975), 66f, he attributes chance to existence. Most Thomists seem content to attribute the contingency inherent in change, which of itself need not surpass the form-matter composition in the essential order, to existence. Cf G Klubertanz, SJ, *Introduction to the Philosophy of Being*, second edition (New York: Appleton-Century-Crofts, 1963), 157–160, 196–203; M De Wulf, *An Introduction to Scholastic Philosophy*, translated by P Coffey (New York: Dover, 1956), 108–110; W Collins, *Metaphysics and Man* (Dubuque: Loras College, 1959), 153–156; A Krapiec, OP, *Metaphysics*, translated by T Sandok (New York: Lane, 1991), 337–344, analyses substantial change in terms of the matter-form composition and, 392–396, tries to show how change indicates a deeper essence-existence composition. He can make this transition, even if not rigorously argued, because in his fundamental concept of being, 86–95, essential and existential orders are contained. — L de Raemaeker, *The Philosophy of Being*, translated by E Ziegelmeyer (St Louis: Herder, 1954), 274f, argues in the reverse order: chance arises from finite freedoms which cannot foresee the intentions of others, but to God nothing is 'unforeseen and fortuitous'. Maritain in *Sept Lecons*, 153, 158f, argues against the equation of chance and unforeseeableness, even while insisting on its preordination by God. Maritain prefers at that time a more essentialist emphasis than de Raemaeker.

conformity of the mind with reality that occurs in the passive intellect. Concepts so formed naturally encourage a static perspective on reality and support clear distinctions: between intellect and will, matter and form, body and soul, concept and judgment, world and God, natural and supernatural, reason and faith, etc.[30] Freedom is understood primarily as freedom of indifference: ie in the interplay whereby the intellect informs the will with various abstract *species*, or possibilities of choice, without the will being determined to choose any single one of them because none of them fulfils the unlimited good to which the will is naturally drawn. In mutual causality, whereby the intellect informs the will with a *species*, thereby preventing the choice from being irrational, and the will chooses freely the last *species* that will inform it in the choice, the free act allegedly occurs. Psychologically faithful to the experience of deliberation preceding choice as this explanation may be, it ultimately fails to explain why the will, being blind yet drawn naturally only to unlimited good, chooses to make any particular specie the ultimate one informing it. Precisely because no finite *species* exhausts the good, the reason for the choice is less than totally persuasive and the choice seems arbitrary. Between abstract *species* and the choice of a concrete object there is an infinite distance.[31]

Such a system offers alternatives to Kant. Though sharing a trust in objective, universal knowledge, Thomists finesse Kant by appeal to history. Truths can be historical and contingent as well as universal and necessary. Jesus Christ is then shown to be God's legate, chosen to bring God's message into the world. Christ's veracity is proven by the miracles accomplished and prophecies fulfilled, especially the

---

30. A Gardeil, OP, *Le Donne revere et la Theologie* (Paris: Gabalda, 1910), 9f; — —, 'La Reforme de la Theologie Catholique', *Revue Thomiste* 11 (1903): 643f; Maritain, *Sept Lecons*, 24–27, 71–75; — —, *Bergsonian Philosophy and Thomism*, translated by M Andison (New York: Philosophical Library, 1955), 30–38, 127, 239, 352f. Maritain's notion of being is very complex and in evolution: cf B Ritzler, *Freiheit in der Umarmung des ewig Liebenden* (Bern: Lang, 2000), 51–94, 141–165, 263–281, 285–295, 452–468. For more literature cf J McDermott, SJ, 'The Methodological Shift in Twentieth Century Thomism', *Seminarium* 31 (1991): 245f. Billot's concept of being is also very profound: cf A Cozzi, *La Centralita di Cristo nella Teologia di L Billot* (Milano: Glossa, 1999), 53–78.

31. J McDermott SJ, 'The Neo-Scholastic Analysis of Freedom', *International Philosophical Quarterly* 34 (1994): 149–164.

resurrection, the greatest of miracles which Jesus predicted. In matters of such moment God would certainly not deceive. One accepts therefore revealed truths, the material objects of faith, on the authority of God, the formal object illuminating the intellect.[32] Although these truths are supernatural, surpassing the powers of natural intellect, their incomprehensibility is somewhat attenuated by appeal to analogy. God was good enough to reveal truths in human concepts analogous to natural truths and providing a certain analogy among themselves and with man's final end (DS 3016). Some theologians, stressing the mysteriousness of faith's content, appeal to a theological analogy transcending the analogy of being, but others refuse that step, aware that the truths of faith also concern reality and should fall under the analogy of being.[33]

The problem of unity in diversity of natural and supernatural orders emerges also in the analysis of the act of faith. Though faith is a supernatural gift to be accepted freely, the acceptance cannot be irrational lest it be inhuman. Since the human mind does not directly perceive supernatural truths, rational *praeambula fidei*, ie arguments proving the witness's veracity, have to be urged. These lead to the judgment of credibility, whereby the mind acknowledges not only its natural obligation to believe whatever God reveals but also the actual occurrence of a historical relation. Since the judgment of credibility is produced by natural reason, a supplementary, supernatural judgment of credentity has to be postulated: right here and now the person is called to respond freely to grace and believe. The general recognition of revelation is rendered a concrete obligation to man's freedom.

Such distinctions do not easily stand scrutiny. If natural reason's investigations really result in a scientific, or natural, faith, what can supernatural grace add to the intellect's assent? Surely the universal contains the particular, and the general recognition of revelation's facticity naturally results in the individual's concrete obligation to believe. Recognising the problem, the great Gardeil felt forced to postulate a preliminary natural judgment of credentity before the

---

32. J McDermott, SJ, 'Faithful and Critical Reason in Theology', in *Excellence in Seminary Education*, edited by S Minkiel *et ai* (Erie: Gannon U, 1988), 71–73.

33. McDermott, 'Methodological Shift,' 245–253; this is corrected in our 'La struttura sacramentale della realta', *La Scuola Cattolica* 128 (2000): 277f, n. 8: Maritain and Journet hold for a 'superanalogy of faith' while Gardeil and Penido reject it.

supernatural judgment of credentity.[34] Moreover the certitude of supernatural faith is said to surpass the certitude of natural reason since its source is in God, who neither deceives nor is deceived, and no just cause can justify denial of the true faith (DS 3014, 3017). After all, one is expected to give one's life for the truths of faith, not for the principle of non-contradiction. Yet insofar as the *praeambula fidei* involve natural arguments depending on the first principle of reason, how can the conclusion of faith be more certain than the premises? Scientific faith surely lacks metaphysical certitude and the assent of supernatural faith is based on no further insight or argument. Some theologians distinguished the objective certitude of the revealed proposition (*quoad se et in nobis*) from the subjective certitude of the believer (*quoad nos*).[35] The flimsiness of such a subterfuge becomes evident as soon as one reflects that 'certitude' refers to the state of the knower. There are no discursive propositions certain in themselves apart from human knowers. A further question concerns faith's freedom. If faith's assent is proven by rational arguments, what room is left for freedom? Either the argument is probative and assent follows necessarily or freedom must supply for the want of rational persuasion.[36]

In the face of these and other difficulties, transcendental Thomists seek solutions by constructing their edifice not upon the concept of being but upon the judgment of being. Truth is in judgment; there the mind reaches reality. As an activity of the mind, judgment is ascribed to the active intellect. As a movement, it has a goal. Because the judgment surpasses the concept contained within it, nothing finite can satisfy its implicit desire. Once the finite is recognised as such, it is thereby surpassed. Only the direct possession of God in himself can satisfy man's intellectual desire.[37] Whereas conceptualist theologians

---

34. A Gardeil, OP, *La Credibilite et l'Apologetique* (Paris: Gabalda, 1908), 18–21, 32f; he drops the natural judgment of credentity in the second edition of 1912: cf 50f. R Garrigou-Lagrange, OP, *De Revelatione*, fourth edition (Roma: Ferrari, 1945), I, 504f, actually follows the schema of the first edition while praising and claiming to follow the second edition (398, n. 1, 503, n. 4).

35. Gardeil, *ibid*, 157–163, 172; Garrigou-Lagrange, 399, 403, 423–425, 429.

36. P Rousselot, SJ, 'Les Yeux de la Foi', *Recherches des Sciences Religieuses* 1 (1910): 444–448.

37. McDermott, 'Faithful', 75f; — —, 'Methodological Shift', 253f. We have presented the argument in greater detail in *Love and Understanding: The Relation*

minimise the relevance of Thomas's natural desire for the beatific vision, explaining it as a mere natural velleity or the consequence of supernatural knowledge,[38] transcendental Thomists take Thomas at his word and even employ the desire as the basis of the proof for God's existence. They generally uphold the natural-supernatural distinction by allowing a validity to concepts or ascribing a meaning to the infinite intellectual drive, even if it cannot attain its end without grace. Where concepts distinguish even to the point of division, judgment's motion, a combination of potency and act, overcomes distinctions even while presupposing them. Concepts are relativised within the movement of judgment. Hence the distinction between natural and supernatural, like those between matter and form, body and soul, world and God, intellect and will, remains precarious and admittedly 'paradoxical'.[39]

Within transcendental Thomism, where the intellect seeks the true as its fulfilling good, intellect and will are united in a single dynamism. The indifference of freedom is overcome since freedom is always engaged, or Augustinian, freedom. The will is created to choose the good and is most itself in choosing the good.[40] Conceptualist theologians recognise the validity of such an understanding of freedom especially for the beatific vision. They refuse to say that man's fulfilment, in which the direct vision of God as infinite Good compels

---

of Will and Intellect in Pierre Rousselot's Christological Vision (Rome: Gregorian, 1983), especially 134–139, 224–228; 'Karl Rahner on Two Infinities: God and Matter', *International Philosophical Quarterly* 28 (1988): 450–454; 'The Analogy of Knowing in Karl Rahner', *ibid*, 36 (1996): 201–216; 'Dialectical Analogy: The Oscillating Center of Rahner's Thought', *Gregorianum* 75 (1994): 675–703; 'De Lubac and Rousselot', *ibid*, 78 (1997): 741–751; 'Marechal et Rousselot', in *Au point de depart*, edited by P Gilbert (Bruxelles: Lessius, 2000), 204–217; for Lonergan cf G Rota, *'Persona' e 'Natura' nell'itinerario speculativo di Bernard JF Lonergan SJ.* (Milano: Glossa, 1998), especially 113–165.

38.   Garrigou-Lagrange, 359–376; J Maritain, *The Degrees of Knowledge*, translated by G Phelan (New York: Schribner's, 1959), 283–291.

39.   The references to 'paradoxical' natural-supernatural distinction in the works of Rousselot, Marechal, Lonergan, Alfaro, de Lubac, von Balthasar, Mouroux and Rahner can be found in J McDermott, SJ, 'The Theology of John Paul II: A Response', in *The Thought of Pope John Paul II*, edited J McDermott (Rome: Gregorian, 1993), 63f, n. 36.

40.   McDermott, 'Faithful', 75f; 'Methodological Shift', 253–257.

the will to choose God, destroys freedom; hence they change their definition of freedom from freedom of indifference to freedom of spontaneity, autonomy, or exultation and predicate the same freedom of man's following of God's law leading to the final vision.[41] Some transcendental theologians so stress Augustinian freedom as to deny freedom of indifference. Besides that affront to ordinary experience of deliberation, the transcendental position also involves this difficulty: because God is implicitly affirmed in every judgment and choice, it does not seem possible to reject him and sin mortally. Unwilling to fall into such an absurdity, Karl Rahner affirms man's capability of sinning, without which freedom would be meaningless, and described it as 'a real, absolute contradiction'.[42] Of course a contradiction explains absolutely nothing and its affirmation as real only confirms our earlier argument that evil remains inexplicable to human reason.

---

41. J Maritain, *Trois Reformateurs* (Paris: Plon, 1925), 232–237; — —, 'The Conquest of Freedom', in *The Social and Political Philosophy of Jacques Maritain*, edited by J Evan and L Ward (1955; rpt. Notre Dame: University of Notre Dame Press, 1976), 17f, 24–27; — —, 'The Thomist Idea of Freedom', in *Scholasticism and Politics*, translated by M Adler (1940; rpt. Garden City: Doubleday, 1960), 132–138; R Garrigou-Lagrange, OP, *Reality*, translated by P Cummins (St Louis: Herder, 1950), 225f; Y Simon, *Traite du libre arbitre* (Liege: Sciences et Lettres, 1951), 136–140; O Lotin, OSB, *Morale Fondamentale*, I (Tournai: Desclee, 1954), 80; J Bauscher, 'Liberte', *Dictionnaire de Theologie Catholique*, IX/1 (Paris: Letouzey, 1926), 662f; C Pesch, SJ, *Praelectiones Dogmaticae*, IX, fifth edition (Freiburg: Herder, 1923), 280f; L Janssens, OSB, *Tractatus de Homine*, I (Freiburg: Herder, 1918), 372f, 397. Actually in *Bergsonian Philosophy*, 276, Maritain denies 'all freedom', ie freedom of exercise and of specification, before God in the beatific vision, but allows it with regard to secondary objects; in this he echoes earlier scholastics like G Teppe, SJ, *Institutiones Theologicae*, IV (Paris: Lethielleux, 1896), 704f, and D Palmieri, SJ, *Tractatus Theologicus de Novissimis* (Prati: Giachetti, 1908), 180; but Pesch, *ibid*, claims that the majority are opposed to this view. The same problem occurs in Christology, where Christ enjoys always the beatific vision but must be free to merit man's redemption by some act not owed to God.

42. K Rahner, SJ, *Grundkurs des Glaubens* (Freiburg: Herder, 1976), 44f, 49, 90, 101, 102f, 106–109; cf McDermott, 'Metaphysical Conundrums', 718–726, for more on Rahner. Other transcendental Thomists recognised the need to maintain within Augustinian freedom a place for freedom of indifference, and even Rahner himself had to appeal to freedom of indifference: cf McDermott, 'Struttura sacramentale', 288f, n. 32.

That Rahner is forced to such an admission puts the validity of his system into question.

As the natural-supernatural distinction gradually dissolves, so do the reason-faith and object-subject distinctions. Because truth is known only in judgment, ie in the knowing subject's affirmation, there is no objectivity except over subjectivity. The subjective dynamism is oriented to the supernatural vision of God, and the final cause is already impressing itself upon the dynamism. So the evidence of the senses, the so-called 'natural signs' of credibility, is perceived within a supernatural movement. The natural judgment of credibility is assimilated into the supernatural judgment of credentity. Indeed, it is misleading to call the signs 'natural' insofar as they do not exist objectively in themselves. As B Lonergan claims, there is no 'already out there now'. Objectivity is grasped only in subjectivity; there is no sign without significance. Further difficulties with the transcendental analysis of the act of faith can be enumerated. First, since every intellectual act is *de facto* supernaturalised, any external sign, even 'common, everyday signs', in Rousselot's words, can induce the affirmation of faith. With that the historical mediation of Jesus Christ, so essential to Christian faith, is greatly relativised.[43] Second, since the

---

43. McDermott, 'Faithful', 76–79; 'Methodological Shift', 255–259; B Lonergan, SJ, *Insight* (1958; rpt New York: Harper and Row, 1978), chapter 8; Rousselot, 'Yeux', 258f. To save Jesus' unique, universal mediation of salvation, K Rahner, 'Die ewige Bedeutung der Menschheit Jesu fur unser Gottesverhaltnis', *Schriften zur Theologie*, III (Einsiedeln: Benziger, 1956), 57–59; — —, 'Der eine Mittler und die Vielheit der Vermittlungen', *Schriften* VIII (1967), 229–233, holds that all grace is a participation in his humanity. But there are difficulties: sanctifying grace is a participation in God's own nature, and it is not clear how a finite humanity can replace the infinity of the divine nature, to which, in Rahner's system, all people are oriented. (Cf J McDermott, SJ, 'The Christologies of Karl Rahner', *Gregorianum* 67 (1986): 87–123, 297–327, for a presentation and critique.) The late Lonergan has Jesus as the supreme and most successful realisation of universal openness to God (J McDermott, SJ, 'Tensions in Lonergan's Theory of Conversion', *Gregorianum* 74 (1993): 137f; cf also Rota, pp. 331–350, especially 342–350; A Kelly, CSsR, 'Is Lonergan's Method Adequate to Christian Mystery?', *The Thomist* 39 (1975): 437–470; S de h-Ide, 'Rahner and Lonergan', *Studies* (Dublin) 65 (1976): 63–67; C Skrenes, 'Lonergan's Metaphysics: Ontological Implications of Insight-as-Event', *International Philosophical Quarterly* 24 (1984): 409). Others, like P Knitter, *No Other Name?* (Maryknoll: Orbis, 1985), 166f, 182f, 186–204, and R Haight, SJ,

object of faith is God himself, usually described as 'personal' or 'person', and all conceptual propositions are inadequate formulations of God's infinite mystery, the authoritative dogmas of the church are relativised as the call is made to adapt them to the needs and understandings of modern man.[44] Intellectual chaos threatens. If faith cannot specify its object and make its demands concretely binding, it evaporates into the very thin air of idealistic speculation. The whole finite intelligibility of reality is radically questioned.

The basic difficulty concerns the desire for the infinite God. How can finite intelligence grasp God's infinity? If God is infinitely far, how can the finite creature overcome the infinite gap separating him from God? Any appeal to grace admits that nature cannot complete itself. Such a nature is of itself doomed to frustration and cannot provide the basis for a proof of God's existence. Man becomes, in Sartre's words, a 'useless passion'. If grace alone allegedly makes sense of nature, Catholics fall into a Protestant position and never explain how the beatific vision itself can occur.[45] A further difficulty is this: if God is

---

Jesus Symbol of God (Maryknoll: Orbis, 1999), 162, 353, 357f, 412, n 25, 422, 433, simply abandon the unique mediatorship of Jesus, faithful to a system of thought, not to the gospel.

44. McDermott, 'Faithful', 77–80; — —, 'Methodological Shift', 256–265: in nn. 33, 34, are listed leading theologians who understand faith primarily as a 'personal encounter'. Actually only J Mouroux, *I Believe*, translated by M Turner (New York: Sheed and Ward, 1959), 15, n. 1, noted that when the First Truth is recognised as the object of faith, he can be called a person only 'in the broad sense of a Personal Being'. For the real object is the divine nature which allegedly terminates man's natural desire. Until the others, Rousselot retained revealed propositions as the (material) object of faith: McDermott, *Love*, 143–145, 150f., 153, 190–194.

45. J Sartre, *Being and Nothingness*, translated by H Barnes (1953; rpt New York: Washington Square, 1966), 784. The beatific vision is affirmed on the basis of Scripture (I John 3:2; cf Aquinas, *ST* I, 12, 1–10). But its mystery presents many problems for understanding. How may the finite mind of man receive the infinite God as an informing form, which produces truth by identity, without being absorbed into God? Thomas surely sees the problem that the finite mind of man is not naturally capable of receiving the infinite God directly in an intuition; so he postulates the *lumen gloriae*. But as a created reality the *lumen gloriae* cannot extend the finite intellect to infinity. Moreover, it is not clear whether the *lumen gloriae* is something added to the natural intellect or an intensification of its power of seeing or understanding. In the former case, the *lumen gloriae* would

infinite, he is infinitely close; since judgment is a reflexive act, the subject must be originally self-conscious (*Sein ist Bei-sich-Sein*); the infinite God must be present to him intuitively; but such an intuition is the beatific vision, and such a conclusion contradicts everyone's experience.[46]

This conundrum about the finite-infinite relation shows how well transcendental Thomism is adapted to modern or postmodern thought. As the nineteenth century wearied of its bootless attempts to join the creature to God, Nietzsche proclaimed God dead, irrelevant, and interpreted man's dynamism as perpetual volitive self-transcendence. In view of the continual receding of the infinite horizon of intelligibility before man's quest for truth and objectivity, Heidegger refused all judgment about reality's meaning; meaning allegedly comes from a future that is never attained. Sartre, his pupil, concluded that if no meaning can be found, if the subject cannot know the object in itself, there is no meaning: life is absurd. Nietzsche realised that with God's demise truth also passes from the scene. Heidegger tried to save truth by reinterpreting it as a simultaneous concealing and revealing. Such ambiguity did not long satisfy. Sartre realised that man, as free, is the absolute being who creates his own values, but they die with him;

---

understand, not the human intellect, or both would somehow be understanding together, which is still not human understanding; in the latter case, the mere intensification of a natural power is not supernatural. Clearly the problem of the continuity and discontinuity between natural and supernatural orders reemerges. In addition, the passive intellect is supposed to receive God; but the passive intellect receives forms, and God is pure *Esse*, which is normally known in the judgment, the product of the active intellect. The problem of the beatific vision is all the greater for transcendental Thomists who consider the intellect as primarily active. The active intellect is not passive for reception and its drive to embrace the infinite would be unending and ultimately frustrated, even under grace. Rahner even speaks of the enduring incomprehensibility of God in the beatific vision, perhaps aware of man's continuing potency to grow in knowledge even in the beatific vision: cf K Rahner, SJ, 'Uber den Begriff des Geheimnisses in der katholischen Theologie', *Schriften* IV (1960): 57–59, 75–78. But potency implies imperfection. This is a great mystery, or perhaps the Aristotelian rational psychology is not quite adequate to describe the reality.

46. Rahner might have been aware of this tension in his thought when he wrote, *Grundkurs*, 136, 'The graced spirit moves itself in the goal (through God's self-communication) toward the goal (the *visio beatifica*)'.

and deconstructionalists simply deny objective meaning.[47] Obviously the infinite noumenon is reduced to prime matter, even if it be called 'existence', and everything is referred to its unintelligibility. Finite meaning is dissolved into infinite meaninglessness.

Within such a philosophical horizon supernatural revelation is rejected for the following reasons:

Whatever man knows is limited by the very knowing. Man stands as subject in relation to every object known.

Since man is restricted to knowledge of the finite, he cannot know the infinite God.

Without a knowledge of God no one can recognise him as the source and guarantor of any alleged revelation. Hence no one can pretend to receive or proclaim a revelation from God.[48]

3. Drawing conclusions

In the face of all these rational dilemmas, where do we stand? Squarely in the Catholic tradition. Though we have criticised the conceptualist and transcendental theologies, our questioning should not be understood as an attack upon the faith. Three things must be considered. First, Catholic faith depends not upon the validity of any particular theoretical system but upon the facticity of the resurrection. Second, there is no inconsistency in God and his speaking. The problem is not with revelation but with our understanding. All theological problems are really philosophical problems. Third, the arguments offered by Kant and existentialists against the possibility of supernatural revelation refute each other. Kant absolutised human reason, constituting it the arbiter of all truth. The existentialists, recognising the absurdity of absolutising the finite, have totally relativised reason, admitting its absurdity. When reason itself is absurd, it can hardly prescribe rules excluding God from manifesting

---

47. Nietzsche, *Zarathustra*, 27–31, 44, 74, 91, 273f; — —, *Beyond*, 1–10, 14f, 24–27, 42f, 48–51; — —, *Joyful Wisdom*, translated by T Common (New York: Ungar, 1960), #125, 167–169; M Heidegger, *Sein und Zeit*, tenth edition (Tubingen: Niemeyer, 1963), 218–230, 339–346, 356–366, 372–277, 382–397, 436f; Sartre, 789–798; — —, *Existentialism and Human Emotions*, translated by B Frechtman (New York: Philosophical Library, 1947), 19–28, 39–44, 54f.

48. These arguments are drawn from Sartre, *Being*, 17–30; — —, *Existentialism*. 22–24, 27, 54f.

himself. For that reason modern Protestants utter their 'nevertheless' to the pretensions of reason and affirm revelation as a miracle. God intervenes when and where he wants. But such an answer, by accepting the initial premise that man cannot know God with his natural intellect, engenders theological confusion: how may man interpret God's revelation if human knowing cannot grasp God? What meaning can revelation contain?[49]

The tension between conceptualist and transcendental theologians reflects the opposition between Kantian rationalism and existentialism: a tendency to absolute finite intelligibility versus a tendency to relativise it before the mystery of the infinite God. The best thinkers of both schools: Billot, Gardeil, Sertillanges, Penido, Maritain, Wojtyla, Gilson, de Finance, Rousselot, Marechal, Lonergan, Rahner, de Lubac and von Balthasar see the dangers inherent in exaggerations and attempt to maintain the proper balance between essential and existential orders, concept and judgment, natural and supernatural. The same, sane balance is sought also by other thinkers like Blondel, Przywara, Adam, Guardini, Ratzinger and Kasper.[50] Human truth, like virtue, stands in the middle, between the two interpretations of the Angelic Doctor.

In *Fides et Ratio* there emerges a comprehensive understanding of reason embracing both conceptualist and transcendental presuppositions.[51] With conceptual thinkers the encyclical affirms the distinction of reason and faith (39, 53), insisting on the former's autonomy (45, 48f, 75, 77), its natural capacity to intuit first principles (4), attain universal truth (33, 47, 82), reach an absolute (82, 97), and know God through nature (19, 22, 82). Faith must be accepted before philosophical reason contributes to its speculative illumination (42). For the truths of faith transcend reason (8f, 15, 42, 53, 55, 75). This allows faith and the magisterium to judge the insufficiencies of any

---

49. J McDermott, SJ, 'Jesus', 543–551.
50. We give brief indications of their ultimate concord in our 'Neo-Scholastic', 164f., and 'Sheehan, Rousselot, and Theological Method', *Gregorianum* 68 (1987): 714–717.
51. The numbers in parenthesis refer to the paragraphs of *Fides et Ratio* (1998). The faith-reason relation in the encyclical deserves a more extended analysis. Often presuppositions of conceptual and transcendental theologies are found in the same paragraph; the Pope's vision is not just a simple balancing of two current theologies but an attempt at synthesis.

philosophical system (44, 49f, 52–54). Although faith's truths are accepted on the revealing God's authoritative testimony (13, 55) and help to heal and guide human intelligence wounded by sin (22, 43, 73), the original acceptance of faith is not blind: there are *praeambula fidei*, certain truths available to man's mind which prepare the intellectual ground for faith's assent (67).[52] Alongside this more abstract understanding of natural reason so clearly distinct from supernatural faith is another understanding of reason, much more concrete, dynamic and relative. This sapiential reason, unifying reason and faith (15-18, 105), is primarily a quest for truth, the infinite, and the absolute (24f, 29, 33). It is concerned with the 'ultimate truth' about existence, the 'mystery' or 'insoluble puzzle' of personal existence (12, 38) that generates different philosophical systems and provides the theme of theology (4, 15). This mystery of man cannot be illuminated without reference to the mystery of God (14) and the mystery of Christ, the fullness of truth in history (9f, 13, 15, 80f, 104). This existential reason exists in history, in relation to others (21), from whom it accepts on trust many truths beyond its own experience (31f). This reason is interwoven with love and is influenced by freedom's choices (13, 15, 17, 32, 90, 107). Indeed, faith liberates reason (20). Before the mysteries of suffering, particularly innocent suffering, death (23, 26), and evil (76, 80) reason recognises its limitations and its need of insight surpassing its own power (79). Here faith and reason contain each other (16f, 77, 100), and divine truth possesses an 'innate intelligibility' (66). The cross of Christ provides 'the reef upon which the link between faith and philosophy can break up, but it is also the reef beyond which the two can set forth upon the boundless ocean of truth'. On the one hand, 'the true key-point, which challenges every philosophy, is Jesus Christ's death on the Cross. It is here that every attempt to reduce the Father's saving plan to purely human logic is doomed to failure'. On the other hand, 'reason cannot eliminate the mystery of love which the Cross represents, while the Cross can give to reason the ultimate answer which it seeks'. (23; cf also 12) Thus the original faith in reason, with truths accepted on faith from others, is expanded into supernatural faith in the loving God revealed in Jesus Christ (33f), which is historical and universal (14, 23) as well as the unity of natural and revealed truth

---

52. Among the truths listed is not the soul's immortality, a truth usually presupposed as a natural truth by conceptualist theologians.

(34, 41). For Jesus Christ reveals man to himself and brings to light his most high calling (60).[53]

Without claiming to represent the Pope's thought the following reflections seek to prolong it as they identify the structure of truth and freedom that opens man to historical revelation.

4. Truth and love

Catholic theology recapitulates in theological terms the perennial epistemological conundrum: how may the finite intellect know the infinite? How may the relative know the absolute? The same problem re-emerges in ontology and ethics: how can the finite exist alongside the infinite? How can man be free when God is omnipotent? In short, how does one reconcile the finite with the infinite in knowing, being, and acting? Faced with this conundrum, atheism short-circuits thought. Denying God only intensifies the problem. There remains another infinity resisting thought's penetration: the 'base infinity' which the ancients identified with prime matter, the principle of individuation. The human mind cannot comprehend the individual as such, and since reality is composed of individuals, the mind cannot apparently know reality as such. Human beings have identity crises, being opaque to themselves. But if you do not know who you are, who can tell you your identity? Unless there exists an infinite God who comprehends the base infinity of matter and calls individuals by name, the intelligibility of this world is lost. Many existential and decon-

---

53. These references to suffering and the cross go far beyond usual transcendental theology. Because of its demand that theology be relevant to the subject—theology is anthropology and there is no objectivity except over subjectivity—the problem of evil is scarcely touched by transcendental theology; evil has no intelligibility for the human subject. Actually the Pope's own thought is very heavily concentrated on freedom. This is clear in his magisterial study, *The Acting Person*, translated by A Potocki (Dordracht: Reidel, 1979). It is the person that primarily acts, not the nature; hence freedom is located primarily in the person, not in the natural will. In two articles, 'Theology of John Paul II', 55–68, and 'The Context of Veritatis Splendor', in *Prophecy and Diplomacy*, edited by J Conley and J Koterski (New York: Fordham, 1999), 115–172 (unfortunately the manuscript suffered some mutilation by 'inclusive language', without permission or notification), we tried to show how the Pope steers his way between the two principal Thomistic interpretations while developing his own emphasis on freedom.

structionalist thinkers draw such a nihilistic conclusion, destroying the very reason by which they draw their conclusion. Faced by man's inability to grasp the infinite, other philosophers support a 'faith' in reason.[54] But a faith in something finite is idolatry and doomed to disappoint. Pope John Paul II is more intelligent and sane. Following Vatican I, he recognises the need of faith and reason. Precisely because of his faith in God he affirms the validity of reason. A good God does not destroy man's ability to know and love him. Analogy must exist between God and the world. Without finite intelligibility perceptible to

---

54. K Popper, *The Open Society and Its Enemies*, fourth edition (London: Rutledge & Keegan Paul, 1962), I, 230–234. Admitting that the basis of rational argument is 'an irrational faith in reason' whose origin is 'an irrational decision'. In *Objective Knowledge* (Oxford: Clarendon, 1972), 4f, 9, 29f, 106, 111f, 116, 126, 143f, 154–156, 158–161, 317f, Popper thinks that his own method escapes irrationalism. Though rejecting metaphysics as a pseudo-science and refusing to see any statement as more than a hypothesis, Popper sees the need of truth as an objective basis of critical science. So he postulates an objective knowledge existing without a knowing subject, 'a kind of Platonic (or Bolzanoesque) third world of books in themselves, theories in themselves, problems in themselves, problem situations in themselves, arguments in themselves, and so on'. Yet he admits that this 'third world', allegedly 'largely autonomous' and mediating between the first world of physical objects or states and the second world of states of consciousness, is a human product but 'has no similarity whatever to human consciousness'. Similarly he wishes to provide a means for the critical evaluation of theories by trial and error-elimination in view of 'verisimilitude', ie 'better or less good approximation to the truth'; this implies truth as correspondence between mind and reality functioning as a regulative ideal, but he also denies any criterion of correspondence for true propositions. It would be so much less fatiguing and more rational to believe in a God beyond human reason, as did CS Peirce, whose acuity Popper greatly respects. Cf V Potter, SJ, ''Vaguely Like a Man': The Theism of Charles S Peirce', in *God Knowable and Unknowable*, edited by R Roth (Bronx: Fordham University Press, 1973), 241–254. — M Polanyi, *Science, Faith and Society* (1946; rpt. Chicago: University of Chicago Press, 1964), 9, 11, 15–17, 44f, 61, 63, etc, stresses that scientists and their supporting societies have to believe in truth and its accessible objectivity, even if they will never be able to express it adequately nor demonstrate it compellingly to others. Science then is a *fides quaerens intellectum*. Truth has to be accepted a reality existing independently of one's knowledge, yet accessible to all (81). In holding this position, Polanyi is open to an affirmation of God's existence as the ultimate ground of truth (82f).

human reason God cannot be known and freedom is reduced to a useless passion constructing human projections of which, like a spoiled child, it soon tires and destroys.

God can be known by human reason.[55] But how? Here we propose our solution: not by absolutising reason but by love. Human beings primordially accept that existence has a meaning not because a philosopher convinced them at the age of three by irrefutable arguments, but because their parents loved them. Without love babies die. Their parents' love mediates a meaning which harsh experience and rational conundrums later put into question. Love is the basis of morality because the love bestowed creates the obligation of a response. As one does not choose one's parents but is called to love them in return, so obligation precedes right. Five main characteristics of the moral experience can be enumerated: it is absolute, supra-rational, personal, free and liberating. *Absolute* signifies that the doing of the good involves total dedication; one must be prepared even to die, to go to apparent non-being rather than to deviate from what is right. All the attractions of this world are as nothing before the claims of duty. Such absolute commitment cannot be effected merely by a rational argument; one person cannot be argued into loving another person; for every argument can be relativised in view of the infinite-finite conundrum; so the commitment must be *suprarational,* trans-cending reason. Then it must be *personal,* ie both the moral subject and the one loved must be endowed with intelligence and freedom; human ideals exist only as abstractions elaborated by reason, and no one should give his life for something subhuman. The moral experience is *free* because it depends upon a *should,* not a *must,* and experience quickly testifies to human failures. Finally it is *liberating* insofar as every finite reality and value is relativised by the commitment unto death; nothing else matters but fidelity to the moral summons. Such moral commitment can be found in antiquity in the conduct of Phintias and Damon, Achilles' acceptance of death for the sake of Patroclus,

---

55. The following reflections were first spelt out in our 'A New Approach to God's Existence', *The Thomist* 44 (1980): 219–250, and slightly revised in 'Proof for the Existence of God', in *The New Dictionary of Theology*, edited by J Komonchak *et al* (Dublin: Gill and Macmillan, 1987), 708–710; the proof was also presented again from within the Protestant-Catholic dialogue in 'Struttura sacramentale', 273–299.

and Socrates' self-sacrifice for his fellow citizens. It is manifested most clearly in Jesus' teaching and death: 'Greater love no one has than to give his life for his friends' (John 15:13).

Philosophers can find the fly in this ointment: how can a finite man perceive something absolute? Do not values exist only in relation to individual human beings? As relational, they are limited by the one perceiving them. Sartre considers love an illusion, only a subjective projection designed to make oneself loved.[56] Is love only an illusion designed to warm and cover our cold, naked loneliness? Is there no hope of a meaning transcending us? After rejecting love as an absurdity, Sartre rejects reason as absurd. But if reason is absurd, its judgment on love cannot be valid. Cannot then the tables be turned on Sartre? Love manifests the structure of infinite and finite: an absolute claim made on a finite freedom. Recurrently the same tension between infinite and finite appears in the structure of reason. Man needs some absolute in order to think at all, but his intellect is finite. Instead of employing reason to judge love and then fall into hopeless confusion, cannot love save reason? The structures of love and reason manifest the same polar tension between absolute and relative, infinite and finite. If love is reality, then the structure of reason reflects the structure of love, which is the structure of reality. Truth is the correspondence of reason and reality and it is attained in the acknowledgment of love's reality. Of course love can be recognised as real only by the person who gives himself over to love and runs its risks. Praxis and theory go together as do freedom and thought. Here the Greek notion of truth as conformity is synthesised with the Hebrew notion of truth as fidelity. 'He who does the truth comes to the light' (John 3:21). Only the one faithful to love can affirm its truth.[57]

---

56. Sartre, *Being*, 474–491.

57. *Fides et Ratio* 82–84, 95f., has rightly insisted on the value of concepts and propositions and the enduring validity of dogmatic formulae. Space does not permit here the justification of concepts and the propositions in which they are employed, but this may be said: insofar as human knowing involves always a finite intelligibility (a concept), concepts do really mediate reality, even if they do not exhaust it; furthermore the structure of all Catholic theology is found in the tension of freedom between finite and infinite, and that structure as given in Christ's humanity and the eucharist was affirmed definitively at Nicea and Chalcedon.

Since no finite person can ground the absoluteness of love's demand, God is revealed as the One calling people to himself through the other finite person, his image. Human beings reflect the love of God to each other and in their love God is present. Thus is established the sacramental structure of reality, ie in and through a finite figure the infinite God makes himself present, calling people to the total dedication of love and upon man's response depends his eternal salvation or damnation.[58] Marriage is the 'sacrament' of creation in which Adam and Eve mediate God to each other. This structure entails its perpetuation not only in its openness to children as love's super-abundant, self-sacrificial fruitfulness but also in everlasting life. For the moment in which a person acknowledges God's absolute claim of love and goes to death in obedience to that claim cannot involve his annihilation. God has all power over him but it is exactly divine omni-potence which awakens man's freedom and makes him live the life of Love, which is God. Dr Johnson once remarked, 'When a man knows he is to be hanged in a fortnight, it concentrates his mind wonder-fully'.[59] So much the more does the free acceptance of death imply the greatest self-awareness as well as mark the greatest realisation of freedom. God does not destroy what he creates. So the one who trusts himself to God's love and shares in that love shares God's triumph over death.

The 'proof' of God's existence briefly sketched here is not a rational demonstration. A rational demonstration presupposes an absolute, undeniable premise. Otherwise no conclusion follows necessarily. The conclusion of an absolute God's existence cannot be deduced from a contingent premise. There is no finite absolute. Were there such a reality or principle of reason, there would be no need of God as the necessity grounding contingency. Our 'proof' consists merely in laying open the structure of reality. If God is not present at the beginning of an argument, he will not be present at all. God does not force himself upon man's reason through an irrefutable rational argument. One must have the eyes of love to perceive the God of love. One must recognise existence as a gift and an obligation. One must have faith in

---

58.   *Fides et Ratio* 13 refers also to 'the sacramental character of Revelation' without specifying it more closely.

59.   J Boswell, *The Life of Samuel Johnson* (1791; rpt. New York: Modern Library, nd), 725 (19 September 1777).

love's reality in order to recognise the validity of reason. There must be a faith in reason which derives from the more fundamental faith in love and in the Love that is God. Without faith in God human reason becomes meaningless, a mere sophistical tool to deceive the unwary and protect oneself against love's reality.

On the basis of creation it would be possible to affirm God's love. But creation no longer breathes forth its pristine freshness and love. Looking around this world, we see so much lovelessness: man's exploitation of man and its justification in terms of economics, psychology, evolutionary theory, politics. Children are abused, promises unfulfilled, oaths broken, lies told, marriages destroyed, people repressed, tortured, and killed, and there is so much indifference as we are bombarded with horror stories by a media intent of making a profit and pushing an ideology. Is love real? Who can assure us of love's reality? Once the idealistic enthusiasm of youth, so blind its own failings, has given way to reality and we are forced to look at our own twisted hearts, can any of us, on the basis of our experience, testify authentically and authoritatively to the reality of love? We need a witness who surpasses our broken condition. Such is Christ. The infinite was made man in order to renew the image of God among us and testify infallibly to Love's reality. Incarnate Love testifies in his own person to the reality of Love, which he has from the Father in the Holy Spirit. This testimony occurs not only in word but also in deed. Jesus gives his life in obedience to his Father and out of love for us. In going to death, heeding the command of Love, he is not abandoned. On the third day he rises to show us that Love is stronger than sin and death. That is the basis of Christian faith. Jesus is the concrete, historical proof of our 'proof' of God's existence. In his death and resurrection we know that Love is a concrete reality, a reality that transcends our ambiguous experience. Because Jesus died and rose we can have a faith in Love that is stronger and surer than any faith in love and reason based on our experience of a fallen creation. Hence Christian faith is more certain than the certitude of reason.[60]

---

60. The Christian response to suffering is the only one that makes any sense out of suffering. I have tried to indicate it in the *Bible on Human Suffering* (Middlegreen: St Paul, 1991) and 'Sofferenza', *Dizionario di teologia fondamentale*, edited by R Latourelle, R Fisichella (Assisi: Cittadella, 1990), 1154–1160 (I would make reference to the English edition of the same if the

Faith is more than a belief in a message. God's word is creative, effecting what it proclaims (Isa 55:10f). Love engenders love. By giving his all for us, Jesus causes our total response of love. Union with Jesus is union with God. Thus the new humanity in Christ restores the original unity of man with God and among people lost by original sin. The salvific, total union, involving body and spirit, comprises the church, the body of Christ, assembled around Jesus' eucharistic body. Here the sacramental structure of reality is renewed and preserved. Here the two types of freedom, indifference and engaged, are reconciled. The finite figure preserves the distance necessary for freedom of indifference; it is possible to reject God. Yet before the offer of prevenient love no neutrality is possible: all are called to respond to God. God is present in every exercise of freedom, calling men to himself. As the locus of freedom in a fallen world, the church unites in herself the strengths of the various religions of mankind. She demands obedience since love demands concrete commitment. While love presupposes human freedom, it cannot be earned, but must be received as a gift. Love's commitment is not blind. On the contrary, without love reason makes no sense. Love preserves an intellectual structure, even while its mystery encourages further investigation. Love leads to the mysticism of union since it unites persons most closely, even while preserving their distinction: 'Now live no longer I but Christ lives in me' (Gal 2:20). While being most intimately individual, love is also mediated historically and socially. Its sacramental structure involves a social body and finds expression in sacraments whereby God is present, offering himself and calling for love. In short Catholicism is the faith for all, for it alone preserves meaning and freedom, gifts bestowed on us in Christ.

---

publishers had not changed my text, without permission or notice, in favour of 'inclusive language' — which unfortunately excludes women from mankind — and thereby distorted my intention and even ascribed to me the heretical opinion that 'the eternal Son became a human person').

Fides et Ratio et . . .

Kevin Hart

I

'Faith' and 'reason' belong to an open network of concepts that Christianity has been developing since the formation of the New Testament. Because the New Testament itself draws profoundly from Jewish Scripture and Semitic styles of interpretation, as well as from Greek culture, it is hard to say precisely when these concepts first took on distinctive Christian forms. *Pistis* goes back to classical Greek and gains a positive religious meaning only in the New Testament where it continues and redirects the sense of *he'emin,* the Hebrew word for faith. *Logos* also has a deep past in classical and Hellenistic Greek, and also cuts a figure against a Hebraic ground. In its sense of 'reason', rather than 'word', it is less important in the New Testament than in reflection on it. Indeed, it is *ratio* rather than *logos* that enters Catholic theological debate; and it needs to be noted that there are more difficulties in translating *logos* as *ratio* than *pistis* as *fides.* Christianity did not develop by simply expanding or regulating a network of concepts but by folding old concepts into new ones, thereby changing the sense and function of what had been received, or by unfolding concepts only to fold them in another way, along with new concepts. And so it goes on endlessly, in ways that can be brutally simple and exquisitely complex. This is how a tradition is made, even one that is based on a revelation of God.

I use the word 'concepts' in a very general sense. In a longer and more exacting study, I would have to distinguish kerygma from dogma, *theologoumenon* from dogma, the faith of the people from the doctrines of the church, as well as ordinary and extraordinary acts of the *magisterium.* In that study I would need to show in detail how some concepts are linked, how some serve as contexts for others, and how these framings change over time, sometimes by dint of local religious practice, sometimes under the pressure of theological debates, and sometimes under the weight of ecclesiastical concerns. These concepts are not always equally valued in liturgy, theology and personal devotion. The doctrine of the Trinity, for instance, was not prominent for much of the eighteenth and nineteenth centuries, even though that doctrine is firmly embedded in the creeds.[1] And Karl Rahner is certainly right to observe that today 'despite their orthodox confession of the Trinity, Christians are, in their practical life, almost mere "monotheists"'.[2] There are other times when a concept circumscribes the whole of the faith: contemporary paschal Trinitarian theology provides an example. Yet difficulties arise when attempts are made to frame the faith completely: a heavy emphasis on the crucified and resurrected Christ in his relations with the Father and the Spirit, as occurs in neo-orthodoxies, can obscure Jesus' preaching of the *basileia*. It could be pointed out that the gospels represent Jesus before his passion as intimately involved with the Father and the Spirit, and of course it can be noted in reply that the gospels were written in the strange and compelling light of Easter. Yet no one would suggest that the preaching of the *basileia* is itself simply an expression of the newly won paschal faith.

This late in Western history each of 'faith' and 'reason' comes to us in a very creased condition. One might say that the unity 'faith and reason' has been less frequently handled than either of its terms, although one would have to recognise that the larger theme of 'grace and nature' has been folded into it in various ways. St Augustine, so the story goes, marks the culmination of patristic thought about the relations of faith and reason in *De Doctrina Christiana* and *De Trinitate*. And, likely as not, we will be asked to recognize the firm hand of St Thomas Aquinas in giving the doublet its definitive shape. Nevertheless, for most Catholics today 'faith and reason' has a nineteenth-century air about it that does not cling to 'grace and nature'. Some people will recall the condemnation of Georg Hermes in 1835 for an overly rational account of the faith developed on Kantian grounds. If that comes to mind, so too will how Louis Bautain was required to sign a formula in 1844 to make very plain that faith could not rightly squeeze reason from orthodox religious practice. John

---

1.   See John Henry Newman, *Fifteen Sermons Preached before the University of Oxford*, third edition (London: Longmans, Green, and Co, 1892), sermon 13 ('Implicit and Explicit Reason'), and Matthias Joseph Scheeben, *The Mysteries of Christianity*, translated by Cyril Vollert, SJ (London: B. Herder, 1946), Part 10, chapter 29.

2.   Karl Rahner, *The Trinity*, translated by Joseph Donceel (London: Burns and Oates, 1970), 10.

Henry Newman's nuanced discussion of faith by way of explicit and implicit reason belongs to this cultural world, as does Matthias Scheeben's careful work on the roles of faith and reason with respect to mystery.[3] Many who have little interest in nineteenth-century Catholic theology, however, will know that Vatican I (1869–70) concerned itself not only with papal infallibility but also with relations between faith and reason; and this discussion, cast as the dogmatic constitution *Deus Filius* (1870), forms the backdrop to all later reflections on the topic.

There can be no doubt that the encyclical *Aeterni Patris* (1879) is a clear and concerted extension of Vatican I's dogmatic constitution. The Aquinas who is commended by Leo XIII as exemplary for Catholic theology is the master who blended philosophical realism and supernatural faith. Pius XII confirmed his predecessor's judgment of the Angelic Doctor's excellence in *Humani Generis* (1950), while Vatican II's Constitution on Divine Revelation, *Dei Verbum* (1965), follows the earlier constitution's insistence on maintaining a balance of faith and reason. John Paul II's *Fides et Ratio* (1998) belongs to the same sequence or, more accurately, gathers the earlier documents into a tradition. In doing so the encyclical bypasses other perspectives on faith, including 'faith and dialogue' which interested John Paul II in 1972 when he was a cardinal commenting on *Dei Verbum*.[4]

At first glance one might think that the very existence of *Humani Generis*, *Dei Verbum* and *Fides et Ratio* in the second half of the twentieth century signals a renewed interest in the question how faith and reason are to be linked. Yet it is striking how little concerned each text is to refresh discussion of 'faith and reason' by reference to central currents of twentieth-century thought. To a greater or lesser extent all the documents look back to the nineteenth century. This is not to say that the church should take its cues from contemporary ideas, for each

3.   See John Henry Newman, *Fifteen Sermons Preached before the University of Oxford*, third edition (London: Longmans, Green, and Co, 1892), sermon 13 ('Implicit and Explicit Reason'), and Matthias Joseph Scheeben, *The Mysteries of Christianity*, trans. Cyril Vollert, SJ (London: B Herder, 1946), Part 10, chapter 29.

4.   See Karol Wojtyla, *Sources of Renewal: The Implementation of the Second Vatican Council*, translated PS Falla (London: Collins, 1980). Part I is mostly concerned with faith; however, the main emphases are on faith as *habitus* (27) and the relation of faith and dialogue (34). Even when commenting on DV6, which claims that God can certainly be known 'by the light of human reason', Wojtyla does not focus on the theme of 'faith and reason'.

age overvalues itself in one way or another. The church moves in larger, slower rhythms than any century; and partly because of this it can seem, from deep within the ecclesiastical hierarchy, as though its central concepts move undisturbed through history, as *tradita* rather than *traditio*. From anywhere else, though, these concepts are seen to be reset, sometimes very minutely, when religious and secular contexts change. This is not historicism; it is simply the realisation that there is an irreducible hermeneutic aspect to all preaching of the gospel. In attending to both Scripture and tradition, the church has always acknowledged this, although, to be sure, more than this has always been at stake in leaguing tradition with Scripture.

'Faith and reason' is important in the church because it falls within the broad commitment to tradition as well as Scripture. If it trusted in Scripture as the sole source of revelation, the church would have to content itself with a biblical theology, although that theology would doubtless generate its own traditions. The revelation of Jesus as the Christ might be definitive but it is not unconditioned; it was received and shaped linguistically, culturally and religiously from the very beginning. No sooner do we ask how revelation and revealability are related than the theme of 'Scripture and tradition' begins to resonate. As things stand, however, there is a double link between tradition and 'faith and reason'. For when the church speaks of the content of tradition it identifies a heritage which, especially after Vatican I, is often summarised by 'faith and reason', and which we can abridge even more tersely as the 'A' list of Catholic theology: Augustine, Anselm and Aquinas. And when the church speaks of 'tradition', considered as a medium, it identifies a style of historical transmission that is guaranteed first by faith (it is overseen by the Holy Spirit) and second by reason (it is conducted consciously, explicitly and rationally). Already, then, it has become apparent that 'faith and reason' has at least two major senses: a deposit of the faith, and the privileged way in which that faith elaborates itself.

I would like to explore this a little further, and so I ask, What does 'faith and reason' signify within the tradition? We need to be aware of the limits within which this conjunction should work; and therefore I also want to ask, What are the dangers of relying improperly or overly upon this conjunction? I do not pose this question while looking askance at the recent encyclical *Fides et Ratio*, although the encyclical does not always speak precisely; and so I wish to raise the question, How is *Fides et Ratio* to be understood? These are large questions, and I will not be able to answer them at all fully. Yet it seems to me that, taken together, they suggest a theme of their own which I can summarise as '*fides et Ratio et. . .*'

II

As soon as one begins to unfold the expression 'faith and reason' it starts to take up one's entire study. Even a cursory glance at the doublet reveals that at the beginning, namely in the Hebrew Scriptures, faith [*he'emin*] is not associated with reason but with truth ['*emet*].[5] The truth is constant, and faith is a relation of trust in that absolute reliability. Since the Jewish scriptures present Yahweh as the one who will act to save Israel, only those who trust him will be safely grounded in life. 'If ye will not believe, surely ye shall not be established', declares the prophet (Isa 7:9). At the other beginning, namely in Plato, things are indeed otherwise: for the truth is constant in its timeless self-identity, and the proper relation to have with it is not faith but knowledge. One uses true belief in scaling the dialectical heights yet converts those beliefs into knowledge when descending from the Good: such is the lesson of *Republic* 511b–c. It would be misleading to see the Jewish and the Greek models as diverging approaches in all respects, for faith in Yahweh's actions is trust that one will come to know the truth at last. Even so, the distinctions between faith and truth, and knowledge and truth, help to establish the network of concepts in which Christianity has developed.

With hindsight, it appears inevitable that a division would arise between faith and knowledge. Some have found it as early as St Paul who first spoke of 'the preaching of the cross' as being no more than 'foolishness' to unbelievers (1 Cor 1:18) and then darkly quoted Isaiah 29:14, 'I will destroy the wisdom of the wise' (1 Cor 1:19). Paul should not be taken to be deriding logical argument or the human capacity for reasoning. His quarry is those philosophical minds that misuse knowledge in order to exclude faith. That said, in the first and second centuries of the common era both Jews and Christians were criticised for supposedly having jettisoned all reason. Galen (c 130–200), for one, sneered at the faithful of both religions for not grounding their belief in

---

5.   The point is made very clearly by Wolfhart Pannenberg in his *Systematic Theology*, trans. Geoffrey W Bromiley, 3 volumes (Edinburgh: T&T Clark, 1998), I, chapter 13, II, §1.

God in natural law, as he had done, but for advising one another, 'Just believe'.[6] Undoubtedly some Christians had said exactly that, but the church saw its task as bringing faith and knowledge into some sort of harmony.

'Possibly we may be rightly said to believe everything we know, but not to know what we only believe.'[7] So wrote Augustine in his early *Soliloquies*. As figured here, faith is secondary to knowledge, and the Bishop of Hippo never wished to transform it into certainty. That was what we must hope for in the life to come. Here and now we must stretch toward that full knowledge by always living in terms of a dialectic. In Augustine's words this comes to be, 'Faith seeks, understanding finds' [*Fides quaerit, intellectus invenit*], a formulation which was to be mirrored centuries later by St Anselm and which was to influence all later Catholic theology.[8] This description of Christian life is a very long way from the injunction 'Just believe', not least of all because it turns on two senses of 'believe'. Christian life begins with an act of faith which makes the truth available to the believer, though not in a comprehensible manner. One begins to uncover that truth, insofar as it is possible, by the exercise of reason, and in doing so one comes to understand what is believed. The passage is from *fides qua* to *fides quae*,

---

6.   Richard Walzer, *Galen on Jews and Christians* (Oxford: Oxford University Press, 1949), 48. Plainly Galen had not encountered the writings of Justin Martyr or Clement of Alexandria, both of whom sought to establish relations between Christianity and Greek philosophy.

7.   Augustine, 'The Soliloquies', in *Augustine: Earlier Writings*, edited and translated by John HS Burleigh, The Library of Christian Classics, VI (London: SCM Press, 1953), 28.

8.   Augustine, *On the Trinity*, translated by Arthur West Haddan, in *The Works of Aurelius Augustine*, 15 volumes, edited by Marcus Dods (Edinburgh: T&T Clark, 1873), VII, 378. The expression has been refigured many times in both Catholic and Protestant contexts. In the latter, *fides* is usually implicitly taken as *fiducia*. Emily Dickinson, for instance, recasts it as 'Faith bleats to understand — ', *The Poems of Emily Dickinson*, variorum edition, 3 volumes, edited by RW Franklin (Cambridge, MA: Belknap Press of Harvard University Press, 1998), I, 301. Augustine's formulation has also generated intriguing variations of no particular religious persuasion. For example, the Argentinian aphorist Antonio Porchia writes, 'He who does not know how to believe, should not know', *Voices*, translated by WS Merwin (Chicago: Big Table Publishing, 1969), 31.

and it offers a profound satisfaction. 'For understanding is the reward of faith' [*Intellectus enim merces est fidei*].[9]

Now the rubric 'faith and understanding' is not quite the same as 'faith and reason', and this should make us pause before accepting the old line that Augustine marks the culmination of patristic thought on 'faith and reason'. The truth is a little more complex, and in order to glimpse it we need to return to our man's understanding of faith. If we ask Augustine what he means by 'belief' his final answer is 'consideration with assent'.[10] There is no faith without thought, and human beings think because we have been created in the image of God. In particular, we use reason to gain knowledge. That Augustine prizes reason in the quest for understanding is evident from his writings on the subject, although it would be a wild error to convict him of intellectualism. *The Confessions* tell us how the reasoning that prepared for his act of faith was embedded in experience, and how this preparation was itself shaped by desire and imagination. Also, as Etienne Gilson rightly points out, 'the Augustinian doctrine of the relations between faith and reason gives formal expression to a moral experience'.[11] The passage from *fides qua* to *fides quae* does not occur in a vacuum. Gilson puts the matter very well: 'The adherence of the mind to God's authority implies humility, but humility in turn presupposes a confidence in God, and this in itself is an act of love and charity' (31). In other words, Augustine's 'faith and understanding' is not reducible to 'faith and reason'; it could be better summarised as 'faith and reason and . . .' [*fides et ratio et. . .*].

Could one say the same of Thomas Aquinas? Since the publication of *Aeterni Patris* he has become the Catholic theologian most prized for an exemplary balancing of faith and reason. This phrasing needs to be underlined. Thomas should not be commended as exemplar but as exemplary.[12] The *Summa Theologiæ*, for instance, should not be held up

---

9. Augustine, *Lectures or Tractates on the Gospel According to St John*, trans. James Innes, in *The Works of Aurelius Augustine*, X, 405.

10. Augustine, *On the Predestination of the Saints*, translated by Peter Holmes and Robert Ernest Wallis, in *The Works of Aurelius Augustine*, XV, 124.

11. Etienne Gilson, *The Christian Philosophy of Saint Augustine*, translated by LEM Lynch (London: Victor Gollancz, 1961), 31.

12. The distinction is Otto Weber's although, so far as I am aware, he did not use it in conjunction with Thomas Aquinas. I am indebted to Elisabeth Moltmann-Wendel for

as a model to which Catholic theologians are to conform in all respects
but as an example that illustrates how theology can be done in a
courageous, creative and responsible manner. To some extent *Fides et
Ratio* confirms this in saying that Christianity has no official
philosophy.[13] That Thomas valued both faith and reason is obvious to
anyone who reads a page by him. Indeed, his view that one cannot
possess the same truth by both faith and reason is central to his
thought. People have sometimes taken this to generate oddities in his
system, suggesting, for instance, that a philosopher who establishes the
unity of God by logical argument cannot properly confess at mass, 'I
believe in one God'. Putting such questions aside, what needs to be
noted is that for Thomas faith is an imperfect knowledge, one that
cannot be perfected by the appropriate use of reason.[14]

One might be tempted to say that, for Thomas, a bracing of faith
and reason is necessary for developing a theology but not essential to
the practice of religion. This would be an inaccurate statement of
matters. For Thomas, everyone who is in a position to do so should
seek to establish that God exists, and therefore should separate the
preambula fidei from what is revealed solely by supernatural means.
Also, Thomas insists that faith is not just a matter of a personal relation
with Christ; it has a propositional structure. For although faith is a
theological virtue, a free gift of God, and therefore surpasses reason, its
content can be distinctly stated. The believer should assent to the creed
regarded as a series of propositions even though the realities it
presents will one day be revealed to us by intuition alone.[15] Thomas
does not place undue stress on this aspect of faith: only theologians are
required to have explicit belief in a wide range of articles, while both
the learned and the unlearned enter into the life of God through

introducing me to Weber's distinction. See her *Autobiography*, translated by John
Bowden (London: SCM Press, 1997), 24.

13. John Paul II, *Fides et Ratio* (Strathfield: St Paul's Publications, 1998), 107.

14. Aquinas, 'It is clear, however, that imperfection of knowledge belongs to the very
nature of faith', *Summa Theologiæ*, Ia2ae 67.3, translated by WD Hughes, Blackfriars
edition, volume 23 (London: Eyre and Spottiswoode, 1969).

15. Aquinas, 'Then, that vision will not take the form of a proposition, but of a simple
intuition', *Summa Theologiæ*, 2a2ae 1.2, translated by TC O'Brien, Blackfriars edition,
volume 31 (London: Eyre and Spottiswoode, 1974).

faith.[16] We are drawn to the articles of faith and the eternal life they proclaim by the divine love itself, and we assent to them not through the exercise of reason but by a movement of the will. Certainly Thomas thinks that we can discover that God exists by natural reason and that we can enter the divine mystery by faith, but he does not propose a particular arrangement, 'faith and reason', as the way in which divine love must be approached or accepted. Negative theology plays too big a role in his doctrine of God for that to be so: we are unable to know 'the divine substance', he writes, 'Yet we are able to have some knowledge of it by knowing *what it is not*'.[17] For Thomas, what we call 'faith and reason' is properly understood as a relationship between theology and philosophy. The former has gained a high profile in large part because it stands under the authority of the latter. If that is the case, it is only reasonable to ask if this framing can skew the faith.

III

It would be a mistake to answer this question by looking for a species of reasoning that occurs outside philosophy. Some philosophers have very high hopes for reason—Plato, Descartes and Hegel come to mind—while others content themselves with more modest claims on its behalf: Kant and Wittgenstein, for example. Besides, philosophy has no strict borders. One can find its grounding motifs at work even in disciplines that believe they have loosened all ties with it. So a possible world in which 'love and exegesis', 'sacrament and hope', 'faith and imagination', or 'faith and dialogue', had the same status in Christianity that 'faith and reason' has in ours would still be a world in which reason would play an important role. I do not want to suggest that these conjunctions provide better alternatives than 'faith and reason', only that, strictly speaking, 'faith and reason' cannot be conceived without involving them also. Properly understood, *fides et ratio* should be heard as *fides et ratio et. . .*

I think this needs to be stressed. Unless 'faith and reason' is embedded in a context that shows its connections with love and

---

16. Aquinas, 'those who have the office of teaching others are held to an explicit belief in more things than others are', *Summa Theologiæ*, 2a2ae 2.6; 'faith is that habit of mind whereby eternal life begins in us', *Summa Theologiæ*, 2a2ae.4.1.

17. Aquinas, *Summa Contra Gentiles*, 5 volumes, translated by Anton C Pegis (Notre Dame: University of Notre Dame Press, 1975), I, 14, 2.

sacrament, any commendation of it by the church can give the false impression that Christian existence has neither flesh nor blood. With that in mind, some caveats about how 'faith' and 'reason' can be presented might be in order. We know that reason can be set in sharp contrast to experience: rationalism provides an example. It may never have been the church's intention to set a gulf between experience and natural reason, although her official pronoucements, especially those made with modernism in mind, can mislead the unwary. Even an encyclical that has been sifted as carefully as *Fides et Ratio* talks of a 'crisis of rationalism' (72) rather than a 'crisis of rationality' or even a 'crisis of reason'. One must ensure that too strong an emphasis on discursive reasoning does not allow Christian experience to slip out of focus and become a blurry background against which we see the sharp contours of 'faith and reason'. Similarly, faith is frequently defined against experience, often as a direct response to the authority of Hebrews 11:1 ('Now faith is the substance of things hoped for, the evidence of things not seen.'). And so, as Gerard Ebeling suggests, we may find ourselves saying that 'Faith believes in the face of all experience' without recognising that 'experiences offer themselves which are peculiar to faith'.[18] I do not propose to engage the question whether faith opens experiences that are unavailable to non-believers or whether it creates an allegiance to Christ that helps the believer negotiate experiences that are common to all.[19] All I wish to point out is that, if 'faith and reason' is regarded as a directive that is essential to the Christian life, and if both 'faith' and 'reason' are defined against experience, *Erfahrung* as well as *Erlebnis*, Christianity is quietly removed from the company of flesh and blood.

Such an abstraction would ill suit a religion grounded in the incarnation of God and elaborated in the sacraments. Indeed, it is precisely in his 'On the Incarnation of the Word' that Anselm observes, 'he who does not believe will not experience, and he who has not had

---

18. Gerhard Ebeling, *The Nature of Faith*, translated by Ronald Gregor Smith (Philadelphia: Fortress Press, 1961), 158.

19. See respectively Eberhard Jüngel, *God as the Mystery of the World: On the Foundation of the Theology of the Crucified One in the Dispute between Theism and Atheism*, translated by Darrell L Guder (Grand Rapids: Eerdmans, 1983), 32, and Tom Wright, *What Saint Paul Really Said: Was Paul of Tarsus the Real Founder of Christianity?* (Oxford: Lion, 1997), 157.

experience will not know'.[20] The idea of setting 'faith and reason' against experience has the air of one of those lopsidedly intellectualistic theology manuals that haunt the imaginations of some contemporary theologians, and has a sense of recoil brought about by the strictures against modernism in *Pascendi* (1907) and *Lamentabili* (1907) or, more recently, by a distrust of charismatics. Such a recoil would be regrettable, however. For Jesus taught that God reveals himself in our experience of the *basileia*, and since the *basileia* is never simply here but is always also to come it follows that our experience of God is never given simply in the present. In general, Christianity teaches that experience and transcendence are not always to be opposed. Of course, in the Catholic faith experience of God is centred on the sacraments considered as the body of Christ. Just as the incarnation was not the first moment of the life of Christ but his whole existence on earth, including his existential condition, so too our lives are to be wholly sacramental in character, not merely punctuated by baptism, Eucharist, marriage, and the others.[21] To have been baptised into the faith is to be called to live in such a way that *basileia* and *ekklesia* may become one. Similarly, to be married or ordained a priest is to have entered profoundly into the salvation offered by Jesus, and each and every moment that follows the reception of the sacrament offers an opportunity for that reception to be individually confirmed and deepened.

We can distinguish, then, between the validity of a sacrament, the life it opens, and the individual confirmation of that sacrament and that life. An ordinary experience like peeling an orange for one's child is not a sacrament; it is a reaffirmation of the sacrament of marriage. It takes place in a relationship that is borne along by the paschal mystery. The experience occurs within that mystery and affirms it. In a world of sacraments there is no event that, in principle, cannot be part of Christ's saving activity; and this runs across the spectrum from daily chores to unmerited mortal suffering. Nothing occurs simply within a horizon of calculation, and no theology of sacraments could entertain

---

20.   Anselm, 'On the Incarnation of the Word', in his *Trinity, Incarnation and Redemption: Theological Treatises*, edited by Jasper Hopkins and Herbert Richardson, revised edition (New York: Harper and Row, 1970), 10.

21.   See Edward Schillebeeckx, *Christ the Sacrament of the Encounter with God*, n. trans (London: Sheed and Ward, 1963), 26.

the idea. It would be a return to the misunderstanding of sacraments being efficacious because of the priest's sanctity. The scholastic expression *ex opere operato* is sometimes unfairly regarded as the ground of this view. Yet it means something else: the sacraments are always efficacious because Christ always acts in and through them. As it happens, this gives us an insight into how reason and faith enter into a relationship. Considered philosophically, a sacrament can be regarded as validly performed if the proper prayers are said in the appropriate context by an authorised person. Also, one can say with strict philosophical rigor that for an event to happen there must be a possibility of the unexpected occurring.[22] (Everyone has stories of things going wrong at baptisms and weddings.) One steps outside the economy of philosophy, though, when saying that the divine mystery enters into the conferring of a sacrament. And one remains outside philosophy in saying that God can unexpectedly enter any event in life. Peeling an orange for one's child is, as I have said, a response in faith to the sacrament of marriage; and it is by no means impossible that seeing a man peel an orange for his daughter could stir an observer to believe or deepen belief in God. In a scene quietly and invisibly charged with grace, a gesture of the man's hand, the way he turns to look at his daughter, or the tone of simple words exchanged between the two, could be the avenue for an observer to crystallise a decision about God. A philosopher will say that no event is bounded by a single, uninterrupted horizon of expectation, while a theologian will add that this same point acknowledges the freedom of God.

IV

I do not think that the church's reflection in the twentieth century on 'faith and reason' has sought to bypass or reduce the role of the sacraments. Yet experience that occurs within the space opened by sacraments needs to be acknowledged whenever one presents 'faith and reason' as a theme. That doublet is invoked, especially in *Fides et Ratio*, partly to reiterate that the separate terms form a unity and partly to affirm the importance of metaphysics. I would like to register a couple of reservations about how 'reason' is used in the encyclical, and

---

22.   On the question whether an event or encounter can be anticipated, see Jacques Derrida, 'Mes chances: au rendez-vous de quelques stéréophonies épicuriennes', *Confrontation*, 19 (1988), 23.

then, before considering the remarks on metaphysics, pose the general question of what is involved in reading a document such as this.

The first thing that strikes me in *Fides et Ratio* is its double relation to modern discussion of the scope, status and strength of reason. On the one hand, there is a fear that a 'crisis of rationalism' will inevitably lead to 'nihilism'(72). I have already noted that the word is 'rationalism' rather than 'rationality' or even 'reason'. The allusion, I take it, is to the firm shaking that David Hume's skepticism gave to Kant while enjoying his dogmatic slumbers as a Wolffian rationalist. Now the critical philosophy attempts to provide a transcendental ground for the human understanding, and this has two consequences: the theoretical use of reason is limited, and a gap is introduced between faith and reason. The ontological argument for the existence of God received a very severe blow, and not even the best continental doctors have been able to put it back on its feet. Since we cannot prove that God exists, we have to rethink the existence of God, freedom and immortality—the three postulates of pure practical reason—by way of faith.[23] Ecclesiastical faith will not suffice, Kant thought, for it is merely empirical and external. Only a moral faith can generate a rational faith.[24] Now Kant's response to the 'crisis of rationalism' is usually taken to lead to theological liberalism, not to nihilism. One significant exception is Nietzsche, for whom the critical philosophy leads ineluctably to nihilism understood as the devaluation of all values.[25] In a strange way, perhaps Nietzsche and the Vatican passed

---

23.   Kant, *Critique of Judgement*, translated by James Creed Meredith (Oxford: Clarendon Press, 1952), 142–44.

24.   Kant, *Critique of Pure Reason*, trans. Norman Kemp Smith (London: Macmillan, 1933), 650; *Religion within the Limits of Reason Alone*, translated by Theodore M Greene and Hoyt H Hudson (New York: Harper and Row, 1960), 99.

25.   See Friedrich Nietzsche, 'How the "Real World" at Last Became a Myth', in *Twilight of the Idols and The Anti-Christ*, translator and introduction by RJ Hollingdale (Harmondsworth: Penguin, 1968). Heidegger distinguishes 'crude nihilism (eg Bolshevism)' from 'nihilism' in the philosophical sense of the word. *Fides et Ratio* appears to take the word in a more general sense than either. Heidegger's warning to Christianity is worth noting. He tells us that 'The most disastrous nihilism consists in passing oneself off as protector of Christianity and even claiming for oneself the most Christian Christianity on the basis of social accomplishments' when people today should recognise that the prevalent state of being is 'that all *goals* are gone'. How Christianity is to weather this abandonment of being is not made clear. What the

through one another in 1998 while nonetheless heading in opposite directions.

On the other hand, *Fides et Ratio* shows little interest in what twentieth-century thinkers have said about reason. Philosophers have various understandings of reason, and it is common for these to be criticised by other philosophers without anyone seriously thinking that rationality is being abandoned or assailed. Let us consider two people who have been considered to be unfriendly to reason. Martin Heidegger may attempt to rethink 'human being' by way of a relation to being rather than by way of 'rational animal', but he does not conduct his project in an unreasonable manner.[26] Similarly, Sigmund Freud's placing of reason in the context of a distinction between the conscious and the unconscious does not amount to a plea for irrationalism. In dismissing the description of man as a rational animal, Heidegger's intent was to ground *Dasein* in concrete practice, and this kept irrationalism more surely at arm's length, he thought, than do those philosophies that invest humans with only a theoretical faculty of reasoning.[27] And in investigating the unconscious, Freud was seeking to make sense of human desires so that we could live with our neuroses rather than have them live us. Neither thinker may fit into the history of ideas that is tightly folded inside *Fides et Ratio*, yet neither dismisses reason. Moreover, an understanding of relations beween *Dasein* and being, and of unconscious desires, may well serve to clarify the scope, strength and status of reason. And this would be of help for the faithful in understanding the sense and function of 'faith and reason' in the church today. We may not all be touched by the Heideggerian rethinking of human being but, as WH Auden remarked over sixty years ago, Freud has become 'a whole climate of opinion'.[28] Interestingly enough, he has remained so, despite a failure of confidence in the curative powers of psychoanalysis.

---

church can learn from Heidegger, however, is that nihilism is not necessary simply outside the practice of Christianity. See Martin Heidegger, *Contributions to Philosophy (From Enowning)*, translated by Parvis Emad and Kenneth Maly (Bloomington: Indiana Univesity Press, 1999), § 72.

26.   See Heidegger, *Nietzsche*, IV, edited by David Farrell Krell, translated by Frank A Capuzzi (San Francisco: Harper and Row, 1982), § 21.

27.   Heidegger, *Vom Wesen der menschlichen Freiheit. Einleitung in die Philosophie*, *Gesamtausgabe*, 31 (Frankfurt am Main: Vittorio Klostermann, 1982), § 26b.

28.   WH Auden, 'In Memory of Sigmund Freud', in his *Selected Poems*, edited by Edward Mendelson (London: Faber, 1979), 93.

No sooner does one begin to comment on *Fides et Ratio*, though, than the question arises as to what sort of text it is and, accordingly, what degree of exactness one should expect of its formulations. Without being disrespectful, one must say that it is not an essay in philosophy, the history of philosophy, theology, or the history of theology, although, to be sure, it draws on all these disciplines. The encyclical is a letter, not an essay, and a glance at its notes will show that its principal references are ecclesiastical rather than scholarly. The letter is signed—John Paul II's handwritten signature as Pope is reproduced—and while we know that encyclicals are drafted by theologians, read by the Curia, and then redrafted many times, so that, in a sense, the document is written by the church, it is nonetheless possible to find traces of Karol Wojtyla in the text. Since it is a letter, the document is addressed: not to the faithful at large but to 'My Venerable Brother Bishops'. Priests, religious, and lay Catholics, not to mention other Christians, are put in the slightly awkward position of reading someone else's mail. Yet it is fully expected that we will read it. Like many encyclicals, this is a letter that is sent to its addressees in the full awareness that many others will read it and that they should read it.[29] The address and signature are nevertheless important, for they remind us that the encyclical is first and foremost an ecclesiastical document. Once the character of *Fides et Ratio* is evident, we should consider it in terms of the church's self-understandings before and after Vatican II, keeping in mind John Paul II's developing sense of that council's vision of the proper relations between hierarchic authority and cooperation among theologians.

I do not have the time in this short paper to show how Vatican II, or even the former Cardinal Wojtyla's commentary on it, *Sources of Renewal*, is tucked into *Fides et Ratio*. All I can do is briefly ponder two of John Paul II's observations about metaphysics that are ventured under the sign of 'faith and reason'. The first is that 'A theology without a metaphysical horizon could not move beyond an analysis of

---

29. Some of John Paul II's encyclicals—*Laborem Exercens* (1981) and *Redemptoris Missio* (1991), for instance—are addressed to 'Venerable Brothers and dear sons and daughters', while others such as *Veritatis Splendor* (1993) and *Fides et Ratio* (1999) are addressed only to his brother bishops. The latter documents tend to be more explicitly concerned with questions of faith and morals, though the distinction would be hard to maintain in all John Paul II's encyclicals.

religious experience, nor would it allow the *intellectus fidei* to give a
coherent account of the universal and transcendent value of revealed
truth' (119). And the second is the judgment that metaphysics provides
'the path to be taken in order to move beyond the crisis pervading
large sectors of philosophy at the moment' (119). I find these puzzling
remarks for several reasons. It is not clear what 'metaphysical' means
here, nor is it certain who or what is being criticised. Also, there has
been a curious shift in the encyclical: what seemed to be a letter about
'faith and reason' has turned into a text about 'faith and metaphysics'.
Let me begin, then, by trying to clarify matters.

One reason why people are likely to be confused is that
'metaphysics' means quite different things in different contexts. For
Aristotle, the word denotes what comes after [*meta*] the study of
nature. It is first philosophy, the explanation of what is the case, and at
its most fundamental it is the study of being and unity. Thereafter,
even those who kept faith with Aristotle tended to take *meta* in a
stronger sense, so that 'metaphysics' came to mean the study of that
which transcends nature. It has been inflected in many ways in
modern times: Descartes, for instance, construes it as a general science
that undergirds all others, while Kant regards it as *a priori* speculation.
If John Paul II has in mind that theology must address what transcends
nature, then there can be no doubt that for him theology must be
metaphysical in this sense. One must pass, he writes, 'from *phenomena*
to *foundation*' (118), meaning that one should neither remain at the
level of empirical study nor allow empiricism to set the limits for
study. No prescription is given about what kind of 'foundation' is to be
determined or where it is to be. At this level of generality it could be in
the human subject or in God. This metaphysics—the study of what
transcends nature—may not have much to do with metaphysics in any
other sense, except of course the philosophical lexicon that constitutes
book D of Aristotle's *Metaphysics*. For even Karl Barth freely uses
words like 'being' and 'unity'. 'If we open our mouths, we find
ourselves in the province of philosophy', he said, although he freely
admitted to being a gypsy there.[30]

When John Paul II characterises philosophy as in a state of crisis, he
recalls Edmund Husserl's 1935 lecture at the University of Prague,

---

30.   Karl Barth, *Credo: A Presentation of the Chief Problems of Dogmatics with Reference
       to the Apostle's Creed*, translated by J Strathearn McNab (London: Hodder and
       Stoughton, 1936), 183.

'Philosophy and the Crisis of European Man'. What animated Husserl in that lecture, and in all his last work, was the spectre of 'the seeming collapse of rationalism'.[31] This was nothing to do with rationalism itself, he thought, but with 'its exteriorization, its absorption in "naturalism" and "objectivism"' (191). Europe would end either 'alienated from its rational sense of life, fallen into a barbarian hatred of spirit' or rise again 'through a heroism of reason that will definitively overcome naturalism'(192). Transcendental phenomenology, he had no doubt, could be this 'heroism of reason'. The Pope's interest in phenomenology is well known: his second doctorate was an evaluation of Max Scheler's ethics from a Thomist perspective. He has testified to how his 'Aristotelian-Thomistic formation was enriched by the phenomenological method' and has noted that phenomenology 'is rich in christian inspiration'.[32] *Fides et Ratio* speaks of a crisis in ways that recall Husserl, as well as evoking 'new and unsuspected horizons' (104), a phrasing that instantly puts one in mind of Martin Heidegger. Like Husserl, the Holy Father wishes to save human reason in order to prevent the success of 'a barbarian hatred of spirit'; and like Husserl he sees a metaphysical philosophy—for phenomenology became a metaphysics with *Ideas I* (1913)—as the only way in which our spiritual weariness and despair can be overcome.

That someone or something is being chastised in *Fides et Ratio* is unmistakable, but exactly who or what is not immediately apparent. An example will make the situation a little clearer. Karl Barth certainly envisaged his *Church Dogmatics* to be without a metaphysical horizon, and that extraordinary work certainly reaches far beyond an account of religious experience and attempts to give a coherent account of revealed truth. Faith supplies its own ground in the Logos, Barth tells us, and its reasonableness cannot properly be derived from anywhere else: 'the ontological order demonstrates itself in the noetic'.[33] We

31. Edmund Husserl, 'Philosophy and the Crisis of European Man', in *Phenomenology and the Crisis of Philosophy*, translated and introduction by Quentin Lauer (New York: Harper and Row, 1965), 191.

32. Pope John Paul II, *Gift and Mystery: On the Fiftieth Anniversary of My Priestly Ordination*, n. trans (New York: Doubleday, 1996), 93–94; [Karol Wojtyla], *Sign of Contradiction*, translated by Mary Smith (Middlegreen, Slough: St Paul Publications, 1979), 14.

33. See Barth, *Church Dogmatics*, III: 1, edited by GW Bromiley and TF Torrance, translated by JW Edwards *et al* (Edinburgh: T&T. Clark, 1958), 349. The importance

should talk not of an *analogia entis*, for that inevitably restricts our knowledge of God to human terms, but of an *analogia fidei*. Notice though that Barth does not reject analogy, and he certainly does not reject reason: in exploring faith we are dealing with an analogy, and so we are required to reason with respect to *Gleichheit* and *Ungleichheit*, identity and difference, equality and inequality. Important as human reason is for Barth, it is not put in the service of constructing a metaphysics. That said, it is unlikely that John Paul II is objecting to Barth or his Catholic admirers, Hans Urs von Balthasar being not the least among them.[34] He may not agree with all that Barth has to say—the status and the role of the *analogia entis* remain sticking points—but there is perhaps more common ground between Basel and Rome than there once seemed.

More likely, John Paul II has in mind those Catholics who follow liberals and modernists in regarding faith, not revelation, as the ground of theology. This, for him, would be a consequence of 'the crisis of rationalism'. And surely he also has in mind those liberation theologians and advocates of political theology who in practice give precedence to establishing a unity of 'faith and politics' rather than of 'faith and reason'.[35] *Fides et Ratio* is adamant that there is to be no 'uncritical adoption' of 'opinions and methods drawn from Marxism' (81). What a 'critical adoption' would be remains undeveloped in the encyclical. Which aspects of Marxism would have to be criticised by a Catholic theologian before the social vision of Marxism could be of use

---

of Anselm for Barth on this issue needs to be underlined. 'God gave himself to him [Anselm] to know and he was able to know God', writes Barth. *Anselm: Fides Quaerens Intellectum*, translated by Ian W. Robertson (London: SCM Press, 1960), 170.

34. See for instance Hans Urs von Balthasar, *The Theology of Karl Barth*, translated by John Drury (New York: Holt, Rinehart and Winston, 1971). John Paul II wished to raise von Balthasar 'to the dignity of the cardinalate' but the theologian died before this could occur. See 'Telegram from Pope John Paul II', *Hans Urs von Balthasar: His Life and Work*, edited by David L Schindler (San Francisco: Ignatius Press, 1991), 289.

35. Johann Baptist Metz, for instance, has been sharply critical of the Augustinian dialectic of faith and reason, arguing instead for Christianity to learn from the Jewish people's reliance on reason and memory. See his 'Anamnestic Reason: A Theologian's Remarks on the Crisis in the *Geistewissenshaften*', in *Cultural-Political Interventions in the Unfinished Project of Enlightenment*, edited by Axel Honneth, Thomas McCarthy, Claus Ofe and Albrecht Wellmer, translated by Barbara Fultner (Cambridge, MA: MIT Press, 1992).

to Christianity? It is no easy question because there are several Marxisms, some of which respond to the positive influence of Christianity's vision of society more openly and more benignly than others. Marxism's debts to Christianity are more extensive than a prophetic vision of social justice, however. It draws on a heritage of metaphysics from the Presocratics to Friedrich Schelling, as folded by Hegel and then refolded by Marx.

The example of Marxism brings another sense of 'metaphysics' to mind, what is now commonly called 'the metaphysics of presence'. It is primarily associated with Heidegger, although one must be careful to distinguish the early philosopher who, even as late as his *An Introduction to Metaphysics* (based on lectures given in 1935), was sympathetic to the project, from the thinker who shortly after came to regard it as an impediment to thought.[36] This later Heidegger came to the judgment that to think about beings in general and the highest being in particular, as metaphysics has done since Aristotle, is to become trammeled in a notion of being as permanent presence. Now 'presence' spawns a rich lexicon in Heidegger—*Anwesen, Anwesenheit, Gegenwart, Parousia, Präsenz, Vorhandensein*—and it would take some time to detail it fully. In brief, what Heidegger seeks to question is not the flux of coming-into-presence, *Anwesen*, which Heraclitus and Parmenides experienced, but rather the hardened presentness, *Anwesenheit*, which to a greater or a lesser extent marks all philosophy thereafter and the consequence of which is modern technology's preoccupation with *Vorhandensein*. Historically, it is *Answesenheit* that has generated, among other things, the ghostly image of a static, supersensible world.[37] Indeed, it is in a history mostly characterised by *Anwesenheit* that human being has been figured as the rational animal. 'As long as man remains the *animal rationale* he is also the *animal metaphysicum*', Heidegger tells us.[38] Only if we seek what

---

36. The expression 'metaphysics of presence' is taken up by Jacques Derrida, who shows the strength, scope and status of this metaphysics far more thoroughly than Heidegger does. See the central chapters and appendix of my *The Trespass of the Sign*, exp edition (New York: Fordham University Press, 2000).

37. Heidegger, *Nietzsche,* III, translated by Joan Stambaugh, David Farrell Krell, Frank A Capuzzi, edited by David Farrell Krell (San Francisco: Harper and Row, 1987), 133.

38. Heidegger, 'The Way Back into the Ground of Metaphysics', in *Existentialism from Doestoevsky to Sartre*, edited by Walter Kaufman, revised and expanded edition (New York: New American Library, 1975), 267.

grounds metaphysics itself, the question of the truth of being, can we refigure human beings by way of our relation with being.

It is possible to see Heidegger's dismantling of metaphysics, in his sense of the word, as a complicated folding of Martin Luther's *Heidelberg Disputation* (1518) which itself refolds St Paul's warning to the Corinthians which has already folded Isaiah's vision of Yahweh's sentence, 'I will destroy the wisdom of the wise'.[39] That may be so, although rather more than Luther's sense of *destruuntur* is enclosed in Heidegger's word *Destruktion*. Heidegger has no doubt that the Christian understanding of God has been partly shaped by this metaphysics. It was not one of his concerns to show just how this occurred or to release the reality of the living God from the metaphysical concept of God as absolute ground. He admitted that this was one path to follow, while he pursued another; and one can only regret the neo-paganism of his later writings. The first path, though, has been variously marked out. The work has been undertaken to stress the freedom of God with respect to his determination as being (Jüngel), to show that God presents himself under the horizon of the gift rather than being (Marion), to stress that Thomas's understanding of *esse* is not simply metaphysical (Caputo), to revive an originary sense of faith (O'Leary), to elaborate a new understanding of the sacraments (Chauvet), and to emphasise that negative theology places God beyond the categories of being and non-being (Hart).[40] All I wish to take from this complex body of work is this: the metaphysics of presence does not so much illuminate the Christian God as postulate him as the highest value, the *ens supremum*, the ground of all entities.

---

39. Martin Luther, *Heidelberg Disputation* (1518) in *Luther's Works*, 55 volumes, gen edition Helmut T Lehmann (Philadelphia: Muhlenberg Press, 1958–86), 31: *Career of the Reformer* I, editor Harold J Grimm. John van Buren offers an illuminating account of Heidegger's investment in Luther's appropriation of 1 Corinthians 1:19 in his *The Young Heidegger: Rumor of the Hidden King* (Bloomington: Indiana University Press, 1994), 160–65.

40. See for example Jüngel, *God as the Mystery of the World*; Jean-Luc Marion, *L'Idol et la distance* (Paris: Grasset, 1977) and *Dieu sans l'être* (Paris: Fayard, 1982); John D Caputo, *Heidegger and Aquinas: An Essay on Overcoming Metaphysics* (New York: Fordham University Press, 1982); Joseph S O'Leary, *Questioning Back: The Overcoming of Metaphysics in Christian Tradition* (Minneapolis: Winston Press, 1985); Louis-Marie Chauvet, *Symbol and Sacrament: A Sacramental Reinterpretation of Christian Existence*, translated by Patrick Madigan, SJ and Madeleine Beaumont (Collegeville: The Liturgical Press, 1995); and my *The Trespass of the Sign*.

To construe God is this way is to allow him to be subsumed by a human dream of completeness and permanence where the divine being cannot be thought as becoming, and, ultimately, to reduce him to the status of an idol.

Fides et Ratio cites the expression 'the end of metaphysics'(82) with disapproval although without making it plain whether the object of criticism is logical positivism, which wanted to dissolve metaphysics, or those philosophers like Heidegger and Jacques Derrida who draw deeply, if critically, from phenomenology. The one is linked to a project of philosophical modernism, while the other is leagued with what people have come to call 'postmodernism'. Certainly the encyclical shows considerable unease about what it dubs 'postmodernity' (127), and censures 'destructive critique of every certitude' (127). Yet it remains unclear who or what is being referred to here. It has been loosely suggested in the media that the Pope has Derrida in mind. Were that so, Vatican theologians would be relying more on caricatures of the French philosopher than on reading his writings with the closeness they deserve, for Derrida takes pains to show that deconstruction is affirmative, not 'destructive', is not a species of 'critique', and is to be aligned with justice.[41] Derrida's rich analysis of the gift should be of deep interest to anyone interested in the theology of grace, while his reflections on faith and testimony might be a useful reference point for debate among fundamental theologians.[42] And in time his essays on forgiveness and hospitality

---

41. Plainly this is not the place to distinguish Derrida's thought from 'destructive critique of every certitude'. Suffice it to say that Derrida writes of 'deconstructive (ie affirmative) interpretation', *Spurs: Nietzsche's Styles*, translated by Barbara Harlow (Chicago: The University of Chicago Press, 1979), 37. In an interview he notes that 'Deconstruction is also a deconstruction of critique. Which does not mean that all critique or all criticism is devalued, but that one is trying to think what the authority of the critical instance signifies in history', *Points. . . Interviews, 1974–1994*, translated by Peggy Kamuf and others (Stanford: Stanford University Press, 1995), 212. Considering the distinction between law and justice, he observes that 'Deconstruction is justice' in 'Force of Law: The "Mystical Foundation of Authority"', *Cardozo Law Review* 11: 5–6, 945.

42. See Derrida, *Given Time: I. Counterfeit Money*, translated by Peggy Kamuf (Chicago: University of Chicago Press, 1992) and *The Gift of Death*, translated by David Wills (Chicago: University of Chicago Press, 1995), and his discussion with Jean-Luc Marion in *God, the Gift, and Postmodernism*, edited by John D.

are likely to elicit discussion among moral theologians.[43] I would
hope, then, that official disapproval is limited to the earlier, modern
call for 'the end of metaphysics'.[44] Positivism confidently announces
the meaninglessness of ethics, metaphysics and theology; while the
thought that stems from phenomenology—which, as we have seen,
John Paul II knows very well indeed—attends to the closure, not the
end, of the metaphysics of presence.[45] Christians of quite different

---

Caputo and Michael J Scanlon (Bloomington: Indiana University Press, 1999).
Robyn Horner broaches a rethinking of the deity along the lines of the gift in her
Rethinking God as Gift: Marion, Derrida, and the Limits of Phenomenology (New
York: Fordham University Press, 2001). With regard to Derrida on faith, see his
essay 'Faith and Knowledge: The Two Sources of "Religion" at the Limits of
Reason Alone', translated by Samuel Weber in *Religion*, edited by Jacques
Derrida and Gianni Vattimo (Cambridge: Polity Press, 1998). My reservations
about Derrida's account of faith are noted in '"Absolute Interruption": On Faith',
in *Questioning God*, edited by John D Caputo, Mark Dooley, and Michael J
Scanlon (Bloomington: Indiana University Press, 2001), 186–208. See in
particular Derrida's response and my reply on 200–202. My reservations about
Derrida's notion of 'religion without religion' are indicated in my
Postmodernism: A Beginner's Guide (Oxford: Oneworld, 2004), 123–27.
Derrida's remarks on testimony can be found in *Demeure: Fiction and Testimony*
bound with Maurice Blanchot, *The Instant of My Death*, both translated by
Elizabeth Rottenberg (Stanford: Stanford University Press, 2000).

43.   See Derrida, 'To Forgive: The Unforgivable and the Imprescriptible', *Questioning
      God*, 21–51, and his comments in the roundtable 'On Forgiveness', that follows.
      Also see his *On Cosmopolitanism and Forgiveness*, trans. Mark Dooley and
      Michael Hughes, preface by Simon Critchley and Richard Kearney (London:
      Routledge, 2001) and his discussion with Anne Dufourmantelle, *Of Hospitality*,
      translated by Rachel Bowlby (Stanford: Stanford University Press, 2000.

44.   The encyclical is critical of other tendencies that are perhaps more evident in
      analytical than continental philosophy: empiricism, historicism, pragmatism and
      scientism. In general, its language suggests sympathy for the phenomenological
      and hermeneutical tradition. The brief remarks on postmodernity are far too
      cautiously and imprecisely formulated to offer any guidance. Even here, though,
      there is nothing said that captures the thought of Heidegger or Derrida. Indeed,
      'nihilism' seems to be linked to 'a certain positivist cast of mind'. Plainly, John
      Paul II regards (and rightly so) the legacy of positivism as having outlasted the
      logical positivist school.

45.   See AJ Ayer, *Language, Truth and Logic* (London: Victor Gollancz, 1936) and
      Derrida, *Of Grammatology*, translated by Gayatri Chakravorty Spivak (Baltimore:
      The Johns Hopkins University Press, 1976), 4.

stripes have noted that this closure does not precipitate nihilism but rather reinvigorates discussion about theology.[46]

Overall, my sense is that, although 'faith' and 'reason' have passed into each other over the millennia, the conjunction 'faith and reason' is essentially a nineteenth-century phenomenon, a projection of 'grace and nature' upon the axis of epistemology. Even *Fides et Ratio* does not focus steadily upon its title; it talks of rationalism and faith, along with metaphysics and faith, while not defining either sharply. The looseness of definition is intentional, I suspect, for quite rightly the church has no wish to specify a particular philosophy as the vehicle of the faith. What the church needs to stress is that rationalism and fideism are equally unfaithful to the Catholic tradition, and the encyclical indicates this very plainly. The tradition is one in which faith and reason are valued but do not arrange themselves in a formula: they always presume at least another 'and', and that 'and' bespeaks love and sacrament, hope and exegesis, imagination and testimony—in a word, 'experience'. I think this would be palpable if Catholics read Augustine, Anselm and Aquinas both as a whole and more closely. Perhaps what *Fides et Ratio* tries to say, in a voice that is by turns authoritative and cautious, is that seminarians and theologians should attend ever more closely to our tradition. It is right to say that. It is also right to suggest that this tradition must remain open to what is thought throughout the centuries. In saying so, it whispers a fundamental truth of the Catholic faith, *fides et ratio et. . .*

---

46. See for example *Phenomenology and the 'Theological Turn': The French Debate* by Dominque Janicaud *et al*, translated by Bernard G. Prusak, Jeffrey L Kosky and Thomas A Carlson (New York: Fordham University Press, 2000). François Nault offers a useful overview in his *Derrida et la théologie: Dire Dieu après déconstruction* (Montréal: Les Éditions Médiaspaul, 2000). Also see Jean-Louis Chrétien's comments in his 'Rétrospection', *L'inoubliable et l'inespéré*, second edition (Paris: Desclée, 2000), especially 172–73.

A Response to the Papers by John McDermott and Kevin Hart

Gerald Gleeson

1. Introduction

Whenever we reflect on the relationships between faith and reason, we must first clarify our starting point and intellectual perspective. Are we, as theologians, reflecting on the methods and results of human reasoning from the perspective of Christian faith, or are we, as philosophers, reflecting on the reality of faith from the perspective of human reasoning? This question of intellectual starting point, in other words 'the hermeneutical question', is the most general issue raised for me by the two papers this morning. In this response I will seek to show, in the light of suggestions by John McDermott and Kevin Hart, that the standpoints of faith and reason are irreducible and need to be held in a mutually enriching tension. My remarks will be in keeping with what I believe to be the central message in *Fides et Ratio*, viz that theological activity grounded in faith should include and embrace philosophical activity, while, for its part, philosophical activity should be positively open to insights deriving from faith and revelation.

I first take up the standpoint of faith and theology. The question here is: What should Christian faith make of human reasoning?

2. Faith reflects on human reasoning

Since the act of faith involves—among other things—an intellectual assent to revealed truth, it raises for a believer the question of how, if at all, human reasoning is exercised in relation to this act of faith. John McDermott has reminded us that whereas in the Protestant tradition faith is solely God's work, in the Catholic tradition the grace of faith includes within itself the human response, viz truly cooperative activity on the part of intellect and will. It is this *doctrine* which underpins Pope John Paul II's argument in *Fides et Ratio* that 'It is an illusion to think that faith, tied to weak reasoning, might be more penetrating' (48). Writing as a bishop (not as a philosopher), the Pope urges us to have confidence in the power of human reasoning, convinced that unless it is allied to the use of reason, faith itself will suffer, indeed will wither into 'myth or superstition' (48).

One task for Catholic *theology*, therefore, is to probe this doctrine and so to show how and why the use of reason should be intrinsic to the response of faith, to explain why respect for the conclusions of natural reasoning should enhance faith as a supernatural activity. Yet this task can have no systematic resolution for, as McDermott has also reminded us, neither 'conceptualist Thomism' nor 'transcendental Thomism' has been able completely and systematically to coordinate the relations of faith and reason, grace and freedom, within the assent of faith. We are dealing here with what Karl Rahner in a seminal essay famously characterised as 'mystery' in the properly theological sense: there is no third term to link faith and reason, there is no independent vantage point from which the respective roles of faith and reason, grace and human response, could be apportioned and coordinated.[1]

Moreover, Kevin Hart has reminded us that when faith is our starting point, it must not be narrowly conceived simply as intellectual assent. Thomas Aquinas identified three elements within the complex act of faith: *believing truths* revealed by God, *relying on God* as one who reveals truly, and *clinging to God* with one's whole being. Hart situates this complex act more widely within the rich tapestry of *Christian experience*, which encompasses exegesis, sacrament, imagination, practice, dialogue and hope. Hart makes the important point that the restricted conjunction 'faith and reason' is a nineteenth century construct reflecting the problematic of the time, a problematic with which *Fides et Ratio* is still dealing, and to which the two great recent schools of Thomistic thought mentioned above have sought to respond: viz the neo-Thomism which emphasised the validity of human *concepts* as a grasp of the finite intelligibility of creation, and the subsequent transcendental Thomism which emphasised the dynamism of human *judgments* as reaching out to the infinite horizon of being, there to meet the self-communication of God. In the ultimate insufficiencies of both systems McDermott sees demonstrated the tension between finite and infinite which defies neat systematisation, and which constitutes a genuine 'mystery'.

---

1. Karl Rahner, 'The Concept of Mystery in Catholic Theology', *Theological Investigations* volume IV, translated by Kevin Smith (London: DLT, 1974).

Having noted that 'faith' should be read inclusively—inclusive of sacrament and experience, exegesis and dialogue, imagination and experience—Kevin Hart also alerts us to the real danger that human reason in its various philosophical guises will distort faith. This is the danger of *rationalism* to which Catholic theology is perennially exposed. In what is almost an aside, Hart suggests that theology's 'high profile' derives from the fact that it stands under the authority of philosophy, ie that theology's intellectual credentials depend on its being a philosophically shaped enterprise.

But for many that is precisely the problem. Hart's particular concern is the way a 'metaphysics of presence' distorts the reality of God affirmed in faith. This is the metaphysical view on which being or reality is equated with the presence of an object or thing, of 'the real already out there to be discovered'; on which the human being is exhaustively circumscribed as a rational animal; on which the transcendent is 'the ghostly image of a static world, supersensible world'; and finally, on which God is equated with the 'supreme being', the ground of being, and the highest value. In such a metaphysics God becomes an idol trapped within the net of human reasoning as it aspires to a totalising, comprehensive understanding of reality.

Of course Catholic theology at its best has always been aware of its limitations, of the 'negative moment' which undercuts the 'positive moment'. For Thomas Aquinas, no sooner have we come to affirm that God is, than we must also confess that we cannot know who or what God is. For Thomas, faith joins us to God as to one unknown. Yet Hart's 'negative theology' is more radical than that of Thomas, for although he speaks of the sacramentality of ordinary experience, such that seeing a man lovingly peeling an orange for his daughter might be the (sacramental) event which stirs an observer to believe in God, it is not clear that this moment of faith involves an affirmation on the part of *reason* which might lend itself to subsequent *philosophical* articulation.

To reflect on the difficult question of how philosophy may enter into the understanding of faith, without distorting it, we need to begin again from the vantage point of philosophy. From the standpoint of natural reason and philosophy the question is: What should reason make of religious faith?

3. Philosophy reflects on the response of faith

As John McDermott has noted, modern philosophy has been notoriously harsh in its judgment on religious faith. Modern philosophy began with the turn to the human subject, and it typically explores human reason and experience 'from within', and concludes that since human reason is only exercised validly within its own proper limits, limits it cannot transcend, faith is either superfluous (if God is indeed accessible to reason), or is irrational and immoral (if God is truly beyond human reason). Just what the valid limits of human reason are said to be varies from philosopher to philosopher, eg from Kant's moral rationality to the sense-data of the positivists. McDermott helpfully generalises the issue in terms of the fundamental tension between finite and infinite. That finite human reason can in some way grasp, or at least affirm, the infinite God, is one of the *theological* presuppositions of *Fides et Ratio,* and this is why John Paul II urges philosophers not to foreclose on the possibility of revealed truth. Furthermore, as McDermott argues, it is precisely because of the limitations of reason in the face of the key mysteries of human existence—evil, suffering and mortality—that we look to the answers of faith.

4. The tension between faith and reason

How then should these two perspectives, those of faith and human reasoning, relate to each other? How should the limitations of reason and the proper humility of faith impact on each other? In this regard I was struck by McDermott's remark that 'All theological problems are philosophical problems'—they turn on the inability of human reason to master the mystery of God and God's self-communication. To this lapidary remark, I can imagine Kevin Hart responding that 'theological activity' involves much more than a quest for intellectual mastery, and that the true 'theological problem' is that one must live one's faith without the backing of philosophical solutions. And yet this response (if indeed it would be Hart's response) is not so far from McDermott's own proposal of a 'sacramental' understanding of reality, in which the most readily accessible paradigm of reality's structure is the experience of human love and the moral response it elicits.

Our two speakers are thus agreed that the structure of reality is not to be derived from reflection on 'things', on static finite essences or 'objects out there', but is rather to be discerned in the structure of human experience as 'sacramental', as intimating that which escapes it, viz the unbounded mystery of God. In the experience of being loved by a finite other, and of being summonsed to love in return (as perhaps in Hart's example of seeing a man lovingly peel an orange for his daughter), McDermott argues that a person may encounter something absolute and unconditional—the infinite Other, God, who is thereby made present.

I take it John McDermott is speaking here as a theologian, from the vantage point of faith. From the vantage point of philosophy, the idea of the finite perceiving the infinite remains problematic. And yet, perhaps some forms of philosophy can nonetheless help faith remain true to itself in this regard. In speaking of the finite as sacramental, we must acknowledge, with Louis-Marie Chauvet, that sacraments mediate the *absence* of God as much as the *presence* of God. That is to say, sacraments only mediate the presence of God on the condition that we remember they are sacraments, and not God. Chauvet writes: 'To accept [a sacrament's] mediation is to agree that [the] vacancy [of God] will never be filled.'[2]

This theme—that being is never fully present, that reality always escapes our grasp of it—is the recurring theme of those twentieth century philosophies and theologies to which Kevin Hart draws our attention. He mentions Jüngel, Marion, Caputo, O'Leary, Chauvet and his own proposals for a 'negative theology', and regrets that *Fides et Ratio* does not examine any recent 'post-metaphysical' construals of human reason, which deploy such themes as freedom, gift, *esse* as relational, sacrament etc. However, I think Hart may be a little too 'charitable' to his own approach when he reads *Fides et Ratio*'s strictures on the 'end of metaphysics' as applying only to positivism, and not to more recent deconstructionist philosophies. There is more than enough mention of postmodernism and nihilism for me to conclude that philosophies of deconstruction are being criticised (but as usual, papal documents rarely name names).

2.   Louis-Marie Chauvet, *Symbol and Sacrament, A Sacramental Reinterpretation of Christian Existence*, translated by Patrick Madigan SJ & Madeleine Beaumont (Collegeville: Liturgical Press, 1995), 177ff.

5. What kind of metaphysics do we need?

Fides et Ratio affirms the need for metaphysics in theology, for a philosophy capable of transcending the empirical to attain something absolute (83), and indeed of a philosophy of being which grasps, albeit imperfectly and analogously, the 'ontological, causal and communicative structures' of reality (97). Although John Paul II does not endorse any particular metaphysical system, his language remains largely that of conceptualist Thomism with its strongly 'realist' concerns, and it remains unclear to me just how much scope he thinks there is for approaches to 'Christian metaphysics' like those advocated by our speakers today.

The Pope acknowledges the hermeneutical problem and looks to philosophy to deepen our understanding of the relationship between concepts, language and truth (96). May I suggest that John McDermott and Kevin Hart, in different but related ways, are well embarked on this task, and are already quite a way ahead of the kind of traditional 'realist metaphysics' that *Fides et Ratio* adumbrates. I think that is a good thing, but I would like to ask both speakers whether they do agree with me that their approaches have indeed moved beyond the kind of metaphysics endorsed in the encyclical. For my part, I believe that the kind of irreducible polar tension that John McDermott finds between finite and infinite applies equally to the relationship between reasoning and faith. Believers find themselves *in the midst* of this tension, at one moment allowing faith to complete reason and prompt its further explorations, at another moment allowing reason to illuminate and even to critically refine and purify faith.

In conclusion, I would summarise the fundamental message of *Fides et Ratio* in this way: since the object of faith is the reality of God, our exploration of faith should welcome and draw upon our best insights into the nature of reality itself. In drawing on our best philosophical insights there are, however, two dangers in particular. First, there is the danger that our insights will reflect a too limited view of reality, thereby either restricting faith to what we can understand ('scepticism' or 'rationalism from below') or, conversely, abandoning faith to the domain of the irrational ('fideism'). Secondly, there is the danger that our insights will be too ambitious, thereby circumscribing faith, making God an idol in metaphysical dress ('rationalism from above'). I thank our speakers today for helping us to explore ways in which we may avoid these dangers, and so ensure that Christian faith is truly faith in the living God, not worship of an idol of our own philosophical construction.

Faith and Reason: Friends or Foes in the New Millennium? A Response to McDermott and Hart

Anthony Fisher OP

1. For whom?

It is with some fear and trembling that I, a Dominican, enter the fray on the topic of grace and freedom with a Jesuit. Our two orders do not have a particularly good record when it comes to discussing such things. For nearly two hundred years until 1773 our best theologians and philosophers were locked in combat on *de auxiliis* of tribal proportions to rival even that between supporters of opposing Melbourne football teams. Eventually we had to be formally forbidden by Pope Paul V from calling each other heretics! Instead, the Jesuits called us quietists and Jansenists and we called the Jesuits Pelagians and laxists. However, I have found my Dominican soul much comforted by John McDermott's insistence that 'God is present in every exercise of freedom, calling men to himself'—a doctrine entirely compatible with the Thomistic doctrine of the total dependence of human freedom on the *concursus* of God. I was also delighted by his exploration of the interdependence between knowledge (both of faith and of reason) and freedom, and of love as a precondition of both. McDermott strikes me as neither Pelagian nor laxist.

Well, *Fides et Ratio* was not written for battling Dominicans and Jesuits, so whom was it written for? Kevin Hart notes that it is formally a letter to bishops, but wonders who the real target is: he suggests it might be 'liberal Catholics' and liberation theologians. I don't think that quite gets it. For one thing, not all encyclicals are addressed to bishops: the one before *Fides et Ratio, Evangelium Vitæ,* for instance, was addressed to all the faithful. Might John Paul have particular reasons for addressing the bishops in particular here? One reason might be that bishops are the chief preachers and teachers in the local churches and John Paul II is here exhorting them to join him in his task as critic and evangelist of modern culture. Another might be that bishops are

responsible for the Catholic universities, theological and pastoral
institutes and John Paul II is exhorting them to do certain things with
respect to those institutions. And a third might be that bishops are
called to be pastors of academics and ordinary people who are
constantly engaging in informal theologising and philosophising.

But Hart is obviously right to think that there is more to the story
that an exhortation by the Pope to the bishops. One way to discover
this is to do something which would horrify a writer of detective
novels such as Professor McInerny: that is, to go straight to the end of
the story to find out how it all resolves itself. *Fides et Ratio* ends with
some remarks in turn for theologians, for those responsible for priestly
formation, for teachers of philosophy, for scientists, and lastly for
every seeker after truth and meaning.

For philosophers, there is a closing declaration that 'The church
follows the work of philosophers with interest and appreciation; and
they should rest assured of her respect for the rightful autonomy of
their discipline'. But there is a plea here also: that philosophers have
the courage to recover their place in a long tradition, that they open
their horizons to 'the range of authentic wisdom and truth,
metaphysical truth included', that they 'always strive for truth, alert to
the good which truth contains'. There are reasons in the letter, and
elsewhere in John Paul's writing, to think that he thinks philosophers
are not always so broad or deep or courageous.

For theologians, to whom he says his 'thoughts turn particularly',
there is encouragement also to breadth and depth, but there is also a
particular exhortation to recover a sense of 'the intimate bond between
theological and philosophical wisdom' which is 'one of the Christian
tradition's most distinctive treasures'. Clearly the Pope thinks some
Catholic theology at least lacks philosophical rigour or insight. He also
echoes St Bonaventure's critique of those who engage in 'reading
without repentance, knowledge without devotion, research without
the impulse of wonder, prudence without the ability to surrender to
joy, action divorced from religion, learning sundered from love,
intelligence without humility, study unsustained by divine grace,
thought without the wisdom inspired by God'.

With respect to those responsible for priestly formation, whether
academic or pastoral, he echoes an oft-sounded caution that seminaries
and ecclesiastical faculties neglect sound philosophical grounding at
the peril of their charges. 'I have myself emphasized several times the
importance of this philosophical formation for those who one day, in

their pastoral life, will have to address the aspirations of the contemporary world and understand the causes of certain behaviour in order to respond in appropriate ways.' Obviously, once again, John Paul has not chosen this audience at random. He is all too aware of the wholesale abandonment of philosophy in many theologates since Vatican II and the risks of this for the passing on and development of the Catholic tradition and for the formation of critical minds amongst future priests and laity. Courses in spirituality and social sciences are, in his view, no substitute as a foundation for theological studies. And like the myth of value-free science still naively or self-interestedly proclaimed by some, theologies without overt thinking about their underlying philosophical basis far from being philosophy-free will inevitably have underneath them some unexamined covert philosophy, or some minestrone of leftovers of past and present ideologies, possibly ill-suited to understanding faith.

John Paul then has words for scientists and ordinary faithful whom he calls as the church to join the rest of humanity in a humble but confident search for truth and meaning. The church has long seen its task not as excluding either faith or reason but as bringing them 'into some sort of harmony'. Yet as Hart notes, individual Christians have not always demonstrated such good sense. Galen, he tells us, sneered at Jews and Christians for not grounding their belief in God in natural law, as he had done, but for advising one another 'Just believe'. Perhaps our age is more inclined to Galen's pole, making a religion of human reasoning, human effort and human pride, unpolluted by divine revelation. Yet as recent press accounts of cults alive and well here in Australia luridly demonstrate, the fideistic 'just believe' recurs throughout Christian history both amongst simple Catholics who find the musings of academics offensive to pious ears, and amongst some simple Protestants who think mundane reason unavoidably deceiving or simply unnecessary.

In Evelyn Waugh's novel *Brideshead Revisited* Rex, a Protestant, wants to marry Julia, a Catholic, and so decides to become a Catholic himself. He presumes this is a simple matter of signing a form and paying a membership fee, but is told he must first receive instruction. One of McDermott's brothers, a Jesuit father, renowned for his triumphs with obdurate catechumens, is chosen. After the third meeting Julia's mother inquires of Fr Mowbray how he finds her future son-in-law.

'He's the most difficult convert I have ever met.'

'Oh dear, I thought he was going to make it so easy.'

'That's exactly it. I can't get anywhere near him. He doesn't seem to have the least intellectual curiosity or natural piety.

'The first day I wanted to find out what sort of religious life he had till now, so I asked him what he meant by prayer. He said: "*I* don't mean anything. *You* tell *me*". I tried to, in a few words, and he said: "Right. So much for prayer. What's the next thing?" I gave him the catechism to take away. Yesterday I asked him whether Our Lord had more than one nature. He said: "Just as many as you say, Father."

'Then again I asked him: "Supposing the Pope looked up and saw a cloud and said 'It's going to rain', would that be bound to happen?" "Oh, yes, Father." "But supposing it didn't?" He thought a moment and said, "I suppose it would be sort of raining spiritually, only we were too sinful to see it".'

As the story progresses Fr Mowbray decides to treat Rex as a semi-imbecile, as he accepted anything and everything the priest told him and remembered some of it. His instruction came to something of a crisis, however, when Julia's naughty baby sister Cordelia took Rex aside and told him that in addition to the catechism there were other, more important arcane Catholic doctrines, which were being kept from him. For example: you have to sleep with your feet pointing east because that's the direction of heaven, and if you die you can walk straight there; that one of the popes made one of his horses a cardinal; that there is a box in the church porch into which pound notes are placed with people's names on them to get them sent to hell; that there are sacred monkeys in the Vatican; and so on.

The story is an amusing one, but my point in quoting it here is that Rex thought that a good Catholic would accept on faith anything the priests told him, no matter how irrational, and that one should not complexify things any further. Why worry if the realm of empirical reality, grasped by the senses and human reason, and the realm of religious reality, known by faith and church authority, contradict each other? Indeed, ever since the fathers of the 'Enlightenment'—from Hume and Voltaire through to Dawkins and Philip Adams—declared faith and reason opposed, the irrationality of the Christian religion has often been presumed not only by intellectual elites outside the church but even by the faithful and perhaps secretly by some ecclesiastical academics. It is for them, as much as anyone, that the encyclical is therefore written.

2. How?

So how are we to relate faith and reason? With what intellectual resources? At this conference there has already been plenty of discussion of the various Thomisms which have informed much Catholic magisterial thought in the lead-up to *Fides et Ratio* and which McDermott points out are proposed as antidotes to the dualism, reductionism and other ill-effects of Enlightenment philosophies such as that of Kant. Far be it from me to say anything to discourage the Thomist turn: it is a rare case of Catholic academy leading rather than following in the modern world and a delight to live in a time when new books on Aquinas are appearing every few weeks. But Kant was and perhaps still is rather too much a boo word in certain Catholic circles the way Thomas and Wojtyla are in Catholic circles of a rather different hue. Outside the Catholic academy people may wonder what all the fuss is about and find much of value in each. What would neo-Kantians such as O'Neill, Korsgaard, Shermon, Hermann, Baron, Louden, Sullivan and others make of the Kant so often denigrated by some Catholic thinkers and uncritically adopted by others? They would, I suspect, offer much more complex and subtle accounts of Kantian moral psychology and very different readings of Kant on questions such as the supposed disjunctions or oppositions between morality and desire, or between faith and morality, and so on. While not necessarily agreeing with all their readings of their master's texts or the value of their own positive contributions, one can still appreciate the importance of reading them to enrich our thinking or sharpen our critique.

In a similar vein Hart complains that the tone and sources of *Fides et Ratio* are very nineteenth-centuryish. I found the document at once much older and much younger in its feel. Older, because the faith and reason doublet is so much older, appearing as it does, for instance, around twenty times in the *Roman Catechism* which was prepared the last time there was a Dominican saint-pope—which as you might guess was a long time ago, more than four centuries ago in fact. Hart recognises the influence of 'the A team' (Augustine, Anselm, Aquinas), and therefore of a long patristic and scholastic tradition. Yet he deplores the failure of *Fides et Ratio* and many other recent Catholic magisterial documents 'to refresh discussion of "faith and reason" by reference to central currents of twentieth-century thought'. Of course that may just be because many of those 'central currents', far from being sources of refreshment, are more like the rips that regularly drag Australian surfers out to sea. The corrosive cynicism and nihilism, pervasive mendacity and will to domination which speakers at this symposium from a variety of perspectives have identified as crises of the academy and the broader society are, I suspect, often fed by those very currents of modern thought and thus understandably feared in Roman quarters. But I do not find a complete absence of twentieth century thought in *Fides et Ratio* such as Hart implies: there are various glimpses of Continental thought, especially of phenomenology and personalism; there is an unparalleled invitation (unparalleled in magisterial documents that is) to consider the wisdom of the East and of indigenous cultures; there is the enthusiasm for the church joining contemporaries of all religions and none in a partnership in pursuit of meaning; and various names are recommended who are to a lot of us Anglo-Americans not because they are nineteenth-century names but because they are Continental European or even Russian names. If John Paul II stands prophetically against the perennial temptation to jump into bed with the zeitgeist and for the need to sift the latest ideological fashions carefully and not ignore treasures of more traditional wisdom, he does so while at least as well informed about, and as dependent upon, the currents of twentieth century thought as the best of us are.

Hart concludes that 'faith and reason' are properly valued but do not arrange themselves in a formula: they always presume at least another 'and'.' I wonder if we shouldn't be thinking of a different conjunction or preposition, such as faith and reason 'via', or 'from' X 'to' faith and reason. In many situations adding perception, or humility, or love, or sacrament, or hope, or exegesis, or imagination, or testimony, or experience would only confuse a doublet offered, not to exhaust all that matters in human life, but rather to describe the different but hopefully compatible ways of knowing, of access to truth, with distinct ends and means. It is of course very important to be aware that there's a lot more to life, that faith and reason must reflect *on something*, be informed *by something*, be sensitised and inspired and tutored *in something*, and the something here will be experience or love or flesh and blood or whatever. Both our lecturers today in their own ways have shown how important love and the experience of love are for our knowledge of God. There is no suggestion in John Paul's work that faith or reason are somehow in opposition to or to the exclusion of experience or love: *Fides et Ratio,* like all his works, ends with a kind of love poem-prayer, in this case to the Seat of Wisdom.

3. Why?

Why bother with faith and reason? McDermott insightfully identifies what I suspect is a central concern motivating many of John Paul II's intellectual and pastoral efforts: a genuine fear that 'intellectual chaos threatens' Western civilisation. Why worry? many moderns would respond. Is not anxiety about the truth just the concern of a controlling, tidy-desk, military-curial sort of mind-set? Is not the Roman anxiety about intellectual chaos just another symptom of its loss of authority since the advent of academies and academics and ideologies beyond ecclesiastical control, the age of revolutions and the loss of papal states, and so on? Isn't a good deal of mess—physical, psychological, intellectual, moral, spiritual mess—just the way of things and rather fun at that? Would not the Pope benefit from the wisdom of the pop song 'Don't worry, be happy'?

In the Catholic tradition a sound faith and sound reason, each informing and correcting the other, are thought to be intimately connected with happiness in this life and salvation in the next. 'Just believe' is such bad advice because we so easily believe in mirages. The great lies can do such terrible harm in this life and deflect people from their ultimate goal in the next; the great truths can edify and point the way to true happiness in this life and the life beyond. Far from being the product of tidy-desk bureaucracy or ecclesiastical thought police, Christian wisdom about the importance of truth goes right back to the work of the Creator-spirit hovering over primaeval chaos and bringing order out of disorder, light out of darkness. It goes right back to Christ's contest with ignorance, sickness, sin and every other kind of death.

Another reason for thinking truth matters so much is because of our fundamental curiosity, our need to know (whether it is about ourselves, our fellows, our universe or our Creator). Much contemporary Roman apologetics, including *Fides et Ratio,* begins with the claim that certain fundamental questions—for McDermott the 'three conundrums of evil, suffering and personal immortality'—constitute, as he puts it, 'decisive questions of interest to most human beings because they pertain to their fate and provide the horizon of meaning within which their choices are made'. Neither John Paul nor his Jesuit commentator are denying, of course, the crisis of confidence in the intelligibility and liveability of the truth among many of their contemporaries, nor the temptation to put truth out of our minds when it is threatening and go for something more comfortable. But they seem to be to underestimate the effects of contemporary society, economy and culture upon many moderns in making them simply not care. Many people today seem to live in a kind of permanent moral sedation, even anaesthesia—whether induced by those literal narcotics so readily available within metres of the new campus of Australian Catholic University in Melbourne, or by the umpteen equally effective means of mind-numbing available. 'Don't worry, be happy', says the pop culture. 'We have the quick fixes', says techno-commercialism. Hard thinking will only give you a headache, or as Ecclesiastes put it so nicely, 'of making many books there is no end, and much study is a weariness of the flesh' (12:12).

In so many of our contemporaries, and perhaps in many of us much of the time, there is a kind of insensitivity, a stupor, a boredom, with big questions such as suffering and souls. Fewer and fewer young people can be bothered with those endless undergraduate discussions in bars and cafes about how I know I exist or whether anyone's moral opinions are better than anyone else's, let alone take to the streets or invade the vice-chancellor's office. Nor is it just the young who increasingly lack any manifestation of passion for the big questions. At a conference held in this very theatre a week ago on the future of the universities, many academics present seemed to me unable to see what was really at risk, how precious and fragile is truth and the vocation of its pursuit, and how dulled is the passion of this age for it. It might not be such a bad thing for Jesuits and Dominicans to work up the sweat to call each other heretics again! Maybe John Paul II is too optimistic about human nature—not just about its ability to grasp and live the truth, as Professor Adams has complained—but also about its interest in doing so. But perhaps his talk of our native wonder and curiosity is more aspirational than descriptive and amounts to a call to conversion to all humanity to faith and reason, to freedom and love, and a plea to its intellectuals to give leadership in evangelising hearts to recover their wonder and awe, their passion for truth and love.

Was Thomas Aquinas a Deconstructionist? The Gift of the Spirit and the Experience of Grace

Tony Kelly CSsR

Fides et Ratio conveniently introduces our topic. One of the aims of the encyclical is to encourage an assured comprehensive or sapiential intellectuality. Hence, it seeks to counter all kinds of diffident realism which go under the names of scepticism, relativism, pluralism, nihilism, postmodern indeterminacy, and by implication what has become known as 'deconstructivism' [46; 81; 90; 91]. Needless to say, it calls on the authority of Aquinas for his uniquely confident combination of faith and reason. The Pope stresses the role of wisdom, both as a gift and as a philosophical habit of mind. He writes:

> Another of the great insights of St Thomas was his perception of the role of the Holy Spirit in the process by which knowledge matures into wisdom. From the first pages of his *Summa Theologiae*,[1] Aquinas was keen to show the primacy of the gift of wisdom which is a gift of the Holy Spirit which opens a way to the knowledge of divine realities. His theology allows us to understand what is distinctive of wisdom in its close link with faith and knowledge of the divine. This wisdom comes to know by way of connaturality; it presupposes faith and eventually formulates its right judgment on the basis of the truth of faith itself: 'The wisdom named among the gifts of the Holy Spirit is different from the wisdom found among the intellectual virtues. This second wisdom is acquired through study but the first 'comes from on high', as St James puts it. This also distinguishes it from faith, since faith accepts the divine truth as it is. But the gift of

---

1. See Thomas Aquinas, *Summa Theologiae* 1,1, 6.

wisdom enables judgment according to the divine truth (*ST* 2–2, 45, 1 ad 2; 2–2, 45, 2).

Yet the priority accorded to this wisdom does not lead the Angelic Doctor to overlook the two other complementary forms of wisdom—*philosophical* wisdom which is based upon the capacity of the intellect, for all its natural limitations, to explore reality, and *theological* wisdom which is based upon revelation and which explores the contents of faith, entering into very mystery of God.

Implicit in this reference to the gifts of the Spirit, and the special wisdom that they bring, is a nice question: Does *Fides et Ratio* allow sufficiently for the radically negative moment in Aquinas's presentation of wisdom's experience of God? After all, as we shall see, the gifts of the Spirit, including wisdom, are said to operate 'beyond the mode of reason'. In its aim to reassure contemporary thinkers concerning the validity of human reason and wisdom, the encyclical is hardly likely to dwell on the supra-rational mode in which the gift of wisdom operates—at least in Aquinas's understanding. Nonetheless, I think that acknowledgment of the 'positive' negativity of Thomas's doctrine is of special importance. There is what might be correctly termed a 'deconstructive' mode of deferral to the Spirit's action and of surrender to it that exceeds the rational mode, and, to that degree, always eludes the comprehension of a rationally constructed theological system.

By clarifying some aspects of the 'deconstruction' inherent in Aquinas's theological thinking, I would hope to promote a more fruitful dialogue among the representatives of faith and reason, and so to get beyond the caricatures in which both are too often represented. As *F&R* states, quoting Thomas, 'whatever its source, Truth is of the Holy Spirit' (*omne verum a quocumque dicatur a Spiritu Sancto est*) (*ST* 1–2, 109, 1 ad 1).

Well, it all depends, you might say, on what deconstruction means! For many, Thomas is the very exemplar of onto-theology, the paradigm of presentiality and systematisation. His metaphysical framework comprehends even psychology in its ambit, as human 'nature' operates through the spiritual 'faculties' of intellect and will, which, in turn, are perfected by 'virtues' proportioned to various goods, thus enabling all the variety of human 'acts' specified by their respective objects; and so on. Still, it should not be forgotten that Aquinas's explorations unfold in questions, not theses. The realism of his open, questioning mode of exploring is underscored with the recognition that it is quite basic to his theology that we do not know what God is in this life (*ST* 1, 12,1), and that even the believer is united to the divine as to one unknown (*ST* 1, 12, 13 ad 1). Analogical discourse was the only way (*ST* 1,13,5),[2] when it appears that the most appropriate way of affirming the unknowable infinities of God was in the judgment that God is sheer Be-ing, or *ipsum esse subsistens* (*ST* 1,13,11)—God affirmed as verb, outside of all genus (*ST* 1,3,5), every giving being, but unknown and incomprehensible save through the giving and the gifts: *amor Dei est infundens et creans bonitatem in rebus*: 'The love of God is pouring forth and creating goodness in things' (*ST* 1,20,2). In this sense, there is always an endless deferral in our knowledge of God. Our judgments reach far beyond concepts, going beyond the ideality of mere conceptions, however lofty, in an intending of what cannot be expressed or immediately intuited, but is, nevertheless, affirmed and lived.

These are huge matters for discussion.[3] I will here concentrate on one or other modality of Thomas's account of theological reason. I will

---

2.   On this topic of analogy, a case can be made that Derrida's whole deconstructionist project owes its origins to his desire to work out the terms of analogy. He realised early on that univocity is clearly a dead end, and that equivocity would lead nowhere. For this see his *An Introduction* to Edmund Husserl's *Origin of Geometry*, translated by John P Leavey Jnr (Lincoln: University of Nebraska Press, 1989). Note the following remarks:
     Husserl never ceased to appeal to the imperative of univocity. Equivocity is the path of all philosophical aberration. It is all the more difficult not to be hasty here, as the sense of equivocity in general is itself equivocal.There is a *contingent* plurivocity and multisignificance and an *essential* one (100–101).

3.   This exposition must be set in much larger contexts.While I have chosen just two comparatively small examples, there is a lot more ground to be covered. A foremost consideration is Thomas's quasi-definition of God as sheer 'to be', *ipsum esse subsistens*. If some, like the early Marion, insist in interpreting 'being' in a Scotist mode, whereby 'being' is a kind of super-concept identical with *esse commune* englobing all differences, then it must appear as a conceptual idol and as alien conceptual intrusion into the data of faith. If, on the other hand, granting the data of faith, Thomas's affirmation of God as *ipsum esse* is not taken as a concept but as a judgment intending the non-conceptualisable limitlessness of God, as horizon and indeed the dynamism of his theological hermeneutics, then

spend most of the time on his doctrine of the gifts of the Spirit and their relationship to reason. I shall leave to a later time a more contemporary application of this question. It would entail an investigation of the rich phenomenology of 'the gift',[4] a more precise exploration of the meaning of deconstruction and the presence of God, as say in Kevin Hart's, *The Trespass of the Sign*.[5] Thirdly, we would need to register the complex question of the phenomenology of 'Spirit'—as brought out by Derrida in his *Of Spirit. Heidegger and the Question*.[6]

It is illuminating, I would suggest, before coming to Thomas's doctrine on the gifts to note how he answered the question of what, to him, and to all Christian believers was, most pertinent: How might we know that we were in the grace of God ? (ST 1–2, 112, 5).

He sees three possibilities. First, that it is not beyond theological imagination that in special circumstances someone could receive a special revelation from God in this regard, eg, St Paul in 2 Corinthians 12:9. Secondly, and this is where things become interesting, there is the theoretical possibility of scientific knowing, a certitude resulting 'when through non-demonstrable first principles we arrive at demonstrable conclusions'. But Thomas says this is impossible, since that would mean knowing God as the transcendent source of grace. The upshot is that we can never be scientifically or rationally sure of our good standing before God!

If the first way of knowing is infrequent and unpredictable—at least for theologians—and the second is impossible, there remains a third way: *coniecturaliter per aliqua signa* ('conjecturally, by means of signs'). This is an intriguing little phrase: there is no vision, no certitude, no systematic assurance, no possession. Christian conscious-

---

things are different. And *pace* Heidegger, the forgetfulness of being not only does not apply, but a definite recollection or remembrance of Be-ing is called for. This, I say, is a much bigger project, since the Thomist project is intrinsically deconstructionist to any system of conceptual rationality . . . if only for the reason that God belongs to no kind of genus. For more on these points see my '"The Horrible Wrappers" of Aquinas' God', *Pacifica* 9 (June 1996): 185–203.

4.   See Robyn Horner, *Rethinking God as Gift* (New York: Fordham University Press, 2000).

5.   Kevin Hart, *The Trespass of the Sign. Deconstruction, Theology and Philosophy* (Melbourne: Cambridge University Press, 1989).

6.   Jacques Derrida, *Of Spirit. Heidegger and the Question*, translated by Geoffrey Bennington and Rachel Bowlby (Chicago: University of Chicago Press, 1989).

ness and conscience for that matter is left with conjecture: inasmuch as we are experiencing ourselves taking delight in God, turning from 'worldly things', and have no conscience of mortal sin, then we can proceed in peace. Here, though Thomas speaks of certain 'sweetness' (*dulcedo*) in this experience, it is a radically imperfect way of knowing.

As I say, it is useful to bear this conclusion in mind since it throws considerable light on the meaning and purpose of the gifts. The believer does not live in a universe of grace save through a form of self-surrender and continuing self-transcendence. Certainly, there is no rational mastery of the situation when neither the divine Spirit, nor his gifts, nor his giving is possessed with rational certitude.

This suggests an approach to Aquinas on the gifts of the Spirit. Admittedly, such a consideration is usually tucked away in specialised soundings in the history of Christian mysticism. But I think it will prove to have a more general relevance, even to current 'deconstructionist' concerns to free faith from conceptual idols and to subvert the totalitarian pretensions of any system of thought.[7] Essentially, the theological problem is set for us in Paul's description of the 'spiritual' person described in 1 Corinthians:

> 'What eye has not seen, nor ear heard, nor the human heart conceived, what God has prepared for those who love him'—these things God has revealed to us through the Spirit; for the Spirit searches everything, even the depths of God. For what human being knows what is truly human except the human spirit that is within? So also no one comprehends what is truly God's except the Spirit of God. Now we have received not the spirit of the world, but the Spirit that is from God, so that we may understand the gifts that are bestowed on us by God. And we speak of these things

---

7.   As a matter of fact, some twenty-five years ago I was invited to write an article in a series commemorating the seven-hundredth anniversary of St Thomas' death. It was entitled, 'The Gifts of the Spirit: Aquinas in the Modern Context'. I did not realise, as I outlined the main elements this theme and attempted to transpose it into a variety of 'modern contexts' (Lonergan's intentionality analysis, Macquarrie's existential theology, Heideggerian *Gelassenheit*, and the intercultural phenomenologies of the self), that I was biting off more than I could chew. The 'modernity' I took for granted was to explode into 'postmodernity'!

in words not taught by human wisdom but taught by
the Spirit, interpreting spiritual things to those who are
spiritual (1 Cor 2:9–13).

Considering these and similar texts (eg 1 John 2:27), theology is
always somewhat at a loss, in its efforts to name or explain what is so
intrinsically elusive. That is why Thomas is interesting. His
philosophical categories are Aristotelian, and his theological goals are
rigorously intellectual: *sacra doctrina* is, after all, to be elaborated as a
scientia (*ST* 1, 1, 2–3). And yet, at some point, there is a gifted excess
both in understanding and in deliberation. This is the sphere of the
gifts of the Spirit, in which the graced subject acts 'beyond the human
measure' (*III Sent* d34, q1 a1): 'The Holy Spirit moves the human mind
to act in a manner that surpasses reason' (*ST* 1–2, 70, 4). Let us locate
this movement or experience more closely:

> Clearly the human virtues perfect human agents in that
> they are natively to be guided by reason in both their
> interior and exterior operations. And so it is fitting that
> there be in human beings higher perfections according
> to which they are disposed to be moved by God. These
> perfections are called gifts, not only because they are
> infused by God, but also *because of them the human*
> *person is so disposed as to be readily moved by divine*
> *inspiration to acts that are higher than the acts of the virtues*
> (*ST* 1, 68, 1).

We might note how there are levels of conscious activity implied.
At one level, there is deliberate 'rational' activity; and a higher level,
consciousness is waiting, as it were, for divine inspiration to act in a
way that surpasses the normal deliberative mode of virtuous action.

In focusing on this disposition to be moved by a divinely given
instinct, Aquinas is in fact bringing together three strands of tradition.[8]
First, the traditional patristic commentaries on Isaiah 11:2–3 describing
the many gifts (six in the Hebrew, seven in the Septuagint) that
descend on God's Anointed [His main *auctoritas* was Gregory the

---

8.   See *The Gifts of the Spirit*, in the Blackfriars edition of the *Summa Theologiae*,
      Volume 24 (Ia2ae. 68–70) edited and translated by Edward D O'Connor, CSC
      (London: Blackfriars, 1974), 80–110.

Great, especially to the *Moralia II*, c 49 and 56 (*PL* 75, 592; 598)]. Then there is the Pauline doctrine of the 'spiritual' person, in 1 Corinthians 2 and Romans 8. On the philosophical level, there is the Greek doctrine of enthusiasm, divine possession and of divine 'instinctus'. This is basically a Platonic theme which found its way to Thomas through the *Liber de Bona Fortuna*, a Latin translation of the younger Aristotle's *VII Eudemian Ethics*. In fact, despite the richness of the theological tradition on the *gratia septiformis Spiritus Sancti*, only at the beginning of the thirteenth century, with Philip the Chancellor's *Summa de Bono*, was any clear distinction drawn between the virtues and the gifts. For Philip the gifts are given to facilitate the action of the virtues. Albert the Great took this further: the gifts not only perfect the virtues but they are the principles of a higher mode of activity since God acts directly through them. It would seem that the experience of grace, of that transformation of human existence that was working itself out in history, had begun to suggest a more differentiated theoretical appreciation of Christian consciousness. On the one hand, it registered the experience of the laborious, deliberative, horizontal mode in which so much of life is conducted. On the other, it came to respect, and even to expect, the vertically given, transformative moments or states of experience and action.

This is the background in which Thomas addressed the subject of the gifts. In his combination of the tradition and the immediate past, Aquinas's key principle is the peculiar immanence of the Spirit to human freedom and action. He conceives human action as affected by a twofold principle, *duplex principium movens*: 'There is within the human being a twofold principle of motion. One is more interior, and that is reason; the other is more exterior, and that is God' (*ST* 1–2, 68, 1). Clearly, Thomas is in no way eroding the freedom of the human agent. He seems to candidly assume that we human beings remain in charge of our own house, as it were, as we experience our own acts of deliberation and reason. And yet there is that 'more exterior' source of movement within what is 'in' us. It corresponds to another of level of the consciousness of grace. A deliberative activity 'from below', as it were, reaches up to and awaits a movement 'from above'. In indicating this realm of especially gifted operation, Aquinas invites the human

subjects to appropriate the full potentiality of their immanent life, and
to allow for what exceeds the rational or deliberative mode.[9]

In terms of that inner domain of reason and its mode of activity,
virtues are cultivated and even divinely given so that the authentic
rationality can be extended through all the faculties, as the human
person moves toward the ultimate good and seeks the means to
achieve it. Yet the divine originality remains. It is not restricted to the
limits of human deliberation. The dimensions of both the divine
immanence and transcendence are what the notion of the gifts is
attempting to respect. In a gifted state of responsiveness to the supra-
rational possibilities of the Spirit's initiative, the human agent
transcends the limited and provisional mode proportionate to the
resources of reason. Open to what surpasses reason, human life yields
to the initiative proper to God's own activity (*ST* 1–2, 68, 1).

In this higher mode of operation, the gift of understanding leads to
a negative kind of penetrating knowledge resulting in a 'cleanness of
heart' in regard to the distorting images and notions that detract from
an authentic understanding of divine things (*ST* 2–2, 8, 1–8). The gift of
knowledge, similarly negative, ponders on the meaning of creation in
the light of God, as the mind recognises the deep ambiguity and
fragility of the world. It results in a kind of mourning over the vacuity
of a world turned against God (*ST* 2–2, 9, 1–4). The gift of fear brings
with it a radical poverty of spirit, and reverent sensitivity to the divine
action, in ways that are compatible with a loving relationship, as
believers look beyond themselves and all created things to surrender to
God (*ST* 2–2, 19,1–12). With the gift of counsel, the special activity of
the Spirit is registered in the domain of practical action (*ST* 2–2, 52,
1–4). The graced agent transcends the usual prudential mode of moral
discernment in surrender to the Spirit, the 'regula suprema' of all

---

9.   While the terms 'interior' and 'exterior' are employed, the transcendent
       immanence of God is more immanent than the interiority of reason, and more
       transcendent than a complementary or super-added divine motion. See *ST* 1–2,
       9,4. A couple of articles later we read, 'God moves the human will as the
       universal mover to the universal object of the will which the good. Without this
       universal motion, the human agent cannot will anything. But through it the human
       subject determines itself to will this or that' (*ST* 1–2, 9, 6 ad 3). The theology of
       the gifts is a specific instance of the more general metaphysics of human action
       and freedom. The divine 'instinct' or motion is presupposed. There is a domain of
       categorial human action under our control; but our transcendental orientation to
       the good is through the divine instinct moving the will to act.

morality. Fortitude is an experience of the Spirit manifest in resolute-
ness in overcoming the fears that are inevitably associated with the
realisation of the Christian vocation (*ST* 2–2, 139, 1). Piety is associated
with the guidance of the Spirit affecting a person's filial relationship
with God in gentleness and calm.

But, for Thomas, the gift par excellence is that of wisdom, *sapientia*
(*ST* 2–2, 45, 1–6). Those gifted with this wisdom can act in a way that
transcends the perfect use of reason, for their judgment draws its
evidence from a loving connaturality with the things of God (*ST* 2–2,
45, 2). Wisdom, in this sense, is a kind of feeling for the divine
mysteries arising out of love's union with God, and thus supplying a
special evidence of the divine reality.[10]

Thomas recognises that believers must in some measure suffer a
certain strain or dislocation due to their God-given destiny—which is
beyond all the proportion of natural possibilities. While there is a
native aptitude for the pursuit of the good and the truth proportionate
to our being in world, such a 'connaturality' is lacking when it comes
to our divine vocation—which, after all, is to participate in God's own
life. A necessary complement, therefore, to our vocation to the divine
life are the gifts of the Spirit attuning us to milieu in which we are
called to live. Only through these gifts can the divine life be lived and
integrated into human existence:

> The person can act through the judgment of reason in
> regard to those things which fall in the domain of
> reason in the pursuit of the end that is connatural to us.
> In moving toward the ultimate good which is beyond
> the reach of nature, reason does act—in that it is in
> some imperfect way formed by the theological virtues.
> But this movement of reason is not sufficient unless
> there is given from beyond it the instinct and
> movement of the Holy Spirit (*ST* 1–2, 68, 2).

Only the Spirit of God can move humankind to its destiny in God.
The person is united to the Holy Spirit through the theological virtues
of faith, hope and charity. These radical God-given and God-directed

---

10. Compare with John Macquarrie, 'The Seven Gifts of the Holy Spirit', *Studies in
    Christian Existentialism* (London: SCM, 1965), 246–273.

capacities lead to an objective immediate contact with the giver of such grace. In this the theological virtues are the 'roots' of the gifts (*ST* 1–2, 4, 3). But it is one thing to have an objectively supernatural horizon through the virtues, and another to move within it restricted to the resources of reason alone. If the believer is not given a more lively, supple and receptive attunement to the Spirit's interior action, Thomas seems to fear that our sense of God will be taken over by, or reduced to, the rational mode, whereas, in the order of grace, the rational pattern of activity should in fact find its fulfilment in surrendering itself to the divine instinct.[11]

Here there is a precious further point. The gifts, as dispositions to the movement of the Spirit, owe their special character to the affectivity that the gift of charity inspires in the human heart and spirit. To this degree, the seven gifts are quasi-metaphysical descriptions of our consciousness as taken over by the demands of mystical and moral love as it realised in the person in the state of grace. Sharing in the divine life and attuned to the divine action, believers are enabled to follow the instinct of love in every aspect of their being.[12] Thomas writes:

> All powers of the soul are disposed through gifts in reference to the Holy Spirit who lives in us in charity, as we read in Romans 5:5. So, as the moral virtues are interconnected through the virtue of prudence, so the gifts of the Spirit are interconnected in charity (*ST* 1–2, 68,5).

When the human agent is moved by the Spirit through the gifts, there is obviously not only a special passivity implied, but also a new level of activity. The mode of human activity characteristic of the gifts is described as 'supra human' or even as a 'divine' mode of action,

---

11. In the theological virtues are the literally radical condition for the operation of the gifts, it is especially in charity that the movement of the Spirit is recognised: 'faith is about what is not seen, hope is concerned with what is not possessed, but the love of charity concerns the one who is already possessed, for the beloved is somehow within the lover, and also the lover is affectively attracted to be united with the beloved' (*ST* 1–2, 66, 5).

12. Since the gifts are so intimately connected to the gift and activity of love, Thomas postulates that they remain even in the fullness of life, *in patria* when the human subject will be 'totally given over to God', *totaliter subditus Deo* (*ST* 1–2, 68, 6).

certainly beyond the rational and deliberative mode. In his early commentary on the Sentences, Thomas wrote, 'the virtues enable acts to be performed in a human manner, but the gifts work beyond the human manner' (*III Sent* d 34 q 1). In a maturer phase, however, he expatiates with greater clarity on how the gifts affect our actions: 'Virtues bring a perfection to the human subject who natively acts according to reason. It is fitting however that there be higher perfections through which we are disposed to be moved by God' (*ST* 1–2, 68, 1). In his earlier treatment Thomas focuses on the ultra-human mode of action; in his later exposition, with a more explicitly theological emphasis, the accent is on the special movement of the Spirit. Not 'reason', but God himself becomes the *regula* of human action. Reason as most immanent and essential to human existence is experienced, through the immanence of the Spirit, in it openness to the divine initiative. The human cooperates with the divine at a new level, outstripping the limitations of human deliberation, ie 'the rational mode'. Illustrating this new level of operation, an acute Thomistic commentator especially in matters psychological, John of St Thomas, bequeathed to the theology of the gifts a telling metaphor: 'Although the forward progress of the ship may be the same, there is a vast difference in its being moved by laborious rowing of the oarsmen and its being moved by sails filled with strong breeze.'[13] It is as though the galley slaves can join the captain on the bridge! Apart from that dubious association, such an influential metaphor, while making its point, unwitting opens the door to some distortions. The gifts are about new modes of self-surrender to the movement of God, and, while they escape some of the limitations of human action, they are far from being a free ride. It is significant that fortitude is numbered amongst them! Moreover, it is not as though the 'gifted' can now rest on their oars; for, in attentiveness and unconditional surrender to the workings of the Spirit, they must also put up the sails . . . to await the unpredictable movement of the holy breath or wind.

Far from destroying or compromising human liberty, the inspiration of the Spirit of the gifts enlarges and completes it. The person remains a free agent. In his *Commentary on the Romans*, we find

---

13. John of St Thomas, *The Gifts of the Holy Spirit* (London: Sheed and Ward, 1951), 56.

Thomas's best description of the manner in which human liberty is completed through the gifts:

> The spiritual person is not only instructed by the Holy Spirit on what they should do, but also their heart is moved by the Spirit. And so there is more to be understood in the phrase, 'whoever are moved by the Spirit of God'. Those things are said to be moved when they are stirred by some higher instinct. Hence we say of brute beasts not that they act but that they are acted on because they are moved by nature and not from their own movement to their actions. Similarly the spiritual person is stirred principally by the Holy Spirit to do something. But this does not exclude that these Spirit-possessed persons act voluntarily and freely because the Spirit causes in them that movement of will and freedom as we read in Phil 2:13 (*Epist Ad Romanos*, VIII, lect 3).

The 'spiritual' are not merely inspired in what they should do but moved by the Spirit in the actual execution of the inspiration. In this there is a certain analogy with the movement of instinct in the order of nature.[14] The animal does not so much act, but is acted on, or moved by the impulse or instinct of nature toward some natural end. The spiritual person, analogically speaking, is similarly affected by a God-given instinct to attain the goals of a supernatural vocation. Despite the similarities, there is a difference: the human agent is moved to act freely, while the animal is not. Human agents are moved to act out of their own immanent liberty, but in a freedom that is enlarged, adapted and perfected with regard to a supernatural goal and the manner of attaining it. God works within us both the will and the deed (Phil 2:13). There is a certain passivity in relation to the action of the Spirit implied

---

14. Under the influence of this *instinctus* — for Thomas a category found at all levels of life — certain human beings 'have no need to resort to human deliberation for they follow an interior instinct, moved as they are by a higher principle' (*ST* 1–2, 68, 1). JH Walgrave, 'Een Proeve Tot Thomas Interpretatie', *Emphemerides Theologicae Lovanienses* XLV (1969) 417–431, contends that only in his later writings did Thomas give an important role to the *instinctus divinus*. It fits into the larger field of divine providence which moves the natural world by instinct as well.

here, but this liberates liberty rather than stunts it. God acts that the human agent can act with a more perfect freedom. Human liberty reaches its highest manifestation when its it is dynamically open to the surprises of God.

This supra-rational mode of acting through the gifts is presented as a new dimension, or both height and depth, for human liberty. It recasts the meaning of rationality and suggests modes of operation flowing from a special attunement to the divine action. There must be room for the incalculable. When the gifts suggest a divine initiative working in human liberty they are akin to other workings of grace precisely as operative, giving an instinct to act in a way that goes beyond any rationally established horizon. The examples here are when the will makes its first choice of the unlimited good, and, in the grace of conversion, when the sinner returns to God, and the heart of stone is dissolved, and replaced by the heart of flesh. In such situations, the free act is not the outcome of a prior human action: it happens by the gift of grace. Only a divine liberty can activate and perfect the finite liberty of the human (*ST* 1–2, 111, 2; 3, 86, 6).

A Lonergan-type intentionality analysis can bring all this down to earth in a number of telling ways. Though an experiential depth is implied in the Thomist account of the gifts, the main concern was to get beyond the symbolic modes of common sense discourse to the metaphysically modulated theory. A fruitful retrieval of the theology of the gifts may occur through a more critically grounded inten-tionality analysis as theology attends to the data of consciousness in a more refined phenomenology, and scrutinises moral and mystical experience in an effort to find precise terms to name the trajectory of self-transcendence that appears. Lonergan makes a good point:

> The point to making metaphysical terms and relations not basic but derived is that a critical metaphysics results. For every term and relation there will exist a corresponding element in intentional consciousness. Accordingly, empty and misleading terms and relations can be eliminated, while valid ones can be elucidated by the conscious intention from which they are derived. The importance of such critical control will

be evident to anyone familiar with the vast and arid
wastes of theological controversy.[15]

Further, Lonergan's understanding of the threefold nature of conversion as intellectual, moral and religious would tend to lead into further
fruitful discussion on the meaning of the gifts and the plurality of the
aspects that are considered. Horizontal liberty develops along the lines
of traditional formation—of ratio—in this sense. Vertical liberty occurs
when a new dimension—either as breakout or break-in—in terms of
the basic direction of our living.

The Thomist point remains: there is the multi-levelled character of
human consciousness—in the order of grace fundamentally regulated,
not by critical reflection, but by the movement of grace itself, in accord
with the intimate attunement and restless demands of love itself.
Thomas's theology is fundamentally a thinking through of the
experience of the gift of grace. The rational and deliberative mode that
seeks answers to the *quaestio*-driven and analogical 'system' of Thomist
thought, is in some measure subverted. It must yield to another kind of
evidence, and be taken beyond itself—never possessing its object, but
being possessed or moved by it. Thus, the intentionality of faith knows
its own kind of 'deconstruction' or, if you will, something similar to a
Derridean *différance*.

In conclusion, in Aquinas's theology of the gifts we have a glimpse
of theory, systematic in aspiration, yet trying to cope with the unique,
the gift, the always excessively given. Within the limited scope of this
reflection on Thomas's treatment of the gifts, there are questions one
might bear in mind as we touch on the main points: What kind of
experience of faith and reason is implied here? What sense of self and
of God is communicated? What kind of experience is Thomas taking
for granted?

However such questions are answered, Thomas's treatment of the
gifts is an attempt of creative Christian theology to name the
indefinable excess present in the moral and mystical lives of
Christians—and of Christ himself. In him, the gifts are said to exist in
the 'most excellent manner' (*ST* 3, 7, 5) and are objectified in the
beatitudes he uttered. Thomas's doctrine of the gifts of the Spirit are,

---

15.   Bernard Lonergan, *Method in Theology* (London: Darton, Longman and Todd,
       1972), 343.

therefore, one avenue into an appreciation of the psychology of Jesus himself, and of how his mind is in his followers (Cf Phil 2:5).

Meaning, Faith and Reason:
Is Metaphysics the Way?

John Quilter

1. Introductory considerations

1.1 The state of the debate
In the course of the twentieth century, we have seen an explosion of ideas concerning the best way to interpret the talk of religious adherents, their communities and traditions. A survey of the variety of approaches makes the point well that an enormous amount of energy has gone into the task. The following lists are a sample. Among other philosophical approaches we have seen:

- the revival of Analogy Theories of religious language among both Thomists and other religious thinkers like Swinburne
- the non-cognitivism of the Verificationists and other empiricists influenced by them;
- Crombie's parables and Mitchell's bliks
- Malcolm's and Phillips's so-called 'Wittgensteinian Fideism'
- proposals of the irreducibly metaphorical character of religious thought and talk
- Alston has revived a functionalist univocalism about the divine psychology
- various doctrines of theological Realism.

Among theologians we have seen:
- proposals for various Narrative theories
- Hermeneutical approaches of a wide variety, especially in Biblical Studies
- Deconstructionism's influence on theology, and I should mention Structuralism.

Among studies of religion in the social sciences we have seen:
- (social-scientific) functionalist approaches to the meaning of religious language
- 'symbolist' theories of religious language.

Finally, there are the debates from the philosophy of the social sciences about the requirements of understanding another culture's thought and practice: debates about the relevance of explanation in reductive terms, the observation and participation by the field workers in the object culture, and the possibility of sympathetic description in the object culture's own terms.

The list is incomplete but is already imposing. Perhaps the most noteworthy thing about it is that one might have hoped that from this ferment a few points of clarity and light might have distilled around areas of common concern, if not focus. But contrary to the adage, this house divided against itself has risen and risen with all too few bridges built. The debates around these lines of thought go on largely without contacts with each other.

But I suspect the situation is really worse. For, add to this the intensity and variety of work on general philosophy of language that might be thought to cast light on religious thought and talk, and the fact that, by and large, many of the defining debates there[1] have penetrated mainstream discussions of religious language very little; and one is left somewhat overwhelmed by the consideration of what we could make of religious language. Taken at large, the discussion of religious language lacks direction.

A recent book by Dan Stiver[2] tries to remedy this situation to some degree. For, while I would be critical of many of the preoccupations of Analytic Philosophy of Religion, I believe its interest in truth and content in relation to the meaning of religious language is of central importance for the religious life. And it is to Stiver's credit that his study of the varieties of twentieth century philosophy of religious language plausibly connects many of them to those kinds of traditional philosophical concerns with religious language.

Stiver admits that his analyses are tendentious and will not always find the endorsement of the figures he discusses. He is an ecumenist and seeks to discern trends of convergence, opportunities for complementation of one school's lines of thought with another's, and

---

1.   A sample of important themes: Quine's thesis of the indeterminacy of translation; the merits of Tarski-style truth-conditional semantics, Frege's Puzzle, the theory of reference championed by Putnam and Kripke, and the anti-representationalism championed by Rorty and by Brandom.

2.   D Stiver, *The Philosophy of Religious Language* (Oxford: Blackwell, 1996).

therefore, he seeks to reduce the obligation to feel tensions between approaches even where different approaches themselves want to present them. But he shows that the apparent novelty of many recent approaches to religious language conceals relations to more traditional positions on the topic that invite us back to the issues of truth and content.

With others, Stiver argues that in deconstruction and hermeneutic lines of thought, we find echoes of classical debates between negative theology and the High Schoolmen expounding varieties of univocality theories and analogy theories of religious language. He argues that in the thesis that religious language is irreducibly metaphorical, we find reflections of classical views that religious language is semantically equivocal relative to common language. He argues that Narrative accounts raise sharply issues of the assessment of truth in religious discourse. And in all, there are background issues of the relationship between literalness, positive content, truth and whether, in the end, religious language is cognitive, or says anything.

So, without delving into any detailed defence of my foci in this paper, I will simply assert that, despite the richness and diversity of these many important ideas about the nature of religious thought and talk, their significance does not obviate the need for grappling with the more traditional set of concerns which I will be discussing. Indeed, if Stiver is right, there's little progress to be expected for a comparative evaluation of these various lines of thought unless one confronts the issues I want to discuss. Thus, the argument here is intended not just to join debates within a narrowly construed more or less traditional agenda of topics in Analytic philosophy of religious language. I mean the argument here to bear on the assessment of many other, apparently disparate, lines of thought on the topic.

1.2 Overview with caution

If I were forced to state in brief compass what the topic of this paper is, I would hesitatingly say this. In this paper I want to ask whether religious thought and talk is cognitive: does it make any sense or say anything? And if it does, how are we to think of this?

I say 'hesitatingly' because the expression 'cognitive', and related expressions, is a term of philosophical art that has acquired a set of resonances that are unfortunate for the line of argument I want to sponsor. In particular, the notion of a 'cognitive body of thought' is generally understood against an assumed contrast between bodies of thought and enquiry which are objective, susceptible of evidentiary and epistemic appraisal and are answerable to 'reality' and truth, as against bodies of thought which are not properly thought of in just these ways. Contemporary Analytic philosophy tends to describe a philosophical account of the first conception of a body of thought as a 'realist theory' and the second as an 'anti-realist theory'.[3] Thus, distinctions of these kinds are familiar from Meta-ethics, Philosophy of Science and Philosophy of Language.

The structuring contrast is broadly 'Humean': on one hand, there is objective thought that is keyed to and disciplined by attention to the way the world is in itself as our best evidence reflects this, independently of factors such as emotion, desire and idiosyncrasies which interfere with objective thinking; and on the other, there is thought where our registration of evidence and fact is overlain with projections of emotional colour, desiderative attractions and autobiographical or species-specific peculiarities. The former is capable of yielding knowledge, and hence is cognitive, but the latter is not, even though in other ways it may be valuable in life. The former is where one can hope to talk meaningfully about truth, in the ways more or less taken for granted in traditional philosophy. However, in connection with the latter, the use of 'true' is a semantic gaff or it occurs in an entirely different sense from its use in connection with the former; at any rate, what is meant by 'truth' in connection with objective thought is not present in the latter kinds of thought. The latter kinds of thought are too infected with the emotional, the merely psychological, the specificities of culture, traditional ways or prejudices, or those of our human nature, to rate as rational, to rate, that is, as genuinely leading us into understanding the way the world is in itself, to rate as genuinely disciplining our understanding with the constraints of objective thought. It is more or less common ground in the debates about realism and anti-realism that the primary example of the cognitive is the natural sciences. We then tend to try to settle the question about some allegedly problematic kind of thought and talk, in terms of its similarities to the natural sciences (or some natural science).

---

3.   Though Simon Blackburn's colourful terminology of the 'Apollian' and the 'Dionysian' is more appealing; cf his *Ruling Passions* (Oxford: Oxford University Press, 1999).

If, then, I want to discuss whether religious language is 'cognitive', it can seem obvious that we first need to have an idea of what we are asking: what is involved in claiming of a body of talk and thought that it is *cognitive*? The Humean contrast just described would seem to provide us with an answer to this question. We would seem to be asking on which side of this contrast does religious thought fall? Is it more like (some) natural science or is it more like, say, taste in ice-cream?

However, since I am unconvinced by the distinction which informs the understanding of this (and related) terms of appraisal, I hesitate to describe my question this way. I am unconvinced by the distinction for reasons which we do not have time here to consider in any detail. Some of them should emerge as the argument progresses here. This said, however, I will persist in the traditional language, for want of a better one with which to connect with traditional philosophical debates.

The shape of my hesitancy should be clear in general terms. For it seems to me that the distinctions marked by contrasts such as 'objective/subjective', 'knowledge/opinion' and 'taste (preference) /truth (reality)' do not coincide with those between the natural (and mathematical) sciences and such kinds of talk as ethics, aesthetic criticism and other areas of thought typically thought to be problematic. That is to say, it seems to me that in many kinds of discourse (not all) that are culturally specific, tradition-informed or otherwise controversial in ways natural sciences are not, there are the kinds of distinctions and patterns of critical appraisal similar to those in the sciences, though also different from them. Perhaps they do not take exactly the same form or they serve some distinctive point. However, the language of critical appraisal is there.

Thus, for instance, I would urge that we should not look at 'truth' and 'reality' language in the natural sciences, and then ask whether ethical propositions are apt for truth, as if to conceal the qualification *just as the propositions of natural scientific thought are apt for truth*. Finding out that ethics is not *in that way* apt for truth is simply finding out that science and ethics are not the same thing. And that is hardly a discovery. Rather, we should observe the use of 'truth' and 'reality' language in ethical thought and talk and ask how it works in connection with distinctions between appearance and reality in ethics. This may make 'ethical truth' ('ethical reality') *somewhat like* 'natural scientific truth' but in other ways unlike it. Does this mean that ethics is somehow not a 'knowledge yielding' way to think and talk? Saying this is to say that the only way to think and talk that is intellectually respectable is to do so scientifically. And yet to say *that* is hardly a matter of science. It is simply scientism, no matter how sophisticated. And I simply cannot take this seriously.[4]

Therefore, rather than take the distinction between the cognitive and the non-cognitive for granted, our discussion will turn to an examination of uses to which the notion of a 'cognitive body of thought and talk' has been put. I will pursue this in a way that I hope connects with the right kinds of concerns for our discussion of religious language, as well as with more familiar or well-trawled areas where it has been raised, such as in Meta-ethics or Philosophy of Science, which we have just rehearsed.

I will, then, begin by looking at the advantages that, I take it, have been thought achieved by Analogical theories of religious language. Eventually I will argue that these theories fail to achieve what they generally aspire to.

In its stead, I will offer an alternative account of what religious language means and how, along the way developing a criticism of the value of metaphysics for faith and fending off an objection or two to clarify what I am proposing. I think it is fair to describe my proposal as a species of fideism about the semantics of religious thought and talk. I will consider how much this matters, given everything else I have argued.

---

4. There is another important caveat to be urged about our criticism of the Humean distinction. It is that before serious characterisation and understanding of critical terms such as tend to interest philosophers is possible, we have to be attentive to the details and peculiarities of those terms in *particular* outlooks, rather than seeking comprehensive abstract accounts—say, of what 'truth' would have to mean in Daoism. So, in my view we should look at, say, the notions of truth and reality in Buddhist ethics and then in Thomistic ethics, rather than in Ethics-as-a-whole. For it is naive to think Buddhist notions of truth in ethics will simply transfer to Thomistic ones and vice versa. In this paper, however, my interest is in *similarities* between some religious traditions to what in the Christian tradition we call 'faith'. There is no claim to universality. Indeed, it is doubtful whether a notion quite like *faith* can be found in all religious traditions. I do not think there is a notion in Theravada Buddhism similar enough to the Western idea of faith to be characterised along with it.

Finally I will argue that, so understood, religious language deserves to be understood as a cognitive body of thought and talk; and will return to consider this in connection with the idea of cognitivity discussed earlier.

2. Analogy theories

2.1

I think it is fair to say that there are three main points of advantage that, traditionally, Analogy theories of religious language would claim:

(a)   On an Analogy theory, religious language is a literal form of language which describes things as they are in themselves.

(b)   On an Analogy theory, religious language is able to express positive content.

(c)   On an Analogy theory, the content of religious language is neither merely anthropomorphic nor so 'transcendent' that we cannot know what it means and we can give an account of how religious language can work this way.

These three features of Analogy theories form a close-knit group of theses. I want now to make some comments on them and elucidate their relations.

(a) Given the analogical interpretation of religious language, religious thought and talk is a form of literal language, rather than being a metaphorical form of talk or a 'symbolic' kind of language. Of course, this does not mean that an Analogy theory interprets *all* religious language literally and not metaphorically. This only implies that it interprets some—the 'intellectually serious' religious language—in this way. Clearly, it is no part of an Analogy theory that 'God is a fortress and a rock' is to be taken literally. On the other hand, it is part of an Analogy theory that serious *theologumena* like the ancient Trinitarian formulation, 'God is a community of love between subsistent relations' is to be taken literally. It is to be understood analogically, but that is not to say it is a metaphor or somehow 'symbolic' talk.

On this approach, describing something as 'symbolic talk' places it outside the sphere of what can be intellectually made sense of. Symbols function *qua* symbols either merely conventionally and without, *qua* symbols, a descriptive function; or they work rhetorically, poetically or emotionally or the like. Accounts differ at this point:

religious talk *qua* symbolic may move us to action, or evoke community allegiances, or whatever. In any case, they are not, *as such*, a 'work of the mind' but 'of the heart' (or the like), and so, not intellectually contentful. Similarly for irreducibly metaphorical talk—it 'goes beyond' what the literal meanings understood by reason can convey.

On either reading, the non-literal means what it means *equivocally*, relative to meaning the intellect makes sense of. This brings us to the second claimed advantage of Analogy theories.

(b) An Analogy theory does not have to sag into a negative theology. If religious language is equivocal in its semantic value (its *Bedeutung*), with respect to mundane language, we don't know what we are saying in talking religious talk. But there are two problems here: first, if we don't know what we are saying, we could be uttering complete gibberish or, worse or not, self-contradictions. Secondly, it just seems false phenomenologically. We *are* saying something, perhaps woefully inadequately, but we are not either talking gibberish or just saying nothing. That is, from the experience of belief, there is actual, positive content in our utterances. If our religious thought and talk is literal, this can be so. We are talking about God, the incarnation or the like where these are not understood to be pleasant metaphors or 'symbols' of anything else. They are about what they are about; they say about it what they say.

But if our religious talk and thought is literal and its content is positive and not merely equivocal relative to mundane talk, and not merely negative, why is it not simply univocal with our non-religious language? In particular, why isn't it anthropomorphic?

(c) An Analogy theory's next claimed advantage is to offer an account of *how* religious thought and talk is neither merely anthropomorphic, nor so other that we have no idea what we are talking about. For an Analogy theory points to similarities between the *Bedeutungen* of mundane language and those of the divine while insisting, rightly, on differences too. Similarity is not identity, but difference is not utter unintelligibility.

Again, if religious language were equivocal in our sense and incapable of positive interpretation, it would seem to enjoy a kind of quarantine from the outside world. What religious language means shares no 'semantic overlap' with mundane language and so it cannot be said to say more than what is not. However, were this the case, any response to a given religious utterance, which did not merely insert a negation in it, might be thought to be as good as any other. Yet, manifestly religious language is not a purely random set of practices: people use it in patterned ways suggestive of a disciplined form of life. In Christian circles, if we are considering the nature of the incarnation, say, it is hardly apropos to start expatiating on the merits of Oracle databases. In such debates, distinctions are drawn between permissible moves, false moves and irrelevant moves. Presumably, if religious language does anything for its users, it will be emergent from religious forms of life, even if not saying anything affirmatively formulable. However, if this is so and religious language is equivocal relative to mundane language, its semantics will be in effect hermetically sealed off from the rest of human thought and talk.

So, I want to suggest that this third advantage claimed by Analogy theory is that, on its accounting, religious language is neither anthropomorphic nor quarantined from the rest of human enquiry and practice. It might enjoy a certain autonomy deriving from the mystery of God, but it can manage to say something *responsible to life* while not mere anthropomorphism. From this standpoint, religious language is literal language expressing positive content though not reducible to mundane thought while not unconnected with it. It seems natural, then, to see religious language as apt for truth and so, cognitive.

2.2

I want now to broaden our discussion into the target question: What is it for a body of thought and talk to count as cognitive? When the term was first bandied about by the positivists, it meant something like 'not subject to the disciplines of collecting evidence in its favour', or 'verification'. The history of the failure of the positivists' verificationist criterion of cognitive discourse is too well known to merit recollection here. It is important, however, to understand that the term has not really enjoyed such careful use since that failure. It is useful to survey the field of its occurrences.

Let us start in the debate concerning scientific realism. Van Fraassen uses the notion of the literal as a gloss on 'realist' philosophy of science in connection with the theoretical language of science. In contrast to instrumentalism or operationalism, Van Fraassen suggests that scientific theoretical language is intended literally, in a sense familiar from biblical interpretation in contrast to various non-literalist interpretative schemes of various genres of biblical writing. I take this to suggest that the literal, as the interpretative scheme for the semantics of scientific theoretical language, is a mark of the cognitive, for scientific language is, of course, a cognitive kind of language.[5]

Though I have not got the space to argue this in detail, I would suggest that this is a line of thought informing a great deal of philosophical and other studies of religion. On this view, to the extent that it diverges from susceptibility of literal construal, religious language fails to be a cognitive form of thought and talk, and has to be understood to work as a non-cognitive kind of speech. To be rendered cognitive, one has to analyse it as having a deep grammar which departs from its apparent purport. Perhaps it moves us to high moral ambition, or consoles our bruised hearts or functions socially to manage errant motivations. But it doesn't say *anything* in any sense that makes it intellectually contentful in its distinctively religious aspects.

There is another way in which this notion of the literal helps us connect our question about religious language with its relation to the rest of life. Being construable as literal language, univocally or analogically interpreted religious talk can count as cognitive: it *says something*, expresses a content. In contrast, equivocally, and so, un-interpretable negative, or semantically hermetically-sealed religious language will be non-cognitive.

Therefore, I take the debate concerning the cognitivity of religious language to glom onto these themes. The literalness of religious language will support its claim to being cognitive.

However, there is more to the notion of cognitivity. For the cognitive/non-cognitive distinction has at least the following two connections that also percolate in the background of the literature on religious language.

The first concerns the relation of the linguistic practices to truth, or the good-ordered presence of a truth-predicate in the language in question. Following common practice, let us say that a kind of language in whose interpretation, or in the evaluation of whose utterances, truth is a relevant concern, is a language which is apt for truth. Some sentences of natural language are clearly unapt for truth: questions, imperatives and greetings cannot he true or false. Of course, some such kinds of sentence are not unrelated to truth: if the meaning of a question is the possible answers to it, then, indirectly, questions

5.   B Van Fraassen, *The Scientific Image* (Oxford: Clarendon Press, 1980), 10.

are cognitive, because answers, being declaratives, are apt for truth. Perhaps the situation is similar for imperatives: their meanings are arguably the factual claims that would be descriptive of their satisfaction.

However, the connection between aptness for truth and the semantics of a kind of language usually has more bite than this. For, for example, meta-ethical non-cognitivists like Ayer or Hare mean to claim that ethical language is not apt for truth: such sentences aren't capable of being either true or false. But clearly we can ask ethical questions: for instance, 'What is the right thing to do when you believe your boss orders you to do something wrong?' And clearly, there are sentences which are possible answers to this: 'You should blow the whistle on her', 'You should just do as you are told', 'You should just refuse to do it but don't blow the whistle' and so on. Non-cognitivism wants to say that such answers are not apt for truth: they are insusceptible of being either true or false. Their function is to do something other than state propositions which are true or false, or true or false if properly disambiguated etc: they are not truth-apt. So, one other idea which the idea of cognitivity has served is that of truth-aptness.

Sometimes people put this by saying that there is a 'fact of the matter' to which such language is semantically answerable. There is, for instance, no fact of the matter whether chocolate pecan ice-cream is better ice-cream than rum'n'raisin; or whether roll-on deodorant is better than stick deodorant. All there is is 'different strokes for different folks' as we say. This brings us to our second additional role to which the cognitive/non-cognitive distinction has been put.

Our culture tends to work with a contrast between two extremes of kinds of thought. On one side there are issues like those about the deodorants and the ice-creams. Here, all there is are differences between people which reflect differences in their tastes or preferences or idiosyncrasies of emotion, physique or the like—the merely psychological or individual differences that discriminate people. Disagreements over what is better ice-cream or nicer aftershave, disagreements over preferable foundation garments, and the like, are of this order. It is a silly mistake to search for the truth, the facts of the matter about what is the better ice-cream, or what is the better fragrance: there is no truth about such an issue against which an individual's view on the matter could be determined to be false and in error. Bad taste in fragrances is not disagreement with an objective order. The point of distinguishing good and bad taste in fragrances is not to repel each other and hopefully to please—it is not to achieve any kind of 'match between opinion and reality'. Such discourse is not apt for truth, and disagreement between the malodorous and the rest of us—if so much agreement as this can be got—is merely psychological. It is a matter of the ways we differ in what pleases us. Similarly, other disagreements are 'cultural', or 'matters of personal experience (ways we differ)' or perhaps matters of differences in body chemistry or bodily peculiarities. Differences between men and women in the ways they co-categorise hues may be an example of the latter.

In contrast, our culture treats science very differently. Where some physicists believe in cold fusion, and the vast majority do not, here we think there is a fact of the matter. There are standards of rationality about which there is consensus, whose application will settle the matter. And if they don't conclusively settle the disagreement, as they do in the cold fusion question but do not, say, over the mass of neutrinos—there is something here to be discovered—a fact of the matter to settle. Our procedures for working out what the facts are may be technically beyond us or there may not be sufficient evidence yet assembled, or the bright idea to progress the debate may simply be too hard for us to come up with just yet. However, there's rationality and truth to be got here, reality to be uncovered. Too bad for the cold fusionists, that they just have it wrong. Indeed, the science of a couple of centuries hence might show us up to have been similarly wrong and our theories false about a great deal that we take for true. But that only shows how our best efforts to work reality out can fall short, even radically short, of describing things the way they are. The rational enquirer's epistemological achievement or rationality is one thing, what she is talking about and the truth of her claims about it can be quite something else. Aristotle's theory of gravity concerned gravity, of course, but it was wildly incorrect, even though the best theory going at the time.

On this received way of thinking of science, there are two distinct steps in scientific theorising: establishing what the theory says, and working out whether to believe it or hold it true. The former concerns the meaning of scientific hypotheses, the latter concerns the epistemology of scientific enquiry. Scientific realists disagree about how deeply the latter is related to Truth/Reality, with capital T and R. For the present discussion this is less important than the point that scientific enquiry concerns what the facts of the matter are in a way that tolerates, given the history of science and its changes in deep theory, the conception of a possibly radical disparity between the findings of rational enquiry and what the facts are. This possibility of such a radical disparity is closely related to the distinction between the meaning of a hypothesis and the achievement of rational enquiry into its truth. For the only way we can cash the possibility of radical disparity between what the facts are and what claims rational enquiry can lead us to hold true is by giving examples of it from history: where we can understand, for instance, what Aristotle meant when he said that gravity was pressure downwards towards the absolute centre of the universe, the centre of the earth, a pressure due to the natural motion of earth and water, towards their natural places; where we can understand this, but understand its falsehood by contrasting this representation of the world to ours, in which, among other things, gravity is not a pressure, it is a feature of all matter, not just earth and water, there are no natural motions of particular kinds of matter, but gravity attracts all lumps of matter to all others, in mathematically precise homological patterns; and so on. Moreover, though so wildly wrong, we can still admire Aristotle's rationality—his intellectual achievement in investigating the world as much as he did, of proposing laws regarding physical behaviours, and of systematising his theory into a natural philosophy. We cash the idea of radical disparity between the way things are and rational enquiry by examples such as these, where it is a necessary condition of the examples' serving this point, that the meaning of the false theory is intelligible to us, even though we don't share the intellectual values of the theorist, don't share his epistemology, but can still admire his enquiry for the rational achievement it was. This man's views were not 'merely psychological', though false.

Here we find the cognitive as understood on the received conception: in that concerning which there are facts of the matter to be had, error can be understood without sharing its epistemology but while still admiring such rationality as it had, and where radical disparity between the facts and rational investigation is made intelligible by just such a possibility.

So, from the perspective of received notions of cognitivity, our question is whether religion is more like the latter, scientific cognitivity, or is it more like the earlier matters where disagreement is non-cognitive?

I think we can understand a great deal of the way debates concerning the semantics of religious thought and talk have gone, in terms of the interpenetration of these various conceptual associations with Analogy theories and the notions of cognitivity I have tried to bring out.

3. Can Analogy theories make sense of religious thought and talk?

3.1 Analogy with metaphysics
As I said earlier, there are three points of advantage that Analogy theories of religious language claim:

(a) On an Analogy theory, religious language is literally true, if true at all.
(b) On an Analogy theory, religious language can be used to affirm positive content, not merely make denials.
(c) However, literal religious language is neither anthropomorphic, or more generally univocal or synonymous with the non-religious use of the relevant expressions, but neither is it equivocal with respect to such mundane use or hermetically sealed from the rest of life; and we can show how this works.

Of course, there is quite a number of accounts of the meaning of religious language which describe themselves as Analogy theories, or which borrow the nomenclature.[6] I will focus on what I take to be the broadly Thomistic account as the classical version of the idea.

The starting point is the general notion of an expression the senses of whose various uses are organised into a systematic ambiguity which has a focus of meaning. 'Healthy' is the standard example from Aristotle. I assume familiarity. Perfection terms—for example, 'living', 'understanding . . . ', 'wills . . . ', 'good', 'wise'—and the like are to be understood on this model in application to God. *Secundum esse*, their application to God is the primary or focal one. God is the prime analogate. Of course, *secundum nos*, 'in the order of knowledge', this is not so as our intellects are primarily equipped not to know God, but to know the physical world, and, if things go well, our own nature.

---

6.   See R Swinburne, *The Coherence of Theism* (Oxford: Clarendon Press, 1977), chapters 4 and 5.

Clearly, then, if such terms are to mean anything to us, or figure contentfully in our lives, there has to be some way to bridge the semantic gap, as it were, between, as we might say, the *Bedeutung* of these expressions, their application to God, the (W)Holy Other, and the *Sinn* of such expressions as they function in non-religious language. The risk is that we will be forced to a kind of semantic agnosticism—we don't know what we are saying in using religious language—combined with a dogmatic assertion that these claims that we do not understand are true. Alternatively, we will be forced into a kind of negative theology.

The first resembles the situation Russell sometimes argued we are in with respect to the numbers: we have no idea what we mean in making mathematical claims, but we know they are true. This is a paradoxical predicament, most would agree. If we can avoid it in mathematics, I take it we should also do so in religion. As for negative theology, this seems to me phenomenologically implausible as an account of the understanding of faith: while our understanding of our religious talk is no match for what we are talking about, people of faith generally have the conviction that they are saying something. If we can we should avoid negative theology too.

At this stage classical Analogy theory wheels in some technical notions and some great chain-of-being metaphysics. The key idea is that despite their ontological differences, there exists an ordered relationship between ontological categories of being, which grounds the semantic relationships between the meanings of the expressions as they apply to these different categories of being. Thus, because human nature enjoys an ordered relationship to the divine nature as the latter's creature, and like it, is spiritual, and so on, we can explain that as wisdom is to human nature, so wisdom is to the divine nature.

As Cajetan points out, such an analogy of proportionality can be 'proper' or 'improper', that is, literal or metaphorical. It is metaphor to say that as a king is to his subjects so the lion is to the other wild animals. But God *really* is wise. Thus, we cannot say that such analogy applied to God is *im*proper or not 'belonging to' God. For if we do, we will lose the literalness of the language.

However, it is not obvious that proper analogy of proportionality is enough. For, ordinarily, other proper analogies of proportionality do not yield non-univocal uses of a term; at least as understood in the sentence in which it occurs. So, for instance, 'one is to two as three is to six', does not clarify the meaning of 'three' if we did not know it already and both proportionalities are simply one-half. There is no hint of anything like an 'analogical meaning' in this. Three is simply half of six as one is half of two.

Again 'retrojets are to a plane as an anchor is to a billy cart' does not clarify what 'anchor' means here unless we can see the same meaning in the proportionality on both sides of the equation. Namely, it is a (not very good) method of braking. Likewise with other examples of proper analogy of proportion that I can think of: 'A steel is to a butcher as a grinder is to a shearer', 'A pip is to an orange as an acorn is to an oak', 'The eucharist is to a Catholic as the Torah is to Jew', 'Bradman is to cricket as Jordan is to basketball'. In all of these, we have a univocal relationship on both sides of the comparison. This would seem to render God talk anthropomorphic if it clarified the application of psychological predicates to God at all. Some, of course, defend such a view of the psychological predicates applied to God and see no harm in the univocal nature of such language.[7]

The classical Thomistic reply proceeds to analogy of attribution. This is much the same as the idea of focal equivocity that I have introduced already. The main examples around which debate focused were the so-called transcendental attributes: 'being', 'good' and 'true' as applied across the Aristotelian categories. A substance exists in the primary sense, or is a being, whereas things like a place, a relative attribute, a disposition etc are all beings in a secondary sense, parasitic upon the sense in which a substance is a being. This semantic relation among the expressions is focused on their application to substances, in that ontologically these things in different ontological categories are dependent upon things in the category of substance.

Correspondingly, within the category of substance, God is a being or better being as such, in the primary sense, *ipsum esse subsistens*, *Ens Ipsissimum*. In turn, angels, human beings etc are a being in a secondary sense parasitic upon the sense in which God is, that is, on the sense in which being itself is, in the primary sense. This ordered relationship among beings to Being as such grounds semantic relationship among 'God exists' and, for example, 'Socrates exists', that form a focally equivocal series of senses. This set of semantic relationships is literally true, and, since we understand 'Socrates

---

7.   Cf W Alston, *Divine Nature and Human Language* (Ithaca NY: Cornell University Press, 1989), chapters 3 and 4.

exists', we can understand 'God exists' if we can understand the notion of being as such or '*ipsum esse subsistens*' and the like.

From this ontological grounding, in the metaphysics of *esse*, we can ground the analogical interpretation of the perfection predicates to God. The proportionality that God's wisdom is to God as human wisdom is to human nature is interpreted through the conception of God's being as *ipsum esse subsistens*—the very existential *actus* of existing itself, a substance. As Socrates' wisdom is to human nature so God's wisdom is to *that*. 'Wise' in 'God is wise' means what it means, non-univocally with 'wise' in 'Socrates is wise', by its 'semantic magnification' to 'fit' the very *actus* itself that existing is itself as a substance.

Now, if any of this makes sense—and I'm not *in principle* unsympathetic to it—it has to be admitted that the risks of the non-literal, hermetically sealed religious language are avoided. For, if this line of thought makes sense, there are traceable connections between God talk and mundane talk.

But it is not clear that this approach avoids univocality. That is, it is not clear that appealing to analogy of attribution clarifies why the analogy 'as Socrates' wisdom is to human nature so God's wisdom is to *ipsum esse subsistens*' does not express the same relationship on both sides of the equation. For the resulting proper analogy of proportionality seems to imply that wisdom is such an attribute of being itself as a substance (God) as makes Socrates the wise human being he is. And this *sounds* rather like saying that wisdom is in God what it is in Socrates. Moreover, if *that* is so, even abstracting from any distinctively human connotations of wisdom, it is not clear we avoid anthropomorphism. If this is right, the implication seems to be that if this kind of religious language is both literal and possessed of positive content, it is not analogical but anthropomorphic. One of the claimed advantages of Analogy theory is lost if the other two are preserved.

On the other hand, it can seem to be unclear that we avoid negative theology. For instance, if we gloss '*ipsum esse*' as a pure actuality, we have little option but to elucidate this in turn as the lack of potentiality. Being itself is characterised as the absence, as it were, of room for improvement. Alternatively, if we want to try positively to elucidate '*esse*' directly, I have to confess to having a serious difficulty. One wants to say that *esse* is that by which a being 'be's'. Already that is difficult. Such an invented usage does not obviously connect to other talk by which to introduce it. Moreover, to claim further that we can intelligibly speak of *'ipsum esse subsistens'*—that itself by which a being be's, taken as a substance—from these philosophical practices of metaphysical speculation seems to 'illuminate' by closing the door on a darkened room. For the intellectual credibility of such philosophy cannot be taken as a given. Worse, though this is not a knockdown objection, from a consistently Aristotelian point of view, speaking of a substance as *ipsum esse* is surely self-contradictory. An Aristotelian substance is an individual distinct and independent from other individuals, but *ipsum esse* must be something somehow 'in common' to all that is even if not in a univocal sense.

Thus, it is far from clear that the Analogy theory can at once preserve literalness and analogically grounded meanings for God talk, while also allowing us to interpret its content positively.

3.2 Analogy without metaphysics
Burrell in discussing the Analogy theory,[8] avoids the metaphysics of Thomistic tradition. He proposes Analogy as a rule for *interpreting* religious language, rather than as a semantics grounded on a meta-physics of ontological relations. We are to interpret religious expressions in terms of extensions of use according to the patterns of focally equivocal language.

However, it seems to me that this leaves us with the problems I have already suggested: we either have to accept God talk in the spirit in which Russell accepts mathematical language, and we have to give up positive content; or we have to satisfy ourselves with univocal anthropomorphism. Burrell wants to say that we have some idea of what we are talking about when we talk seriously about God. But at this point, he speaks of the 'irreducible implicitness', 'the contextuality' and 'participatory character' of religious language. He describes this by saying that religious language is 'irreducibly metaphorical'.

If my argument so far is right, then, Burrell gives up literalness as well as the positive content that metaphysics hopes to provide. However, arguably he does not have to, for implicitness, context

---

8.   D Burrell, 'Religious Language and the Logic of Analogy', *International Philosophical Quarterly* Vol 2 (1962): 643–57, 'Beyond the Theory of Analogy', *Proceedings and Addresses of the American Philosophical Association*, vol 46 (1972): 114–21, and *Analogy and Philosophical Language* (New Haven CT: Yale University Press, 1973), chapter 6.

dependence and participatory character of language do not a metaphor make. If it did, 'good' in 'Charity is morally good' would be metaphorical, and perhaps also, it is arguable that the indirect reflective personal pronoun would be metaphorical.[9] So Burrell is not obliged to give up literalness, even if he eschews metaphysics.

However, with or without drawing on the metaphysics, it is not obvious that he can solve the problems to which I have drawn attention. Even if someone deploys analogy as an interpretative rule for the understanding of talk about divine nature (by analogy of attribution of 'being' to clarify the proper analogy of proportionality), it is arguable that there is trouble. The problems are semantic and independent of the metaphysics.

My suspicion is that if there is anything to the notion of *ipsum esse*, let alone *ipsum esse subsistens*, it is 'more than can be said'. Perhaps we should admit that the givenness of existing is inutterable. Nor does it help to say that I just uttered it. For the mere use of words together that separately make sense does not show that I have said anything. I might have said nothing. Making a noise that is grammatical explains nothing.

On the other hand, many words have been used in the attempt to give expression to some such notion, whether in the language of être, *Dasein*, or *esse*. Surely *something* has to be made of such philosophical labours. Wittgenstein's distinction between saying and showing suggests itself. If one's attempts either to say what *esse* is or, more modestly, to speak in ways that enable people to see it for themselves fail to help you to see what I am trying to bring into view by my words, we would have to admit that there is only silence to be had.

On the other hand, perhaps some of my readers will be able to believe themselves to 'get it'. I recall a seminar some years ago where a prominent Sydney phenomenologist was arguing for the virtues of Husserl on the nature knowledge of the external world. She argued that even within the scope of the *epoché*, our primitive notion of being grounds our claim to know a reality beyond the mind. She distinguished this notion of being from the traditional Fregean doctrine. To make the point that the *noema* 'being' was competent for

---

9.   See J Perry, 'The Problem of the Essential Indexical', *Nous* Vol 13 (1979): 3–21,
      H Castañeda, *The Phenomeno-Logic of the I: Essays on Self-consciousness*
      (Bloomington IN: Indiana University Press, 1999), E Harcourt,
      'Interpretationism, the First Person and "That"-Clauses', *Nous* vol 33 No 3
      (1999): 459–72.

such an epistemological role, she marked its importance with heavy emphasis when she uttered the word 'being': '*being*'. When I protested that I had no idea what she meant when she continued to speak the expression with heavy emphasis, she challenged me: 'You know that this table is existing, that it is. You know what I mean'. And I had to admit, though somewhat lost for *words*, that I felt myself to have some inkling. Others seem to agree with this general thought. So, let us assume that those who cannot 'get it' are missing something of an intellectual nature, while conceding that the 'givenness of existing' (I mean the scare quotes seriously) is not a competence in a language, even a technical one. In this way, *esse* is non-intelligible. It is not a notion to be grasped at all. However, it is something to be 'grasped'.

The point of importance for us is that even such a weakened introduction of the notion of *esse* is not of itself an introduction to seeing *God*. People cannot always see God in it, even believers. For many, the givenness of existing, *esse*, isolates and engenders anxiety rather than intimating the worship-worthy. The existentialists seem to witness to such a sense of it. Buddhism and Advaita Vedanta seem to intimate the loss of all such distinctions as feature in the theistic sense of it: there is no I, no Thou, there, only 'no-thing'. The Platonic tradition speaks of that 'beyond being and non-being' apparently in the same spirit as this experience of *esse*.

I conclude that analogy theory of religious language ultimately fails to achieve its aim. Even if the analogy of attribution of being makes sense in some way, it ultimately is not an unambiguous ground for understanding *God* talk. If it is to be understood this way, *that* would be an interpretative step, requiring that God talk already made sense to those who speak theistically of the sense of being. And surely, if this is right, Analogy theory is not able to rescue the cognitivity of religious language in the way it wants to: by showing how religious language has literal, positive content which is neither anthropomorphic nor hermetically sealed off from the rest of life.

4. An alternative

I want to argue that religious thought and talk is a cognitive body of thought, talk and practices. However, while I want to make connections between my suggestion for the cognitivity of religious thought, and the debates so far discussed, I cannot make these connections directly as I would also argue that there are too many problematic assumptions informing the structure of these debates, to take on all at once. So I will simply present the two central features of my proposal and try to clarify my position relative to these received debates in considering some objections that I anticipate.

4.1 Faith as a virtue of interpretation

Broadly speaking, I want to explore the idea that the meaning of religious language arises from forms of life and practices which furnish disciplines of interpretation and utterance. Religious talk is subject to standards of correctness and excellence implicit in those forms of life and practices and not totally explicitisable, and partially constituted by a tradition of valuation and enquiry and patterns of responsiveness within the religious community. In particular, I want to suggest that the notion of faith as a virtue of the believer is a central cipher for the philosophy of religious language, as the notion of faith as a virtue is a, perhaps *the*, notion in which the disciplines of interpretation and utterance of religious thought and talk are given realisation in the forms of life and the practices of a religious community. This general line of thought has found proponents recently in the theory of knowledge, particularly in Zagzebski's *Virtues of the Mind*. I am proposing that we extend the approach to the theory of the meaning of religious language.

What does this involve? I think it involves two main points. The first is that if one is to understand what religious thought and talk means and how it does it, one has to look at *faith's* understanding in a space of evaluative or normative contrasts between the real thing, faith, and on the one hand, various relevant vices or corruptions of faith, and on the other hand, semblances of faith: states of the believer which are like faith but not the full bottle or are somehow immature or the like. Sometimes the difference between a semblance of a virtue and a vice or a corruption is one of emphasis. But the distinction is acceptable as a general one. So, for instance, consider the difference between being in love, and being infatuated. The latter is a semblance, the former a virtue, in a love-relationship. Again, generosity with one's time is a virtue, but if one gives of one's time to others to the point of self-neglect, it is not genuine generosity but a semblance of generosity. And of course, it can become a vice if, for instance, by dint of habit, one uses if to hide from other responsibilities one has. My suggestion is that faith is a virtue in a conceptual space of this general kind. This is hardly a novel idea—it forms the core of scholastic discussions of faith.

But it is an idea that has been undeservedly overlooked in too much contemporary philosophy of religious language. How would this idea work?

To begin, there is a most important difference in the understanding of religious talk marked by a distinction between what we describe as an 'overliteral' interpretation and the right one that a mature faith affords us. There is a story about St Francis which illustrates this. When the young Francis first developed the conviction that God was calling him to work for him, Francis' epiphany took the form of hearing God tell him 'Build up my church, Francis'. The young Francis took this to mean that he physically had to construct a church building, so he spent a long time dragging stone blocks to the building site to work on it. That is, in the immaturity of his faith, at this stage of his life, Francis took the Lord too literally. This was something that he worked out as he grew in his faith. As his faith matured and deepened, so did his understanding of the meaning of the Lord's words. Similar stories are told of the gradual development of correct understanding of Yahweh's calls to various prophets. Similar development of genuine understanding of the meaning of religious revelation is reflected in passages in the Qur'an concerning the prophet's faith in Allah. These immature, literal-minded interpretations are not genuine faith, but a semblance. Not to be disdained for that, just as emerging moral virtue is not to be rejected. However, it is not the real virtue.

Likewise, superstitious and magical interpretations of religious language are not genuine faith. Sometimes magical understandings are semblances—not really bad for faith, or betrayals of God or the like—but hardly mature faith. But sometimes magical construals of religious talk is vicious—for instance, if a Catholic were to use consecrated eucharistic elements to bring down a curse on an enemy. Superstition is probably more controversial. I believe that the wearing of scapulas is usually superstitious and so, not really an expression of faith. That is, people understand the wearing of them as effective in producing outcomes in the afterlife. They are like athletes who must wear the same pair of socks whenever they compete. This could be a semblance of faith—a harmless tolerable missing of the mark. Could it become a vice? Presumably it would if it came to be thought to obviate the need for prayer, nourishing the virtues etc.

Similarly, people sometimes mistake a tribalistic ideology for faith. Some Catholics in Northern Ireland seem to do this. And people with strong sectarian memories of other denominations do too. For them the meaning of one's community's religious ideas is whatever casts the opponents in a vicious or silly light. In more sectarian days in Australia, Protestant sectarians used to interpret their notion of 'the church' by contrast with the alleged anti-patriotism of Catholics under papal governance. So, for them, the church is not a political thing. Catholic sectarians used to interpret transubstantiation in terms of the conflictual history with the Lutherans and the Zwinglians, yet very few Protestants treat the eucharistic elements with the kind of disregard one would hold for old bread destined for the chicken coop. From the point of view of a more mature faith, eucharist is the Lord's supper and there is no need to understand it in such terms as to dodge the wrong side of a polemical divide. The latter is not genuine faith but tribalistic ideology. Is it vice or semblance? I'd say, mostly vice. For it harms Christian unity.

4.2 Faith language as 'to-be-realistically-construed'
Does this framework illuminate the kinds of concern that traditional faith/reason debates are exercised by? I think it does. For, though we do not have a separate terminology for it, it seems to me part of a genuine, mature faith, that it not turn its back on other parts of life. In particular, faith should not have any fear of rational knowledge if, as we say, truth is one, reason is a gift from God, and this world is good. From this perspective, an interpretation of religious talk under the assumption that knowledge of the world and human nature from non-religious sources is unneedful or a vanity is at best a counterfeit faith or even a vice. Equally, uncritically enucleating the content of religious talk under the assumption that anything that parades itself as 'modern thinking' should trump traditional ideas is equally a mistake. Again, it could be a counterfeit of faith, if motivated by the desire to avoid, say a magical religiosity, but it could be a vice of the mind if, say, uncritically trendy. The effort faithfully to engage non-religious knowledge or sources of wisdom and understanding in a critical and intellectually honest way for the sake of deepening and maturing faith is a virtue partially constitutive of faith. This pattern of argument about faith seems to me to apply equally well regarding matters of world-view and morality.

   With this elaboration of faith, which is more mature than a semblance and avoids the vices or corruptions of faith, religious people deploy a vocabulary of critical appraisal. Some of it is familiar from general epistemology: there is concern for the giving of reasons for interpretation, for consistency among ideas, and for various kinds of evidence. There are also other epistemic values in religious thinking. A concern for coherence with tradition is a feature of Catholic thought. This, while unfamiliar to contemporary philosophy (though in this official position, there is a certain amount of self-deception), is also most important to late antique Greco-Roman philosophy, Indian and Buddhist philosophy. A concern for being 'Bible-based' is important to evangelical thinkers. Muslim thinkers hold to the statements of the Qur'an, the example of the life of the Prophet, analogies and the community's consensus as values in their decisions about belief and interpretation.

No one would deny that it takes time and practice to develop competence and mastery of such language. Early stages of learning the competence can be difficult. In particular, it is unsurprising that early stages of faith development require teachers of faith to use ways of inducting learners into faith which simplify and, if taken strictly, mislead as to the genuine content of faith. Arguably, many people who have some religion in their background either never get past these early stages of development or give up working at it because they find it too hard to translate religious language sensibly into other kinds of thought they have become competent in. It is worth noting that one finds a similar pattern in the acquisition of competence in scientific or other specialised language. Loss of faith that has progressed little beyond early stages of development can resemble in important ways the attitude towards science, especially its more theoretical end, of those who think of it with suspicion or as an irrelevance to real life, having given up trying to make sense of it.

Religious thought is a critical style of thinking. It is not all and only the thinking about religious matters of the superstitious or ideological. Religious thought is subject to disciplines of interpretation and expression according to standards of correctness embodied in conceptions of genuine faith sustained by the tradition and practice of a religious community, in a contrastive space of the genuine thing, semblances and vices or corruption.

Moreover, against this kind of background, it is hard not to take seriously the religious believer's general concern for truth and answerability to an objective order, to an order which measures the community's and the individual's efforts to get their interpretation of their religious tradition's vocabulary right. These are the kinds of mark of a form of life and a kind of talk that invite interpretation as a cognitive one. If Anti-Realism is right about religious talk, it would have to be in the form of an Error theory.

Some will complain that this does not suffice to show that religious talk is cognitive or truth-apt. There are two objections I will consider briefly here. The first argument is that there are forms of thought which display such disciplines and distinctions but which are not cognitive, and whose language, therefore, is not apt for truth. However, the only way such an objection could work is by producing examples. One can expect that these examples will themselves be controversial, especially to the extent that they rely on tendentious assumptions about what cognitivity and truth-aptness are.

The second and more serious objection is this. The disciplines of faith subject the believer to certain serious limits to what they may question and demand of the believer a commitment or attachment to the truth of certain claims, that is, in a certain way, unconditional or unprovisional. For instance, the faithful Muslim cannot, while remaining a Muslim, deny the divine origin of the Qur'an. The believing Christian cannot, while remaining a Christian, deny that Jesus the Jewish teacher and healer of first century Palestine, is (somehow) the revelation of God. The argument proposes that any discipline on understanding which requires such unconditional or unprovisional attachment to or belief in the truth of any claim is inconsistent with recognising that discipline as a cognitive one.

My reply to this is that it disproves too much. If all unconditional or unprovisional attachment to a claim is incompatible with treating that thought or thought closely connected to it as cognitive, then too little of our thought is implied to be cognitive. Mathematics will be dismissed (for instance, Peano's Axioms). Certain assumptions within physics (for instance, various symmetry principles) will be dismissed. And much more besides.

I conclude that there is no particular reason from the nature of religious thought itself to deny that it is cognitive and deserving of a construal as truth-apt and there is much in it to invite such a construal.

4.3 But . . .

That was the Realist part of the paper. I am not sure that realists will be happy with the next part. For the next ingredient in the view I want to urge is to press the analogy with ethical thought further, to a point that few meta-ethical realists will find plausible about ethical virtue. In effect, I will be insisting that 'truth-aptness' is not a univocal term in its connection with, say, science, and in it connection with religion.

Earlier I argued that our philosophical culture associates the cognitivity of scientific language, in contrast to the language of gustatory or olfactory rating, with a distinction between the epistemological achievement of rational investigation (assigning truth values to claims), and the understood content of a proposition being entertained in the investigation: it is one thing to formulate a proposition as a hypothesis and another to have rationally investigated its truth-value. The availability of this distinction is a necessary condition of being able to cash out the possibility that the world might be other than as our best efforts at rational enquiry leads us to think. So content is one thing, the relevant epistemic status is another. Understanding and belief are different.

However, this is not true, I argue, in ethics. Socrates, Plato and Aristotle are right: knowledge, true knowledge, that is, of the good is to do it virtuously. There is a difference between what the good person understands in deciding to do something, for the ethical reasons she has, and what the akratic person understands when, as we say, she knows what she should do, but is deflected from it by disequilibriating emotion or passion. Of course, for culpably akratic behaviour, for the purposes of holding such a person responsible, they are properly describable as understanding what they should do. As Aristotle says, 'when water chokes, what will we wash *it* down with?' The best Aristotle can do to make sense of the culpable akratic's behaviour is to say she doesn't 'put what she understands to use' .

But the difference between her and the good person is that the latter understands the good so seamlessly that there is no distinction between will and intellect in her—choice and understanding 'are one': her state of mind is at once *orektikos nous* (conative understanding) that is *noetike orexis* (intellectual conation).[10] What the akratic understands tolerates distinction between understanding and will and *what* the akratic understands in her penetration of the good, is only as a drunk understands Empedocles' verses when he can drunkenly parrot them. His understanding is, we might say, a semblance. Plato overdramatically describes him as ignorant. In any case, in the

---

10.   1139b4f.

determination of the content of a person's ethical thought, it matters what kind of character they have.

I want to argue that the content or meaning of religious language is like this. Just as the understanding of ethical language requires virtue, so too in religion the content/subject distinction does not go deep towards understanding religious thought and talk. In religion, as Philips put it, belief and understanding are one. Or as I would prefer to put it: genuine understanding of religious dicta requires genuine faith towards them. Arguably, then, if this idea cannot be made to fly in ethics, it will be the weaker as an account of religious language.

I do not have the space to argue the point in ethics.[11] Let me, then, simply try to elucidate its application in the theory of religious language and then consider some objections.

The thought I am suggesting is that, as in ethics, the moral understanding of a *virtuous* person is the cipher through which the content of understanding the meaning of a certain kind of behaviour or whatever is revealed; so too, the virtue of faith, the religious understanding of a person of mature faith, is the cipher through which the religious significance of, for example a doctrinal formulation, or a prayer, or ritual words and actions is disclosed. And just as ethics, that is genuine goodness in which the real ethical significance of something is disclosed, so too in religion, true faith is that to which the religious meaning of these formulae, stories, prayers or whatever is shown in the objects of its attention.

Of course, as in ethics, propositional contents can be abstracted from what faith understands, and contemplated in abstraction from the faith that understands them. Just as the akratic, and even the enkratic person, can distil the content of an ethical thought about some behaviour into a proposition and consider it without virtue (in the abstract 'ethical proposition'),[12] so too, propositional contents can be distilled from faith, for consideration in abstraction from faith. The magical believer enjoys comprehension of some such, as does the young Francis, the ideological sectarian Catholic and, arguably the theistic metaphysician when under this hat. But what is understood here is not what faith understands, even when it is a matter such as God's existence or goodness or providential care. These are revealed

---

11.   The reader may compare the argument of R Gaita, 'Goodness beyond Virtue' and 'Evil beyond Vice' in *A Common Humanity* (Melbourne: Text, 1999)

12.   Cf Blackburn *op cit*, chapter 4.

elsewhere—in meditative writing, prayer, extended theological reflections on faith, in the sacraments or rituals of a religion and the like.

My argument is that the semantics of religious language will only be distorted into misconstruing semblances of faith for the real thing, if one insists that propositional contents abstractable from things religious people say *qua* religious and faith filled, and for which are traceable steps of semantic continuity with, for instance, metaphysical claims as per classical Analogy theory (*if* there are such traceable steps), if it is insisted that such abstracted propositional contents are the grounds for the cognitivity and intelligibility of religious talk and thought. This is what I take most natural theology as applied to religious talk and thought to claim.

This distorts what religious talk and thought means because, in faith, as in ethical understanding of the significance of things in life, the intelligibility of content and the cognitivity of the talk and thought is exactly what is revealed in the ways faith *distinguishes* itself from the kind of intellectual achievement and speculative, theoretical posture towards God as metaphysical posit or conclusion of an inference based on alleged facts about this universe, that are the typical fare of metaphysical philosophy of religion. As I have argued, what distinguishes faith from the latter is its 'feeling', and is altogether *sui generis* (although 'feeling' is too mundane and safe a word). More precisely, the distinction of faith is all those things *iman* means in Arabic, *pistis* means in the New Testament and the Hindus mean by *bakhti*: it is the love of God, the awe before the mystery of God's love for one, trust and confidence in God's intimacy, the sense of the sheer goodness one does not deserve to approach but which brings you to it lovingly. I speak with a Christian vocabulary of course. Other religious traditions will explain this differently and these explanations will be constitutive of *faiths*. Generalising from similarities, however, mindful of the limitations of such generalisation, we can say that this is the kind of thing that distinguishes faith from metaphysical thinking about God in Philosophy of Religion. And this is the kind of thing that gives religious language its meaning.

Such language is the stuff that moves the soul and strikes at the heart. It is the kind of expression that Russell complained of at a certain meeting of the Cambridge Moral Sciences Club where, upon a vigorous discussion on religion, the gathered number one by one got up to give testimony to their experience of God's forgiveness or the like. Dismayed with the similarity of the events to a Beach Mission Revival, Russell promptly ceased participating, in the name of reason.

Such discriminants of faith are apt to invite the suspicion of intellectuals. I admit also to suspicion of enthusiasm and much, maybe all, charismatic religion of the emotions. But such a point, even if well made, does not imply that wherever religious thought is imbued with this kind of grand emotion, religious thought fails to reveal anything intelligible and, in its domain, literally contentful. As I have argued, in religion, as in ethics, belief-knowledge-faith is understanding. This gives a particular twist to Anselm's famous dictum *'credo ut intelligam'*. It is only dogmatism to see in the passionate distinctiveness of faith an obstacle to construing the meaning or content of the understood, that it discloses, as so much non-cognitive attitudinal superaddition to the metaphysically expressible facts. Instead, I suggest, faith is a seamless responsiveness in which both understanding and the heart move us in the disclosure and registration of religious meaning that is irreducible either to language univocally related to the mundane (eg the use of psychological predicate to characterise our fellows) or to language extended, analogically, under the disciplines of a metaphysical conception, from such mundane subject matter.

I am satisfied to describe religious thought and talk, so construed, as literal so long as we realise that such an ascription is relative to our target language: it is literal in the language of faith, though not in 'common sense' talk. Just as, in the language of Catholic faith, the believer literally sees Jesus in the eucharistic bread or again, relates to God as our father/mother. Blank looks of incomprehension are the right response when a person challenges such claims by pointing out that what is perceptually obvious is the white disk of bread and that God never had sex with one's mother. Such an observation is, religiously, just silly. It shows that one is not speaking 'God talk' in making it. From the critic's linguistic territory, divine parenthood is, of course, metaphorical. But whether metaphorical or literal is a question of what the home vocabulary and practices are for the particular utterances.

While we fail to attend seriously to real faith—the kind that leads us in prayer to crave the sense of God's presence and finds peace and joy in our rest in her presence—and see in the distinctively affective and desiderative tone of faith, a suspicious element which, by taking the content of religious thought beyond what metaphysical thinking can abstract from faith as an attitude of commitment and love of God, thereby introduces non-cognitive elements into faith, there will be no alternative than either to see faith as a non-cognitive attitude to this world (for traditional metaphysical language of analogy fails to serve religion now) or to try to save its significance by reducing it to a more naturalistic thing, which to me will smack either of superstition or of an intellectually gratuitous overlay on the natural and human world.

5. Objections and responses

(i) To many it seems obvious that we simply can formulate and understand claims about God without the benefits of faith. Indeed, the traditional perspective of Natural Theology and much contemporary Analytic philosophy of religion is that many, though indeed not all, of the truths of faith are susceptible of 'pre-faith understanding' by reason, and can be epistemically assessed under this interpretation. Does this thought not seem confirmed in the very existence of reasoned debate in Natural Theology and Analytic philosophy of religion? Does this not also locate a role for metaphysics in religious thinking?

Moreover, the approach presented here fails to distinguish between propositions of faith that are susceptible of such metaphysical formulation and those which are not. The claims that God exists, that God is all powerful, that God is personal, and the like are formulable in this way. In contrast, claims distinctive of revealed truth—such as that God is a community of love between subsistent relations—cannot be formulated for this kind of epistemic appraisal, prior to the benefits of faith. The approach sponsored here fails to take account of such distinctions.

My reply to this line of thought is this. It is firstly important to realise that it is a philosopher's line of thought. The formulation of propositions with terms appearing in them such as 'God', 'all powerful' and the like are given such content as they have by philosophical clarification or explicitation. Of course, 'clarification' and 'explicitation' is clarification and explicitation of *something* and this something would presumably have to be *somehow* related to the meanings of these expressions in religion (I will come back to this). These expressions are given the discipline of clarification and explicitness by the imposition on them of the tools of trade of philosophical reflection. Thus, for instance, it is argued that from faith we understand that: (G) God (whose concept we understand) is that than which nothing greater can be conceived.

For the purposes of natural theology, this requires translation into the language of philosophical analysis. Here, however, we encounter problems, for in the language of quantificational logic, it is well known that we must make some decisions. This apparently unproblematic piece of religious English can be formulated a number of ways:[13]

(G1) $\exists x$ (Ux & ~$\exists w \exists y$ (Ww &ywGx@)) (There is an understandable being x, such that for no world w and being y does the greatness of y in w exceed the greatness of x in the actual world.)

(G2) $\exists x \exists v$ (Ux & Wv & ~$\exists x Vy$ (Wx & ywGxv)) (There are an understandable being x and a world v, such that for no world w and being y does the greatness of y in w exceed the greatness of x in v.)

(G3) $\exists x$ (Ux & ~$\exists v \exists w \exists y$ (Wv & Ww &ywGxv)) (There is an understandable being x such that for no worlds v and w and being y does the greatness of y in w exceed the greatness of x in v.)

These propositions are not logically equivalent. (G3) implies (G1) but not conversely and (G1) implies (G2) but not conversely. When the Ontological Argument is formulated with (G1) and (G3), it is invalid. Thus, these are unacceptable translations for the purposes of natural theology. When it is formulated with (G2), the argument is valid but it does not imply that God exists in the actual world, only that she could exist. Again, this is not helpful for the purposes of natural theology. Thus, the ontological argument is not the support for religion that natural theology presents itself as being.

Some will contend that the problem is with natural theology. However, this misses the point. I mean only to make an illustration of what is fundamental here. The important point is that a piece of metaphysics has to show that it can pull its weight. Arguably, the ontological argument does not.[14] And that *is* a problem with the

---

13.   Cf D Lewis, *Philosophical Papers Volume 1* (Oxford: Oxford University Press, 1983), 14.

14.   Perhaps another version does have something to offer faith, a version which rejects Lewis's counterpart theory of transworld identity.

ontological argument. However, just as the ontological argument has to show its credentials as having something to offer religious thought and faith, so does any metaphysical proposal. And here, God, we might say, is in the details . . . or not.

Thus, I can concede to the objection that we can indeed formulate metaphysical theses with terms in them borrowed from faith. Moreover, these propositions can be understood independently of faith. But this does not show that they are any help in grounding the content of faith's beliefs. As metaphysics, like the ontological argument, they may just fail: fail to prove their intended propositions or fail to cohere with other elements of a contemporary world-view conditioned by scientific knowledge of nature; or perhaps fail in other ways. The assessment of this is a matter of detailed analysis and evaluation. I for one am pessimistic about the prospects of received metaphysical natural theology in fulfilling its ambitions because, one by one, various attempted versions are arguably not successful even as metaphysics. This obviously requires more argument than one can give here. But one should be open-minded enough to allow that some future proposal might be more successful.

More to the point however, let us imagine a metaphysical natural theology which is successful as metaphysics. Assume, for instance, that it is formulable in a precise and rigorous way, that its arguments are valid and premises plausible under translation into a plausible underlying logic, and that it manages to cohere with scientific knowledge of the natural world. How will it be of help to religion in grounding the meaning of faith's beliefs?

This is the question that plagued Pascal. How does one relate the God of metaphysics to the God of Abraham, Isaac and Jacob? As we have seen, philosophical regimentation with the discipline of philosophical natural theology might start with religious thinking, but it requires a translation into the technical language of philosophical theory. Thus, 'God, my loving father' becomes 'the uncaused cause of pure actuality lacking all potentiality', or 'the modally maximally perfect being-in-a-possible-world in S4 Quantified Modal Logic'. That is, a kind of theoretical identification must be possible for one whose faith is to benefit from this kind of metaphysical natural theology. We can have reasons for theoretical identifications of various kinds: genes with DNA, electrical discharge across a potential difference between the clouds and the earth's surface with lightning. In such theoretical identifications, we must have understanding and reasons that are prior to the identification in order to make it. That is, for instance, we do not need to know what DNA is in order to know that there are inheritance factors and how, functionally, they work: we had Mendel's laws first, and later discovered DNA. We understand what lightning is without needing the benefits of geographical electrodynamics. Both terms of the identification are conceptually autonomous and do not require the identification to be understood. Why should we expect it to be different in religion. Does the unphilosophical believer have to wait for the metaphysician to afford her the benefits of his work, in order to understand her faith? To make the availability of metaphysical natural theology a necessary condition of the possibility of the intelligibility of religious language surely implies she must. And this is a mistake.

Of course, religious faith can benefit from intellectual effort. I take that for granted. But this does not show that the semantics of religious language needs a metaphysical theology for us to be able to 'make sense of religious language'. Where faith does benefit from intellectual work, the relation between the two is more complex than that. Indeed, the only real question is whether the two sets of concepts—those of faith and those of metaphysical natural theology—are similar enough to be profitably related. If they are, it is because faith can see in the concepts of metaphysics something sufficiently similar to what it *already* understands to be worth investigating as a way of expressing faith's understanding in a different language.

Thus, I conclude that we may well be able to formulate intelligible propositions with expression borrowed from religion, that are understandable without faith; and that indeed, a system of such proposition may be of value to faith. However, the work is not done by the metaphysics when it is valuable to faith, it is done by faith. And whether it is valuable to faith is a matter for faith to decide rather than the metaphysics. This seems to me quite contrary to the traditional spirit in which philosophers have sought to do metaphysical natural theology.

(ii) A second objection to the approach of this paper goes like this. If religious talk is in these ways autonomous vis-à-vis metaphysics and other intellectual discourse, two things seem to follow: first, that there can be no reasons for non-religious people to enter a religious form of life; and second, that if faith implies propositions that are irrational or have not discharged their burdens of proof, it need not be unreasonable not to give up on these beliefs. Are these implications not an embarrassment of my position?

My reply is this. I take issue with the description of the situation. I have already said that it is no part of my view of a mature faith that it hermetically seals itself off from other forms of enquiry. So, if the objection questions this, I simply reiterate it.

On the other hand, the objection proceeds from a point of view that is heavily indebted to the dichotomy between reason and science on one side, and religion on the other. My proposal is that there is a kind of reason in science, a kind of reason in ethics, a kind of reason in, say, music, and a kind of reason in religion. Reason does not amount to one way of assessing views, grading proposals, and making epistemic distinctions between ideas and performances. There are the 'reasons of the heart' which are no less reasons for being of the heart than are the reasons of scientific enquiry. So, I object to the assumption of the objection that it is possible in the abstract to have a contentful characterisation of such a conflict between religion and other kinds of thought. *It all depends on the details.* Of course religious ideas can conflict with ideas from other sources. And a mature faith will be truthful about that. But there is no reason in general to suppose that there must be conflict between reason and what religion implies, than there is to suppose that there must be conflict between science, say, and what ethics implies. Again, it just depends on the details of the alleged conflict.

For instance, it would seem to me that there is a conflict between science and such versions of Christian faith as interpret the first few chapters of Genesis as implying that the beginning of the universe was in 4004 BCE. Here, Christian faith of this kind is revealed for its immaturity if it insists on this interpretation against the evidence of science. In this case, religious faith has to find greater intellectual sophistication to be mature. But does this show that *in general*, 'the scientific world-view' (there is just one?[15]) somehow puts into question the intellectual respectability of dwelling receptively in stillness before the consoling presence of the Spirit in my grief at great trauma?

---

15.   Cf T Kasulis, 'Sushi, Science, and Spirituality', *Philosophy of East and West,* vol 45 (1995): 227–48.

The only way the first part of this objection can have any force is with examples of alleged conflict. Since this is a matter for other debates, we can dismiss this part of the objection.

This puts us in a position to answer the second half of the objection. Non-believers may find faith by considering metaphysical arguments for God's existence or philosophical apologetics. Nothing in my approach implies this is not possible. Moreover, nothing in my approach implies that there can be no reason in the emergence of such belief. Whether there is reason in it or not depends on the logical or philosophical merit of the arguments that convince the person in question. And one would be unwise to rule on this in advance.

However, few would believe that a person who has come to faith in this way can rest easy, that there is no more religious growth to go through. It is to be expected, miracles notwithstanding, that such a neophyte's faith has a lot of development to go through. All that my argument in this paper implies is that part of this development will be the learning of a set of religious epistemic terms of appraisal—for want of a better term, the acquisition of religion's reasons, the reasons of faith, which are not necessarily grounded on metaphysics. This objection is misplaced.

(iii) Finally, one might object that my approach is too open. It allows any kind of ratbag religion in as having its own 'reasons of faith' so long as it distinguishes between genuine faith and its semblances and corruptions. Surely, the objection goes, this is too permissive.

Indeed, if this is what my argument implies, it is too permissive. And if one does not have a faith to speak from, and defended such a view, this view would be too permissive. Without any faith perspective from which to adopt a critical stance towards other religions, it is hard to see how one could reasonably exclude certain views and practices as incompatible with true faith, real religion. However, my conception of the meaning of religious language does not have to be like this.

The question of the relation between religions is far too large to embark on here. Suffice it to say that a broadly monotheistic religious commitment aligned with the Judaeo-Christian-Islamic tradition seems to be at least one adequate way to be open to other religions without letting in the ratbags. From the perspective of the shared conception of faith present in that tradition, certain concrete pretenders to faith do not pass muster: for example, those dedicated to the rejection of all enquiry independent of Holy Writ; those dedicated to establishing their preferred religious way at any cost, even by means of violence and murder. Clearly, then, there is no notion of 'really understanding the religious significance' of something that is wholly independent of what is being 'understood' and its relations to other matters. The actual beliefs of a putative religious outlook are relevant to assessing its claim to be a kind of faith.

This makes a point that I have not dwelt on here but is worth making. It is that the ability to recognise in another religion a virtue of interpretation and belief sufficiently like one's own to merit being understood as faith, is something we exercise *in medias res* and will be a matter of controversy. Most of the best things in life are.

Alasdair MacIntyre's Tradition-Dependent Rationality and *Fides et Ratio*

Tracey Rowland

1. Introduction

Concomitant with Henri De Lubac's argument that 'no culture is really neutral' is Alasdair MacIntyre's argument that no conception of rationality is ever really neutral in its relation to theism or competing intellectual traditions. However while MacIntyre acknowledges the genealogical claims that all forms of rationality are 'tradition-dependent', he nonetheless holds that while reason may not be neutral, it can be universal. Indeed, in *Three Rival Versions of Moral Inquiry*, MacIntyre went so far as to argue that 'reason can only move towards being genuinely universal and impersonal insofar as it is neither neutral nor disinterested'.[1]

Such a conception of rationality represents a dramatic break with the strategy of the neo-Thomists to defend their tradition by reference to Enlightenment conceptions of rationality. Criticisms of their strategy may be found in the works of scholars associated with the so-called *Nouvelle Théologie*, and in Etienne Gilson's histories of Thomist thought. In a letter to de Lubac, Gilson criticised the Dominican theologians from Hervé Nedellec right up to Cajetan and beyond of 'emasculating' the doctrine of St Thomas and of making his theology a 'brew of watered-down *philosophica aristotelico thomistica* concocted to give off a vague deism fit only for the use of right-thinking candidates for high school diplomas and Arts degrees'.[2] Similarly, Yves Simon observed:

> Today we consider it a paradox that Thomists have ever accepted a division of philosophy which was initiated by Wolff, consolidated by Kant, popularized by the Eclectics of the school of Cousin and was

---

1. Alasdair MacIntyre, *Three Rival Versions of Moral Enquiry* (London: Duckworth, 1990), 59–60.
2. Etienne Gilson, *Letters to Henri de Lubac* (San Francisco: Ignatius, 1986), 24.

fundamentally at variance with that upheld by Saint Thomas.[3]

Thus while all Thomists agree that there is a relationship between faith and reason and that it is a perennial interest of their tradition to defend the complementarity of the two orders, the contemporary challenge of postmodern scholarship is forcing Thomist scholars to think more deeply about how their understanding of rationality differs from the Enlightenment-derived alternatives on the one hand, and from the genealogical tradition on the other. To this end this paper is focused on an account of Alasdair MacIntyre's notion of a narrative tradition and its relationship to ideas found within the encyclical *Fides et Ratio*, particularly John Paul II's reference to 'principles of an implicit philosophy'.

2. The influence of RG Collingwood

MacIntyre's notion of a tradition-dependent rationality derives in part from the early influence of historiographer RG Collingwood. Although Collingwood was sympathetic to the kind of continental liberalism espoused by Guido De Ruggiero, it was not Collingwood's political philosophy which inspired MacIntyre, but rather his theory of history. Collingwood argued that past ideas could not be studied without reference to the historical context in which the ideas originated, and thus that historians should reconstruct in their own minds the situations in which the great philosophers found themselves.[4] MacIntyre presents the issue as one of understanding the 'social embodiment of concepts' and argues that 'to abstract any type of concept, but notably moral concepts, from the contexts of the traditions which they inform and through which they are transmitted is to risk damaging misunderstandings'.[5] From this perspective the task of philosophy is to articulate for a particular cultural and social order 'its concepts and beliefs in a manner which enables those who inhabit that culture to learn both what criticisms of those concepts and beliefs require a rational answer and to what degree such an answer can be

---

3. Yves Simon, *Maritain's Philosophy of the Sciences* (New York: Sheed & Ward, 1943), 159.
4. RG Collingwood, *The Idea of History* (Oxford: Clarendon Press, 1946).
5. Alasdair MacIntyre, 'Interview with Cogito', *Cogito*, vol 2 (1991): 69.

provided'.[6] In an essay on Aquinas's critique of education, MacIntyre summarises this methodology thus:

> [W]ith Aquinas's texts as with those of many philosophers a crucial question is always: Against whom is he writing here? Within what is this or that particular contention to be situated? Philosophers characteristically invite us not simply to assert *p*, but to assert *p* rather than *q* or *r*, and we will often only understand the point of asserting *p*, if we know what *q* and *r* are.[7]

Concretely, MacIntyre argues that the position in which Aquinas found himself when a young teacher at the University of Paris was not merely that of having to reconcile the theological tradition of the Fathers (principally Augustine and his *credo ut intelligere* principle) with the philosophical tradition of Aristotle; but also of having to formulate jurisprudential principles to deal with the jurisdictional conflicts of the time. These included the power of the papacy, the powers of the sainted Louis IX in France and the excommunicated anti-papal Frederick II in Sicily, and the powers of episcopacy.[8] For MacIntyre, the fact that Louis IX sent royal archers to the University of Paris in 1255 to ensure that a Dominican master could safely deliver his inaugural lecture was one of a myriad of historical events in the life of St Thomas which would have provided the background data against which he formulated his theses. Moreover, when providing an account of Aquinas's treatise on law, MacIntyre develops his arguments by reference to the contrasting attitudes of Louis IX, Frederick II and Aquinas, on the social influence of *jongleurs*. These provide MacIntyre with a case study in which to examine Aquinas's approach to the question of: 'To what extent ought a ruler enforce the practices of Christian morality?'

---

6.   Alasdair MacIntyre 'Precis of *Whose Justice? Which Rationality?*', *Philosophy and Phenomenological Research* 51 (1, 1991): 150.

7.   Alasdair MacIntyre, 'Aquinas's Critique of Education,' in *Philosophers on Education: New Historical Perspectives*, edited by AO Rorty (London: Routledge, 1998), 96.

8.   Alasdair MacIntyre, 'Natural Law as Subversice: The Case of Aquinas', *Journal of Medieval and Early Modern Studies*, vol 26 (1,1995): 61–63.

Another illustration of MacIntyre's methodology may be found in his treatment of the Scottish Enlightenment. Just as the scholastic system was forged by Aquinas's synthesis of Aristotelian philosophy with the theology of Augustine, MacIntyre views the main dynamic of the Scottish Enlightenment as an attempted synthesis of Aristotelian philosophy with the theology of Calvin. And just as MacIntyre argues in the above example that the principles endorsed by Aquinas are better understood by reference to the jurisdictional conflicts of his time, he argues that it is important to understand that the educated class which effected the Scottish Enlightenment was torn between English culture on the one side, and the culture of the Gaelic Highlands, on the other. It had to formulate principles for a common moral system, based on an authority completely independent of the rival cultures in Scotland. And while the ideas of Louis IX and Frederick II were used by MacIntyre in the *jongleurs* case-study to bring into sharper focus the nuances and complexities in Aquinas's thought, so too in the Scottish context MacIntyre refers to the ideas of Anglo-Hibernian writers (Blackstone and Burke) to highlight the distinctive features of the position in Scotland.

This use of the historical methodology of Collingwood by a Thomist is not as arbitrary or eccentric as it might at first appear. Aspects of Collingwood's theory of the history of ideas were also shared by Werner Stark (1909–85), a Thomist sociologist and economic historian. Stark developed the theme that in order to examine the seminal ideas within different systems of thought, it was necessary to consider how these ideas made sense within the framework of the social conditions out of which they grew.[9] In the context of the sociology of knowledge, Stark was in a position very similar to MacIntyre in that he was trying to reconcile theories of the 'social determination of knowledge' with a quest for trans-historical truth. Other Thomist scholars in the early twentieth century who sought to acquire a better historical understanding of the work of St Thomas included: Martin Grabmann, Pierre Mandonnet, Fernand van Steenberghen, and James Weisheipl, each of whom are acknowledged

---

9.   Werner Stark, *The Sociology of Knowledge: Toward a Deeper Understanding of the History of Ideas* (London: Transaction Publishers, 1991); *The Social Bond*, volumes I–IV (New York: Fordham), 1978–1987); *The Ideal Foundations of Economic Thought* (London: Kegan, 1944).

by MacIntyre in his Gifford Lectures as adopting a methodology with affinities to his own.[10]

A reference to the tension between a Collingwood-style approach to intellectual history and the Thomist quest for a trans-historical truth may be found in a recent address by Joseph Ratzinger. After giving an outline of historicist approaches similar to MacIntyre's account above, Ratzinger went on to say that 'behind this form of historical interpretation lies a philosophy, a fundamental perspective on reality, which says that it is in fact pointless to ask about what is; we can only ask ourselves what we are able to do with things' and further, that 'this philosophy contains a false humility that does not recognize in the human person the capacity for the truth'.[11] MacIntyre's position, however, like that of Stark, does not deny the capacity for knowledge of the truth. Rather he asserts: (i) that the quest for truth always takes place within a particular tradition, that is, that conceptions of truth are tradition-dependent, (ii) that traditions can be tested for rational coherence, (iii) that there is a universal human nature and consequently a transcultural standard of human flourishing otherwise defined by the principles of the natural law, and (iv) that the Thomist tradition is the only tradition which is rationally coherent and able to yield an account of the principles of the natural moral law. In so doing, MacIntyre's 'postmodern' development of the tradition does not seek to repudiate the natural law doctrine and seeks to avoid the specific flaws of historicism which were the subject of criticism in *Fides et Ratio*.

3. The concept of a narrative tradition

Implicit within the methodological parameters outlined above is a rejection of the idea that it is possible to understand concepts in laboratory conditions, as it were, abstracted from the traditions in which they were originally formulated. Rather, MacIntyre promotes a

---

10.   Aidan Nichols has also drawn attention to the significance of historical factors for de Lubac's understanding of the development of the doctrine against the 'logicist' positions of neo-Thomists. See: *From Newman to Congar: The Idea of the Development of Doctrine from the Victorians to the Second Vatican Council* (Edinburgh: T&T Clark, 1990), 195–213.

11.   Joseph Ratzinger, 'Culture and Truth: Reflections on the Encyclical *Fides et Ratio*', 627. cf: *Fides et Ratio* (87).

conception of rational enquiry as one embodied within a tradition.[12] Significantly, his understanding of a tradition is much richer than that of a mere conceptual framework. MacIntyre argues that 'beliefs are expressed in and through rituals and ritual dramas, masks and modes of dress, the ways in which houses are structured and villages and towns laid out, and of course by actions in general'; and as a consequence, 'the reformulations of belief are not to be thought of only in intellectual terms; or rather the intellect is not to be thought of as either a Cartesian mind or a materialist brain; but as that through which thinking individuals relate themselves to each other'.[13]

Such an understanding of the elements of a tradition builds upon ideas which were already developed in the latter half of the nineteenth century and first half of the twentieth century, by John Henry Newman and Maurice Blondel. In particular, MacIntyre's account of a tradition shares the typically Blondelian emphasis on the relationship between doctrine and practices as two essential elements of a tradition, but adds to this emphasis Newman's interest in the role of masters of a tradition in handing on the theory and practices of the tradition, and in the resolution of crises within the tradition.[14] This latter idea—that traditions develop through the resolution of crises—is acknowledged by MacIntyre to be one of the central themes in John Henry Newman's *Essay on the Development of Doctrine*.[15] Blondel defined a tradition as the 'living synthesis of all the speculative and ascetic, historical and theological forces', that is, 'the data of history, the efforts of reason and

---

12.   Alasdair MacIntyre, *Whose Justice? Which Rationality?* (London: Duckworth, 1988), 7.

13.   *Ibid*, 355.

14.   Cf Kenneth Schmitz, *The Gift: Creation* (Milwaukee: Marquette University Press, 1982), 55: 'A tradition is a chain of actual benefactions. It is not parentage in general that gives life, or technical insight that invents a tool; rather it is *this* giver and *that* receiver'.

15.   Alasdair MacIntyre, *Whose Justice? Which Rationality?* 8, 353–4, 362. cf: John Henry Newman, *The Development of Christian Doctrine* (London: Sheed and Ward, 1960), 264: 'Doctrine is percolated, as it were, through different minds, beginning with writers of inferior authority in the Church, and issuing at length in the enunciation of her Doctors'.

the experiences of faithful action'.[16] A tradition in this sense is not merely a theoretical framework but the embodiment in practices of the principles of the framework, and the practices in turn foster a culture:

> Christian practice nourishes man's knowledge of the divine and bears within its action what is progressively discerned by the theologian's initiative. The synthesis of dogma and facts is scientifically effected because there is a synthesis of thought and grace in the life of the believer, a union of man and God, reproducing in the individual consciousness the history of Christianity itself.[17]

The alternative idea—that truth can be pursued outside the framework of a tradition—is attributed by MacIntyre to an account of rationality going back to the Sophists. With reference to Plato's warning in the *Phaedrus* about those whose relationships depend upon writing, MacIntyre suggests that: 'What *is* condemned is *all* writing that has become detached from the author who speaks in and through it, so that the author as author cannot be put to the question along with her or his text'.[18] MacIntyre then considers whether this means that all writing is to be condemned once the author is dead, and concludes that the answer is 'perhaps not if someone else is able to stand in the author's place, to supply the needed authorial voice, and to respond to interrogation by others'.[19] From this judgment MacIntyre formulates the following theses: (i) if writing is to escape condemnation, it must function as subordinated to and only within the context of a spoken dialogue; and (ii) thinking always involves thinking in the context of some particular and specific public, with its own institutional structure.[20] From these theses he concludes that the key question is: 'within what kind of public with what kind of institutionalized

---

16.   Maurice Blondel, *The Letter on Apologetics and History and Dogma*, translated by Alexander Dru and Illtyd Trethowan (New York: Rinehart & Winston, 1964), 215.

17.   *Ibid*, 287.

18.   Alasdair MacIntyre, 'Some Enlightenment Projects Reconsidered', in *Questioning Ethics: Contemporary Debates in Philosophy*, edited by R Kearney and M Dooley (London: Routledge, 1998), 245–258 at 250.

19.   *Ibid*, 250.

20.   *Ibid*, 250.

structures will we be able to identify the limitations imposed on our particular enquiries as a prelude to transcending those limitations in pursuit of the goods of reason?'[21]

Notwithstanding John Paul II's and Ratzinger's warnings against historicism and cultural relativism in certain approaches to philosophical questions, the fact that it is possible to consider the historical dimensions of an issue without ending in a position of historical and/or ethical relativism is reflected in the recent International Theological Commission statement entitled 'Memory and Reconciliation: the Church and the Faults of the Past'. This statement of Ratzinger's office recommends a methodology consistent with MacIntyre's two theses. The authors of the document summarise their methodology thus:

> Bringing to light the communality between interpreter and the object of interpretation . . . requires taking into account the questions that motivate the research and their effect on the answers that are found, the living context in which the work is undertaken, and the interpreting community whose language is spoken and to whom one intends to speak.[22]

What such a methodology and account of rationality does is to reject the idea that knowledge can be transmitted in a cultural vacuum. It highlights the importance of institutional cultures and personal relationships for the transmission of knowledge, and in particular, for the transmission of a knowledge of the practices of a tradition and the meaning of doctrinal propositions upon whose authority, or to which end, the practices were founded and are directed. Its significance can be illustrated by reference to elements of the 'explosive problematic' created by the various interpretations of Conciliar documents.[23]

First, it suggests that the document's authors were naive in their assumption that the key concepts in the documents would be accorded

---

21.   *Ibid*, 252.
22.   International Theological Commission: 'Memory and Reconciliation: the Church and the Faults of the Past', *The Pope Speaks* 45 (4, 2000): 208–249 at 224.
23.   John O'Malley, *Tradition and Transition: Historical Perspectives on Vatican II* (Delaware: Wilmington, 1989), 67.

the same content, regardless of whether they were read by plain persons or philosophers, Catholics or non-Catholics, Easterners or Westerners.[24] Thus, for example, the word 'humanism', on its own, without the adjective 'Christocentric', 'theocentric' or even 'Christian' placed before it, is likely to be construed quite differently by a plain person than by someone with a knowledge of Maritain's *Humanisme Integrale*. Similarly, the concept of 'relevance' will mean something different to a person with a knowledge of Heidegger's philosophy from someone who lacks a knowledge of Heideggerian concepts, and in particular lacks a knowledge of the influence of Heidegger on Karl Rahner's theology and of Rahner's theology on the Conciliar documents. This kind of knowledge depends upon an immersion within a tradition—an education which cannot be presumed of many of those to whom the document was in part directed. Secondly, MacIntyre's account of a tradition highlights the problems with John XXIII's assumption that it is easy or even possible to distinguish between 'the substance of the ancient doctrine of the *depositum fidei* and the formulation of its presentation' or, in other words, the idea that it is always possible to distil doctrines from the tradition which embodies them and then re-present them in the idiom of an alternative tradition—in this context, the idiom of the 'modern man'— without in any way changing the meaning of the doctrines.[25] This particular aspect of the problematic has been addressed by Francis George:

> Implicitly, Pope John's statement seems to support an
> instrumental view of language, regarding language as

---

24.   This issue was also a problem at the time of the First Vatican Council. In a letter to Ambrose Phillipps de Lisle, John Henry Newman wrote: 'Theological language, like legal, is scientific and cannot be understood without the knowledge of long precedent and tradition, nor without the comments of theologians'. See: *Letters and Diaries XXVII*, 153 as cited by Fergus Kerr in 'Did Newman Answer Gladstone?', in *John Henry Newman: Reason, Rhetoric and Romanticism*, edited by David Nicholls and Fergus Kerr (Bristol: The Bristol Press, 1991), 136.

25.   John XXIII, 'Opening Address to the Council', *AAS* 54 (1962), 792. cf: *Gaudium et spes* 62. The post-Conciliar trend which derives from these assumptions is characterised by Aidan Nichols as the belief that it is possible to 'hand down authentic Tradition while manifesting insouciance towards the forms in which Tradition is embodied'—'the immemorial rites and customs that compose Catholic Christianity's received culture'. See: Aidan Nichols, *Christendom Awake* (Edinburgh: T&T Clark, 1999), 59.

the means whereby a speaker gives expression to thoughts which exist independently of language, through the employment of words whose meanings are the object of explicit agreement between prospective speakers. By contrast, an expressivist view of language holds that thought has no determinate content until it is expressed in a shared language.[26]

MacIntyre's preference for the expressivist view is evident in his argument that to 'abstract any type of concept, but notably moral concepts, from the traditions which they inform and through which they are transmitted is to risk damaging misunderstandings'.[27] The alternative position—the instrumental view of language—may be criticised, as George acknowledges, as rationalistic. George concludes that:

> Cultural forms and linguistic expressions are, in fact, not distinguished from the thoughts and message they carry as accidents are distinguished from substance in classical philosophy. A change of form inevitably entails also some change in content. A change in words changes in some fashion the way we think.[28]

Not only was a rationalistic or instrumental account of language implicit in some pronouncements of John XXIII, but as Fergus Kerr has demonstrated there are similarly Cartesian presuppositions in the linguistic philosophy of the most influential theologian of the Conciliar period, Karl Rahner. Kerr observes that 'Rahner's natural assumption —that communication comes after language, and language comes after

---

26.   Francis George, *Inculturation and Ecclesial Communion: Culture and Church in the Teaching of Pope John Paul II* (Rome: Urbaniana University Press, 1996), 88.

27.   MacIntyre became interested in the issue of the translatability of languages in the early 1940s when George Thomson, a Professor of Greek, was engaged in a project of translating Platonic dialogues into Irish. See: Giovanna Borradori, 'Interview with Alasdair MacIntyre', *The American Philosopher* (Chicago: University of Chicago Press, 1994), 141.

28.   *Ibid*, 47.

having concepts—is precisely what the Cartesian tradition has reinforced'.[29]

What this means in effect is that the tendency in post-Conciliar thought and practice, especially in the fields of catechetics and liturgy, to attempt a transposition of Catholic doctrine and practice into 'modern' and 'contemporary' idioms, has been naive and has risked a dimunition of the rich complexity of the narrative tradition, that is, of those elements of the tradition for which there is no equivalent in the non-specialist, non-philosophical, non-theological, non-Thomist and non-liturgical language of 'modern man'.[30] An understanding of elements of the narrative tradition may also be lost through mistranslation in circumstances where different traditions apparently share some linguistic concepts, but actually invest those concepts or words with a partly or wholly different substance or nuance.

The significance of this critical concept of a 'narrative tradition' should thus not be underestimated in any evaluation of MacIntyre's contribution to the recent and future development of the Thomist tradition. Perhaps more effectively than any before him he has demonstrated the need of broadening the concept of a tradition to include much more than just timeless, spaceless doctrinal principles, so as to include the time- and place-bound practices which embody and are directed towards the achievement of the principles. He has also emphasised the importance of 'masters', (even of 'scholar-saints'), within such a narrative tradition, in whom there is found the 'perfect synthesis of thought and grace' and to whom the responsibility of

---

29. Fergus Kerr, *Theology after Wittgenstein* (Oxford: Basil Blackwell 1986), 11.

30. An illustration of the expressivist theory may be found in tests which require persons of one culture to explain the texts of another where a common language is apparently shared but not a common culture. For example, the following words from the first verse of 'Waltzing Matilda', Australia's unofficial national anthem are all English words but are almost inexplicable to non-Australians: 'Once a jolly swagman camped by a billabong, under the shade of a coolibah tree/And he sang as he watched and waited while his billy boiled/You'll come a Waltzing Matilda with me'. The terms, 'billy', 'billabong', 'swagman' and later in the song, 'troopers', 'squatters', 'jumbuck' and 'tuckerbag' can to some degree be translated as watercan, water-hole, tramp, police, farmers, sheep and lunchbox, but the rich nuances are lost. A squatter, for example, is not merely a farmer, but a person who occupied a very particular and socially controversial place within Australian history.

resolving the crises within the tradition falls.[31] As Hibbs has observed, the 'Christian tradition embraces and extends the ancient view of pedagogy, which required as its starting point submission to a teacher, to a tradition of enquiry, and to the discipline of dialectic'.[32] From this perspective, authority is not an impediment to inquiry, rather it is a constitutive element of it.[33] In re-emphasising the importance of a narrative tradition, and a conception of pedagogy which requires the student's submission to the authority of the teacher, MacIntyre steers Thomism away from the lure of the Kantian conception of enlightenment free from constricting traditions and authorities, toward a position which is in accord with that of the theologians associated with the *Nouvelle Théologie*. Von Balthasar, for example, consistently emphasised the importance of scholar-saints as bearers and developers—the masters—of the tradition. The following quotation illustrates this point as well as encapsulating much of the above analysis about the importance of speech and language in the transmission of a tradition:

---

31. MacIntyre tends to use the expression 'masters' rather than 'scholar-saints', but the latter expression has been chosen to emphasise the idea, common to MacIntyre and Schindler and von Balthasar, that 'mastering a tradition' is as much an exercise of the will and the memory, as of the intellect. In other words, to master the Thomist tradition one needs to be holy, not just intellectually gifted.

32. Thomas S Hibbs, 'MacIntyre's Post Modern Thomism: Reflections on Three Rival Versions of Moral Enquiry', *The Thomist* 57 (April 1993): 277–299 at 292.

33. A significant issue which has not been directly addressed by MacIntyre is the relationship between the magisterial authority within the Catholic tradition and that of scholar-saints in the resolution of crises within the tradition. An oblique reference to the issue is found in *TRV*, 125: 'Except for the finality of scripture and dogmatic tradition, there is and can be no finality [to a tradition]'. Implied here is the idea that there is a core to the tradition which cannot be changed and for which there is no possibility of development since the core is derived directly from revelation which ended with the death of the last of the apostles. Since MacIntyre is a self-described 'orthodox Catholic' it may be presumed that he regards the magisterium as the final tribunal in questions of faith and morals, above that of the scholar-saints in a juridical sense, although in all probability, in the resolution of any 'crisis' within the tradition, the magisterium will call upon the scholarship and judgment of the scholar-saints.

> Christianity is not strictly speaking a 'Blood religion'; it
> is the religion of the Word, but not uniquely, not even
> primarily, of the Word in its written form; it is the
> religion of the *Logos*, not written and mute, but the
> incarnate and living *Logos*.[34]

Furthermore, the idea of individual self-enlightenment penetrating
the meaning of free-floating concepts is inconsistent with a theological
framework such as David Schindler's Trinitarian 'identities-in-relation'
logic. The genius of Plato's Academy and the medieval universities
and religious orders is that they provided a culture which facilitated
the transmission of the tradition in their institutional relationships and
practices. Plato had the culture of the Academy, Augustine the
Episcopacy, and Aquinas the Dominican Order. MacIntyre argues that
each of these institutional cultures embodied four principles: (i) a
conception of a truth beyond and ordering all particular truths; (ii) a
conception of a range of senses in the light of which utterances to be
judged true or false and so placed within that ordering are to be
construed; (iii) a conception of a range of genres of utterance, dramatic,
lyrical, historical and the like, by reference to which utterances may be
classified so that we may then proceed to identify their true senses; and
(iv) a contrast between those uses of genres in which in one way or
another truth is at stake and those governed instead only by standards
of rhetorical effectiveness.[35]

Within such institutions a *Geist* or *ethos* was generated by practices
formulated with reference to the internal ends of the tradition, which
included the transmission of the practical and intellectual elements of
the tradition to up-coming generations. The practices also had their
own onto-logic or *logos* consistent with the ends of the tradition, and
thus fostered a particular type of self-formation or *Bildung, Paideia* or
self-formation based upon the tradition's own philosophical and
theological anthropology. In such communities there was an
'acknowledgment of truth as a measure independent of the tradition

---

34.   Hans Urs von Balthasar, *The Theology of Henri de Lubac* (San Francisco:
      Ignatius, 1991), 76, fn. 52. cf Kenneth L Schmitz, 'The Language of Conversion
      and the Conversion of Language', *Communio* 21 (Winter, 1994): 742–765 at 763:
      'I distinguish between the accumulation of detailed scholarly knowledge brought
      about by historical research, including the use of the historical-critical method,
      and the effective memory carried forward by a concrete living tradition'.
35.   Alasdair MacIntyre, *Three Rival Versions of Moral Enquiry*, 200–201.

which aspires to measure itself by truth', but there was nonetheless 'no thesis, argument, or doctrine to be so measured which was not presented as the thesis of this particular historically successive set of tradition-informed and tradition-directed individuals and groups'.[36]

The kind of community which is here described is not merely that of a group of individuals united around a few common objectives, such as a group of persons concerned about health-care for the aged or shelter for the poor, but of an entire order in which certain practices exist simultaneously as elements of the tradition and of the culture in which novices would be formed and masters perfected. Tradition and culture are therefore symbiotic and are essential elements and a context for self-formation. For the flourishing of such a community nothing could be more toxic than the introduction of a counter-culture of 'forced or deliberate forgetting'. The idea that each successive generation of novices needs to re-create the tradition, rather than merely develop it so that they can claim to be 'authentic' and 'autonomous' in the sense promoted by the theories of Rousseau and Kant, or so that they can be 'relevant' to the needs of 'modern man' in the sense promoted by Heidegger and Rahner, is hostile to an Augustinian-Thomist understanding of the processes of rational and cultural formation. According to the classical conception, part of what is transmitted by the masters to the novices is the truth contained in the historical memory of the community: to reject the value of historical memories is thus to reject the truth itself.

To argue that a culture of 'forced or deliberate forgetting' is hostile to intellectual and moral and hence cultural formation is not however to promote a nostalgic or static conception of tradition. With each successive generation the tradition matures and develops to deal with new issues which arise. In the present context, the 'new historical situation' is the predicament of aspirant Thomist selves caught within the contradictions of the culture of modernity. It is this particular problematic which the masters of the tradition currently need to address and resolve.

---

36. *Ibid*, 201.

4. 'Smudging the boundaries' between philosophy and theology

This introduction of the concept of a narrative tradition into the Thomistic framework, or highlighting of where it was already implicit, raises the question of the implications of such a concept for the relationship between philosophy and theology. In the following sub-section it will be argued that MacIntyre's mature works exhibit a tendency to 'smudge the boundaries between theology and philosophy' and that it is precisely this notion of a narrative tradition which brings the boundaries together and overlaps both.

In *Difficulties in Christian Belief* published in 1959, MacIntyre drew a very sharp distinction between 'secular' and 'Christian morality'. The first, which he associated with the work of Kant, he quickly dismissed as not having *any* affinity with the Christian position. There is not, he argued, 'any neutral standpoint from which we can judge between Christianity and its alternatives', or any 'neutral standing ground between Christian morality and other moralities'.[37] However, once MacIntyre moved beyond Barthian Presbyterianism his work began to exhibit what Deal Hudson calls the 'romantic tendency' to 'smudge the boundaries between philosophy and theology'.[38] In doing this he does not reject the 'no neutrality ' thesis, but he does allow room for some overlap between an Aristotelian 'open to revelation' position, and a fully developed Thomism. This is particularly evident in his interview with Dmitri Nikulin. In response to questions from Nikulin regarding the possibility of an ethic of virtue without a concept of God, MacIntyre replied that he followed Aquinas in the assertion that human nature has the capacity to acquire the natural virtues, without understanding that they bring with them special theological obligations. However, he also followed the Thomistic argument that the supernatural life is the form of all the virtues, and that such a life is impossible without love and grace. Accordingly, he concluded that 'the virtues can only be complete with a theological understanding, however the practice of the natural virtues and the understanding of them, of what makes for their excellence, is compatible with

---

37.   Alasdair MacIntyre, *Difficulties in Christian Belief* (London: SCM Press, 1959), 107–108.

38.   Deal Hudson, *The Future of Thomism* (University of Notre Dame Press, 1992), 21.

atheism'.[39] This means that while there can be 'no virtue without grace', the virtuous person need not be self-consciously aware of the operation of grace for it to be effective. Such a position is further developed in his 1998 John Coffin Memorial Lecture, wherein he argues that embedded within Christianity are the elements of a moral philosophy, that can be detached from theological claims to revealed truth on moral matters.[40]

In other words, MacIntyre acknowledges that, at least *to some degree*, there is a role for philosophical analysis which is not *directly* dependent upon theological claims. However, in other contexts, MacIntyre appears to concur with the Nietzschean claim that there is no philosophical position which is neutral in its stance toward the question of the existence of God, and that the mere belief in the principle of non-contradiction is an inherently pro-theistic position. In response to Nikulin's question 'Can the highest good that the end of the virtuous life offers be without a specific reference to God?', MacIntyre responds that 'the consequence of an Aristotelian virtue-ethic is the obligation to remain open to the possibility of divine existence'.[41] The difficult theoretical issue is that of how one can accept simultaneously the Nietzschean argument that the mere belief in logic, for example, is itself a pro-theistic position, that is, the 'no neutrality' thesis, along with the idea that there is a 'way of understanding morality that can be detached from theological claims to revealed truth on moral matters'.

One possible way of asserting both propositions is to adopt what Aidan Nichols has identified as a common Catholic position. According to Nichols:

---

39.   Alasdair MacIntyre, 'Interview with Dmitri Nikulin,' *Voprosy Filosfii* 1 (1996): 91–100 (in Russian) *Deutsche Zeitschrift für Philosophie* 44 (1996): 677 (in German) and for an English translation of most sections see: Tracey Rowland, 'The Reflections of a Romantic Thomist: Alasdair MacIntyre's interview with Dimitri Nikulin of *Voprosy Filosfii*', *Political Theory Newsletter* 9, 1 (March 1998): 47–54.

40.   Alasdair MacIntyre, 'What Has Christianity to Say to the Moral Philosopher?', John Coffin Memorial Lecture, University of London May 21, 1998, 21.

41.   *IDN*, 677.

> From the point of view of theological fruitfulness, a
> good philosophy will consist of, formally speaking, the
> best purely natural reasoning available, but that
> materially speaking or content-wise, revelation could
> help to identify the areas which natural reasoning
> could most profitably be directed. Thus the form of
> philosophy as practised by Christians would have no
> reference to revelation, but its content would.[42]

In other words, MacIntyre's belief that an Aristotelian virtue ethic
requires one to 'remain open to the possibility of divine existence'
means that one's philosophical stand-point cannot be neutral in
relation to the claims of revelation, even though no specific reference to
the claims of revelation need ever be made in the formulation of a
philosophical virtue ethic. The same resolution of the problem has
been indicated by Schindler. Schindler asserts that 'philosophy in its
starting point and all along the way, will always—willy-nilly—bear a
relation to theology (to what has been revealed) that is intrinsic: that
relation can be either negative or it can be positive, but in either case it
will be a relation'.[43] However, this does not mean that the philosopher
who is aware of the truth revealed in Scripture can argue deductively
or inferentially from that truth.

5. *Fides et Ratio*

These issues have, to some degree, been treated in John Paul II's
encyclical *Fides et Ratio*. In this work he asserts that there exists a kind
of 'implicit philosophy' shared by people in a 'general and unreflective
way'.[44] MacIntyre would call the principles of this implicit philosophy
the 'basic intuitions of plain persons'. John Paul II offers as examples,
the principles of non-contradiction, finality and causality, as well as a
concept of the person as a 'free and intelligent subject, with the

---

42. Aidan Nichols, *The Shape of Catholic Theology* (Minnesota: The Liturgical Press, 1991), 48–49.

43. David Schindler, *Heart of the World, Center of the Church. Communion, Ecclesiology, Liberalism and Liberation* (Edinburgh: T&T Clark, 1996), 301–302.

44. David Schindler relates the arguments of John Paul II to the Thomist maxim that 'all things naturally tend to God implicitly'. See: *De Veritate* (Q. 22 a. 2) and *GEI*, 511–540 at 520.

capacity to know God, truth and goodness'.[45] From MacIntyre's perspective such basic principles of an 'implicit philosophy' are those upon which his own philosophical projects are based, and those upon which the judgments of plain persons need to be based.

Nonetheless MacIntyre concedes the claim of the genealogical tradition, to which John Paul II makes no explicit reference, that these principles are not 'neutral' but loaded in a pro-theistic direction, since they assume that there is an order to the universe. While plain persons may arrive at a concept of the person as a free and intelligent subject, with the capacity to know God, truth and goodness through the exercise of reason, they may equally conclude, through the exercise of reason unperfected by faith, that there is little empirical evidence for the proposition that persons are free and intelligent subjects with a capacity for truth, goodness and friendship with God. The widespread occurrence of determinism, atheism and nihilism in Western societies following World Wars I and II is a complex phenomenon which may in part be due to the fact that the evil of these social conflagrations has destroyed the 'self-evidentiary' nature of the principles of an 'implicit philosophy'. Leo Strauss alluded to this when he contrasted pagan atheism with modern atheism. The former he described as motivated by a desire for freedom from the responsibilities imposed by the gods, the latter he described as a kind of stoic intellectual probity.[46]

Not only can the supposedly self-evidentiary principles of an 'implicit philosophy' be undermined by the overwhelming knowledge of the human capacity for irrational behaviour, but the ability to reach an understanding of these principles may also be impaired by personal 'sin' (weakness, confusion, self-interest, passion, and self-delusion), and by, in John Paul II's terms, 'the content of culture and civilization, as a philosophical system an ideology, a programme for action and for the shaping of human behaviour'.[47] Another way of putting this is to say that the basic principles of practical reasoning which the Thomist tradition holds are 'per se nota' accessible to all persons of goodwill and right reason regardless of whether they have accepted Christian

---

45.   *Fides et Ratio* 4 (Homebush: St Paul's 1998), 13.

46.   Leo Strauss, *Spinoza's Critique of Religion* (Chicago: University of Chicago Press, 1965), 30.

47.   John Paul II, *Dominum et Vivificantem* in *The Encyclicals of John Paul II,* Michael Miller (ed) (Huntington: Our Sunday Visitor, 1998): 322–323.

revelation, will not be immediately accessible to persons whose thought and behaviour has been shaped by a 'philosophical system, an ideology, or programme for action' which is atheistic, or anti-realist or irrational. A will whose appetite for goodness has been dulled by the habitual performance of practices which are neither virtue-requiring nor virtue-rewarding, or an intellect that is directed towards power rather than truth, or an imagination satisfied by the bland and ugly rather than reaching out for the beautiful, or a memory which is tormented by despair and foreclosed against the virtue of hope, pre-dispose the person against knowing and applying the basic principles of John Paul II's 'implicit philosophy'. In Schindler's terms the starting point of such a will, intellect, memory or imagination is a relation of opposition to revelation; while in MacIntyre's discourse, the predic-ament of such faculties highlights the problem of the relationship between virtue and the discernment of the principles of an 'implicit philosophy'. It emphasises the fact that the discernment of the principles of practical reasoning and ultimately of the natural law is not simply a matter of ratiocination, like finding a solution to a quadratic equation, but requires the cooperation of all the faculties of the soul. If any faculty has been perverted through such practices and dispositions (including despair and presumption), the ability of plain persons and even philosophers to discern the basic precepts will be impaired. Rational enquiry 'depends for its success on the virtues of those who engage in it, and it requires relationships and evaluative commitments of a particular kind'.[48] Schindler and Nichols would add that these 'evaluative commitments' include a commitment to a view of life centred upon participation in the forms of the true, the good and the beautiful—forms so little experienced in 'mass culture' as to make many people almost impervious to evangelisation.[49]

MacIntyre therefore acknowledges, in a manner consistent with principles espoused in *Fides et Ratio*, a legitimate realm for the work of philosophy. He rejects the Calvinist interpretation of Aquinas as a

---

48.   Alasdair MacIntyre, *Dependent Rational Animals* (Illinois: Open Court, 1999), 156–157.

49.   See, for example, Aidan Nichols, *No Bloodless Myth* (Edinburgh. T&T Clark, 2000), 4: ' . . . to appreciate a form aright, to receive aright its message, depends in some way or other on our having appropriate dispositions. Without a basic readiness to receive what the form has to offer, a willingness to entertain its message, the dialogue between the eloquent appearing of being and human language is more than likely to be at cross-purposes'.

proto-modernist who conceded too much ground to philosophy; but he also believes that even conceptions of finality, causality and non-contradiction, and the human capacity for knowledge of God, truth and goodness, will differ according to the tradition from which they are derived. Some traditions are fundamentally 'open to the possibility of divine existence', others are fundamentally closed to the same possibility. Even among those who are open to the 'possibility of divine existence' the conclusions which are likely to be reached regarding the principles of an 'implicit philosophy' will differ according to whether, for example, one takes a Lutheran or Thomist interpretation of the effect of the fall on the human capacity for knowledge of God, truth, beauty and goodness. These problems are not directly addressed in the encyclical and in this respect it fails to engage the Nietzschean and 'postmodern' Thomist and Augustinian arguments.[50] What would seem to be required by the Thomist tradition at this juncture in its history is a deeper understanding of the extent to which the tradition agrees with the genealogists that conceptions of rationality are tradition-dependent; and further, a deeper understanding of how an immersion within a cultural order which is more or less resistant to grace and hostile to virtue undermines the ability of plain persons to reach an understanding of the principles of John Paul II's 'implicit philosophy'. While MacIntyre has not provided a conclusive treatment of this issue, his work has at least drawn attention to the problematic and indicated the directions in which research needs to be undertaken.

At a more general level of analysis, John Paul II has suggested that the relationship between theology and philosophy should be construed as circular.[51] Looked at in this manner, MacIntyre's tendency to 'smudge the boundaries' between philosophy and theology occurs at points on the circle where the two converge. Moreover, MacIntyre's apparent untidiness with respect to such demarcations may well stem from two important factors. First, MacIntyre believes traditions need to be taken as a whole and not severed into component parts which assume the status of unbridgeable disciplines. Secondly, there is the tension inherent within the Thomist tradition between its Aristotelian

---

50.   This criticism of *Fides et Ratio* can also be found in Anthony Kenny, 'The Pope as Philosopher', *The Tablet* (26 June, 1999): 874–876 at 875.

51.   *Fides et Ratio*, 104.

and Patristic elements. The Patristic elements are responsible for the more historicist and revelation-specific dimensions of MacIntyre's work, while the Aristotelian elements are responsible for his insistence that there is a normative way of being human and a philosophically discernible list of basic goods of human flourishing and of norms of human action.

6. Harmonising Aristotelian and Patristic elements

When speaking of the methodology of moral discernment MacIntyre has a tendency to emphasise the Aristotelian aspects of the Thomist tradition, but when speaking of the moral formation of plain persons, it is the Patristic elements which are brought to the fore. This is not to say that MacIntyre is in any sense a modern disciple of Averroës. He does not subscribe to a position of a philosophic truth for the philosophers and the principles of revelation for plain persons, since he believes that plain persons need to be 'enough of a philosopher' to work out the first principles of practical reasoning for themselves, and philosophers need to be formed within a narrative tradition before embarking on their own developments or critiques of the tradition. There are not two different truths, but merely two different approaches to the one truth. Therefore, depending on the context, MacIntyre alternates between an emphasis on the Aristotelian and Patristic, especially the Augustinian, dimensions of Thomism. The Patristic elements are stronger when the issue is the importance of cultural factors in moral formation, while the Aristotelian aspects tend to dominate in considerations of what might be called the 'practices of philosophy'. The first type of issue is encapsulated by the German term *Bildung*, while the second is more narrowly defined as 'moral philosophy as an intellectual practice'.

In his exposition of the difference between the Augustinian and Aristotelian approaches to philosophical questions, MacIntyre makes the following observations:

> The **Augustinian** is committed to one central negative thesis about all actually or potentially rival positions: that no substantive rationality, independent of faith, will be able to provide an adequate vindication of its claims.[52]

---

52.   Alasdair MacIntyre, *Three Rival Versions of Moral Enquiry*, 101.

From the Aristotelian point of view an understanding
of oneself as having an essential nature and the
discovery of what in one belongs to that nature and
what is merely *per accidens* enters into the progress of
the self . . . even though that understanding and
discovery may take place in a way that presupposes
rather than explicitly formulates the philosophical
theses and arguments involved.[53]

MacIntyre's Augustinian claim that all alternative 'rationalities' will
either 'fall into ineradicable incoherence or be compelled to
acknowledge points at which there is an unavoidable resort to
attitudes of unjustified and unjustifiable belief', is exemplified in the
Augustinian analysis of John Milbank's *Beyond Secular Reason* wherein
he deconstructs so-called 'scientific' sociologies into their mythic
components.[54] It is also consistent with the argument of *inter alia*,
Vatican II, de Lubac, John Paul II, David Schindler and Angelo Scola,
that the human person only attains full self-knowledge through an
understanding that Christ is the archetype of perfected humanity.
Without this understanding those plain persons who are proto-
Aristotelians may, through the exercise of the principles of an 'implicit
rationality' grope their way towards the truth, but they will always
reach an impasse without the knowledge acquired through revelation
mediated by Christian scripture and tradition. However, at the same
time, MacIntyre's description of Aristotelian analytical processes is
compatible with the idea that it is through participation in virtue-
requiring and virtue-engendering practices that one most quickly
grasps an understanding of one's own form, potential and *telos*. With
Aristotle one can get at least as far as the *preparatio fidei*.[55]

---

53. *Ibid*, 138–139.

54. This is not to infer that MacIntyre and Milbank are in complete agreement.
Milbank criticises MacIntyre for making an argument against nihilism by
reference to the relationship between virtue, dialectics and the notion of tradition
in general and instead Milbank wishes to 'detach virtue from dialectics'. See:
John Milbank, *Theology and Social Theory: Beyond Secular Reason* (Oxford:
Blackwell, 1990), 326–377.

55. Alasdair MacIntyre, *Three Rival Versions of Moral Enquiry*, 140–141: 'A Pauline
and Augustinian account retrospectively vindicates that in Aristotle which had
provided a first understanding of the core of the moral life'. To this statement

Although MacIntyre does not offer a systematic account of precisely how one is to transcend the contradictions of the culture of modernity—that is, whether one starts in an 'Augustinian' fashion, submitting one's intellect and will to the truths of the Christian (especially Thomist) tradition, or whether one is simply immersed in a culture and through a more 'Aristotelian' reflection upon its practices, comes to an appreciation of the value of the truths and/or ideologies forming the substance of that culture: it may be that the appropriate approach will vary according to how one is placed in life, that is, in history. Those who are immersed within the *praxis* of the Augustinian-Thomist tradition from childhood will come to an appreciation of the principles of that tradition, partly through a process of self-conscious reflection, and partly through what Michael Polanyi called the 'acquisition of tacit knowledge'. Historically this is how many 'plain persons' acquired an appreciation of the Augustinian-Thomist tradition. However, MacIntyre also acknowledges that one can come to an understanding of the tradition through a dialectical process of the elimination of all other traditions. This is more typically the route of the philosopher and the convert.[56]

Either way it is clear that for MacIntyre the notion of a tradition and of a particular ethos associated with this tradition is essential. Theory and practice cannot be separated and one understood apart from the other. Hence MacIntyre's statement that any particular tradition must

---

could be added that included within the Augustinian account of virtue is the idea that some practices which would be classified as 'virtuous' by Aristotelian standards, may not be by the 'higher' Augustinian standards, which include a judgment of the subjective dimension of actions, that is, the intentions and motivations behind the performance of the apparently virtuous act. For a discussion of the difference between Aristotelian and Augustinian virtue, see: G Scott Davis, 'The Structure and Function of the Virtues in the Moral Theology of St Augustine', *Congresso internazionale su S Agostino nel XVi centenario della conversione*, volume III (Rome: Institutum Patristicum Augustinianum, 1987), 9–18.

56.   The extraordinary number of leading twentieth philosophers and theologians who actually came to Thomism from outside the tradition by a process of intellectual discernment (in cooperation with the work of grace) bears testimony to the value of what MacIntyre calls 'culture transcending tradition-dependent rationality'. A roll call of such persons includes: Elizabeth Anscombe, Peter Geach, Christopher Dawson, John Finnis, Michael Dummett, Frederick Copleston, Gabriel Marcel, Jacques Maritain, Raissa Maritain, Aidan Nichols OP, Benedict Ashley OP, Adolf Reinach, Max Scheler, Edith Stein, and to some degree, MacIntyre himself.

be capable of a social expression, that is, of being embedded within a particular community, and his argument that even philosophers can only come to an understanding of the arguments of a tradition by an association with communities in which those arguments or principles are embodied. Milbank makes a related point when he observes that the argument for the Christian tradition is not merely a series of theoretical propositions, but also the 'story of preachings, journeyings, miracles, martyrdoms, vocations, marriages, icons painted and liturgies sung, as well as intrigues, sins and warfare'.[57] This perspective is also encapsulated in von Balthasar's statement that 'the saints are Tradition at its most living', and John Paul II's statements in *Fides et Ratio* that 'the martyrs are the most authentic witnesses to the truth about existence' and that 'truth is attained not only by reason but also through trusting acquiescence to other persons who can guarantee the authenticity and certainty of the truth itself'.[58]

7. Certainty as 'rational coherence'

This conception of certainty differs from the kind of certainty based upon mathematical proofs typical of post-Cartesian thought. It is best described as a kind of 'rational coherence'.[59] Since MacIntyre set out to analyse the culture of modernity and, in particular, the effect of this culture on the formation of the self, he arrived at the conclusion of the certainty of the truth of the Thomist tradition only after a consideration of all the theoretical alternatives. This methodology which does not

---

57.   John Milbank, *Beyond Secular Reason*, 347.

58.   Hans Urs Von Balthasar, *A Theology of History* (San Francisco: Ignatius, 1994), 110, and *FR*, 52–53.

59.   Again there is a relationship here between MacIntyre's idea that Thomism is philosophically vindicated by being the only tradition which renders the integrity of the self a possibility and the *modus operandi* of Newman. Newman argued that when all the evidence points to one conclusion, converges on one exclusive explanation, then the mind should assent to that one conclusion without fear of the truth of its opposite. Similarly, for Belloc, although no one factor determines history, only one tradition—the Christian Greco-Roman tradition—renders history intelligible. See: Frederick Wilhelmsen, *Hilaire Belloc: No Alienated Man* (London: Sheed & Ward, 1954), 69: 'Bellocian history depends for success on a vital tradition acting like a road the historian can travel down and back again at will—the Bellocian concept of history might well be called Anselmian: historical understanding follows faith'.

begin with the principles of Christian revelation, but rather from an examination of the contradictions of the culture of modernity and a search for an escape route from the either/or tragic options offered by the modern 'severance' or 'mutation' or 'heretical reconstruction' of the classical-theistic order, is one of the factors which gives MacIntyre's Thomism its 'post-modern' quality.[60] MacIntyre himself acknowledged the difference between his own approach and that of classical Thomism in his 1990 Aquinas Lecture:

> We inhabit a time in the history of philosophy in which Thomism can only develop adequate responses to the rejections of its central positions in what must seem initially at least to be un-Thomistic ways . . . in order to restate and defend those [Thomistic] positions in something like their original integrity through an internal critique of those theses and arguments which have displaced them a critique dictated by Thomistic ends, but to be carried through in part at least by somewhat un-Thomistic means.[61]

The 'un-Thomistic means' is arguably MacIntyre's approach of starting from the 'Self' rather than from God, and working out the principles by which the self can possibly retain its integrity. In the final analysis MacIntyre's strongest argument for the Thomist tradition is that the self which embodies the principles of any other tradition is destined to fragmentation and even vacuity. To *some degree* this lends credence to the judgment of John Milbank that the truths of Christianity cannot ultimately be defended at the bar of reason, but rather that the scientific *mythos* of the Enlightenment and any alternative neo-pagan *mythos* employed by the genealogical tradition can be out-narrated. MacIntyre's position is not however that it is either impossible or hubristic to seek to mount a philosophical defence

---

60. Such an approach was foreshadowed by the Italian Thomist Cornelio Fabro in *God in Exile* (Toronto: Newman, 1964) at 69: 'Just as the Christian message of salvation could appear more radiant to the man of classical tragedy, it may without presumption be hoped that the free highway of a better-founded hope, may open up to present-day man out of the holocaust-mottled dead-end in which he sees the *cogito* consuming itself'.

61. Alasdair MacIntyre, *First Principles, Final Ends and Contemporary Moral Issues* (Milwaukee: Marquette University Press, 1990), 2.

of the rationality of the Thomist, or more generally Christian tradition.[62] Rather he seeks to broaden the notion of a tradition to include both its theoretical and practical dimensions. On the one hand, when emphasising the practical dimension, MacIntyre would agree with Milbank that Christian practices are an argument for the tradition or, as Andrew Louth argues, the tradition of the church is not like the traditions to which the gnostics appealed, simply some message, truth or ideology, but 'the whole character of the Christian community, its rites, its ceremonies, its practices, and its life'.[63] However, MacIntyre also argues that the belief that the human intellect is rational (albeit fallen and less than angelic) is a fundamental element of that tradition, and further the fact that the Thomist tradition can be rationally demonstrated to be the *only tradition* which offers any hope for the formation of an integral self is itself a very strong argument for both the truth of the tradition and the merit of philosophy as an intellectual practice. The tradition of Thomism is not merely a history of dialectical encounters, but dialectical encounters are one important aspect of the tradition which seeks an intellectual explication and defence of Christianity. It should be emphasised however that while MacIntyre's defence of the Thomist tradition begins from the perspective of the self, his account of the process of self-formation requires, as a principle of epistemic priority, the existence of a narrative tradition and the self's immersion within that tradition. This means that, while MacIntyre employs a very Aristotelian 'reflection upon practice' methodology in his examinations of the predicament of the various types of modern self, his solution to the predicament is quintessentially Augustinian.

8. Conclusion

The concept of the tradition-constituted rationality embedded within social practices and transmitted from generation to generation by the masters of the narrative tradition is the key 'Post-Modern' concept in MacIntyre's 'Post-Modern Augustinian Thomism'. Unlike much of

---

62. To hold otherwise would be to concede the inverse of Nietzsche's claim that 'it is our preference that decides against Christianity—not arguments'; or in other words, that it is our preference which decides in favour of our Christianity—not our arguments. For a discussion of this issue, see: Henri de Lubac, *The Drama of Atheist Humanism* (San Francisco: Ignatius, 1995), 49.

63. Andrew Louth, *Discerning the Mystery* (Oxford: Clarendon Press, 1983), 73–96.

neo-Thomist scholarship which sought to engage the proponents of the encyclopaedist tradition with arguments drawn exclusively from the Aristotelian currents in Thomism, MacIntyre's idea of a tradition-dependent rationality differentiates the Thomist understanding of rationality from the encyclopaedist conception, and thus sides with the genealogists in their argument that at the basis of any account of rationality, and indeed of any philosophy, is a mythology or theology. Nonetheless, MacIntyre does not concede the Nietzschean argument that the choice for or against Christianity is a mere matter of preference—of differences in personal temperament. Unlike Milbank, with whom MacIntyre is generally in accord, MacIntyre retains a role for dialectics, and hence, 'natural philosophy'. Through his explanation of the operation of a narrative tradition he seeks to unite the theoretical and participatory levels of human experience, as well as the realms of faith and reason. If the notion of the narrative tradition is taken away and philosophy and theology are pursued as completely separate disciplines, then the tradition of Thomism begins to fragment. While theoretically it may be possible to distinguish philosophy and theology, those who consistently work only within the philosophical field risk adopting the logic of 'secular rationality' as they lose sight of where their philosophical questions fit within a theological framework. Alternatively, those who eschew any role for philosophy in theological analysis run the risk of ending in a position of pure fideism. This has historically not been a problem within the Thomist tradition, but it remains a risk for any self-consciously Christian philosophy.

MacIntyre's tendency to 'smudge the boundaries' between philosophy and theology should thus be perceived not as an intellectual inconsistency, but rather the result of his argument that both are intrinsically related, though they may take different priorities depending upon the intellectual context. Further, in engagements with the genealogical tradition, a reference to the theological dimensions of Thomism will not give rise to the same problems as it has in engagements with the encyclopaedist tradition. Whereas the encyclopaedists deny epistemological legitimacy to theological arguments, the genealogists believe that philosophical arguments are at root inescapably mythological. The battle-lines thereby change to a focus on the theological dimensions of an issue. In this sense MacIntyre's tendency to 'smudge the boundaries' may be a necessary corrective to the overly zealous attempts of the neo-Thomists and others to narrow the horizons of the tradition so as to meet the epistemic standards of the encyclopaedists.

What are the practical consequences of this analysis for the Thomist tradition? It raises the question of the prudence of the strategy which has been pursued of adopting elements of the conceptual apparatus of the rival liberal tradition. In particular, MacIntyre's analysis raises the question of whether there can be any such things as 'universal values', understood in the sense that there is a set of values which are of general appeal across a range of traditions, including the Nietzschean, Thomist and liberal traditions. Further, while it does not deny the existence of principles of an implicit philosophy, it does emphasise that these principles are more readily discernible by those immersed within cultures built upon such principles, and this in turn raises typically Augustinian themes about the theological significance of alternative cultures, and the role of a narrative tradition and the faculty of the memory in moral formation.

Contributors

Marilyn McCord Adams is Regius Professor of Divinity, Christ Church, Oxford .

Peter Coghlan is Senior Lecturer, School of Philosophy, Australian Catholic University, Melbourne.

Anthony Fisher OP is Auxiliary Roman Catholic Bishop of Sydney; Episcopal Vicar for Life and Health in the Archdiocese of Sydney; Professor of Bioethics and Moral Theology in the John Paul II Institute for Marriage and Family (Melbourne) and Vice-Chancellor and Faculty Member of the Catholic Institute of Sydney, Sydney.

Raimond Gaita is Professor of Philosophy, Australian Catholic University and Professor of Moral Philosophy, King's College, University of London, London.

Gerald P Gleeson is Senior Lecturer in Philosophy, Catholic Institute of Sydney and Research Associate, John Plunkett Centre for Ethics and Health Care, Sydney.

John Haldane is Professor of Philosophy and Director, Centre for Ethics, Philosophy and Public Affairs, University of St Andrews, Scotland.

Kevin Hart is Professor of English, University of Notre Dame, USA.

Anthony J Kelly CSsR is Professor of Theology, Australian Catholic University, Brisbane.

Winifred Wing Han Lamb is a teacher in Canberra and is a Visiting Fellow in Philosophy at the Australian National University, Canberra.

Michael P Levine is Professor of Philosophy, University of Western Australia, Perth.

John Michael McDermott SJ, STD, is Adjunct Professor, Pontifical College Josephinum, Columbus, Ohio, USA.

Ralph McInerny is Michael P Grace Professor of Medieval Studies and Director, Jacques Maritain Centre, University of Notre Dame, USA.

Fr John Hilary Martin OP teaches in the History of Religions, Core Doctoral Faculty of the Graduate Theological Union, Berkeley, USA.

Gregory Moses is Chairperson of Philosophy and Humanities, St Paul's Theological College, Brisbane College of Theology; Auxiliary Lecturer, Australian Catholic University and Visiting Fellow, School of Theology, Griffith University, Brisbane.

Graham Oppy is Associate Professor, Department of Philosophy; Head of the School of Philosophy and Bioethics and Associate Dean of Research in the Faculty of Arts, Monash University, Melbourne.

John Ozolins is Head of School of Philosophy, Australian Catholic University, Melbourne.

John Quilter is Lecturer, School of Philosophy, Australian Catholic University, Sydney.

Hayden Ramsay is Professor of Philosophy at the John Paul II Institute for Marriage and Family (Melbourne) and is Academic Research Fellow of the Roman Catholic Archdiocese of Sydney.

Tracey Rowland is Dean and Permanent Fellow in Political Philosophy and Continental Theology of the John Paul II Institute for Marriage and Family, Melbourne.

Index of Names

Abraham 22, 226n22
Achilles 242
Adam 238
Adam (Biblical) 217n3
Adam and Eve 7, 166, 244
Adams, Marilyn McCord 3n1, 19-22, 147, 147n19, 284
Adams, Philip 280
Adams, RM 147
Albert the Great 291
Alfaro 232n29
Allah 321
Alston, William 53n24, 168, 300, 315n7
Alter, Robert 134
Angelico, Fra 61
Anscombe, Elizabeth 98, 358n56
Anselm, St 1, 9, 16, 17, 21, 30, 250, 252, 256, 263n33, 269, 282, 328
Aquinas, St Thomas 9, 12, 21, 23-24, 25, 26, 30, 33, 34, 35, 36, 97, 102, 127, 198, 199, 200n29, 219, 219n6, 220n8, 222, 223n16, 228n29, 232, 235n45, 248, 249, 250, 253-255, 266, 269, 271, 272, 281, 282, 285-299, 336-337, 338, 339, 348, 350, 354; Angelic Doctor 35, 238, 249, 286
Aristotle 24, 27, 35, 36, 44, 65, 200n28, 203n39, 219, 262, 265, 291, 311, 312, 313, 325, 338, 357

Armstrong, D 201n32
Ashley OP, Benedict 358n56
Atlas, S 226n24
Auden, WH 260
Augustine, St 15, 16, 17, 32, 66, 108, 217, 248, 250, 252-253, 269, 282, 338, 339, 348
Aurelius, Marcus 123
Averroës 356
Ayer, AJ 210n54, 268n45, 310

Bach 61
Bacon, Francis 75
Balthasar, Hans Urs von 222n14, 232n39, 238, 264, 347n31, 347-348, 359
Baron 281
Barth, Karl 80n8, 83n21, 89n32, 90, 91, 218, 218n5, 262, 263-264
Bauscher, J 233n41
Bautain, Louis 227, 246-247
Beethoven, Ludwig van 60-61, 64, 66
Belloc, Hilaire 359n59
Berkeley, Bishop George 19
Billot 229n30, 238
Blackburn, Simon 303n3, 326n12
Blackstone 339
Blake, William 61, 67
Blondel, Maurice 238, 341-342
Boethius 26, 123n15
Bonaventure, St 9, 25, 26, 278
Bonnetty 227

Index of Subjects